Praise for *Swipe to Unlock*

The #1 Amazon bestseller

Swipe to Unlock is the go-to guide for learning the important trends, concepts, and strategies driving the tech industry.

— Morgan Brown, author of *Hacking Growth*

Swipe to Unlock is our generation's Rosetta Stone — letting even non-engineers peer into the machines and code that are changing our lives every day.

— Jeremy Schifeling, founder of Break into Tech

Praise for *Bubble or Revolution*

The #1 Amazon bestseller

A brilliant overview of what could the next big thing in tech, authored by leaders at today's top tech companies.

— Nir Eyal, bestselling author of *Hooked*

Whether you are bearish or bullish on crypto, *Bubble or Revolution* brilliantly articulates both sides of the argument and offers well-researched insight on the future of blockchain technology.

— Mike Novogratz, former partner at Goldman Sachs

Bubble or Revolution is a must-read for anyone interested in understanding both the immense potential of, AND profound obstacles associated with, blockchain technology.

— Mike Rowan, Chief Product Office at TechStars

PRODUCT MANAGEMENT'S SACRED SEVEN

PRODUCT MANAGEMENT'S SACRED SEVEN

THE SKILLS REQUIRED TO BE A WORLD-CLASS PM

NEEL MEHTA

PARTH DETROJA

ADITYA AGASHE

Product Management's Sacred Seven

pmsacredseven.com

1st Edition, 4th Revision
October 5, 2021

ISBN–13: 978–0–578–74058–4

To everyone who's helped us through this long journey
—NM, PD, & AA

Contents

Preface xi

Introduction xiii

I Product Design **3**

1 Building vs. Scaling 11

2 Solving the Right Problem 27

3 Hypothesis Testing 39

4 Minimum Lovable Products 63

II Economics **85**

5 Business Models 89

6 Market Entry 105

7 Moats 117

8 Unit Economics 123

9 Customer Economics 137

10 Segmentation 149

11 Market Failures 161

III Psychology **175**

12 Pricing Psychology 181

13 Motivation 213

14 Getting the Click 229

15 Stickiness 243

IV User Experience **275**
16 Cognition 281
17 UX Principles 313
18 Usability 341
19 Customer vs. Business 361

V Data Science **379**
20 Distributions of Data 383
21 Experiments 395
22 Metrics 421
23 Metric Models 441
24 Storytelling with Data 463

VI Law & Policy **479**
25 Antitrust 483
26 Intellectual Property 505
27 Platform Liability 519
28 Privacy 531
29 Employment in the Gig Economy 551
30 Accessibility 555

VII Marketing & Growth **565**
31 Branding 569
32 What Are You Hunting? 593
33 Advertising 607
34 Growth Hacking 625
35 Persuasion 639

Conclusion to the Sacred Seven 657

Acknowledgments 663

Citations 667

Preface

WE'VE BEEN FORTUNATE ENOUGH to meet thousands of current and aspiring product managers who have read our first two books, *Swipe to Unlock* and *Bubble or Revolution.* Perhaps the most common question we get from these readers is, "what makes someone an exceptional product manager?"

A few years ago, we decided to hunt down some answers to that important question. At every conference and talk we went to, we made a habit of asking this question to every head of product, hiring manager, or other executive we could find. The question was so broad that we soon started splitting it into two halves for simplicity:

1. What knowledge separates interview candidates you hire from those you don't?

2. What hard skills help PMs move up in their careers the fastest at your company?

When we met up one weekend to compare notes, we realized that we'd interviewed a total of 67 product leaders from 52 companies spanning 14 countries. This little project had gotten a lot broader than we'd expected. We opened up our notebooks and started reading out the answers.

Given that we'd talked to everyone from hiring managers at the FAANG companies to heads of product at Asian unicorn startups, we expected to see no clear pattern in the responses. A growth PM at TikTok, a financial tech PM at Coinbase, and an emerging-markets PM at

Grab probably have very different perspectives on product management, after all.

But to our surprise, we kept hearing the same seven disciplines mentioned over and over: product design, economics, psychology, data science, user experience, law and policy, and marketing and growth. As one Amazon hiring manager put it, a standard PM is good about maybe two or three of those seven: a fresh business school grad might be an expert at marketing and economics, while a more artistically-inclined person might be better at design and UX. An outstanding PM, though, has a strong grasp of all seven.

We mentioned this insight to a new friend at a conference in Zurich, who quipped that things of historical and religious significance often come in sets of seven (Seven Wonders, Seven Seas, Seven Heavens, etc.). Product management is hardly a religion, but we thought the notion was clever and quickly started calling the seven subjects we'd found the *sacred seven*.

We initially thought we'd write a few blog posts on the matter and call it a day, but after digging deeper into these seven subjects in follow-up interviews, devouring books on the subjects we knew less about, and reflecting on our own "war stories," our notes grew to several hundred pages in length. And so we returned to our familiar stomping grounds: we had to put it into a book.

What you're about to read is the end product of everything we've learned from this endeavor. Through a combination of case studies, mental models, theory, and tactical tips, we'll help you gain the hard skills and knowledge you'll need to excel at all of the *sacred seven*. We hope you enjoy the book!

—Neel Mehta, Parth Detroja, and Adi Agashe
August 2020

Introduction

WHAT MAKES a great product manager? You can rattle off a long list of ingredients: technical prowess, a strong grasp of business strategy, soft skills and leadership ability, vision,[1] analytical skills,[2] product sense, and a dash of entrepreneurial mojo.

Those are all important, but beyond a certain point, they become table stakes. Many PMs forget the importance of being well-read beyond the usual fields of technology and business strategy. You can't build a popular product without understanding how the human mind works; you can't sell products without knowing the science of marketing and growth; and you can't generate a strong business model without a firm grasp of economics and business concepts. If you really want to come up with creative product ideas and launch successful companies, you have to be well-read in a variety of disciplines.

Having a diversity of knowledge pays off in other ways, too. Being able to speak the language of engineers, lawyers, designers, and other cross-functional professionals is key to earning their respect and working together effectively.[3] And that's not to mention that knowledge of these subjects will help you rise above the generic answers that most PM interview candidates will give.

If you want to be a truly exceptional product manager, you have to know the "sacred seven" disciplines that we found to be the most important: product design, economics, psychology, data science, user experience, law and policy, and marketing and growth.

What's inside

This book is split into seven parts, one per subject. We've arranged the parts according to their rough position in the product development process:

I. We'll kick things off with **product design**, where we'll take a broad view of disruption, strategic and technical innovation, hypotheses and prototypes, and product-market fit. At the end, we'll be able to think through how to find the right market, the right problem and the right solution.

II. Then we'll apply the science of **economics** to learn how to evaluate and enter markets and then generate sustainable business models. We'll then learn how to use unit economics, revenue metrics, segmentation, and barriers to entry to maximize your growth and profitability.

III. Then we'll apply **psychology** to learn how to attract and retain users. We'll learn how to build habits and make products "sticky," motivate users to use your product, and use psychological tools to win sales and signups.

IV. Next, we'll dig into **user experience** to understand how users develop mental models, the four things that make a great user experience, and how the nuances of human cognition should factor into your designs. The end goal is to build products that are usable and useful for all.

V. We'll then tackle **data science** to learn how to scientifically measure and grow products. We'll talk about A/B testing, measuring experiment results, north-star metrics for the five main business models, and identifying common distributions in data.

VI. We'll start rounding off the development process with **law and policy**, where we'll understand how to comply with laws and actually use them to your advantage. We'll cover intellectual property, antitrust, privacy, and a host of laws that PMs need to know, from GDPR to DMCA to Section 230 to AB5.

VII. Finally, we'll discuss **marketing and growth** to learn how to scale your product and reach the masses. By the end, we'll know how to develop compelling brands, run effective advertising campaigns, influence user behavior, and master the art of growth hacking.

You don't have to follow our order, though. Because each part is quite hefty, we've designed each part to be mostly independent of the rest. Thus, you can feel free to jump around the book or skim parts that discuss topics you already know a lot about.

Along with the main content, we've also included dozens of pieces of bonus content throughout the book, including interview tips and case study videos. Some of this bonus content is online; scan the included QR codes with your phone to pull it up.

Who this book is for

We've designed *Product Management's Sacred Seven* to help everyone from aspiring product managers to established product leaders to tech entrepreneurs in their quests to become world-class product managers and leaders. We think the combination of case studies, theory, and mental models will prove useful no matter where in your product journey you are.

Note that this book is explicitly *not* a book of interview questions and answers. If you're interviewing for a new job, we think that the tools you'll gain from this book will be instrumental in helping you craft strong answers to whatever interview questions you come across. Being able to cite economic theories, growth-hacking case studies, internet law history, and the like will put you at a decided advantage.

To help you even more with interviews, we've also included dozens of case studies so you can talk intelligently about the companies you're interviewing at, along with tactical interview tips to help you avoid common pitfalls and apply what you've learned in the interview setting.

More interview resources

If you *are* looking for classic interview prep materials — strategies to land interviews, tools to crack common questions, and sample answers — we'd suggest you check out the Product Alliance's interview prep courses and free resources at **productalliance.com.** We, the authors of this book, worked with a team of PMs from top tech companies (from Uber to Facebook to Amazon) to create this site, so we think it's the best PM interview prep resource out there.

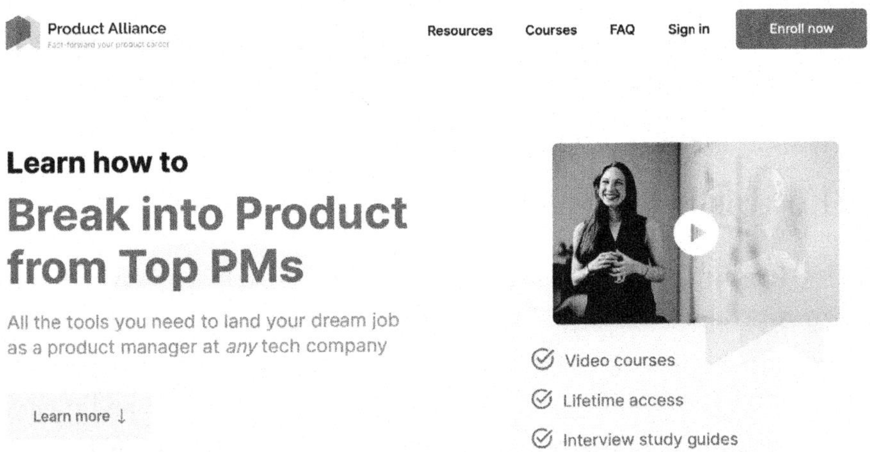

Two more pieces of foundational knowledge for PMs — technology and business strategy — are so deep that we couldn't do them justice in a single part of this book. We'd suggest checking out our first book, *Swipe to Unlock*, which packs dozens of case studies to help you understand these key concepts, explain them fluently, and intuit what the future of the industry might look like.

These two books are complements: think of *Swipe to Unlock* as the foundational information that any PM should know and *Product Management's Sacred Seven* as the added knowledge that will help you excel.

About the authors

The three of us are excited to bring this book to you and hope it'll serve you well on your product journey. Here's a bit more about us.

Neel Mehta is a product manager at Google and formerly worked at Microsoft, the US Census Bureau, and Khan Academy. He is also an instructor for the Product Alliance courses. Neel earned his AB in computer science from Harvard.

Parth Detroja is a product manager at Facebook and formerly worked at Amazon, Microsoft, and IBM. He earned his BS in applied economics from Cornell.

Aditya Agashe is a program manager at Microsoft, was the founder of the software consultancy Belle Applications, and is the host for the Product Alliance courses. He earned his BS in computer science from Cornell.

Feel free to stay in touch with us on LinkedIn; we always enjoy engaging with our readers!

- Neel: **linkedin.com/in/neel-a-mehta**
- Parth: **linkedin.com/in/parthdetroja**
- Adi: **linkedin.com/in/adityaagashe**

Thank you!

Thank you for choosing to read this book. We hope you'll find it informative, thought-provoking, and maybe even fun. From all of us — enjoy!

I

Product Design

Define yourself by your client, not your competitor.

— Ginni Rometty, former CEO of IBM

Introduction

THE YEAR WAS 1978, and Steve Jobs wanted to take a bold new step at Apple. The Apple II, released the previous year, was hailed as a revolution in computing, the first truly personal computer.[1] Previous computers required customers to supply their own case and chargers, but the Apple II came with everything you needed right in the box.[2] Most famously, the computer even had color graphics, a big step from the ugly black-and-white displays from before.[3]

The Apple II was a resounding success, selling hundreds of thousands of units and becoming a reliable moneymaker for the company[4] — a *cash cow*, as it were. But Jobs knew that competitors would catch up to this innovative new product, and they did.[5] His company was now faced with a choice: keep building on the Apple II line, or take an entirely different tack.

The Apple II. Source: Wikimedia[6]

It was no secret, though, that Jobs disdained the people who wanted to keep iterating on the old-school Apple II. He dismissed these people as "regular Navy" compared to the "artists" and "pirates" who would invent new products.[7] Anyone who wasn't making big, bold bets on the future was an incurious dullard — Jobs called these people "bozos" to their faces.[8]

Jobs stoked a culture war: the "pirates" working on Jobs's new Apple III worked on one side of campus, and the "regular Navy" working on the old Apple II sat on the other side of campus. Hostilities were so high that the street down the middle of campus was known as "the demilitarized zone."[9]

Jobs kept beating up on the "bozos." The trouble was that Apple cofounder Steve "Woz" Wozniak, the genius behind the Apple II, very much wanted to keep working on improving the Apple II line, and was thus classified as a bozo.[10] Woz and his team grew disillusioned with Apple under Jobs's harsh direction, and Woz famously quit in 1985.[11]

So what was Jobs doing with his team of "pirates" and "artists" on their side of campus? Jobs had ambitious goals for his Apple III, the first Apple computer designed for businesses rather than consumers.[12] Jobs insisted that the computer have no cooling fan, since he thought fans were "noisy and inelegant." But that design choice came back to bite him: the computer frequently overheated, which caused the computer chips on the motherboard to pop out of place — the only way to fix the computer was to bash it on a desk until the chips popped back into their sockets.[13]

Chapter 1

Building vs. Scaling

THERE'S NO one-size-fits-all approach to designing good products. The fundamental divide is between creating something entirely new (known as *0-to-1 innovation* or *vertical progress*) and iterating on an existing product or business model (known as *1-to-N innovation* or *horizontal progress*).[1] Your goals at each stage are different, as are the maturity of your idea and the amount of resources you have at your disposal. So you, as the product creator, have to vary your approach.

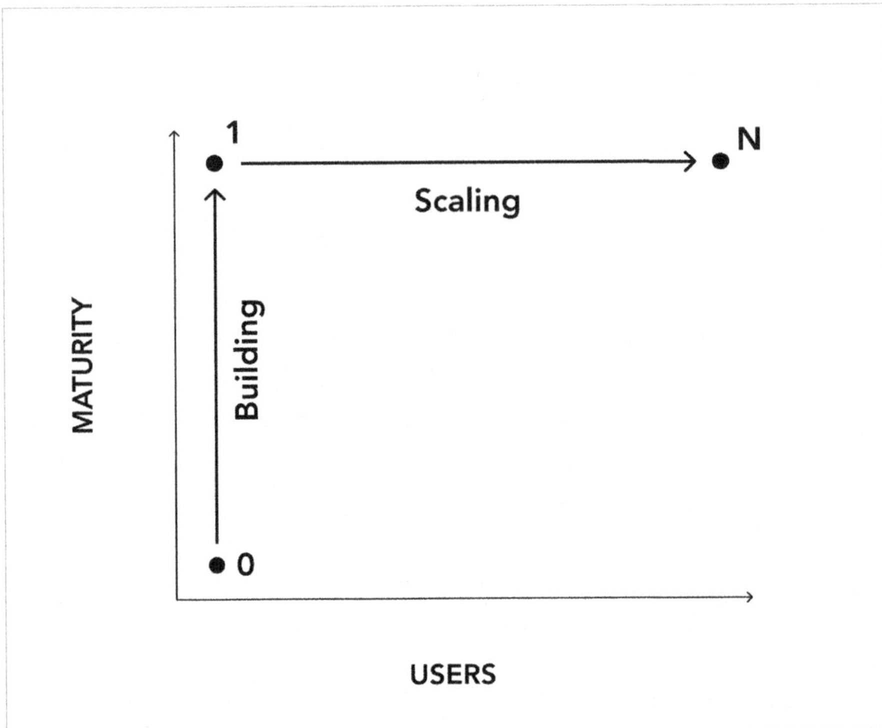

Building a new product is going from "0 to 1," while scaling an existing product takes you from "1 to N."

0-to-1

Products in the 0-to-1 stage are just getting started, looking for their first toehold in a market. Startups' products obviously fall in this category, but established companies often build their own 0-to-1 products, whether it's in "moonshot factories" like Google X — home to projects like delivery drones, internet-beaming balloons, and life-extension projects[2] — or from the brains of a few ambitious product managers.

These products are looking for *product-market fit*: clear proof that markets exist for them, that people in those target markets will use these products, and that the seeds are planted for growth. As the venture capital firm Andreessen Horowitz puts it, if you're launching your dog food company, it doesn't immediately matter if you have a bad business model or production problems. The real question is, "are dogs willing to eat your dog food?"[3]

At this stage, you don't need to be posting *hockey-stick* growth numbers, building your products for scale, or even seeing substantial revenue. You just need enough growth and success to prove to yourself that you'd be able to attain that growth if you were to invest more in the product. Only once you have product-market fit do you need to start scaling and optimizing for growth.[4] 0-to-1 is about building toward product-market fit, while 1-to-N is about scaling. In other words: first ensure that dogs will eat your dog food, then build out all your factories and shops.

Supply and demand

When you're building a 0-to-1 product, it's hard to gain traction if you're selling the same thing to the same people as your competitors. If there's already a pizzeria in town that sells pepperoni pizza to college students, you won't get very far if you set up a pizzeria that gets ingredients from the same suppliers and sells to the same students. It's just hard to stand out.

Instead, you want to find *untapped supply* or *unfulfilled demand* — sellers or buyers whom existing businesses aren't catering to. Since you aren't competing with anyone for these people's attention, it's much easier to win them over.

Many tech companies found unfulfilled demand and built a supply to serve them. E-scooter startups like Lime and Bird found that nobody was serving people who wanted middle-distance transportation (too long to walk, too short to Uber). The startup Brex, which offers company credit cards to startups, found that startups were hungering for such a product but weren't getting any help from the usual financial suspects. And TikTok found that Gen Z (among others) wanted a new way to connect, express themselves, and get entertained, but the existing suite of social media and entertainment products weren't doing it for them.[5]

Plenty of non-tech companies have found untapped stashes of resources, which they could acquire on the cheap and sell at a hefty profit. Whenever someone discovers a new source of oil, diamonds, gold, or other materials, they've found an untapped supply.[a] Tech companies don't usually sell physical goods like these, so finding untapped supply with an existing demand is fairly rare. However, you could argue that finding a new place to put ads is an instance of finding an untapped cache of human attention; the first person to realize that you could put ads in Instagram or Snapchat stories thus behaved a lot like someone who found a new oil reservoir.

Other products found both unfulfilled demand and untapped supply and simply connected the two together. Airbnb found homeowners with spare bedrooms (supply) and travelers who wanted a cheaper place to stay than hotels (demand) and connected them. Uber, similarly, found drivers whose cars were sitting in their garages (supply) and people who wanted cheap rides (demand) and helped them meet. [6]

Those *two-sided market* products, which match buyers and sellers, are the textbook example of products that match supply and demand. Other products achieve this in a more subtle way. Quora matches people who need their questions answered with experts who want exposure; Facebook matches huge amounts of user data with advertisers hungry to target consumers more effectively; the App Store matches app developers with people who want to download apps; and so on.

Generally speaking, your product will take one of two forms: a tool or service that builds the supply for an unfulfilled demand, or a platform that matches untapped supply with unfulfilled demand. (As we men-

[a] For instance, the Spanish carted away massive amounts of gold once they colonized the Americas. The gold wasn't quite untapped, since indigenous Americans had long been using it, but no other Europeans had had access to it.

tioned, finding an untapped supply with an existing demand is rarer.) A key part of your research in the 0-to-1 stage, then, should be finding these untapped supplies and unfulfilled demands and figuring out how you can serve them.

The importance of being 10x

New products don't just have to be better than the competition — they have to be *far* better than existing solutions to overcome customer inertia and gain adoption. You can't settle for 10% improvements; your product has to be *10x* better or *10x* cheaper, in Silicon Valley slang.[7]

A classic example of 10x price reductions comes from watches. The Swiss had long been experts at making mechanical watches, which used an intricate system of miniature cogs and gears to tell time. In the 1960s, these watches could sell for upwards of $9,000 in today's money.[8]

But in 1969, a Japanese watchmaker named Seiko introduced the world's first quartz watch, an electronic gadget that used the vibration of a crystal to keep time.[9] The first quartz watches were pricey,[10] but nowadays you can get a quartz watch for as little as $7.[11]

The internals of a quartz watch (bottom) are much simpler and cheaper than those of a mechanical watch (top). Sources: luginbuhlta via Pixabay[12], *Wikimedia*[13]

While the old-school mechanical watchmakers could keep churning out small improvements, nothing could compare to the revolutionary price reductions of quartz watches. Mechanical watches were still valuable as art pieces, but quartz watches became the new standard for timekeeping. By 1977 Seiko was the largest watchmaker in the world,[14] while Swiss watchmaking employment fell from 90,000 in 1970 to just 28,000 in 1988.[15]

An example of 10x product improvement comes from Elon Musk. Musk, when writing about Tesla's plans for self-driving cars in 2016, insisted that he'd only launch self-driving mode once it became ten times safer than human-powered driving[16] — any less and people wouldn't switch.

So when you're designing a 0-to-1 product, you can't settle for slightly improving on the status quo. Adding a feature or two isn't going to convince people to switch over. You want to create something that's shockingly different from the current set of products. Ideally you'd be entering a market that's never been touched before — that is, tapping entirely untapped supply and filling entirely unfulfilled demand.[17] But, even if you aren't the first on the scene, you can still do well if you're enough of a step up from the current entrants; after all, Google wasn't the first search engine, and Facebook wasn't the first social network.

When you're thinking about designing these 0-to-1 products, then, you shouldn't be thinking on the level of specific features. You have to be thinking much bigger-picture, since fighting for a feature or two isn't going to get you to 10x.

1-to-N

Meanwhile, 1-to-N products have already attained product-market fit, so their main goals are scaling up and continuing to improve. Anyone who's worked on a mature product at a big company can tell you the challenges that these products face: staying relevant, keeping profit

loop is an engine of progress for Amazon, but it's hard for competitors to keep up if they start from a smaller baseline.

Sixth is switching costs. If you're paying for an Amazon Prime subscription, it's hard to justify shopping anywhere but Amazon, since you feel like you're throwing away money. Thus, it's hard for competing ecommerce companies to get customers onto their subscription services, or even onto their websites in the first place.

Seventh is knowledge of processes. Amazon is a logistics powerhouse, with unparalleled knowledge of warehouse management,[26] shipping, and order fulfillment.[27] Competitors could certainly build up the expertise to run ecommerce programs as effective as Amazon's, but that would take a lot of time (or poaching).

Last are captured resources. Amazon has over 10,000 patents spanning digital payment infrastructure, delivery logistics, and warehouse automation.[28] And with about a million employees,[29] the sheer amount of manpower (and womanpower) at Amazon's command is hard to replicate.

When you're looking to design new features or new directions for a 1-to-N product, your overarching goal should be to hit as many of the trio of delight, hard-to-copy advantages, and margin enhancement as possible. At Netflix, Biddle gave each feature idea one point for each category it hit. Features with all three points were marked green, features with two were yellow, and features with one or zero were red.[30]

Disrupt yourself

Following that three-part model is useful for improving your product and business, but far too often, companies have obsessed over climbing the nearest hill while totally ignoring the much taller mountain in the distance. If you're too afraid to disrupt yourself, someone else will!

The classic example is Kodak, the 20th-century photography company that was once so powerful that it's known as "the Google of its day."[31] Kodak sold film for analog cameras and thoroughly dominated the market; at one point, Kodak controlled 90% of the film market and 85% of the camera market.[32] At its peak in 1996, Kodak earned over $16 billion a year in revenue and stood as the world's fifth-most valuable brand.[33]

But in the 1990s, digital cameras took off. While Kodak was busy trying to milk money from their analog and film businesses, smaller competitors like Fujifilm jumped on the digital train.[34] Digital camera sales surpassed analog cameras in 2002 and never looked back.[35]

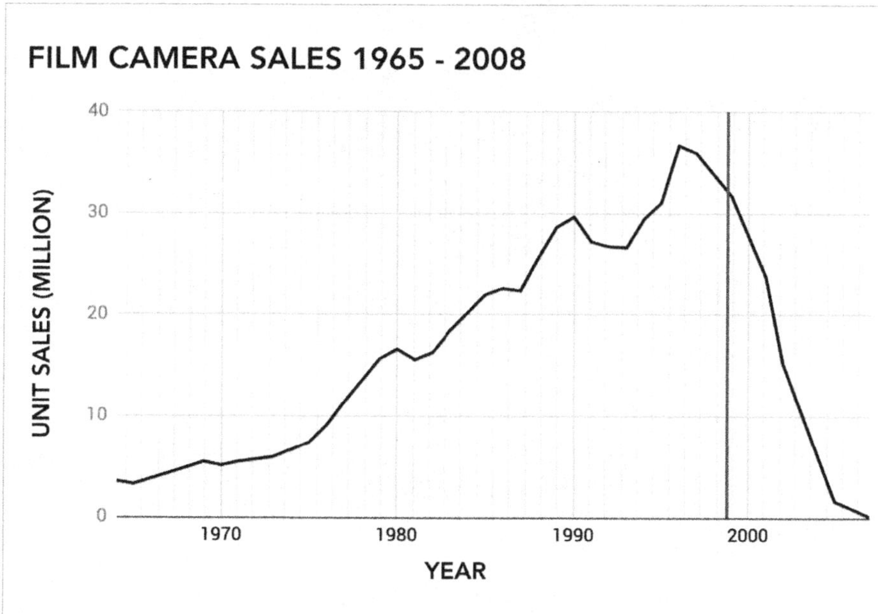

Film camera sales crashed after digital cameras were introduced (the vertical line around 1999). Source: Photography Life[36]

By 2010, film sales were less than a tenth of their 1990s peak, and virtually zero analog cameras were sold.[37] By 2011, Kodak was reduced to a pile of useless patents, and in 2012 the company went bankrupt and was taken off the New York Stock Exchange.[38]

The ironic part was that Kodak had actually *invented* digital cameras in 1975! An engineer at the company had created a prototype digital camera, but company leadership squashed the idea, fearing that these filmless cameras would disrupt their profitable film business.[39]

Steven Sasson's famous 1975 prototype of the first digital camera. Source: Burnick via Flickr[40]

The Kodak story goes to show that companies that are comfortably in the 1-to-N phase are often hesitant to adopt disruptive technology — but this very same technology, harnessed by a competitor, can come back to destroy them in the future. If you're working for a company whose main products are in 1-to-N phase, you have to watch out diligently for this shortsighted trend, which author Tim Wu dubbed the *Kronos effect*, after the Greek god who ate his children out of fear that one of them would overthrow him.[b][42]

[b]In Greek mythology, one of Kronos's children — Zeus — survived, and Zeus freed

Balancing 0-to-1 and 1-to-N

The bigger takeaway is that companies can't be exclusively focused on 0-to-1 products or 1-to-N products. If you, like Kodak, are solely focused on 1-to-N products, you'll miss out on the 0-to-1 products that are essential to the future of your business.

But if you're solely focused on 0-to-1 products, you won't have the steady amounts of cash on hand needed to develop these products. Consider MagicLeap, the augmented and virtual reality startup that was white-hot when it raised $2 billion in funding in 2016.[43] The company had no reliable 1-to-N products; it was all-in on a risky, inventive headset. So when the headset flopped, the company had to slash half its jobs and axe its flagship product.[44]

Successful companies have a balanced portfolio of 1-to-N products that earn steady revenue and 0-to-1 "moonshots" that could be the next big thing. The money from the 1-to-Ns funds the development of the 0-to-1s, and the development of the 0-to-1s ensures that the company has a future once the 1-to-Ns are obsolete. This is the reason why the companies that have succeeded the most in mixed-reality headsets are the likes of Facebook (with Oculus[45]) and Microsoft (with HoloLens[46]), which have funded the experimental technology with the revenue from their traditional *cash cows* like the Facebook app and Office.

The term "cash cow" is actually used to explain the importance of this diversification strategy. The famous *BCG growth-share matrix* compares cash cows to other categories of products.[47]

---

his siblings and killed Kronos in retribution.[41] You can see how this rhymes with the Kronos effect working out badly for Kodak.

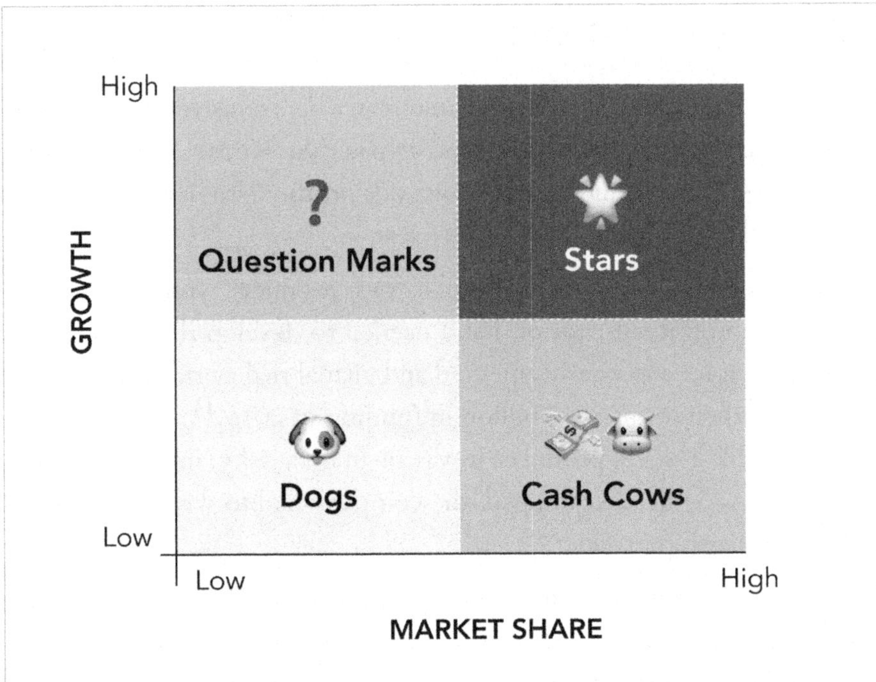

BCG's famous growth-share matrix. Source: NetMBA[48]

Cash cows are low growth but have a strong starting position, so you can "milk" them for a while until they run dry. But the matrix shows that you can't just invest in cash cows; you have to also invest in *question marks*, which are the 0-to-1 products that start off small but have a high growth potential. Ideally you'd get products into the rare *star* category, where they're large and quickly-growing, but even stars will eventually slow down their growth — nothing can grow forever — and become cash cows.

So companies need to balance their 0-to-1 question marks with their 1-to-N cash cows. The corollary is that companies need two types of product managers: the "dreamers" who can grow 0-to-1 products, and the "doers" who can take on 1-to-N challenges. When you're thinking about career development, consider which one you'd rather be; you don't have to strictly be one or the other, but it's useful to specialize in one.

Chapter 2

Solving the Right Problem

When you're building a 0-to-1 product, it's tempting to do what Steve Jobs did with the Apple III and decide ahead of time what you're going to build, what features it's going to have, and who it's going to be sold to. But it's fairly likely you'll realize that you got something wrong — it's very hard to predict any of those things ahead of time, and trying to dictate it just commits you to a path that will probably not be completely right.

Leaders' pet projects, which become company priorities even though they aren't seriously vetted, are some of the worst offenders here.[1] The graveyard of dead products is littered with the corpses of these projects. Just consider Google+, the massive social-networking project that Google started in 2011[2] when Vic Gundotra, then the head of Google Search, was convinced that building a Facebook rival was critical for Google. It was a huge investment: Google shoehorned a Google+ integration into many of its products and even tied all employees' bonuses to the product's success.[3] But the product never reached product-market fit and slowly fizzled out[4] until it was finally laid to rest in 2020.[5] Gundotra should have known better than to go all-in on such a foolhardy project.

So how do you avoid jumping on the wrong problem? You have to start from the bottom up — in other words, let your users, rather than your leaders, drive product design.[6]

Finding a motivated market

Designing a 0-to-1 product begins by finding a target market. The stereotypical advice is to solve a problem that you yourself are facing — *scratching your own itch*[7] — but the first thing you learn when doing user research is that most people are nothing like you, and people like you are only a small slice of the population.

Finding your own pain points is certainly a valid approach, but the approach we prefer is to find a small group of people who are highly-motivated to do something but highly dissatisfied with the existing solutions.

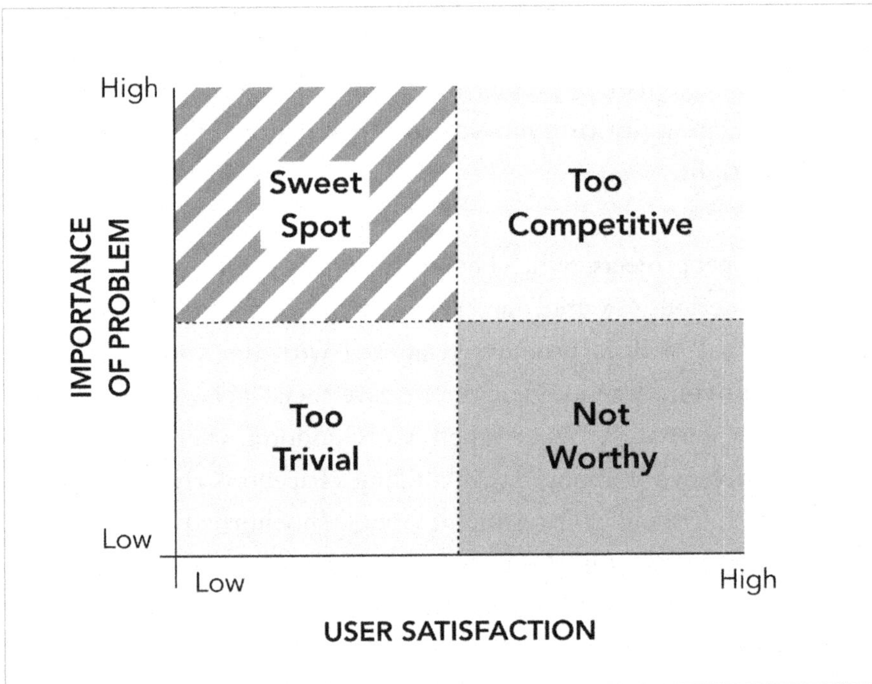

The best product opportunities happen when users are dissatisfied with the current solution to a very important problem (the "sweet spot" in this 2x2). Source: Productized[8]

Interview tip

If you're pitching product ideas to a big company like Facebook or Google, you don't want to be *too* niche. There are plenty of niche, ten-million-dollar ideas that you could pitch, and while these would be great for a five-person startup, they would only be a distraction to these mega-corps. One rule of thumb: if an idea can't make at least $100 million a year or get 100 million users, it's probably not worth a big tech company's time.

If your problem isn't very important to people, they probably won't go out of their way to try a solution for it, even if they aren't very happy with the existing options. That's not to say that super-niche businesses aren't worthwhile — a "magic spoon" that aimed to "reinvent cereal" once got $55 million in funding[9] — but the upside isn't that high.

Meanwhile, if people in the market are happy with the existing solution, it's hard to imagine that you can be 10x better than them. You can still do relatively well if you can carve out a tiny slice of a huge market — like the many small-time Airbnb clones[10] — but it's hardly going to become a $100 million business.

You want to find people who will vocally complain about a problem; that's a sign that both the problem is important to them and that they're dissatisfied with existing solutions. For instance, the Etsy founders were originally freelance web developers, and when they started building an online forum for craft makers, they found that one of the most common posts was people complaining about how awful Ebay was. The fees were high, it was a pain to use, and eBay wasn't responsive to customers. People on the forum literally said, "I wish there was a place I could sell my crafts" other than eBay. That was as sure a sign as any that there was a strong market opportunity — and Etsy worked its way up to a $2 billion valuation in less than a decade.[11]

Another useful method is to find people who are so desperate to do something that they'll take painful actions to do it — that is, people who are *crawling over broken glass.*[12] For instance, Drew Houston, the founder of Dropbox, noticed that people needed online file storage so badly that they'd fill up their entire inboxes by emailing files to themselves.[13]

Another example: the founders of the personal finance tool Mint found that people were spending hours every week categorizing their expenses in tools like Quicken or Microsoft Money. Organizing expenses was so important that people would spend hours on this tedious work — a crystal-clear sign that a product that did this automatically (like Mint!) would appeal to them.[14]

Keep it niche

The market that you'll find through this method is probably quite small. You might be tempted to broaden the market — no startup with 100 users is going to become a unicorn — but, at the start, you have to suppress that urge and stay niche.

This is because products succeed when they can monopolize a market, and smaller markets are (naturally) easier to monopolize than bigger ones.[15] As the saying goes, it's better to be a big fish in a little pond. Indeed, many successful products started by winning over small markets: Facebook started at Harvard before spreading across the world, Lyft and Uber started in just San Francisco, Amazon started its retail empire with books, and Netflix (back in its DVD-mailing days) started by winning over the fringe networks of DVD buffs in the 1990s.[16]

There's also a practical reason to start small: you probably won't have the funds, staff, or notoriety to take on a huge market at the start. You have to build a *flywheel* of growth that will get you there, and you have to kickstart that flywheel by starting with a small market. Once you earn some money from a small market, you can progressively tackle bigger and bigger ones.

Tesla provides the perfect example. Elon Musk had walked away from PayPal with millions, but even that wasn't enough to create the next Ford or GM.[17] Tesla started out by selling just a luxury sports car, the Tesla Roadster. The cars sold for over $100,000, and there were just 500 in the original batch.[18] But with the money from that batch, Tesla was able to move to progressively larger markets:[19] over the next decade, Tesla launched the Model S sedan, the Model X SUV, and then the relatively cheap Model 3.[20]

The original Tesla Roadster. Source: Wikimedia[21]

Why did Musk start at the high end of the car market? For one, it was a smaller market and thus easier to win. But more importantly, cheap mass-market goods require you to have a super-optimized supply chain and great economies of scale.[22] New products don't have that yet, so they won't be able to hit a competitive price for the mass market. Only customers in the top end of the market will be happy to pay a premium for an experimental new product that isn't cost-optimized.

Another reason to start in a niche is that any new product needs a small cohort of diehard fans to keep it afloat. These fans will be happy to try out unpolished features, use your product every day, voluntarily give you plenty of feedback, and even pay for your product when nobody else will. These things are all essential to building a good product, so you need to make sure you've chosen a niche and problem where you'll be able to find these users. As Kevin Kelley, the founder of *Wired* magazine, puts it, you need *1000 true fans* — people who will go to any length to use your product and would be devastated if it was gone.[23]

You'll probably have to be scrappy when trying to get these first 1000 fans. Take the country music star Taylor Swift as an example. At the start of her career, she had to grow her fan base from zero. She responded to every single person who posted on her MySpace page and gave autographs to anyone who asked. She even did a seventeen-hour-long meet and greet where she took pictures with 3000 people.[24] This effort was not at all sustainable, but it got Swift a few thousand diehard fans. After that, her fanbase grew naturally through word-of-mouth, concerts, and the like, but she had to do a lot of manual work to kickstart that loop. Diehard fans are hard to get, but they'll be the basis for all your future growth.

Your users may not be who you think

Most product managers will naturally build products for people like themselves, simply because they're most familiar with their own problems. Combine this with the fact that people in the San Francisco Bay Area love technology and are eager to try new products, and it's no surprise that so many new products are aimed explicitly at youngish, urban, white-collar professionals (nicknamed *yuppies*[25]) in coastal cities. This is why you have so many dog-walking apps, food-delivery platforms, and so on.

To be fair, marketing to young professionals and the tech intelligentsia has worked: Twitter got its start at the SXSW tech conference, a top gathering spot of this class of people.[26] But other products have realized that their true markets look and behave nothing like the founders: the founder of Pinterest originally aimed his product at his tech-loving friends but realized that the people who really grew to love the product were everyday people who wanted to do simple things like gathering meal ideas and redecorating their houses.[27]

Indeed, all kinds of valuable products solve problems for people that the average techie might never meet. Consider Flexport, the freight forwarding startup that raised $1 billion in 2019. You may not know anyone who works in commodities, exporting, or logistics, but Flexport found that it was a very big market (and one that badly needed tech).[28] You could argue that finding a market that most techies overlook is actually a competitive advantage; there are probably a lot more health tracking startups than shipping logistics startups.

Avoiding the high-tech trap

Once you've found a market and found problems that they're eager to get solutions for, it might be tempting to jump straight into building a high-tech solution. As product managers, we all love building shiny technology — but you'll find that, many times, you don't need it, and it might not actually be the wisest strategic move.

Pan Am and American

Take the example of airlines. Pan American World Airlines, nicknamed Pan Am, was the most glamorous airline in the United States for most of the 20th century, and the largest in the country from its founding in 1927 until its bankruptcy in 1991.[29] Pan Am *was* America for many years. It was used by American politicians and diplomats and called the country's unofficial "flag carrier[30] the same way Air Canada, Spain's Iberia, and Germany's Lufthansa are the official airlines of their respective countries. When notorious fraudster Frank Abagnale wanted to impersonate a pilot in the 1960s, his airline of choice was Pan Am for the worldwide prestige it commanded.[31]

A Pan Am jumbo jet from the 1990s. Source: Aero Icarus[32]

Pan Am's dominance was based in large part on its incredibly advanced airplane technology. It ushered the United States into the jet age,[33] working with Boeing to create ever-larger and ever-faster airplanes to shuttle Americans across oceans and continents. In 1955, Pan Am was the first airline to commission Boeing's 707 airplanes[34] and was the first to order the famous 747 in 1966. (Pan Am even worked closely with Boeing to design the planes!)[35]

For many years, Pan Am dominated the American airline industry because nobody could keep pace with it technologically. But in the 1970s, competitors started catching up, and when the 1973 oil crisis sent fuel costs skyrocketing, Pan Am started taking heavier and heavier losses. The downturn in demand also meant Pan Am's expensive 747s were increasingly sitting around empty.[36] By 1991, the company was losing $3 million a day, and that year it finally went bankrupt.[37]

The moral of the story: if you live by technical innovation, you die by technical innovation.

Compare this to the story of American Airlines, which in the 1970s was just an average airline and had nowhere near the same level of elite planes or cultural cachet as Pan Am. American didn't want to compete on technology.[38] Instead it took such unsexy steps as introducing discount "Super Saver" fares in 1976,[39] removing a single olive from every dinner salad served on their planes (which saved the airline $40,000 per year),[40] negotiating with the pilots' union to reduce salaries,[41] adding one of the first loyalty programs,[42] and launching one of the first computerized reservation systems.[43]

American's reservation system, called Sabre, is an especially interesting case study. American gave this system to travel agents across the country. Sabre just so happened to list American Airlines flights above the rest — so it should come as no surprise that American got 50% more revenue from travel agents who used Sabre than those who didn't.[44] And since Sabre charged a small fee every time a travel agent used it to make a booking, by 1985 American was earning more profit from Sabre than from all its flights![45a]

The reason American Airlines was one of the few airlines to survive the 1970s wave of airline deregulation and become one of the world's largest airlines today[46] had nothing to do with its airplanes. Instead, it was a series of savvy business moves that kept the company in the air.

Technical and strategic innovation

We tell the Pan Am and American parable to show that building the highest-tech solution isn't always the best way to solve the problem in

[a]This is quite similar to how Ford makes as much money from its finance arm (which makes loans to dealerships and car buyers) as it does from its actual car sales. Thus the joke that Ford is a bank that has a car lot out back.

front of you. Sometimes, it's better to innovate on the business model, which isn't as flashy but can be even more impactful.

Many of the top tech companies have never had particularly innovative technology, instead opting to combine existing technology in clever ways. When Uber launched in 2010,[47] iPhones had already had GPS and 3G for two years,[48] and taxicabs had been around for hundreds of years. Uber's innovation, rather, was finding ways to put these technologies together so users could hail cars from their phones.

To take another car example, consider Tesla. Electric vehicles have been around since the electric tricycle was created in France in 1881,[49] and the first mass market electric car was launched in 1996[50] — a full decade years before Tesla launched its electric sports car, the Roadster.[51] Tesla was hardly the first to make an electric car, but it was the first to make an electric car that wealthy and influential people wanted to buy. The car's design, branding, and marketing were the real reason for its success, not any major invention.

Oftentimes, products get their start with a technical innovation but really grow to dominance once they find a clever strategic innovation. Google's web page ranking technology was revolutionary, but at its start Google was just a cool PhD project. In fact, by 2000 the company was burning cash because its founders, Larry Page and Sergey Brin, were hesitant to add ads to search results.[52]

Google's fortunes started to turn once Page introduced ads on Google Search later in 2000 (this ad platform would later become AdWords).[53] Google started letting website owners run ads on their websites through AdSense in 2003.[54]. Buoyed by the iconic duo of AdWords and AdSense, Google's revenue grew from $400 million in 2002 to $3.2 billion in 2004,[55] the same year it IPO'ed at a valuation of $23 billion.[56]

That's not to say that technical innovations can't become economically successful. Just consider self-driving cars, machine learning, and even blockchains, each of which have launched major industries and countless startups. But as Google shows, it often takes a savvy business move to properly commercialize these inventions.

Once you've found the problem you want to solve, make sure you don't leap to start looking for some sexy new technology — that's rarely enough, and in many cases you may not need fancy new technology at all.

▶ Watch this

Neel, one of your humble authors, did a mock interview to show how a PM might design the web experience for Lyft. You'll find that the most difficult part is figuring out which problem you want to solve in the first place. And, surprise surprise, cutting-edge technology isn't strictly necessary.

Scan this QR code with your phone, or pull up the link below, to watch the video. (We'll also reprint this QR code at the end of Part I, so feel free to skip this for now.)

productalliance.com/videos/product-design

Chapter 3

Hypothesis Testing

ONCE YOU HAVE a rough idea of what problem your target market wants solved, it's time to create a product that solves that problem. But you shouldn't run off and start building right away. Every product idea is built on many assumptions, some of them hidden. If you're going to be successful, your assumptions have to be valid — so your first step has to be finding and validating your assumptions.

For instance, Slack had found a clear need for a better alternative to email. But if it was going to succeed, it had to prove that companies were willing to pay for a product that employees love but IT teams didn't care about (quite a bold assumption!). TikTok clearly had cool content and mechanics, but it had to prove that the crowded Western social media space had room for one more titan. And so on. If you can't voice and validate your assumptions, you'll never be sure if your product has a realistic shot at success.

Listing assumptions

The first step is voicing your implicit assumptions; you can't validate an assumption you don't know about!

These implicit assumptions are hard to dig out from the back of your mind, so it helps to have a systematic way to catalog them. We like to group assumptions for new products into five buckets:[1]

Bucket	Typical phrasing
Problem	"I assume that user group or stakeholder X has a problem with Y."
Solution	"I assume that X product category is the best way to solve this problem, and not another category."
Feasibility	"I assume that a product like X can be feasibly built and that Y user group will use it."
Team	"I assume that my team has the skills, reputation, and resources to build X."
Economics	"I assume that we could turn a profit by building a business around X."

The five buckets should serve as a useful starting point. Your challenge is to rack your brain for assumptions in each bucket.

As an example, let's take the original product of the finance tech company Square: a small square device that would plug into a phone's audio jack and let the phone thus read a credit card. Jack Dorsey, the founder of Twitter, created Square in 2009 when his friend, a glassblower, told him that he'd lost a $2000 sale because his business was cash-only and a customer wanted to pay by credit card.[2]

The original Square reader, which attaches to a phone and reads credit cards. Source: Rosenfeld Media[3]

Dorsey and his glassblower friend probably had the following assumptions (among others) in mind:

Bucket	Assumption(s)
Problem	Small merchants across the globe lose sales because they can't accept credit cards. The standard ways of getting a credit card reader are too hard or expensive for these small merchants.
Solution	A credit card reader that plugs into a phone is the best way for merchants to make up for these lost sales.

Feasibility	You can read a credit card with nothing but a phone add-on. Banks will allow this, and businesses and customers will trust this tiny reader.
Team	Dorsey has enough money from his Twitter founding to bootstrap the company, including creating the first batch of readers.
Economics	The company can earn more money from these readers than it costs to produce and support them.

At this point in the process, you've probably only found the market and their problems, so you can only really fill in the first bucket of assumptions. In the rest of this chapter, we'll flesh out the rest of the assumptions and then test them.

Learn from users

To figure out the type of products that your target market needs to solve their problems, it's useful to observe or talk to your target users. You might find that the class of products you were thinking of isn't actually what your users needed.

For instance, the consumer goods company Procter & Gamble was trying to find a way to create a breakthrough new product in the stagnant cleaning products business in 1994.[4] The chemistry team got to work on creating a more efficient cleaning fluid so people could mop more effectively.[5]

But another team went to observe how people were cleaning their homes. One person spilled dry coffee grounds on the floor. Instead of reaching for a mop, this person swept up the grounds with a broom and used a wet cloth to pick up the straggling crumbs. The team were shocked and realized where they'd gone wrong: they'd assumed that the solution was a better mop, when really the best solution was *not* a mop![6]

In fact, the best solution was an absorbent, dry device paired with a slightly damp device. The Swiffer products were born:[7] a new kind of anti-mop that could alternate between "dry" and "wet" heads to clean up household spills.[8] Procter & Gamble now sells $500 million of Swiffer products a year,[9] and many young people have never tried cleaning with an old-fashioned mop and bucket.

Simply observing how users tried to solve their problem helped P&G reverse one of their incorrect assumptions, which was the key to creating an incredibly successful product.

This is why user studies are so important — you may not immediately realize that you're holding incorrect assumptions until the lived experience of another person helps you break out of the rut. Sometimes, as in the case of Dorsey's glassblowing friend, you can draw from your own experience to validate your assumptions (in Square's case, that merchants need credit card readers.) But even then, you'll want to do broader-scale user research to make sure you aren't too biased toward your own experience.

A day in the life

The classic way to understand potential users and customers is to bring them to your offices for structured user research sessions or talk to people on the street. These approaches work, but the problem is that they take the research subjects out of context. You can't reduce the user for an enterprise product to the eight hours a day they spend in the office or the sum total of emails they send, and you can't reduce a social media user to the five-minute chunks they have waiting for the bus.

A more holistic approach to understanding your users comes from the *day-in-the-life* method, where you track a real user throughout their day to understand the context in which they face their problems and in which they might use your product.[10] Without this, you might just be building for a fantasy user in an unrealistic use case.

Take Quibi, the short-form video startup that drew $2 billion in funding upon its launch in 2020[11] and boasted new shows with star-studded casts.[12] Quibi's quirk is that episodes are only 5-10 minutes long and can only be watched on your phone;[13] the idea is that you can sneak in a quick show while you're waiting for the rice to cook or the subway to reach your office. It looked like a terrific way to move TV into the era of short attention spans and phone-centric life.

But Quibi's creators didn't understand the context in which we watch shows. We rarely "single-screen" TV — most of the time, Netflix is running in the background while we're doing something else, or we're scrolling through Instagram on our phones while a show blares on the big screen.[14] People watching Quibi videos would naturally want to reach for their phone to do something else — but their screen was already dominated by the video. Quibi's creators were playing to an imaginary audience that would stay glued to their phones, watching the tiny screen for five to ten minutes straight — when even a single trip into the average person's living room would have shown them that that was a fantasy.

After an initial burst of excitement, Quibi quickly stumbled, falling out of the top 50 iPhone apps a week after launch, netting only a few million active users.[15] Company leaders started leaving,[16] and the company fell into a downward spiral. Though Quibi was plagued by mediocre shows,[17] not understanding the context in which people watch videos put Quibi at a permanent disadvantage.

In other words, Quibi didn't question its Use assumption that people would watch TV shows exclusively on their phones — even when observing potential users in action would have shown them that it was wrong.

Contrast this with Tinder, which realized that traveling Tinder users would often open up the app as soon as their plane landed in a new city[18] — even before checking their texts! They'd hurry to lock down fun plans for the very night they landed.[19] Tinder realized that people on Tinder weren't just Tinder users: they were also solo travelers and frequent flyers. In doing so, Tinder verified the Problem assumption that people needed a way to date while traveling and, in 2015, launched Tinder Passport, a paid feature to let users swipe in a city before they flew there.[20]

Getting a holistic view of a user helps you not only with validating assumptions but also with every other stage of the product development process. The alternative to understanding example users inside and out is to construct *personas*, which are archetypal users who you flesh out with a picture, backstory, demographics, interests, and such.[21] The problem with personas is that they're fundamentally fake people, one-dimensional and empty. It's much easier to reason through whether the person you shared beers with would pay for a particular feature than to wonder if your imaginary Frequent Flyer Freddie would do the same.

Finding people to talk to

Big companies usually have structured programs to recruit a representative sample of users for its product managers to talk to. Google, for instance, recruits people into a massive database of potential research participants, algorithmically chooses participants, and invites chosen people into local Google offices (or sends researchers across the world in Google-branded vans).[22]

If you're developing a new product at one of these huge companies, you can reliably use these methods to find users to talk to. If you're at a smaller company (or no company at all!), your best bet to find users in your target market is to go where these users congregate. In the real world, you can go talk to college students outside lecture halls or talk to commuters at train stations.

Online, you can find specific forums or websites to see people in the target markets talking to each other — you can direct message people there to set up an interview, or you can observe their behavior without them even noticing you're there. As we've mentioned, Etsy's founders stumbled upon the idea by overhearing people in crafting forums talk about how much they hated selling their wares on eBay.[23]

Another useful way to observe people's conversations is to use Twitter, LinkedIn,[24] GitHub, Reddit, or other places where people with specific interests talk to each other. Twitter and LinkedIn have powerful advanced searches that let you narrow down the people you want to observe and talk to: if you're launching a design tool out of Carnegie Mellon University, you could use LinkedIn to find design consultants in Pittsburgh. Reddit is even better for observing people's discussions, since they helpfully self-organize into hyper-specific subreddits.

Product Hunt and Hacker News are also good places to find what opinionated tech enthusiasts are talking about — you can figure out the *zeitgeist*, so to speak. Since these people might be your early adopters, it's instructive to see what problems they want solved.

The downside, of course, is that the people you see here may not be a representative subset of the population. Reddit's audience famously skews young and male,[25] while Twitter users are far more likely to pay attention to news and pundits than the average person.[26] Tech forums, predictably, cater to tech people, who might be your early adopters but don't at all resemble broader markets.

If you'd like to get a broader view of how the world at large is thinking, you can check out Google Trends, which shows you the most popular search trends on Google.[27] It's a good way to find fads like fidget spinners, which get spikes in attention but immediately tail off,[28] as well as longer-term trends, like a slow and steady increase in interest for mascara.[29] You can slice and dice this data by geography to find potential niches or by time of year to see if demand for a product fluctuates with the seasons.[30] Because pretty much everyone uses Google, the data you see will be representative of the world at large, but the downside is that you won't find individuals to talk to in greater depth.

If you want to gather more quantitative data, such as by running a survey, your best bet is to use Amazon's Mechanical Turk, the "human intelligence" platform that lets you farm out simple tasks to an army of workers across the globe. You can easily put together a survey in something like Google Forms or Qualtrics and pay workers a few cents for each completed survey.[31]

Mechanical Turk lets you get a high volume of information, but isn't great for microtargeting users because you can't really restrict who gets to complete the task. Thus, it's better suited for understanding broad market trends (e.g. how much time people spend on YouTube every day) than getting insights into a particular market.

If you want to run a slightly more targeted survey at scale, you can try Google Surveys, which lets you use "screening questions" to limit your survey to people who fit particular criteria.[32] For instance, you could publish a survey to just iPhone users who like investing in stocks.

Tools like SurveyMonkey are more heavyweight, but you can use them to find people to fill out surveys as well.[33]

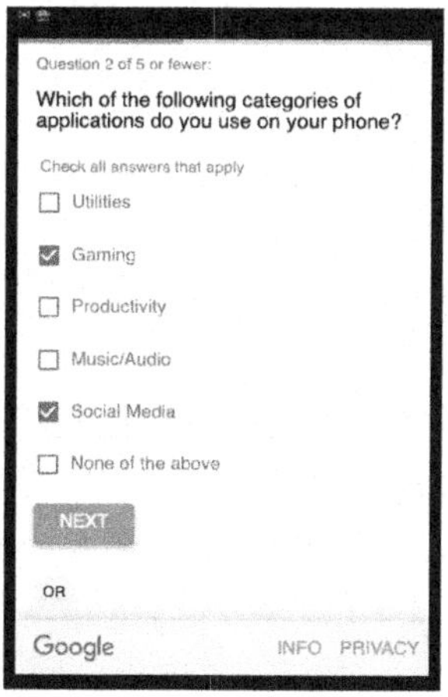

An example survey published with Google Surveys. Source: Google [34]

Methods

We won't get too deep into user research methodology — that could fill up a whole book — but it's worth knowing some major ways to do user research:[35]

Method	Description
Surveys	They're good ways to test your Problem assumptions, but because they aren't great for qualitative feedback, they won't open your eyes to ideas you hadn't thought about before.
Interviews	These one-on-one discussions give you a good look inside the user's mind and can thus reveal new insights. Don't rely on them for quantitative feedback, though, since you can only run so many of these.
Field studies	These involve observing a person as they go about their everyday life, whether micro (observing them do a particular behavior like cleaning their house) or macro (following them through a whole day).
Focus groups	These let you draw out people's opinions and beliefs, since people will reveal more in a free-flowing discussion with peers than when they're being peppered with questions from an interviewer.
Diary studies	Here, you ask participants to record various aspects of their life over time. For instance, you could ask people to write down every time they opened a mobile banking app or prepared coffee in the morning. This gives you a lighter-touch lens into user behavior and lifestyle than physically following them around.[36]

For all of these, one rule of thumb is to ask open-ended questions as much as possible. Closed-ended questions (those with a finite set of answers, like "yes" or "no") don't let the participant reveal much additional information.[a] The true insights, user empathy, and useful context will come from asking questions that let the participant speak at length.[38] For instance, instead of asking, "would you order groceries through an app?" you can ask something like, "what goes through your mind when you're deciding how to buy groceries?"

Early prototyping

Once you've observed and talked to users, you'll probably have a good handle on your Problem assumptions and some Solution assumptions. You'll know, for instance, that merchants really do suffer by not having credit card readers and that they'd rather take credit cards than, say, set up a PayPal. To test your remaining assumptions, you'll have to create and test prototypes of your product.

Early prototypes can (and should) be very low-fidelity. The simplest type of prototype is the *Post-It prototype*, where you sketch the rough flow of your product on sticky notes. You draw the key screens and show how they connect.[39] By doing this, you can show testing participants the gist of your product. (Another way to do user testing with Post-It prototypes is to show participants one Post-It and ask them to "tap" on a button. Then you swap in a new Post-It to simulate the screen switching.)

For example, the Post-It prototype of a peer-to-peer payment app like Venmo would have sticky notes for the screens to view your balance, get payments, and pay friends. The exact screens you show depends on what assumptions you're trying to validate. Venmo would presumably

[a] If you want the full picture, don't just ask yes/no questions. A fun example comes from the movie *The Pink Panther Strikes Again*. The bumbling Inspector Clouseau is checking in at his hotel and sees a dog near the check-in desk. He asks the receptionist, "Does your dog bite?" The man says no, so Clouseau goes to pet the dog, but the dog promptly bites him. Clouseau looks angrily at the man. "That is not my dog," says the receptionist.[37]

want to test whether people would feel comfortable sending money with an app, so showing payment- and bank-related screens might be more important than showing the login screen, which will be uncontroversial.

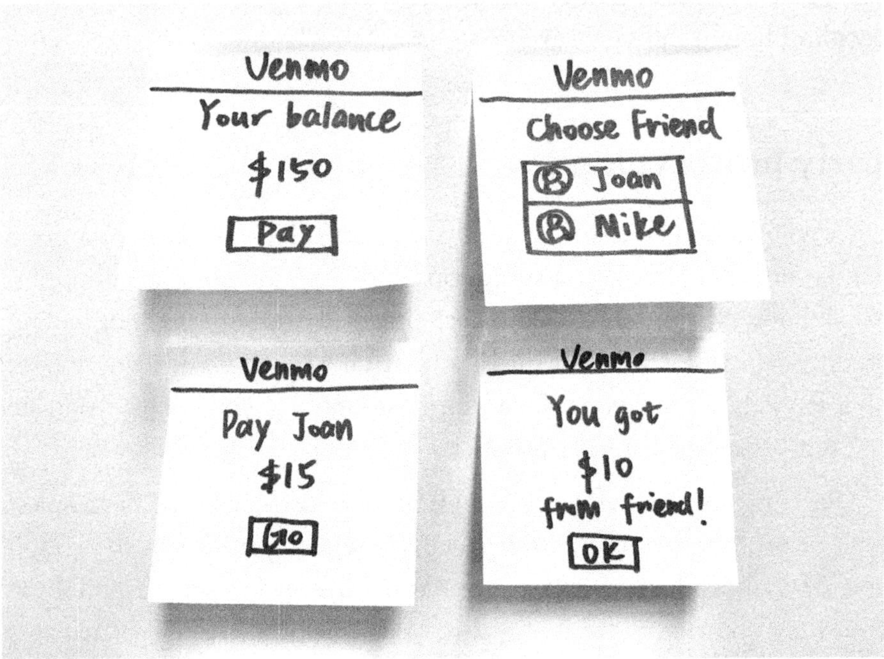

An example Post-It prototype for Venmo.

You'd be surprised at how much feedback you can get with a prototype that takes five minutes to sketch. But you can only really reason about your Solution assumptions at this point.

To validate your Feasibility assumption, you'll need to have something more fleshed out. Post-It prototypes tell you nothing about usability and whether your real product would make sense to people. At this point, it's a good time to invest in a higher-fidelity prototype like *wireframes,* where you lay out the locations of screen objects more formally with a computer, or even a clickable prototype, which you can create with a tool like Figma.[40]

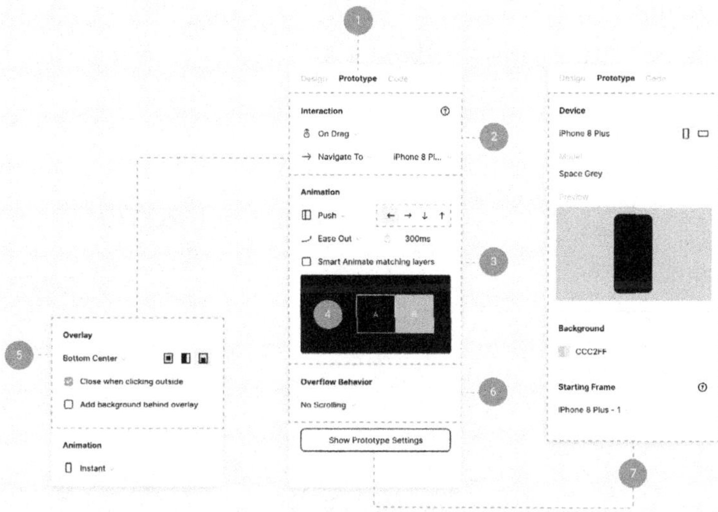

A clickable prototype made in Figma. Source: Figma[41]

Clickable prototypes require little or no code to build — they're mostly created with drag-and-drop tools. The benefit is that you can get a reasonably accurate simulation of what your product might look like with little investment, and you can easily share it with friends and family online to start getting feedback on the user experience. Clickable prototypes also force you to define the entire user flow; you can't get away with omitting certain steps or items like you might with Post-It prototypes or wireframes.

The MVP

Post-It prototypes, wireframes, and clickable prototypes should give you good insights into the Solution and Feasibility assumptions we talked about earlier. But to really test those assumptions, and to test the Economics assumption, you'll have to build something that's a very rough approximation of the actual product. This is the famous *minimum viable product*, or *MVP*.

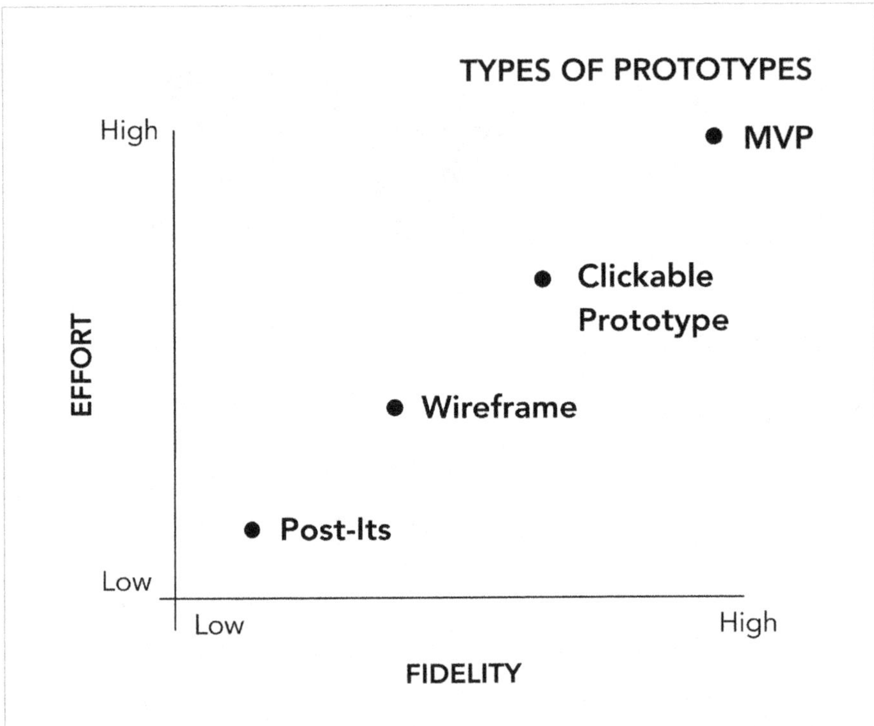

A comparison of the various stages of prototyping. The higher-fidelity your prototype, the harder it is to build.

The MVP is one of the most misunderstood tools in the PM's arsenal, so let us be clear: you aren't going to launch your MVP to the world. You aren't going to do publicity blasts or launch parties. The MVP isn't a "version 1.0" — instead, it exists solely as a testing vehicle.

Your MVP doesn't have to be fully functioning; in fact, it shouldn't be. You can (and should) replace the complex parts of your product with simple but non-scalable alternatives for now.

The Concierge MVP

A great example is the food-delivery company Doordash. Their MVP didn't actually include the whole digital ordering, pickup, and delivery infrastructure that the current app does — that would have required too much investment before the core idea was even borne out. Instead, the MVP, launched to Stanford students, was a simple website where the founders posted the PDF menus of popular websites in nearby Palo Alto. When a customer called, the founders would order pickup from the restaurant, head to town to pick up the order, and deliver it to the customer's dorm room for a $6 delivery fee.[42] That's right: they did the most technically complex part manually. It was hardly scalable, but it was a simple way to prove out the fundamental Economics assumption: that students would pay a third party a delivery fee to order food online.

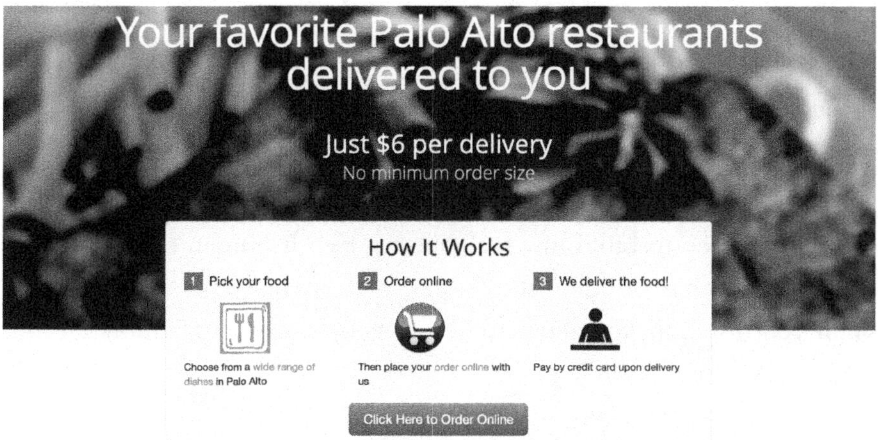

DoorDash's MVP — paloaltodelivery.com — in 2013. Source: Internet Archive[43]

The online shoe retailer Zappos, which is now owned by Amazon, did something quite similar when it launched in 1999. A young entrepreneur named Nick Swinmurn thought that the web was the future of the $2 billion mail-order shoe industry. He was having trouble getting venture capitalists to invest and couldn't convince Tony Hsieh, the man he wanted to become his cofounder, that people would buy shoes online without ever getting to see them or try them on.[44] This was the fundamental Economics assumption that had to be true if Swinmurn's idea was to succeed.

To test this hypothesis, Swinmurn didn't start out by building a giant ecommerce website, supply chain, and warehouse network. Instead, Swinmurn took his camera to a local mall, photographed pairs of shoes in the shoe store, and uploaded the photos to zappos.com. When a customer placed an order for the shoes, Swinmurn would go back to the mall, buy the shoes, and mail them to the customer.[45][46]

This minimal MVP worked enough to get some customers — and it was enough to get Hsieh on board.[47] The rest, as they say, is history: a decade after its founding, Zappos was bought by Amazon for $1.2 billion.[48]

This type of MVP is actually quite common, and it's known as the *Concierge MVP*[b] or *Wizard of Oz MVP*.[50] [c] With these MVPs, you replace a complicated backend (which would require a lot of engineering time and money to build in a scalable way) with human elbow grease. It's a lot easier than building the proper solution, but it gets the job done when you just want to validate whether people would pay money for a product like yours.[51]

The fake door test

Another useful way to judge if people will use and pay for your product (and thus to validate the corresponding assumptions) is to create a landing page that includes all the screenshots, testimonials, copy text, and other

---

[b]So named because concierges at luxury hotels can do all sorts of tasks, from mailing packages to buying tickets, on behalf of guests.[49]

[c]"Pay no attention to the main behind the curtain…"

items you'd use to convince someone to sign up for your product. You even run ads to draw visitors to your landing page.

The catch is that you never actually build the product — when the user goes to sign up, you thank them for their interest and tell them they'll be the first to know once the product is ready.

This is known as the *fake door test*, and it lets you see if your proposed solution resonates with your target market before you build anything.[52] As a bonus, you also collect the email addresses of hardcore fans who can become your first customers as soon as you launch your product for real.

A classic example of fake door testing comes from the social gaming company Zynga, which churned out dozens of popular games like FarmVille starting in the late 2000s. Whenever they had an idea for a game, Zynga would write up a five-word summary of the idea and plaster ads for it on Facebook and other popular websites. They'd only actually build the game if the ad got enough clicks.[53]

Zynga ran multiple fake-door tests at once to ensure that they'd only build out the very best ideas. You can (and should) do the same. Perhaps you aren't sure whether it's better to target your product at consumers or enterprises, or you aren't sure what the best *value proposition* is.[54] Whatever your question is, you can create a variety of ads and a variety of landing pages, let them loose, and compare the results to figure out which one is a winner.

Be careful using fake door testing, though: some users might have gotten their hopes up and been dismayed to see the product wasn't available, and they may think they were tricked.[55] Using the fake-door trick to advertise an entertaining video app is probably going to draw fewer complaints than a fake-door trick advertising a lifesaving medical device; in other words, think through the potential downsides before committing to the trick.

The Riskiest Assumption Test

The MVP is still a flawed term, since people take it to mean anything from "the simplest possible prototype" (too low fidelity, in our view) to "the smallest thing you can test" (decent) to "a good version 1.0" (too high fidelity). The latter is especially problematic. In other words, many PMs take "MVP" to mean building out a bloated prototype, adding in more and more features until they've effectively built the real product without ever stopping to test.[56]

A slightly better phrasing is the *Earliest Testable Product* (*ETP*), which shows that your goal is to create something simple that will let you test if you can address the underlying user need. For instance, if your customer asked you for a car, your ETP could be a skateboard — the simplest possible thing that could solve the underlying need, which is to get from A to B. (Or you could just hand someone a bus ticket!)[57]

The ETP is better, but it's still vague about what, exactly, you're supposed to be testing, rendering it vulnerable to the same scope creep that plagues MVPs. And it isn't very comprehensive. The skateboard example is a way of testing Problem assumptions, but the ETP doesn't help you much with the other types of assumptions.

Instead, our favorite alternative to the MVP is the *Riskiest Assumption Test* (*RAT*). The RAT makes clear that you don't have to build anything that remotely resembles the finished product. Instead, you need to figure out which of your assumptions is the riskiest — the most likely to be wrong — and do the simplest thing you can do to test it.[58]

The RAT is great because it explains many successful startups' prototypes very well. For Airbnb, the riskiest assumption was that people would pay to sleep in a stranger's apartment — so the cofounders set up a simple website that let people pay $80 a night to sleep on an air mattress in their apartment and eat a Pop-Tart for breakfast.[59] People had been buying things online for a while by this point (2008), so the assumption that people would pay for this experience online wasn't that risky and thus wasn't that important to test.

Or take Zappos. Even in 1999, it wasn't too risky to assume that people knew how to operate ecommerce sites, including the concepts of carts, profiles, accounts, and uploading payment credentials. Amazon had been around since 1995, after all.[60] Swinmurn knew that the riskiest assumption was that people would be willing to buy shoes sight-unseen off the internet — and that's exactly what his clever mall-hunting strategy tested.

Finally, consider the personal finance tool Mint, which is now owned by Intuit. The founder, Aaron Patzer, went to a train station and handed out flyers advertising his idea: a website where you could connect all your bank accounts, credit cards, etc. and track your financial state in one place. (He hadn't actually built the website yet, so this was a textbook example of the fake door test.) Patzer asked people what they thought about the idea and found that people's biggest hangup was that they didn't trust some random website with their banking credentials.[61]

Patzer had found his riskiest assumption — so in future iterations of his prototype, he focused on designing the website to convey an impression of trust (he used plenty of pictures of locks). People didn't doubt that a tool like Mint would be useful, and they didn't doubt it would work — so Patzer didn't need to spend as much time clarifying the *value proposition* or proving out the technical stack.[62]

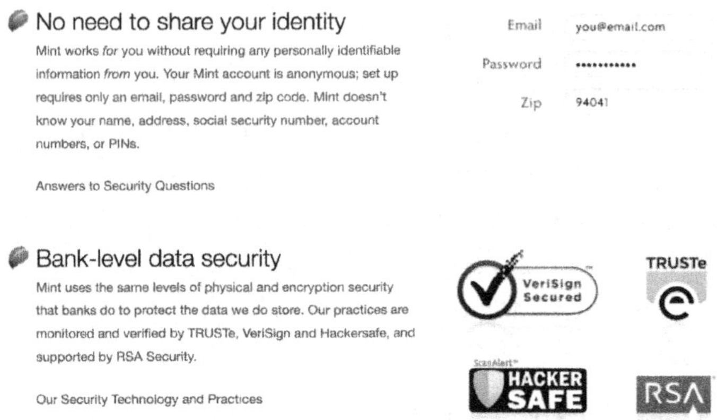

The "Safe and Secure" tab of Mint's website back in 2010. Notice how much it emphasized the company's security credentials. Source: Internet Archive[63]

In short, the RAT trains you to focus on proving out just the most important assumptions while explicitly de-emphasizing the less-controversial assumptions. When you're doing the RAT, be clear about what you're *not* going to do, since that's the best way to avoid creating a bloated prototype.

💼 Interview tip

Your interviewers will probably have heard the "make an MVP, iterate, and launch" technique a million times. If you're discussing how to create a new product, you can certainly mention the MVP, but you should spend the bulk of your time talking about the riskiest assumption and how you'd validate it. That'll be a refreshing — and maybe even surprising — change of pace and will help you stand out.

In practice, the RAT and the MVP might look similar — creating an incomplete version of the product for testing. But we suggest using the

RAT to guide your thinking, since it makes it much easier to remember your goals and avoid scope creep.

Research for 1-to-N products

You may have noticed that most of our advice on hypothesis testing so far has been for 0-to-1 products. That's because 1-to-N products have probably validated most of their core assumptions by now; that's how they got to product-market fit, after all.

The design and development process for 1-to-N products is much more scientific than the qualitative research that you have to do for 0-to-1 products. We'll cover the scientific procedures in more depth later in this book, so we'll touch briefly on the high-level research plan you might follow if you wanted to improve a 1-to-N product.

Finding pain points

Suppose you were tasked with improving the airport experience for Lyft. You'd start off by doing similar user research to what we described above, but chances are good that Lyft has a structured user research program in place so you don't have to be quite as scrappy. You'd probably want to observe Lyft users in the habitat where your product would be used, namely in airports.

You might visit five airports around the United States and watch people's journeys from the arrival gate all the way through leaving the airport (whether by car, train, Uber, or Lyft). You could ask people how they were deciding which method of transportation to take, observe where people stand around waiting the most, and where people seem visibly frustrated.

With that, you can understand and validate the Product assumptions. Then you'd want to think of some potential solutions that might help in this case; remember the importance of creating features that delight users, are hard to copy, and enhance margins.[64]

Suppose you found that people spent too long waiting at pickup points and brainstormed up three solutions. One solution would place signs that say "X minute walk from the pickup point; call your Lyft now" throughout the airport. Another would be to get an exclusivity deal at airports so more Lyfts would be available, leading to a shorter waiting time. The third would be to use a user's GPS location to track their movement through the airport and automatically call a Lyft when their remaining walking time equals the time it'll take for the car to arrive.

Your validation table would then look like something like this:

Solution	**Delights?**	**Hard to copy?**	**Enhances margins?**
"X minute walk" signs	No[d]	No	Maybe
Exclusivity deal	Maybe[e]	Yes	Yes
Auto-call Lyfts	Yes	Maybe	Yes

(Notice that, in the 1-to-N stage, you're mostly researching new features rather than entire new products.)

Prototyping and testing

At this point, you can do a Post-It or clickable prototype, but the companies behind 1-to-N products want to see data to back up assumptions. So your main task would be to set a metrics goal (whether quantitative or qualitative) and run an A/B test, where you launch the feature to a subset of users and see how different the metrics are from the baseline.

[d] It probably feels more like an ad than a convenience.

[e] The downside is that Uber users will get mad.

Put it together, and your research statement might be something like:

> *We believe that Lyft users spend too long waiting at airports' pickup points, which is frustrating them. We think that placing "X minutes of walking time left" signs throughout the airport could solve this problem. We'll launch this in a few airports, and we'll know we're right if we see a 30% increase in users' average self-reported satisfaction (measured on a scale from 1 to 10), average waiting time decrease by 40%, and number of Lyfts called at the airport increase by 10%.*

From this, you can extract a template that you can use when designing your own research statements:[65]

> *We believe that [user group] faces [problem]. We think [solution] could solve it. We'll know we're right if we see [metrics changes].*

Your metrics can and should emphasize delight, difficulty of copying, and profitability.

Once you've created this statement, you'd run your experiments, gather the numbers, and report on whether you hit the goals you set out at the beginning. If you did, chances are good that you'll be given the go-ahead to launch.

Reference customers

The approach we mentioned above is pretty rinse-and-repeat for straightforward features that you can launch, test, and measure easily. But it would be too chaotic if you launched some features before they were ready, and some features are all about usability and thus aren't well-suited to closed-ended feedback, where individual people's stories won't shine through. The former is especially the case for enterprise customers (they don't like getting, and possibly losing, half-baked features), and the latter is especially the case for redesigns or ambitious new product directions.

In these cases, one of the most powerful tools in your arsenal is *reference customers*: a small set of users who you have a very close relationship to and who you can do small-scale testing with. These customers should represent the breadth of your user base, so they'll give you feedback that's representative of what your broader user base would say.[66] The other benefit is that it's much easier to build for a person or organization you know personally than some abstract ideal customer.[f]

As a case study, Microsoft Azure's customers run the gamut from hobbyists to startups to massive businesses[67] like eBay and Boeing.[68] Adi's team on Azure recruited six reference customers: two startups, two mid-sized businesses, and two large enterprises. His team would talk to each of these customers every two weeks, gathering feedback on how the product was currently serving them and running new features by them. By having a small but wide group of customers providing feedback, Adi's team could quickly understand how everyone in the varied customer base might feel about a change.

For example, consider the seemingly-simple problem of showing a customer's servers on a map.[69] What do you do as the viewer zooms in or out of the map: do you lump nearby servers (e.g. the ones in Montreal and Toronto) into a larger bubble, or do you keep them separate?

You can imagine that a large company with servers across the world would like to lump servers together since they need to get a bird's eye view, but a small company that only had servers in Canada would find this lumping entirely counterproductive. By talking to customers of different sizes, Adi's team was able to figure out solutions for problems like these that accommodated everyone.

[f] As you can see, we don't place too much stock in user personas. If your user research finds five people who fit the same archetype (e.g. the community college student), don't generalize them into a persona — just pick one of those people and build for them. This way, you have a flesh-and-blood person to talk to, and you ensure you don't veer into a fantasy world.

Chapter 4

Minimum Lovable Products

WE'VE KEPT TALKING ABOUT how you shouldn't announce your MVP to the world, because it isn't ready. The reason we say that is that you only get one chance to make a first impression on users, and if you don't do that right, you'll have a hard time getting back on track. You only get one launch party, one big reveal, one first round of press coverage (if you're lucky), one demo day. You have to make it count.

So, when you're thinking about shipping version 1.0 of your product, you should be thinking about your *minimum marketable product* (*MMP*)[1] or *minimum lovable product* (*MLP*).[2] While your MVP (or, properly, RAT) is the simplest thing that will help you get feedback, your MLP is the simplest thing that will impress your users and make them stick around.

Simple but good

Unlike the MVP, the MLP should have sanded down all the rough edges and built in key differentiating features that show the user why they should use (and pay for) your product instead of the others on the market. Your MLP doesn't need to have all the features, but the features it *does* have need to be good.[3]

Case study: Notion's 1.0

For instance, take the information management tool Notion. When version 1.0 launched in 2016, the app was quite simple: just document editing and a small to-do list feature. But the few features it had worked very well: people immediately praised how smooth, well-organized, and well-thought-out the product was. Similarly, it only had a Mac and web app, but those apps drew high praise.[4]

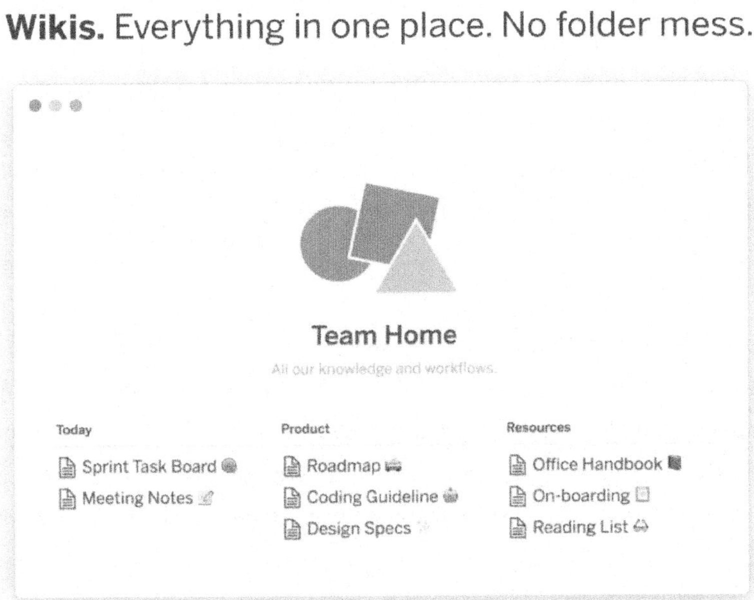

A screenshot from Notion's simple v1 launch. Source: Product Hunt[5]

Features that we might now think of as core, such as the ability to log in with non-Google email addresses and even sharing, weren't added until after this initial launch.[6] Bells and whistles like kanban boards and calendars weren't added until version 2.0 came out in 2018,[7] and even the Android app didn't come out until months after 2.0.[8]

Notion's founder, Ivan Zhao, consciously kept the "surface area" of the app small at the start. Most features weren't there, but the features that *were* there shone. It's better to release a few polished features than to release a bunch of half-baked ones — this is the crux of the MLP concept.

The minimum feature set

How did Zhao decide what would go in his 1.0 and what would be saved for later? He worked backward from his elevator pitch to his feature list. He only built the minimum number of features that would let him prove the value proposition. Here's what he posted on Product Hunt when he announced version 1.0:

> *[O]ur goal is to create the general purpose work tool for a post-file, post-MS Office world... The state of art is either Google Docs/Quip/Dropbox Paper (multiplayer WordPerfect), or rigid SAAS apps (Visual Basic on the web by outsourced IT). To end users, all the knowledge and workflows are trapped in different "silos", the best people can do is to duct-tape everything together, previously with emails, nowadays with Slack.*
>
> *Notion wants to challenge this status quo of "software as silos". For the 1.0 release, we are bundling real-time documents, wiki-like organization, and lightweight tasks into a unified tool that can handle pretty much all your team's knowledge needs.*[9]

Notion was offering a more seamless way to store and manage information. To achieve this, all Zhao had to build was a "wiki"-like system that let you store documents and link them to each other. That was the key innovation behind Notion, and so it's all he had to build up front. Things like sharing and kanban boards, while very useful nowadays, were only incidental to this value proposition and thus not needed for version 1.0.

Core ideas

So the key to building an MLP is to know your minimum feature list, and the key to knowing your minimum feature list is to know the core idea behind your product. Chances are you that this was one of your Solution assumptions from earlier, or even your riskiest assumption from your RAT. As examples, you could phrase the fundamental ideas behind some popular products like so:

- Google Search: PageRank (grading search results by the number and quality of incoming links)[10] is the best way to decide what a search engine should return.
- Airbnb: Staying at a stranger's house is better than staying at a hotel for cost-conscious travelers.
- Bumble: Online dating is better if women message first.[11]
- Trello: The notion of drag-and-droppable kanban cards, originally popularized in Toyota's supply chain management system,[12] can help manage white-collar projects.[13]

Another way to think about it: if you had to describe this product in one sentence at a noisy bar, what would you say? "Yeah, I just downloaded Bumble — it's like Tinder, but the women write first!" That's the core idea behind the product, and that's what you absolutely must have in the MLP. (Chances are you tested that during your MVP and RAT, anyway.)

Experiences, not products

Note that, this whole time, we haven't been talking about minimum *functional* products. We've been talking about minimum *lovable* products. That's for good reason, too: people are buying holistic experiences, not a list of features or even a product. You don't go to Starbucks just for the coffee; you go there for the European coffeehouse aesthetic, to enjoy a "third space" (neither home nor work) where you can hang out and people-watch.[14]

The "product" you think you're selling might not actually be what people care about. For example, guess what draws the most complaints about airlines. Chances are that it's not the plane;[a] the average flyer probably couldn't tell an Airbus A320 from a Boeing 777. People instead pay attention to such seemingly-trivial details as the food served on the planes. In 2020, United announced it would no longer serve the popular Biscoff cookies on its planes.[15] The backlash was so ferocious that United reversed course in less than a week, sheepishly announcing that Biscoff would be here to stay.[16]

For your MLP, you have to make sure you're building in those magical "wow" moments. In most cases, that's more important than the features themselves. Consider the original Nintendo Switch, which by all accounts wasn't the most attractive or functional thing in the world. It had thick bezels, plasticky controllers, a relatively underpowered processor, and a flimsy kickstand.[17]

[a] Unless it's a Boeing 787 MAX.

The Nintendo Switch with its controllers ("Joy-Cons") disconnected. Source: Lin Sinchen[18]

No, what made the Switch have the most successful first year (in terms of sales) of any console in history[19] was just how fun and versatile it was. You can be playing Zelda on your TV, pop it out of its dock, and take it on an airplane and keep playing like nothing had happened. When you're playing in handheld mode and a friend walks in, you can instantly tear off the controllers and start playing in two-player mode.[b] Experiences like these make you overlook the mediocre hardware and made the Switch one of the most beloved gaming consoles ever.[20]

Indeed, most hyper-successful products can generate those magical

[b] Neel's favorite experience: he was playing on an airplane when someone in the row in front of him turned around and asked if he'd like to start a group match. This person brought in his friend, who was sitting many rows ahead, and the three played a pickup game of Super Smash Bros — strangers, and on a plane to boot.

moments. From the day it launched, Uber was inherently cool because you could somehow bring a black car to your exact location at the touch of a button — no need to talk to a grumpy operator or spell out your address.[21] Duolingo lets you learn Klingon, the fictional language from *Star Trek*[22] — not all that practical, but guaranteed to bring a smile to your face. Even the tiny spark of power you feel when you beam your phone screen onto a TV with Chromecast can feel magical.

🎁 Bonus video

Uber was never about just hailing a taxi: it's always been about magical experiences. Watch this bonus video to learn how Uber has maintained the magic since day one.

productalliance.com/videos/uber

Case study: Apple Watch vs. Fitbit

The bad news is that creating these magical moments is an inexact science, and it's a lot harder to do than to toss some barely-functional MVP on the market. But it pays off. In fact, if you ship a product that people truly love, you can get away with being later to the market than competitors.

Consider the Apple Watch, which debuted in 2014.[23] It was hardly the first fitness-focused wearable device for wrists; Fitbit had already launched the Fitbit Flex, a pedometer and wristband, the year before.[24] But the Fitbit Flex was just a utilitarian plastic-and-rubber affair, with subdued colors and a handful of lights.[25]

The original Fitbit Flex wristband, launched in 2013. Source: Wikimedia[26]

The Apple Watch packed more features, including a heart rate sensor and gyroscope (so it could tell what activity you were doing), but what made it such a leap forward was that you could control your iPhone with it.[27] No more need to pull out your phone while running to change the song or check a text — a boon for runners. Being able to read push notifications directly on your wrist made you feel like an important executive, and just owning a watch let you show off all kinds of unusual maneuvers that only fellow Apple Watch users would understand, such as covering your watch with your hand to mute an incoming call.[28] Wearing an Apple Watch made you feel like an important, fit, and sophisticated person — something that let it stand head-and-shoulders above a pedestrian wristband.

Another underrated facet of the Apple Watch is how easily it could become a fashion statement. Rather than forcing you to use dull rubber bands, Apple let you swap in leather bands from the likes of Coach, Hermes, and Kate Spade.[29] Plus, the watch itself is customizable, in suave colors like rose gold, space gray, and stainless steel.[30] Apple even sold a $10,000 watch made of 18-karat gold.[31] The watch was no longer just a fitness tracker — it was an extension of your personality and sense of style.

Apple Watches with luxury leather bands made by Coach. Each is over $100. Source: 9to5Mac[32]

Simply put, the Apple Watch transcends being a tool and becomes a magical experience. The financial numbers show just how effective this strategy has been. While fitness-tracking products have done well, the Apple Watch has been a breakthrough success. In 2019, over 30 million Apple watches were sold — more than the entire Swiss watch industry.[33]

Out-of-box experiences

Your MLP should be relatively polished, but you can get away with some gaps in some of the more obscure parts of your product. (Early Notion versions' wiki functionality was rock-solid, but the drag-and-drop was pretty finicky.[34])

One place you *can't* skimp on, however, is the first impression you make to the user: the *out-of-box experience*, or *OOBE*.[c] Many new products overlook the OOBE because they're dead-set on getting the core features right,[35] leading to a lackluster first-run experience. Nobody's going to use your super-slick core product feature if they don't get past the onboarding flow; people wouldn't try Bumble's clever women-message-first mechanic if they didn't get past the sign-in flow.

For instance, buying an Apple product evokes joy in many people because the device comes in a pearly-white box, perfectly slotted into the grooves. All the irritating manuals and ugly power cords are hidden behind the actual device.[36] It feels less like you're opening a gadget and more like you're opening a treasure chest holding a rare jewel. Meanwhile, imagine if your new iPhone came in that tacky and impossible-to-open plastic shell, or if you were met with a bunch of half-popped bubble wrap and rubber bands upon tearing the box open. You'd love the product a lot less.

[c]Rhymes with "Scooby" from "Scooby Doo."

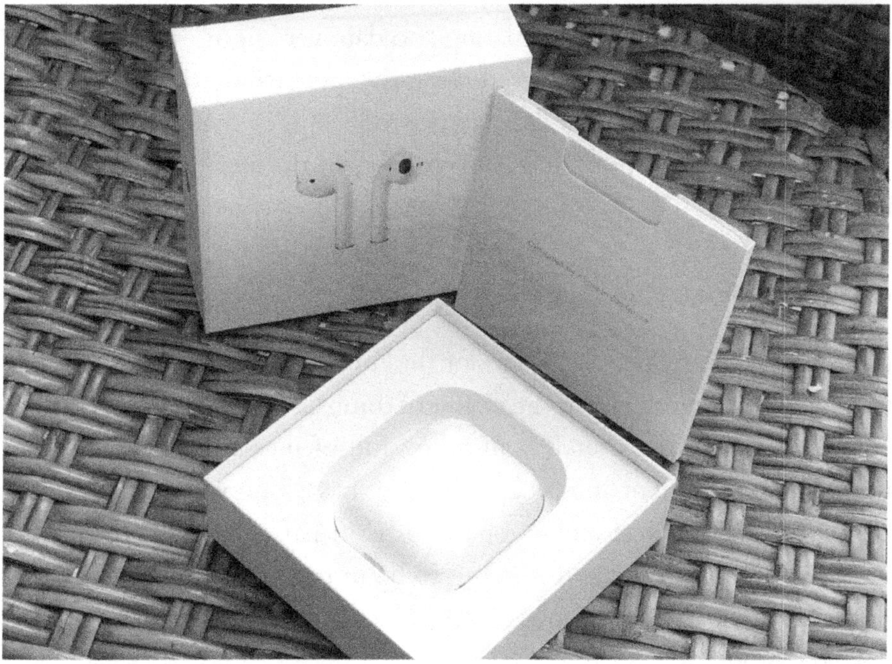

Apple products are the first thing you see when you open their boxes; cables and user manuals are hidden behind them. These small touches give Apple products such wonderful out-of-box experiences. Source: iMore[37]

Investing in the OOBE, which is an afterthought for most products, can yield big dividends. Consider Crashlytics, the former mobile app analytics toolkit. At the time it launched, most similar products hadn't really bothered to make a good OOBE, instead handing new users 10-minute YouTube videos featuring a droning instructor, 30-step tutorials, 10-part forms, or ugly wiki pages full of outdated screenshots. Not a great first impression.[38]

Instead, Crashlytics wanted to make onboarding fast and fun. Installing the tool was as simple as dragging a wiggling red toolbox icon to a particular folder. Then when you fired it up, you saw a dramatic animation that led you to a dashboard filled with example data rather than a blank dashboard with intimidating "no data yet" signs everywhere. It was an instant success: users raved about the onboarding flow, Crashlytics became the biggest mobile analytics tool (bigger than numbers two through six combined),[39] and Twitter bought the startup for $38 million.[40]

Don't start with a bare cupboard

In particular, many people design for the "mature" user: they assume the user has already gotten into the swing of things.[41] Designs of messaging apps assume that the user has an inbox full of messages and plenty of friends; entertainment apps assume the user has a long watch history and a long set of favorites; and so on. This is in part because most of the user's lifetime with the app is going to be in this "mature" state, and in part because it's awkward to even sketch out an app screen that is totally devoid of content.

But, in doing so, you often create an extremely boring, poorly-thought out OOBE. A messaging app with zero threads is boring (and, in fact, intimidating); a social network with no friends feels depressing; and a recommendation system that hasn't been fed any data about the user will spit out generic, impersonal suggestions.[42]

One clever solution to this "cold start" problem is to preload the product with content. Instead of dumping users into a blank dashboard, Trello gives everyone a demo "Welcome Board" to start, full of cards that show what the product can do for you.[43] (This kills two birds with one stone: it gives the user something to play with at the start, and it teaches users how to use the product![44])

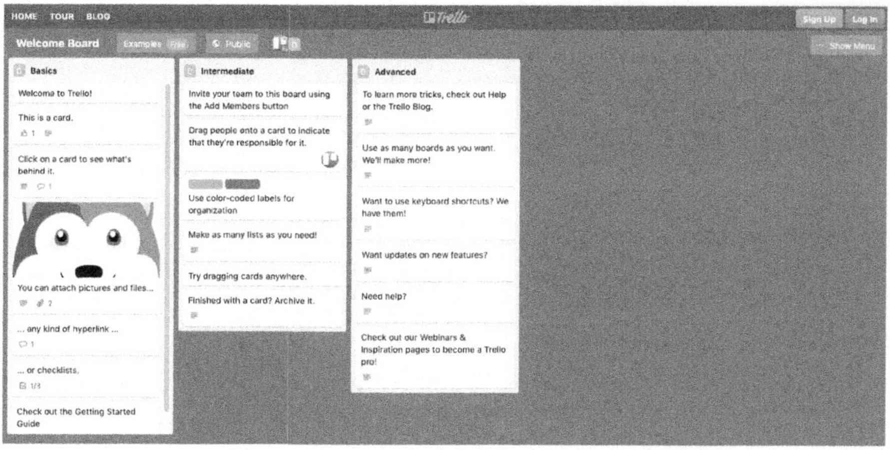

Trello's welcome board, which gives new users something to play with instead of dumping them into an empty UI. Source: Trello[45]

TikTok is the expert in overcoming the cold-start problem, though. While most social networking apps are pretty useless until you start following people, TikTok starts showing you entertaining videos from the moment you open the app — no setup needed.[46] This gets users to appreciate TikTok's value, not to mention its quirky personality, within seconds.

Beyond the first day

What's more, the first few days of a user's relationship with the app are the most critical. The average app loses 77% of its active users within three days of installation and slowly bleeds users for the next few months.[47]

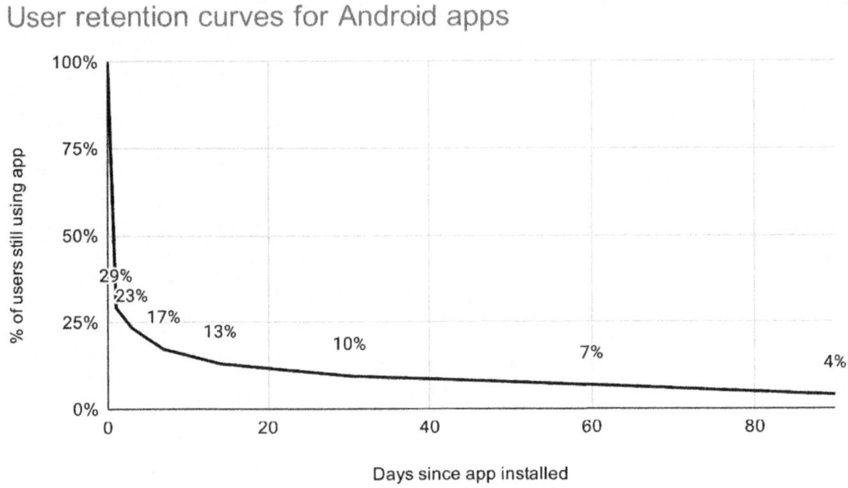

The user retention curves for the average Android app. Source: Andrew Chen[48]

But if you break out the most-downloaded apps on the Play Store, you notice an interesting trend. All apps lose users at about the same rate after the first week or so, but the first week makes all the difference: the top app hangs on to 72% of its user base after three days and 67% after a week, but the average app keeps just 23% and 17%, respectively.[49] The best apps keep almost 13 times as many users as the average app after 90 days — so, all else being equal, they need to spend 13 times less money attracting users.

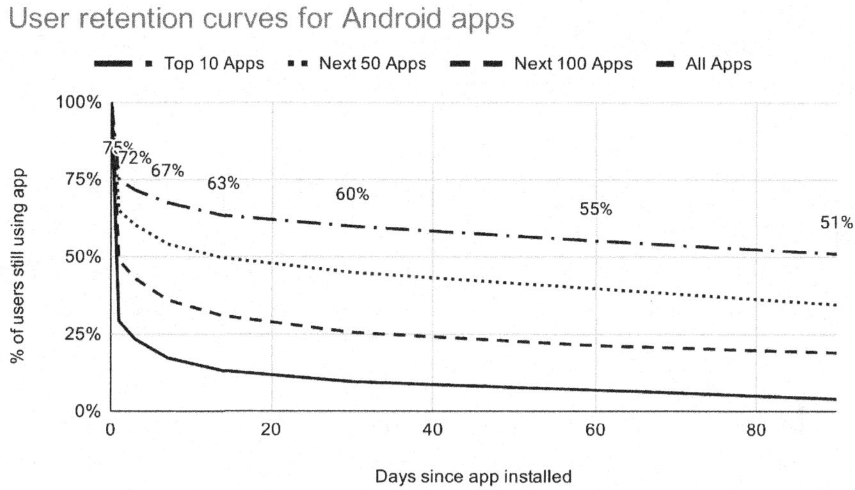

The user retention curves for Android apps, with the top apps broken out. Source: Andrew Chen[50]

This means that your first impression is actually longer than just the first time someone opens the app — the entire first week is just as important. The best way to do this is to make sure users start getting value (productivity, entertainment, etc.) within the first few days, such as by walking users through an onboarding flow that gets everything set up and encourages them to start using your key features. Hinge might want new users to start getting matches within the first few days; Airtable might want users to make two tables and use a few advanced features in the first week.

Interview tip

Notice how none of these first-week goals have anything to do with revenue. That's intentional: you can't expect someone to start paying you until you've shown them your product's value and made them into a fan of your product. Trying to drive sales out of the gate might earn you a few dollars in the short term but miss out on a lot of potential sales in the long term.

Discuss this tension between short-term and long-term profitability with your interviewer. Prioritizing long-term profitability by spending the first week making users happy is usually the best move, and talking about this will show your interviewer that you can think big-picture.

The one thing you absolutely shouldn't do is spam people with notifications and emails.[51] You've probably had this experience: you download an interesting new app but start getting annoying push notifications an hour later. It's very likely that you turned around and immediately uninstalled the app.

Conclusion

IN 1985, Apple was sputtering, and Jobs was the poster child for their failures. Jobs's Macintosh was only selling 10% of its projected volume. John Sculley, who had taken the helm of Apple in 1983, slowly moved Jobs away from the Macintosh and Lisa business, eventually demoting Jobs far enough that Jobs saw the writing on the wall and left Apple.[1] Jobs's stubbornness in designing his computers, not to mention the toxic atmosphere he created, was his undoing.

That year, Jobs decided to take on Apple by creating NeXT, a startup that would sell high-end computers focused on the education market.[2] NeXT was famous for its sleek, boxy, magnesium computers coated in jet-black paint.[3] The hardware was innovative — the Cube ditched the floppy disk a full decade before the iMac did[45] and came with a uniquely high-quality laser printer.[6]

NeXT's iconic computer, the NeXT Cube. It retailed for $6500 and launched in 1988. Source: Wikimedia[7]

NeXT's software was no slouch either: the operating system had full-color graphics and multitasking long before Apple, its developer tools were top-tier, and its apps could interoperate seamlessly.[8]

But NeXT's success was short-lived; their 1990 hardware sold poorly, and they couldn't break through the PC duopoly of Microsoft and Apple. After 1990, the company abandoned hardware entirely and focused only on their programming language, OpenStep[9] The company shuffled along for a few more years until Apple, itself at risk of falling behind Windows 95, bought NeXT for $400 million in 1996.[10d]

But Apple was in dire straits. Apple's market share had sunk below

[d]NeXT's software didn't die with the acquisition: its operating system served as the basis for macOS and, by extension, iOS.[11]

4% as Windows had steadily outpaced it; Apple's last three attempts to reboot its operating system had all failed. The company was about to go bankrupt.[12] After Apple saw its worst financial quarter in history in 1997, Jobs was brought back as CEO in a last-ditch effort to save the company.[13] Jobs was back, and he'd learned from his exile.

Jobs 2.0, as he is now known,[14] now realized that the "bozos" weren't all that bad. Someone had to keep the company running and keep milking the cash cows. So, in 1998, he hired a man named Tim Cook, then a VP at Compaq,[15] then the world's largest PC seller.[16] Nobody mistook Cook for an innovator: he was an efficient operating machine, nicknamed the "Attila the Hun of Inventory."[17]

At the same time, Jobs knew he had to take a risky bet to revive the company. So he tapped an Apple employee named Jony Ive[18] to lead the design of the new iMac G3, a bold, colorful, and bulbous computer that was an instant hit.[19] Computers of the day were beige, boxy, and boring, and it required a lot of expertise to set up and use. Meanwhile, the iMac integrated almost everything into a single fun, colorful box. All you had to attach was the keyboard and mouse that came in the box. It was the first computer that anyone could pick up and play with, and Ive's design brilliance was to thank.[20]

Apple's 1998 iMac G3, which came in delightful colors ranging from Tangerine to Lime to the famous Bondi Blue.[21] *Source: Carl Berkeley*[22]

The iMac, which would go on to be offered in such delicious colors as tangerine, strawberry, lime, and indigo,[23] was only Ive's first hit. He would go on to invent the iPod, iPhone, MacBook Air, and Apple Watch over the next 20 years,[24] while Cook would grow these product lines until Apple became the world's first trillion-dollar company (by market cap) in 2018.[25]

In short, Jobs 2.0 realized that he needed both pirates and the regular Navy. He needed people like Ive to keep creating the next generation of 0-to-1 products, and he needed people like Cook to scale 1-to-N products out enough to fund the next generation of 0-to-1 products. As you can tell, that realization paid off spectacularly.

Most other successful companies have realized this as well. Amazon Web Services is a steady and reliable cash cow for Amazon; it gives

Amazon the funds to fuel its innovative projects in ecommerce, gaming, media, etc.[26] In 2017, in fact, AWS accounted for *all* of Amazon's profit; the ecommerce divisions actually lost money.[27]

Similarly, Facebook's advertising money machine lets it make big bets on billion-dollar projects like Oculus VR,[28] which can take up to a decade to find product-market fit.[29] Remember the hot AR/VR startup MagicLeap: without a steady funding source, it couldn't keep the project going for long enough to reach maturity.

Some companies have even made this a way of life: Google's Area 120 and X divisions are incubators for hot ideas[30] that might one day replace Google Search as the new cash cow. Until then, Google's ad machine will keep printing money to pay the salaries of these experimenters.[31]

As a product manager, you'll be responsible for designing both 0-to-1 and 1-to-N products at various points in your career. Knowing how to do both, and how they fit together, is an extremely important skill. ❦

All QR codes from Part I

In case you skipped over any QR codes from the last few chapters, here's a roundup. Scan them with your phone to watch bonus videos and try interactive demos.

A mock interview where Neel, one of your authors, proposes a design for Lyft's web experience:

productalliance.com/videos/product-design

How Uber creates magical, delightful user experiences:

productalliance.com/videos/uber

II

Economics

Price is what you pay. Value is what you get.

— Warren Buffett

Introduction

IN 2017, the startup MoviePass emerged from obscurity to become one of the tech world's hottest startups when it began offering Americans an incredible deal: nearly unlimited free movies for just $10 a month.[1]

Considering you can spend over $10 on a single movie ticket in many cities,[2] the deal was incredible. MoviePass, which hadn't achieved much of anything since its founding in 2011,[3] suddenly added millions of users within months.[4]

But, for obvious reasons, people started asking immediately if MoviePass was too good to be true.[5] MoviePass argued otherwise, saying that most people wouldn't actually watch more than one movie a month; if true, this would make MoviePass profitable.[6] The logic was like that of a gym: annual passes are so profitable because everyone buys annual passes, goes a few times in January, and promptly drops off once New Year's resolutions are forgotten.

The problem, of course, was that going to the movies was a lot more fun than going to the gym. People watched up to dozens of movies a month, plunging MoviePass into the red: its parent company lost $150 million in 2017 alone.[7]

MoviePass insisted it could still make a profit, saying that it could sell movie viewers' data to theaters and movie studios, sell ads, and land paid promotion deals.[8] But, predictably, they were wrong. Instead of admitting defeat, MoviePass gradually scaled back its generosity, first stopping users from watching popular movies or going to theaters at peak times[9] and later capping users to three movies a month.[10] None of it worked, and MoviePass's parent company went bankrupt in 2020.[11]

MoviePass was clearly a comedy of errors and a flawed company in many, many ways, but their fundamental flaw was a fatal misunderstanding of basic economics. We product managers have to know economics to avoid building the next MoviePass; we have to understand how people make decisions, how to build sustainable businesses, and how to measure our financial success. Let's dive in.

Chapter 5

Business Models

WHEN YOU'RE thinking about launching a product or starting a company, one of the most essential questions you'll have to wrestle with is a simple one: how are you going to make money? Before you start thinking about tactical things like the prices of subscriptions or the locations of your ads, you need to take a step back and think about business models from first principles.

Most companies make money by selling products or services to people. Tech companies tend to focus on products rather than services like accounting or consulting, so we'll only look at products. When you're serving products to people, there are three main ways to make a profitable business: *cost leadership*, *product differentiation*, and a *blue-ocean strategy*. Your business model will probably be based on one of these three, so you should figure out which one applies before you do anything else.

Cost leadership

In this model, your product and all its competitors are pretty much the same; you set yourself apart by selling your product at the lowest possible price.[1]

These highly-similar, interchangeable products are known as *commodities*. There are plenty of well-known, non-tech commodities that you can buy and sell on the stock market: gold, oil, wheat, pork, and so on. They aren't *exactly* the same — one given bushel of wheat might be a bit better than another bushel — but they're close enough that you don't really care who made the product or where it came from. All you care about is the price.[2]

Financiers would say that only items sold on the stock market can be true "commodities," but a looser definition — which most technologists use — includes any category of interchangeable goods. One-liter water bottles, 87-octane gas, and ibuprofen tablets fall in this category. You don't care all that much who made these products, as long as they work properly.[a]

A collection of nearly-identical HDMI cables on Amazon. These are commodity products: all that matters is the price. Source: Amazon[3]

Tech has its fair share of commodities too. Cheap hardware accessories like HDMI cables are differentiated only by price; a gigabyte of cloud storage space is about as useful no matter who (Google Drive, Dropbox, etc.) provides it; and so on. Even ridesharing is a sort of commodity: who hasn't opened both Uber and Lyft and chosen the ride that's a buck cheaper?

[a]This is, incidentally, the foundational logic of the generic drug industry.

One of our favorite examples of tech commodities is the $50 Android smartphone, an unbranded, plasticky, straight-from-the-factory device that does the bare minimum to be called a "smartphone."[4]

To keep costs down, the makers of these phones get cheap parts straight from the makers, install the free-to-use Android operating system, rely on dirt-cheap labor (often in China), and spend absolutely nothing on marketing. They know full well that their customers would abandon them if a competitor made a $49 smartphone, so their mission is to ruthlessly cut costs until they can make a $48 phone.

A collection of cheap phones made by no-name manufacturers in Singapore. Source: Kai Hendry[5]

If you're selling commodities, the only way to keep your prices low is to keep your costs low. You can do this by using *economies of scale*, where your goods get cheaper as you make more of them. Making a higher volume of goods lets you exploit volume discounts, negotiate better deals with your suppliers, and learn how to increase the efficiency of your production process.[6]

Vertical integration, where you buy out all your suppliers, also helps reduce costs, as does cutting out middlemen like retailers by distributing products directly to consumers. (The latter is how Costco, which lets shoppers effectively buy straight from a warehouse, keeps the prices of household essentials so low.)

However, selling commodities isn't a great business to be in, since there's an inevitable *race to the bottom* in prices. If a factory can make USB cables for $2 each, you won't be able to get away with selling them for $3 — someone else will sell them for $2.50 and take your business.

But then someone selling at $2.30 would take all their business, and so on, until the price bottomed out at, say, $2.01 — and, at that point, the winner would be making such razor-thin margins that they'd be unable to stay in business. The only way to win in cost leadership is to have some "secret sauce" that consistently keeps your costs below the competition's.

Product differentiation

On the opposite end of the spectrum is *product differentiation*, where you sell a unique product whose *competitive advantages* justify a higher price. It's the anti-commodity: a company sells a product that's explicitly different from the rest, with a different price tag to match.

Luxury products are classic examples of this strategy. There's an old joke where a person wearing a cheap, plasticky $10 watch needles his friend wearing a Rolex, saying, "My watch costs one-thousandth[7] as much as yours but tells the same time." And yet, people keep buying Rolexes, since Rolex has set itself apart from the commodity products like that $10 watch. Some combination of Rolex's design, superior quality, and elite lifestyle branding justify Rolexes' premium price in buyers' minds.

In tech, iPhones use the same approach. An $1100 iPhone does the same job as a $300 Android phone (and, arguably, those cheap $50 Androids we met earlier), yet millions of people are willing to pay the premium for the phone.

Apple, in this case, has a phenomenal set of services built around the iPhone (like the Health app[8]), fantastic customer service with "Genius Bars" in Apple Stores around the world, a sexy-looking operating system, and even a gorgeous white box that cradles new iPhones.[b] These make iPhones worth the money, in many people's eyes.

The gorgeous white boxes that iPhones come in. Source: KLGadgetGuy[10]

The challenge for companies pursuing a differentiation strategy is

[b]iPhones' pearly boxes are so beloved that people sell them on eBay for up to $10.[9] You'd be hard-pressed to find any Android's packaging up for resale.

staying consistently different from the competition. With enough time and money, anyone could build an operating system as good as Apple's (you can argue that Android has gotten there), great hardware and services (in good years, Samsung's Galaxy line and the Google Pixel rival the iPhone in this regard), and pump cash into marketing. Products need some "secret sauce" that keeps them different.

For iPhones, of course, it's the brand. Toting an iPhone sends a message of wealth, sophistication, and good taste — a message that Apple has consciously cultivated with its marketing and design.

Product managers can build in features that enhance and use the brand, too. Even something as small as a color can make a difference: Android users texting iPhone users get ugly, bright green bubbles, while iPhone users texting other iPhone users get suave blue bubbles.

This creates a subtle social pressure to get an iPhone; green bubbles are stigmatized and seen as a sign that you aren't part of the "in-crowd." This stigma is very powerful: in one study, phone buyers cited not wanting a green bubble as the top reason for preferring an iPhone over Android.[11] (Not to mention the "I don't date green bubbles" memes.[12])

Not all companies can successfully make their product consistently different from the competition. When they can't, their products become *commoditized* — meaning that they become no better than the competition, forcing them to fight on price, which is a surefire way to get razor-thin profit margins.

Uber and Lyft have long had this problem: most people see their products as effectively the same, so few people build loyalty to a brand — they'll just go to whatever's cheaper. When Uber announces unique new features, Lyft just copies them. When Uber announced an Express Pool service in 2018,[13] offering 50% of pooled rides if you walked a few hundred feet,[14] Uber finally had a unique feature — but Lyft added a carbon copy of the feature the next year.[15] It's hard to build brand loyalty if you can't consistently stay different from the rest.

The blue ocean

The third school of thought is to avoid both the cost leadership and product differentiation strategies. With either strategy, you're fighting tooth-and-nail for a slice of the pie, always trying to stay a step ahead of your many competitors. But why not just find a new pie that nobody else is fighting for? Instead of fighting over a crowded market, why not create a new one?

This strategy is called the *blue ocean* strategy — so named because the goal is to find a wide-open sea of possibilities instead of fighting in blood-filled waters (the *red ocean*).[16] By finding a new market, the thinking goes, you can offer *both* low cost and differentiation.

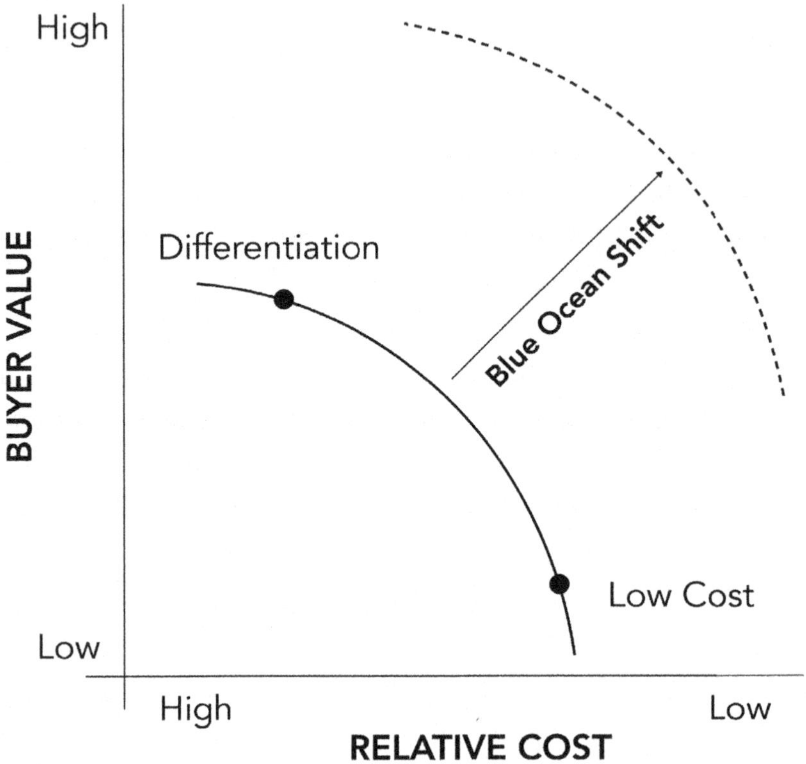

There's usually a tradeoff between cost leadership and differentiation, but a blue ocean shift lets you have both. Source: Chan Kim and Renee Mauborgne[17]

Nintendo

One of the best examples of blue oceans in tech, in our minds, is Nintendo. The gaming company rarely tries to compete head-on with Xbox and PlayStation, two gaming lines that strive to have the most powerful processors, cutting-edge graphics, and intense shoot-em-up games for hardcore gamers. Competing with those two on their own turf would be too hard.

Instead, Nintendo opens up new markets to gaming, letting the company own a space without significant competition.[18] The Wii brought gaming to families[19] — a demographic that Xbox and PlayStation don't even try to target — with its intuitive motion-sensing controllers,[20] casual multiplayer games like *Wii Sports*,[21] and family-friendly gaming franchises like Mario Kart.

It's no surprise that the Wii became one of the best-selling video game consoles of all time, and its games became some of the most popular as well.[22]

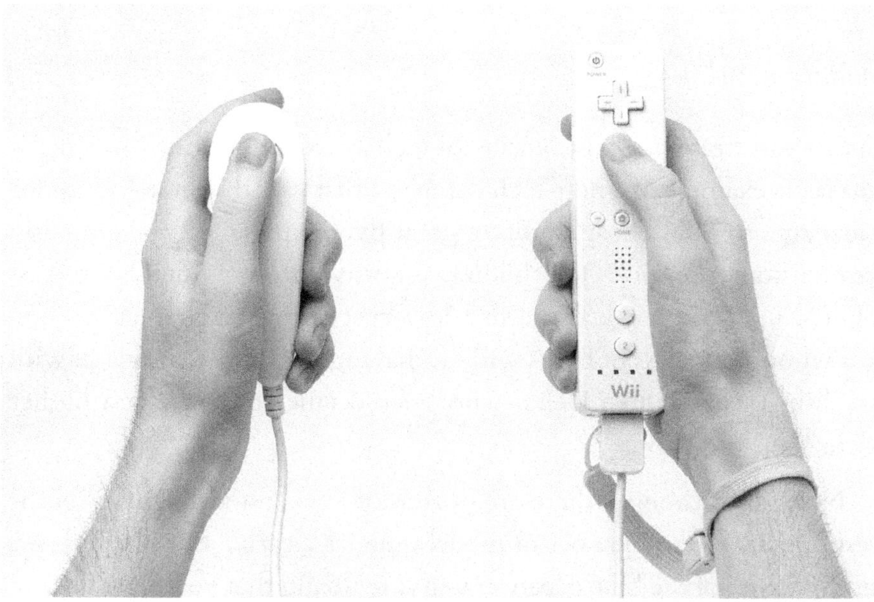

The Wii's famously intuitive, motion-sensing controllers: the "Wiimote" on the right and the "Nunchuck" on the left. Source: Wikimedia[23]

By 2017, the gaming market was split in two: dedicated gamers played on their powerful Xboxes, PlayStations, and gaming computers, while casual gamers played on their phones. Nintendo didn't try to compete directly with either. Instead, it released the hybrid Switch console, which can be played as a handheld or attached to a TV.[24]

With this, Nintendo could uniquely appeal to people who wanted the ability to game in both ways — to play on a small screen on the plane but on the big screen at home.[c] It turns out that there were a lot of people like this — college students, frequent flyers, families with kids, and so on[25] — and neither the Xboxes nor the Candy Crushes of the world could satisfy their needs. The Switch smashed the usual definition of a gaming console, thus appealing to new kinds of gamers, and was rewarded by selling more units in the US in its first year than any other console.[26]

Southwest Airlines

Blue-ocean strategies exist outside of tech as well. Southwest Airlines is the classic example of a non-tech company that uses this strategy[27] since it manages to offer cheap flights, a great flyer experience, *and* famously great customer service. This billing is mostly correct: when Southwest debuted in 1967,[28] it was the first low-cost airline, which let it scoop up a whole new class of flyers without having to compete head-on with established carriers like Delta, who offered fancier service at a higher price.[29]

Nowadays, though, there are dozens of low-cost airlines, so Southwest doesn't fit the blue ocean model quite as clearly. But it still shows another tenet of the blue ocean strategy: realizing that you don't have to trade off between low cost and good service.[30]

While the Ryanairs and Spirit Airlines of the world offer cheap, unpleasant flights and Emirates offers fantastic flights at a premium cost, Southwest found strategies to offer flights that are *both* cheap and high-quality.

For instance, Southwest does away with assigned seat numbers and lets flyers choose any open seat; this reduces boarding time by up to 25%

[c] The Switch's game lineup also deserves a lot of credit. It has both casual games like *Mario Kart* and *Pokémon*, more hardcore offerings like *Fire Emblem*, and games in the middle like *Zelda* and *Super Smash Bros.* It's another way this one product can appeal to a huge range of gamers.

over normal airlines.[31] This cuts Southwest's costs *and* makes boarding less miserable for passengers.

On top of this, Southwest mostly flies "point-to-point" instead of having layovers in "hub" cities, which reduces the amount of time that planes sit idle on runways (thus saving the company money) and helps passengers get to their destinations more quickly.[32] And the company makes a big deal out of treating its employees well, which improves morale and customer service while reducing staff turnover — which, in turn, reduces hiring and training costs.[33]

Our favorite example, though, has to be Southwest's famous policy of giving flyers two free checked bags.[34] It's obviously great for the customer and great for Southwest's brand as a company that refuses to nickel-and-dime customers;[35] "Bags Fly Free" is such a powerful slogan that Southwest once tattooed it on the side of its planes.[36]

A Southwest plane with "Free Bags Fly Here" painted on the side, pointing to the luggage compartment. Source: Wikimedia[37]

But, more importantly for Southwest's bottom line, it massively speeds up boarding. Think about it: how much time have you spent standing in the aisle waiting for someone ahead of you to cram an overstuffed bag into the overhead bin? (Or worse, has someone in the back ever walked way to the front to find a spot for their bag?) Eliminating these carry-on debacles shaves 10 minutes or more off boarding time,[38] which helps Southwest planes squeeze extra flights into the day, thus increasing profitability.

Put all this together and you have one very successful blue-ocean strategy. At the end of 2019, Southwest celebrated its 47th consecutive year of profitability — something unheard of in the airline industry — as well as a half-dozen customer satisfaction awards.[39] You really can have it all, if you're creative.

KaiOS

Finally, it's worth going back to our examples of phone operating systems: there are expensive, differentiated iPhones on one end, and dirt-cheap commodity Androids on the other. The phone OS world is so competitive that it's hard to find a place to fit in. This "red ocean" is littered with the corpses of failed phone OSes: HP's Palm phones running webOS,[40] Mozilla's Firefox OS,[41] and, of course, Windows Phones.[42]

An upstart can't break into the conventional smartphone market; you can't easily beat iPhones on quality or Androids on price. Firefox OS, for instance, tried to compete with Android for lower-end smartphones but was never able to beat Android on price. Without any other differentiating features, Firefox OS shut down within five years of launch.[43]

The only way to succeed in phones is to appeal to a market that neither iPhones nor Androids do. This was the strategy adopted by the emergent KaiOS, a super-simple successor to Firefox OS that powers super-low-end smartphones as cheap as $11.[44] (Yes, you read that right.)

Two generations of JioPhones, the incredibly cheap Indian phones that run KaiOS. Source: Gizmo Times[45]

KaiOS appeals to a whole new market: lower-budget people in developing countries who otherwise couldn't afford a smartphone.[46] For these people, even $50 Android phones were never an option; it was feature phones or nothing.

Of course it makes sense to offer a far cheaper phone than Androids, but it's not easy to develop a phone that cheap. KaiOS does this by breaking some of the foundational assumptions of Android. Gone are the touchscreens[47] and ability to run multiple apps at once.[48] Android relies on these — the whole user interface assumes there's a touchscreen — but KaiOS realized that low-budget phone seekers didn't need these hefty cost-adders.

And while low-end Androids have modest system specifications, KaiOS's specs are puny: a typical screen is 320-by-240 pixels,[49] about 7% as many pixels as a $100 Android phone by Nokia, which packs a 720-by-1520 pixel screen.[50][51]

KaiOS apps run relatively well despite the phones' cheapness, and in many cases they run better than apps on those cheap $50 Android phones.[52] This is because KaiOS apps have to be stripped down, while Android apps, which are normally run on more expensive phones,[53] can normally get away with being relatively bloated.

KaiOS opened up a gigantic new market and has it mostly to itself; its only competition is feature phones, which can't run essentials like WhatsApp. It should be no surprise, then, that KaiOS became the second most popular mobile OS in India within seven months of its launch in January 2018[54] — ahead of iOS — and the third most popular in the world.[55]

Chapter 6

Market Entry

ONCE YOU'VE found a market and a type of business strategy that interests you, you have to choose the right way to get into the market. Whether the market is social networks or video streaming or self-driving cars, you have to find a way to insert your product into the market.

Generally speaking, there are three ways to enter a market: building your own product, borrowing someone else's product, and buying another company's product. Each has its own strengths and weaknesses; you have to vary the strategies you use. The trouble is that various types of people are biased toward using one particular strategy all the time: PMs love building, partnerships folks love borrowing, and M&A teams love buying. You have to take these voices with a grain of salt and think hard about which strategy *really* makes sense in your case.

Build

The most obvious way to enter a market is to build your own product, and this is what engineers and product managers are trained from birth to do.

Compared to buying and borrowing, building makes the most sense if one of four criteria apply to you.

First, building makes sense if your company is new or short on resources. Buying other companies — and even setting up partnerships with other companies — takes a lot of money and employees (to do due diligence, sign contracts, etc.), and the average startup won't have that kind of resources. Building requires a lot of employee-hours, but you're already paying them, so it's not a huge spike in cost.

Second is if buying and borrowing don't pan out. Microsoft reportedly tried buying the corporate collaboration tool Slack for $8 billion in 2016,[1] but when Slack turned them down, Microsoft launched its own competing service, Microsoft Teams.[2] (Slack may have started to regret its decision: Teams had more users than Slack by 2019.[3])

Third is if your company has experience in a similar market. Microsoft has a lot of experience dealing with the litany of data privacy and security regulations that enterprises face,[4] given that Microsoft has been building enterprise software for decades, so the company knew it was especially well-suited to building similar features into Teams. Startups like Slack probably lacked that kind of experience.

Fourth, building makes sense if you can piggyback off your existing products. For Uber, the best way to enter the food delivery market was to build a new product (Uber Eats) instead of buying an existing product, since Uber already had a large network of drivers, a large user base, and the technology needed to tell drivers where to go. (Uber later bought the rival food delivery service Postmates,[5] but that was an expansion play made well after Uber entered the market. Build-then-buy, as Uber shows, is a valuable hybrid strategy.)

Borrow

The second strategy is to partner with other companies to use their products or co-develop new ones. It's probably the least famous of the three strategies, but there are plenty of examples. In 1996, Microsoft, which specialized in online news, partnered with NBC, which specialized in cable news, to create a new media property that would span online and cable; it was called MSNBC.[6] And in the world of gaming, Nintendo licenses third-party video game characters like Sonic the Hedgehog (a

Sega property[7]) to fight alongside Nintendo staples like Link and Kirby in the *Super Smash Bros* fighting series.[8]

Borrowing isn't as common as the other strategies, but it makes sense if one of four criteria apply.

First is if your company isn't an expert in the market, and doesn't want to be. When Facebook wanted to create videos for its new Facebook Watch product (a sort of Netflix competitor) in 2017, it didn't want to get into the business of movie production — that would take a lot of effort to set up, and it wasn't at all connected to Facebook's strengths, or *core competencies*. So Facebook partnered with MLB, National Geographic, and Time, among others, to create shows especially for Facebook Watch.[9]

Second is if you want to lean on someone else's credibility. When Apple wanted to launch its credit card in 2019, it partnered with Goldman Sachs to show that it could be trusted with people's finances.[10]

Third is if you want to quickly patch a hole. Spotify briefly offered free Hulu to premium subscribers in 2019,[11] perhaps because Spotify's audio-streaming competitors — including Apple Music[12] and Amazon Prime Music[13] — were offering free video at a similar monthly price to Spotify. This bundle let Spotify stay competitive, and since borrowing is typically faster than building and cheaper than buying, it was ideal for quickly catching up.

Finally, borrowing makes sense if you want to outsource the less profitable and resource-intensive parts of your business, which would drag you down if you owned them. The classic example here is in semiconductor manufacturing, the industry of making silicon chips like CPUs and GPUs. It takes a lot of time, money, and expertise to run a semiconductor factory (known as a *fab*),[14] so many top chipmakers — including AMD, Nvidia, and Qualcomm — partner with dedicated fabs to manufacture chips instead of trying to build or buy their own fab.[15a]

[a] Intel and Samsung are the main semiconductor makers who have their own fabs.

Buy

Buying another company is the market entry strategy that makes the most headlines. As you've seen, building and borrowing make more sense in many cases, but there are still four good reasons to buy.

One is if you want to remove a competitor from the market or keep the product away from other competitors. When Facebook saw that Instagram hit one million users just two months after the app launched in 2010,[16] it no doubt felt nervous about the rise of a competing social network. And when Facebook learned that Twitter,[17] and possibly Google,[18] were interested in buying Instagram, Facebook knew it had to keep the hot new app out of its competitors' hands — which swiftly led to Facebook buying Instagram for $1 billion in 2012.[19]

They can get away with it since they have such a long track record and so much money, but any newcomer to the space simply doesn't have the time or money to set up their own fab.

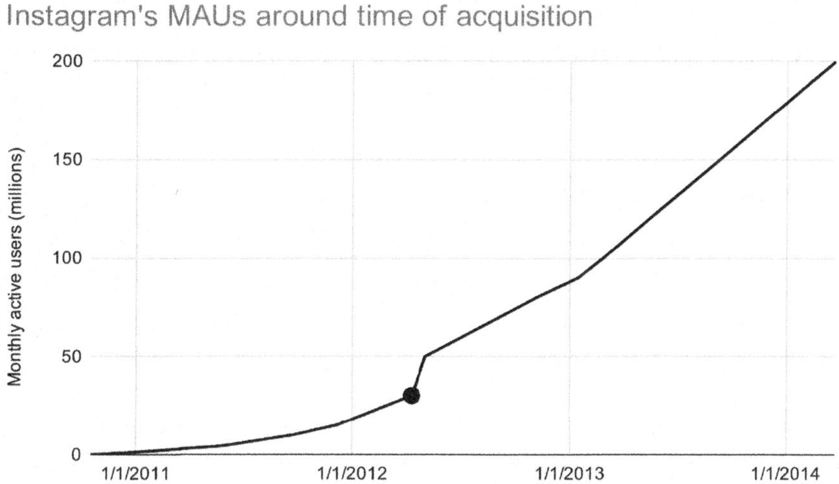

Instagram's Monthly Active Users (MAUs) from 2011 to 2014. The dot, and the beginning of the sudden spike, is when Facebook acquired Instagram. Sources: Business Insider[20], TechCrunch[21], Statista[22], MacStories[23]

Second is if you want to get the company's users. Anyone can rebuild the technology behind an app, but getting users on board is far harder. This is especially true in the case of social networks, which have strong *network effects* — the network becomes more valuable as more people join, which is good for existing networks but makes it very hard to kickstart a new network.[24]

In other words, it's much more effective to buy a social network than to build a new one; the user base is harder to recreate than the app itself. This is why acquisitions are so common in the world of social networking: consider Facebook's buys of Instagram and WhatsApp or Microsoft's $26 billion purchase of LinkedIn.[25] (Building your own social network from scratch is very difficult — just ask Google+.)

Third is if you want to get into a tough-to-enter industry. Amazon, for instance, bought the digital pharmacy PillPack in 2018 because getting licensed to deliver drugs is tough — but PillPack had already gone through all the hassle.[26]

Last is if you want to get special talent, especially if you're a traditionally non-tech company. Walmart, no doubt scared by the rise of Amazon, bought the ecommerce site Jet in 2016 to beef up their online presence.[27] Walmart, despite being a huge employer, probably lacked the kind of in-house tech talent needed to build a good ecommerce platform themselves.

While acquisitions are sexy and make sense in many cases, it's important not to pull the trigger too quickly. Harvard Business School professor Michael Porter said that companies seeking to acquire another need to ensure the proposed purchase passes these three *diversification tests* to ensure they're making the right call:[28]

1. *The better-off test*: do both companies benefit from joining forces? In the case of Microsoft buying LinkedIn, Microsoft's Office products benefited from getting data about professional relationships, and LinkedIn benefited by becoming part of big businesses' standard toolkit (along with Azure, Office, etc.) Meanwhile, HP's blockbuster $25 billion purchase of the computer maker Compaq in 2000 is still considered one of the worst tech acquisitions in history because the two companies had overlapping product lines and thus gained very little — besides a lot of extra salaries to pay — from the merger.[29]

2. *The cost-of-entry test*: is the price right? Or could you build or borrow for less? At the time, Facebook's purchase of WhatsApp in 2014 was seen as not worth the $19 billion price tag,[30] though WhatsApp's growth since then has made the deal look better in hindsight.

3. *The attractiveness test*: Is this new industry a profitable one? Microsoft's $7 billion purchase of the struggling phone maker Nokia

in 2013 is still seen as a failure because Nokia, and thus Windows, stood little chance of succeeding against iPhones and Android. As the critics expected, Windows Phones flopped within a few years.[31]

We like to add a fourth test: *the need-to-own test*. Do you have to buy that company to benefit from the arrangement? Or could you do just as well by establishing a partnership (i.e. borrowing)? Nintendo didn't need to buy Sega to get Sonic the Hedgehog into *Super Smash Bros*; just licensing the character was enough. And Spotify didn't need to buy Hulu to offer video along with music; they could have, but simply partnering to offer a bundle was cheaper (and ultimately easier to undo).

🎁 Bonus video

Build, borrow, and buy are classic market entry strategies, but nowadays there's a fourth: *minority stake investment*. Western tech titans are increasingly finding that it's their only way to get a part of the action in emerging markets like Southeast Asia. Check out this video to learn how this form of investment works and why it's so essential to tech titans' expansion plans.

productalliance.com/videos/emerging-markets

Comparing the options

As you can tell, there's no one-size-fits-all solution for entering a market. As a PM, you'll have to advocate for your company to choose the best tool for the job and not just use the strategy that you've always used. Research backs up the importance of this: one study out of Duke University found that companies that used more than one of build/borrow/buy were 46% more likely to survive over five years than those who just borrowed, 26% more likely than those who always bought, and 12% more likely than those that always built.[32]

One helpful way to summarize the decision-making process is that you should borrow if the product in question isn't core to your value proposition: Facebook isn't a media company, so buying or building a media outlet outright would just distract from the company's core mission. Products that are core to your value proposition should be built or bought; things that are harder to build yourself should, of course, be bought instead of built.[33] This is nicely shown in this 2x2 matrix:[34]

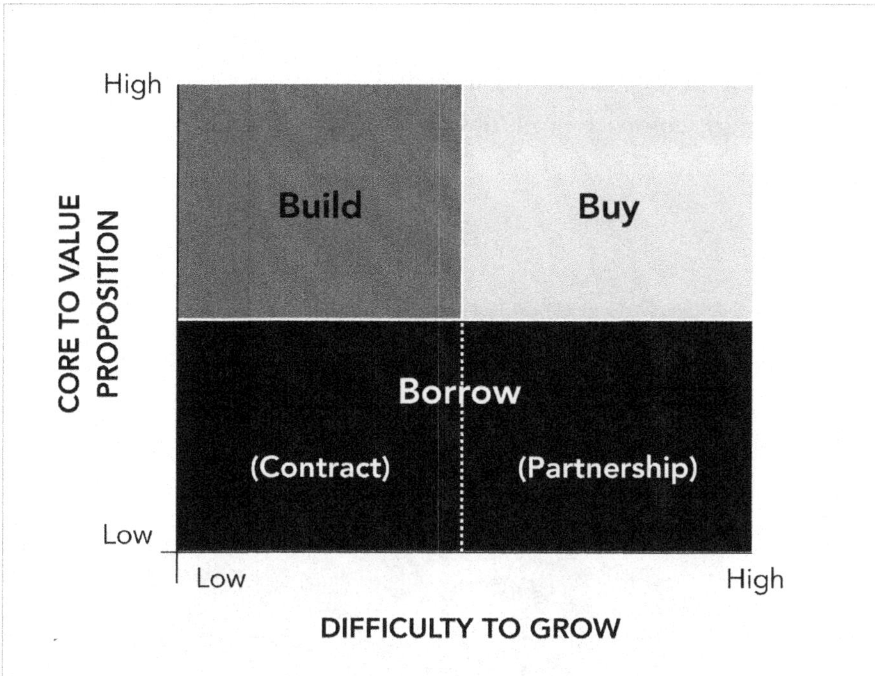

A two-by-two matrix showing the relative merits of building, borrowing, and buying based on the difficulty of growing the desired product and its importance to the company's value proposition. Source: The Power of the 2x2 Matrix[35]

Note that this matrix sharpens the definition of borrowing by breaking it into two parts: contracting, where you make a one-time payment to get something from a vendor, and building a partnership, where you invest in a long-term relationship to co-create something. Contracting is good for small, one-off requests, like hiring an agency to run your rebranding efforts. Partnerships take more time and energy, but they're necessary when the project requires a "high-touch" engagement that spans many years and teams, like when Microsoft and NBC set up MSNBC.

Another useful 2x2 to consider here swaps out the "difficulty to grow" axis for "time pressure." If you're in a hurry, buying and contracting are your go-to methods, since they can be done at the stroke of a pen (relatively speaking), compared to building and forging partnerships, which require a much heavier touch.[36]

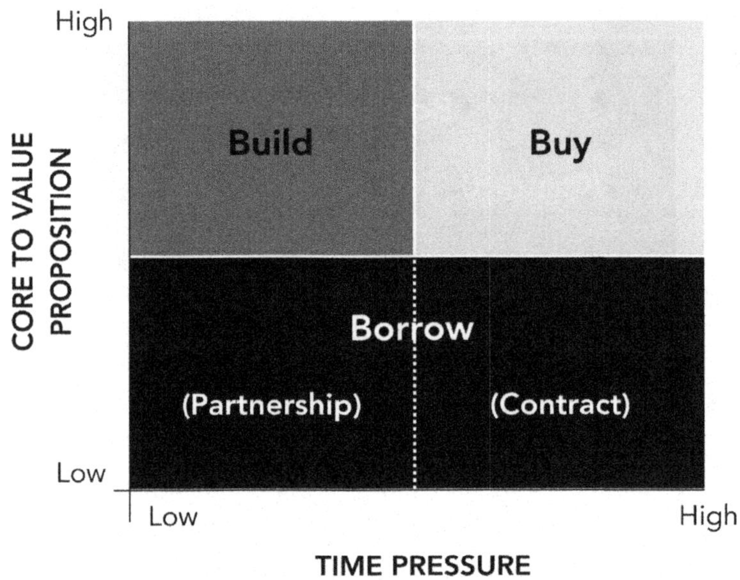

A two-by-two matrix showing the relative merits of building, borrowing, and buying based on the difficulty of growing the desired product and the time horizon in which you need the product to be ready. Source: The Power of the 2x2 Matrix[37]

Interview tip

You might get interview questions that ask how you would build a certain product, whether you would buy a certain company, how you would set up a partnership with a certain company, etc. All these questions assume that you'll use one specific market entry strategy.

A smart move would be to step back, evaluate *why* you're entering the market in the first place, and consider all three strategies instead of just the one that the interviewer mentioned. You'll look more thoughtful and, hopefully, be able to uncover opportunities that would never have crossed other candidates' minds.

Chapter 7

Moats

NOW THAT YOU'VE gotten into a market, you have to defend it. Warren Buffett reached back to medieval imagery to coin a term for this: an economic *moat*, or a sustainable means to stop competitors from "invading" your market.[1] There are two big categories of moats: barriers to entry and barriers to change.

Barriers to entry

These moats make it hard for competitors to enter your market in the first place.

The most notable barrier to entry is cost: an industry that costs a lot to enter is, obviously, going to draw fewer competitors. It's very hard, for instance, to enter industries like airlines (jumbo jets aren't cheap!), oil and gas (mining rigs are hard to set up), and utilities like water or electricity (laying that much wire or piping isn't easy).[2]

The common thread is that all these industries require a lot of infrastructure, which newcomers usually lack the money to set up. For this reason, power in these industries tends to concentrate in the hands of a few massive players, which is why the US airline industry has only a handful of big players. In fact, the cost of entry for local utilities is so high that they are almost always monopolies — because this situation is almost preordained, they're called *natural monopolies*.[3]

Especially with the rise of *cloud computing*, it's not all that hard to enter tech markets — anyone can spin up an app in a weekend and launch a prototype with very little overhead cost. But still, infrastructure is a problem for some tech markets, especially those that deal with the physical world. Amazon's logistics network is so advanced that even big-box retailers, let alone fledgling ecommerce sites, struggle to keep pace with Amazon's lightning-quick deliveries.[4]

Similarly, setting up an internet service provider, or ISP, like Comcast or Spectrum, is so expensive that even Google has struggled to set up its home internet service, called Google Fiber.[5] (Laying fiber-optic cable underground is expensive, and it's hard to justify to local governments when several other ISPs have already done so.)

Another barrier to entry is regulation. As we touched on before, heavy regulation of the digital pharmacy industry makes it hard to get a foothold, which made PillPack even more attractive to Amazon. Healthcare tech is even harder; due to clinical trials, developing a new drug can take over a decade,[6] and becoming profitable can take even longer.[7] That's a turn-off to venture capitalists, who usually seek returns within seven to ten years.[8] Finance, cybersecurity, education, and finance are all heavily regulated as well.[9] Even launching a new cryptocurrency has become harder now that the US's Securities and Exchange Commission, or SEC, has ramped up regulation on the sector.[10]

The last big barrier to entry is intellectual property and patents. Qualcomm's 130,000 patents on wireless connectivity technologies (including 4G and 5G) make it hard for new companies to compete in this space, letting Qualcomm charge all mobile phone makers a 3-5% licensing fee (good for about $6 billion in easy money every year).[11] Google's search algorithm isn't strictly patented, but the sheer amount of knowledge and code that's gone into it isn't easily replicated — making it that much harder for a new search engine to take hold.[12]

Barriers to change

Some moats, on the other hand, are about preventing your users and customers from leaving you — which we call barriers to change.

The most common barrier to change involves *switching costs*, which means locking customers into an ecosystem, making it hard for them to leave.[13] Apple is the master of switching costs. Once you have a few Apple products, you get hooked on services that don't easily transfer out of the ecosystem: iCloud for file sharing, Apple Music and TV, and features like AirPlay and AirDrop, which let you transfer files and videos across Apple devices but are utterly useless with non-Apple devices. A full 21% of all surveyed iOS users said they'd never leave the Apple ecosystem,[14] presumably for this reason.

Social networks also have high switching costs; exporting your Instagram photos, Facebook posts, and Tweets isn't all that easy. Generally, anything that makes users input a lot of information, link a lot of accounts, or store a lot of files is hard to switch away from.

Savvy startups can find ways to cut down switching costs. In 2016, the popular note-taking app Evernote cut down its free tier, letting non-paying users only install the app on two devices[15] and drawing anger from longtime users.[16] Just a few months later, Microsoft's OneNote, a competing note-taking app, launched a tool to let Mac users import Evernote notes to OneNote[17] (and use it for free) — a clever move to snap up disgruntled Evernote users (including us).

Another barrier to change is brand: loyal users are less willing to jump ship to a competing product.[18] Apple is the master of this approach, but other tech (and tech-adjacent) companies have such strong reputations in their fields that they're hard to take down: Tesla for tech-powered cars, Microsoft for enterprise software, Disney for entertainment, American Express for credit cards, and so on.

Finally, there are network effects — as we mentioned earlier, they occur when the product gets more useful as more people use it. This means that powerful products can become juggernauts, while upstart products often have a hard time getting traction. As we saw, network effects are common in social networks, which become more and more useful as more of your friends join. A rule of thumb called Metcalfe's Law says that the value of a social network is roughly equal to the number of users squared,[19] so a social network that's twice as large is four times as valuable.[a]

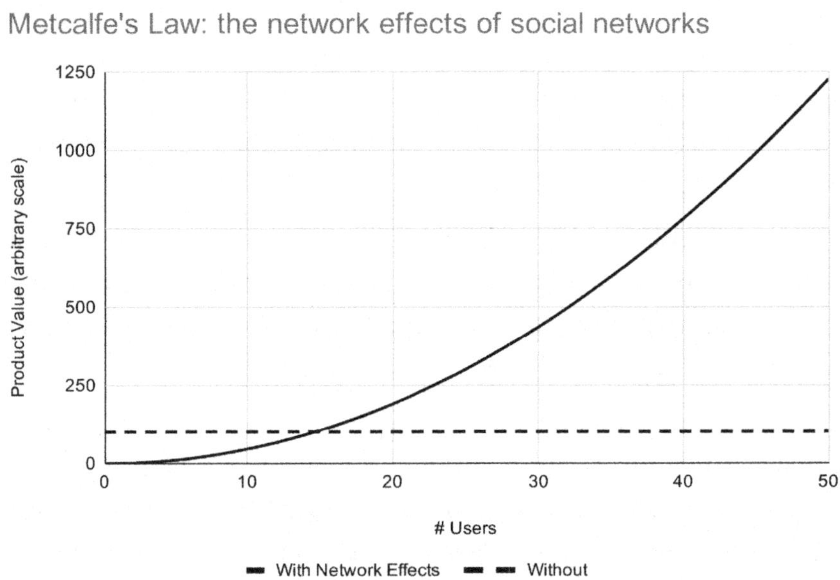

An illustration of Metcalfe's Law, which shows how social networks get far more valuable as they gain users.

Network effects are also prevalent in *two-sided markets*, which match buyers and sellers: think of Amazon, Airbnb, and Uber. These services are useless if there are no buyers or no sellers, but they grow ever more

[a]The actual equation is that $V(n) = n(n-1)/2$, where V is the value and n is the number of users.

useful as more of each join.[20] (You can think of social networks as *one-sided markets*, since there's only one type of user but network effects are still very strong.[21])

Interview tip

Many PM interview candidates fail to realize that some markets are two-sided and only address one side in their answers. For instance, a candidate might only focus on growing the number of buyers on Facebook Marketplace without realizing that they have to grow the number of *sellers* as well. Make sure you're considering all sides of the market when composing an answer.

Network effects also apply when the product itself gets better as more people use it, which is especially common for products that use machine learning.[22] The more people use Google Search, the more Google can learn how to best rank results; the more people use Spotify, the better Spotify can recommend songs to new listeners; the more people ride Lime scooters, the better Lime can figure out where to place scooters. Or, more simply put: more data makes the product better, which draws more users, which brings more data, and so on.

Watch this

One of the less obvious, but more important, challenges when building a two-sided market is *integrity*: preventing scams. We mock interviewed a Pinterest PM to see how she'd stop scams on Facebook Marketplace.

productalliance.com/videos/brainstorming

Chapter 8

Unit Economics

UBER LOST ALMOST $2 billion in 2017 and 2018,[1] but that didn't stop the company from reaching a valuation of $83 billion when it IPO'ed in May 2019, making it one of the largest IPOs of all time.[2] But just after the IPO, Uber revealed that it lost $5 billion in the second quarter of 2019 alone.[3] Uber's stock price plummeted, sinking from an opening value of $42[4] to a low of $25.58 a share by November.[5]

Clearly, investors were more worried about the post-IPO losses than the pre-IPO losses. The reason comes down to economics — specifically, *unit economics*, which measures the cost, revenue, and profit of each *marginal* item a company sells. In the long run, the small amounts of money you make or lose for each sale dwarf whatever amount of money you started with. In other words, your margins are your destiny.

Physical goods

The first thing to know about unit economics is that physical goods and digital goods behave quite differently. By physical goods, we mean products and services that require you to transfer physical, tangible items — selling laptops, transporting humans or meals in a car, building servers and supercomputers, selling pizzas or vitamins, renting out hotel rooms, etc.

These physical goods tend to be expensive to produce, meaning that the amount of *marginal profit* — or just *margin* — you earn on each good is pretty low. The manufacturers of *consumer packaged goods* (packaged items like cereal, hand soap, and tissues) make margins of just 15-25%;[6] electronics manufacturers' margins are even tighter, at 7%.[7] If the materials and labor required to make a product cost you $10, you'll only be able to sell the product to wholesalers[a] for about $12. (The wholesalers and retailers that pass these goods on to consumers earn slightly healthier margins, at about 20% and 50% respectively,[8] but that's only a few dollars of profit per item at best.)

To illustrate the unit economics, it's helpful to take an example. Suppose we set up a business that makes cheap USB flash drives. We can sell these flash drives to wholesalers for $5 a unit. The first flash drive is quite expensive to make ($6 each), but our factory gives us volume discounts the more we sell due to *economies of scale*. Once we make enough, our unit cost bottoms out at $4 a flash drive. We might make a loss on the first few flash drives, but eventually, our margin will be $1, or 25% of our cost.

We can graph our marginal costs, revenue, and profit to show how our margins evolve:

[a]Physical goods typically go from manufacturer to wholesaler to retailer to consumer; each middleman takes a cut. Incidentally, this is how Costco keeps prices so low: you buy straight from the wholesaler, avoiding a round of markups. Direct-to-consumer brands cut out the wholesaler, too, helping them remove even more markups.

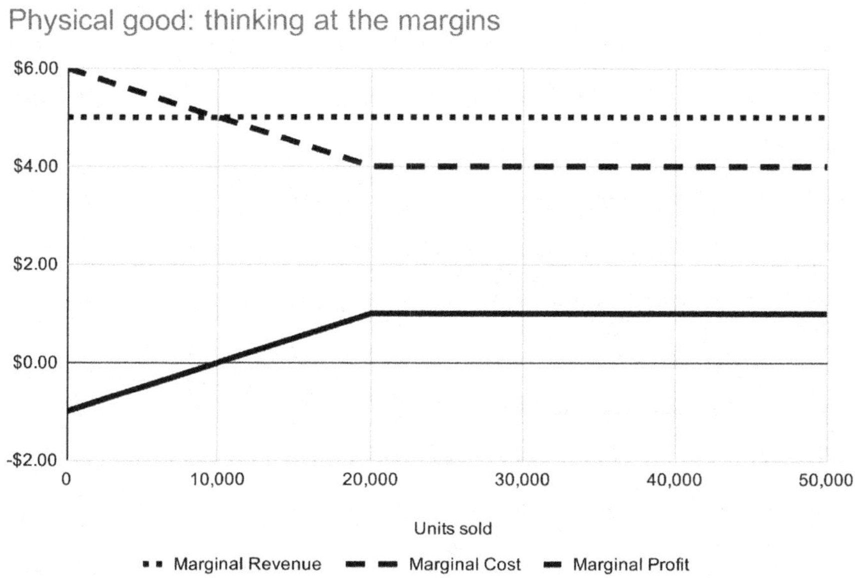

The marginal cost, revenue, and profit for each flash drive we sell in our example.

If we add up the marginal revenues, costs, and profits, we can figure out how much money we'll make in total. We also have to consider *fixed costs*, which we'll have to pay no matter how many flash drives we make. In this example, say it costs $10,000 to set up the factory. We can see our overall situation in this graph:

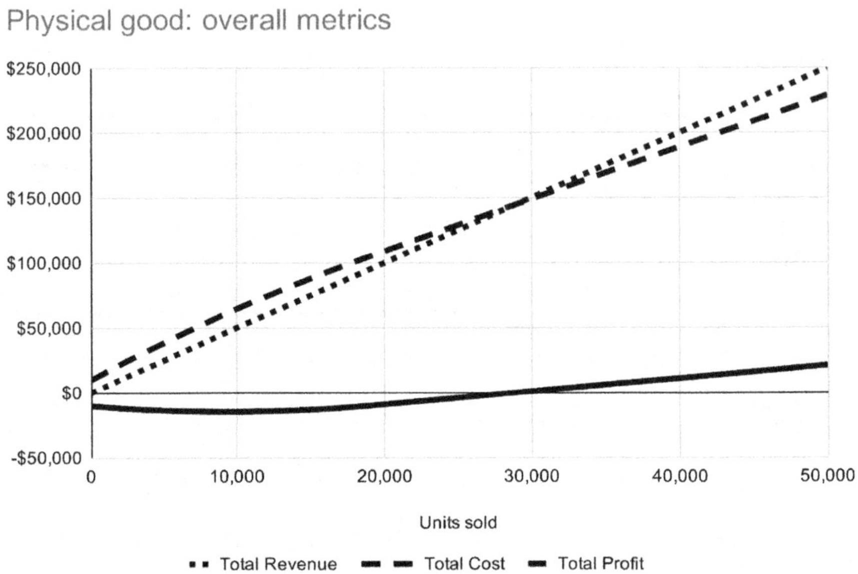

Our overall profitability as we sell our example flash drives.

Note that the combination of fixed costs and high marginal cost means that we won't *break even* until we sell 30,000 units. After that, our profit will grow as we sell more units, but only very slowly. If we want to improve profitability, we could certainly try selling more devices, but we would get a much bigger shift if we managed to shave a few cents off our marginal costs — our profit curve would bend upward quite sharply.

This is why the makers of physical goods work so hard to cut manufacturing costs.[b] To take an example from tech, the manufacturers of consumer electronics like phones and laptops work incredibly hard to optimize their *bill-of-materials* (*BOM*), which lists every item that goes

[b] Yes, this is one reason why outsourcing is so prevalent.

into the device; adding even a dollar can be a dealbreaker.[9]

Digital goods

Digital goods — online ads, enterprise software, movie-streaming services, apps, and the like — are defined by their high upfront, or *fixed*, costs and very low marginal costs. In fact, tech analyst Ben Thompson says that this characteristic is the one thing that unites all tech companies.[10]

This is because, when you sell a digital good, you aren't really selling anything that takes money to produce. Each Google search you make, each Tweet you send, each video game you sell, and each app you put on a user's phone costs you very little — perhaps a fraction of a cent for the additional server storage space and computing power. It's far cheaper than having to produce a physical good like a pair of socks or a granola bar or provide a physical service like an Uber ride.

This means that the unit economics for digital goods are quite different. Suppose we're selling an app for $5 per installation. We have to pay a small amount in server costs, salaries, and the like to support each installation, so the marginal costs are low. Thus, our profit margins are excellent — probably falling just short of $5 per installation.

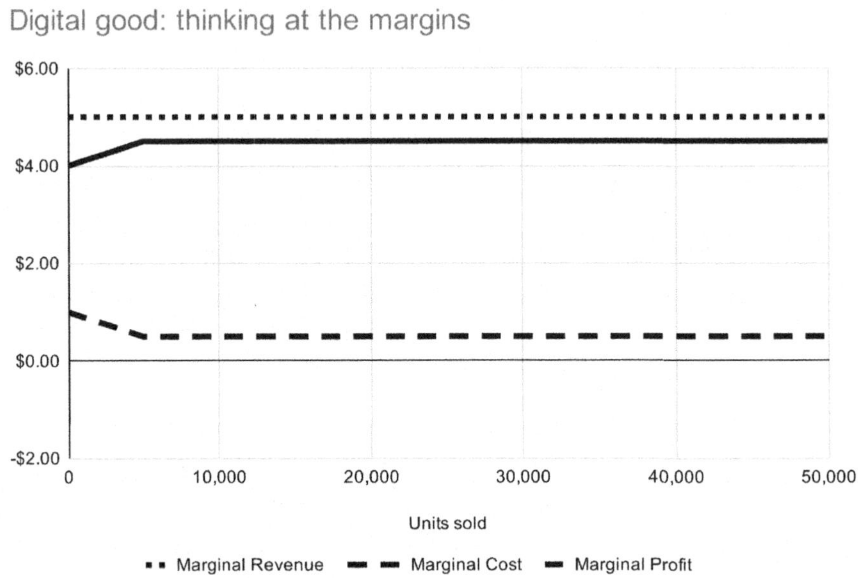

The marginal cost, revenue, and profit for each time our example app gets installed.

On the flip side, the upfront costs to develop and deploy our app — hiring engineers, signing contracts, and the like — are very high. In our example, let's say these upfront costs are $150,000. Our overall financial picture looks quite different than in our USB drive example.

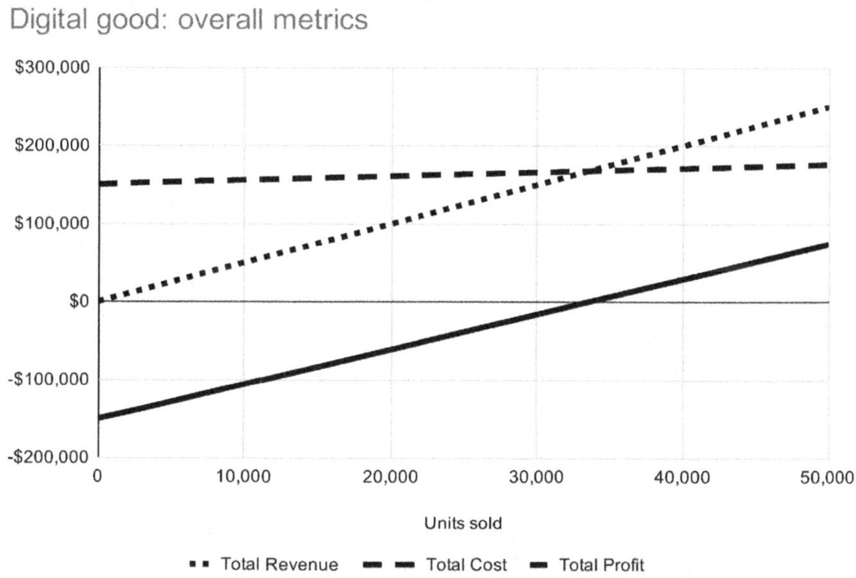

Our overall profitability as we sell our example app.

It'll take us quite a while to dig out of the initial hole, but once we do, we'll be effectively printing money since the marginal costs are so low.

This is why scale matters so much for digital companies: their margins are almost always great, so what matters is getting enough customers to keep racking up profit. Indeed, it's hard to cut marginal costs like physical goods do, because there are almost no marginal costs to speak of!

This is also the reason digital companies often use venture capital. They need an initial influx of money to get started, but if they succeed and get enough users, they can make a lot of money for their initial backers. Meanwhile, the upfront costs for physical-goods businesses are often lower, but their margins are also lower, meaning that they need venture funding less but are also less likely to get it.

Uber's losses

With this lens of unit economics, we can gain a sharper understanding of why Uber's early losses were no big deal but their losses post-IPO were so disastrous. As Uber crept close to IPO, people started paying more attention to the company's unit economics and found that they'd been bad for a long time.

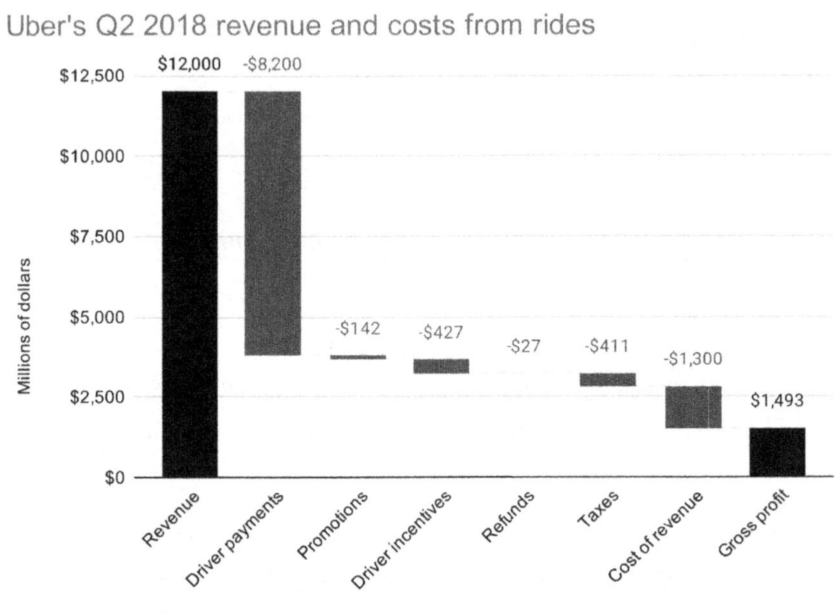

A breakdown of where Uber's revenue went. There wasn't much profit left over at the end. Source: CrunchBase[11]

Consider the second quarter of 2018, almost a year before the IPO. Uber pulled in $12 billion from rides but spent $10.5 billion of it on marginal costs. Paying drivers took up over two-thirds of Uber's ride revenue, and items like incentives for drivers, advertising campaigns, and *cost of revenue* (costs Uber paid to deliver the product,[12] such as the server space and computing power its app demanded) took up most of the rest, leaving just $1.5 billion in *gross profit*[13] — the amount of money Uber took away from its ride services.

Uber's problem was that it had $2.2 billion in *operating costs* (the fixed costs of paying salaries, renting offices, and so on), so ultimately Uber lost $700 million in that quarter (this was its *net profit*).[14]

The topline numbers are bad, but it's important to notice just how slim Uber's margins were. It only made $1.5 billion in gross profit off $12 billion in sales — that's a 12.5% gross margin. That is far, far lower than the up to 80% margins that most tech companies get.[15] The poor margins are due to Uber's high marginal costs, which in turn are due to Uber having to pay drivers.

In other words, Uber was originally valued so highly because people thought it would work like a digital company: high fixed costs but low marginal costs. That excused Uber's poor financials in early years, before the unit economics became apparent. It turned out that Uber behaves a lot more like a physical-goods company, since it had high marginal costs. Each additional user served didn't just cost a few cents of server space and computing power; it cost dollars and dollars because of the need to pay drivers. And these low margins made Uber's future look grim.

In fact, this same problem of high marginal costs affects many tech companies that we think of as "digital." Lyft, Airbnb, and other "sharing economy" companies have to pay a lot of their revenue to the people who provide the physical goods shared on their platforms. Companies that rent out physical goods, like e-scooter companies, have to pay a lot to maintain their fleet.

Media companies like Spotify[16] and Netflix[17] have relatively high marginal costs as well, since they have to pay artists and movie studios to license the content that they offer their users. It's nowhere near as cheap as just serving up a webpage, as low-marginal-cost products like Google

Search and Facebook do.

The fact that these high-marginal-cost companies are still in business shows that their markets are still large enough, and their growth still high enough, that investors think they can eventually dig themselves out of the hole. The news is less rosy for more niche "Uber for X" startups that try to create two-sided markets for things like valets and car washers.[18]

Future cash flows

Uber's case shows that companies that don't turn a profit can still manage to achieve sky-high valuations. This becomes even more puzzling when you realize that steadily profitable companies only scrape by on the stock market. Unit economics, combined with some financial theory, can help us make sense of this seeming paradox.

Let's take the case of Twitter and the New York Times.[19] In 2012, Twitter earned $317 million in revenue and reported a net loss of $79 million.[20] That same year, the New York Times Company reported $1.56 billion in revenue,[21] with $1.28 billion of that ending up as profit.[22]

And yet, the companies' valuations were nowhere close to each other. The New York Times was valued at just under $2 billion in November 2013,[23] but Twitter IPO'ed that same month at a valuation of over $14 billion.[24]

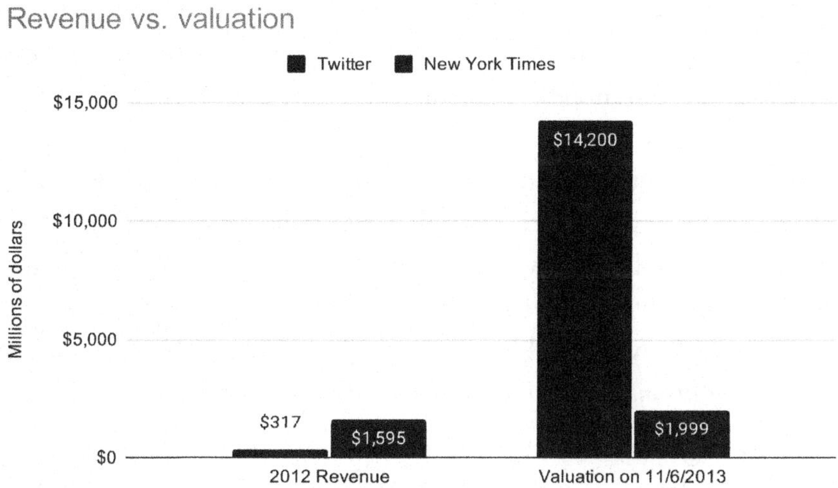

Twitter and the New York Times Company's starkly different revenue and valuations shows that there's more to a company's valuation than its current revenue. Sources: Wired,[25] *MacroTrends,*[26][27] *CNN*[28]

As you can tell, there's more to a valuation than current revenue. To understand this, let's go back to the basics of the stock market. Investors make money off shares of stock either by selling them at a profit or holding onto them and earning *dividends*, which are usually a proportion of the company's profit.[29]

Thus, the higher a company's profit in a given year, the more money investors will earn from holding their shares. Apple pays investors a few dollars per share every year; this amount grew from about $2 in 2016 to $3 in 2019[30] as Apple's revenues and profits ticked steadily upward.[31]

This is why a stock's price is usually correlated to *expected* future profits, since that determines the expected amount of money an investor will earn from dividends in the future.[32]

So when investors see high-growth tech companies like Twitter in

2013, they don't care much about past profit and revenue — they want to see signs that the company will rake in large amounts of profit over time. Meanwhile, an "old money" company like the New York Times might start with a higher base amount of profit, but since it's expected to grow less, its future profits and thus its valuation is lower. (The potential profit can't be too far in the future, though, since financiers "discount" future earnings. One dollar today is more valuable than one dollar a decade from now, since you could invest your dollar today and earn interest over the next ten years. This tendency gives this valuation method its name: *present discounted value*[33] or *discounted cash flow*.[34])

The high growth trajectory of tech startups and the low growth trajectory of companies like the New York Times ties back into our study of unit economics. Digital-goods companies might have huge fixed costs and thus awful financials early in their lifetimes, but because their marginal costs are so low, they have high marginal profit and can thus grow their profit very quickly as they gain users. Thus, investors will overlook short-term financial woes if the company can show that it's on track to dominate its market.

This is why Twitter attained such a strong valuation, as did most other unicorns. We already mentioned Uber, but also consider Lyft, which bled almost $1 billion in 2018[35] en route to a $20 billion IPO the next year.[36] And it's not just startups; Amazon was so hyper-focused on growth that it didn't turn a consistent profit until late 2015 despite pulling in billions in revenue every year.[37]

But, as we saw with Uber, heavy losses are only OK if it's early in the company's lifetime and if the company can prove that it has good promising unit economics. If you're burning money up front, that's fine, but if you're burning money when you're supposed to be scaling up, that's more problematic.

Meanwhile, low-margin businesses like media and physical goods companies have a harder time growing their revenue and profit to astronomical amounts. It can happen — just look at oil companies' occasional trillion-dollar valuations[38] — but it takes a lot more investment. (The massive oil companies need a lot of help from their governments.) And when tech companies start showing signs of poor unit economics, as Uber did in 2019, their expected profits — and thus their valuation — takes a pummeling.

In short, for a tech company, margins are the key to profit — and thus valuations and success on the stock market.

Chapter 9

Customer Economics

UNIT ECONOMICS ISN'T the only way to analyze a tech company's business model. While unit economics focuses on the profit earned per item sold, a toolkit we call customer economics focuses on the profit earned per customer over the customer's lifetime. Customer economics is based on two key metrics: the *customer acquisition cost*, or CAC, and the customer's *lifetime value*, or LTV.[1]

While you have to do a different unit economics analysis for each product in a company's portfolio, a customer economics analysis looks at the business as a whole. And while unit economics focuses on the here and now, customer economics realizes that you may have to take on short-term losses to gain long-term profit from a customer.

CAC

The customer acquisition cost is, on its face, quite simple: it's the average amount of marketing and sales dollars you have to spend to bring a new customer onto your product.[2] If you ran a $1 million marketing campaign and got 100,000 new users, the CAC was $10. In other words, the simplest formula for CAC would be:

$$CAC = (Marketing + sales\ expenses)/(\#\ of\ new\ users)$$

But that simple formula has several flaws. For one, the numerator is incomplete. Bringing on new users doesn't just take marketing and sales dollars. You have to pay the salaries of the people building your product; you have to rent server space and computing power to make your product run; you have to hire a customer support team in some cases; and so on.

The denominator is even harder to get right. For one, what exactly is a customer? If someone signs up for a 30-day free trial, do they count? If someone sits on your free tier forever without ever paying you, do they count? If someone just signs up for your mailing list, do they count? You can usually figure out a crisp definition of a customer, but that takes work and isn't as easy as just sticking numbers into a formula.

And then what is "new"? Sometimes the money you spend is just to bring back old users who quit using the product earlier. Do they count as "new"? Again, you have to answer this question.

The hardest part for the numerator and denominator is understanding the timeframes. It's not like you put money into a vending machine, push a button, and get new users out instantly. Launching a new product or running a marketing campaign takes months, and it often takes months to convince someone to become a customer (this is especially true for enterprise products that have to go through a long sales cycle[3]).

This means that you can't just take a snapshot of a moment in time; you have to look at multi-month windows. For instance, you might spend a lot of money this month and have few users to show for it, but they might all join after next month once your expenses have slowed down. Your CAC this month would be far too high, and your CAC next month would be far too low — you'd have to look over the entire multi-month window.

So, when you put it all together, the better CAC formula could look something like this:[4]

CAC = (Cost of marketing + sales + tools over X month window)/(# of new users added over X month window)

Not nearly as catchy as the simple equation, but it's far more accurate.

Interview tip

If you're trying to be really thorough in your CAC calculations in an interview, you might want to include salaries in the numerator of your CAC equation. Note that it's hard to know exactly how much of your employees' salaries should count against your CAC. 10%? 20%? 50%? It depends on how much of their time they're expected to spend on the project or campaign in question.

Case study: Spotify

Let's say we want to calculate Spotify's CAC for March 1st to June 1st of a given year. Suppose that Spotify's definition of "customer" is a paid Premium customer, and that Spotify's way of getting people to become paying customers is to let them join the free tier for a few months first. So the CAC equation would be:

CAC = (Cost of running free tier) / (# of new non-returning paid customers added during window)

The key number for the numerator is the total cost of operating the free tier for those three months, including the recurring advertising expenses, the salaries of the engineering and product teams that build the free product, the cloud computing costs, and so on. (If you wanted to be extra thorough, you could even account for the monthly rent of the office buildings that the team building the free product sits in, though the typical PM won't need to worry about this.)

Figuring out the denominator is a little harder. Say that half the people who join the free tier will never upgrade to Premium, and those that *do* upgrade take at most six months to do so. To calculate the number of paying users that were brought in by the free tier from March 1st to June 1st, you'd have to look at data from March 1st to *December* 1st, since the users who joined in late May could take up to six months to upgrade. You'd compile a list of all the email addresses who signed up for Spotify's free tier between March 1st to June 1st and then see which of those users upgraded to Premium from March 1st to December 1st. That second set of users would be your denominator.

To make up numbers, say that two million new free users sign up from March 1st to June 1st. Then, by December, you'd expect one million of them to have converted to Premium. So the denominator is one million.

The numerator is harder to figure out: do you consider just March 1st to June 1st (the window of signing up), or March 1st to December 1st (the window of upgrading)? After all, you have to keep paying to maintain the free tier until the user upgrades. Our suggestion would be to split the difference and consider March 1st to September 1st. That means our numerator is the cost of running the free service for six months. Again making up numbers, if Spotify's free tier costs \$5 million to run per month, that means the numerator would be \$30 million.

So, in our example, Spotify's CAC from March 1st to June 1st would be \$30 million divided by one million users, or \$30 per user. Again, these are totally made-up numbers, but the methodology is probably pretty close to what Spotify actually does. (For what it's worth, Spotify's actual CAC in 2017 was \$25.[5])

LTV

The other half of customer economics is the *lifetime value*, known as *LTV*, *CLTV* (the "C" being for "customer"), or, more rarely *CLV*. It's the total amount of money you can expect to make from an average customer over their entire lifetime as a customer — that is, before they quit using your product.[6]

Computing LTV is a bit more straightforward than computing CAC.

LTV is simply the sum of the marginal profits you earn from every action the average customer takes.[7]

If you're selling physical or digital goods, that's the marginal profit you make on all the items you'll ever sell to the average customer. If the average Nintendo customer buys two Nintendo consoles (each for a profit of, say, \$100 for Nintendo) and five games (each earning Nintendo \$40 in profits), the LTV is $2 \times \$100 + 5 \times \$40 = \$400$.

If you're in the advertising business, you don't sell items directly to customers, but you still earn revenue from each ad they click. To make up numbers, if the average Google user clicks on 100 ads in their lifetime, each of which earns Google \$0.50 in profit, the LTV is \$50.

(Note that the LTV is the *profit* you make from a customer over their lifetime, not the *revenue*.[a] If you sold \$100 worth of goods to someone for \$90, that customer isn't very valuable![8])

Lifetimes

The sum-of-all-expenditures method always works, but it's hard to predict exactly how many purchases (or ad clicks, etc.) the average customer will ever make. In other words, it's hard to predict the length of a customer's "lifetime." This is a big deal — Netflix would surely like to know if the average user sticks around for one year or ten.

The standard method to compute customer's lifetimes uses a metric called *churn rate* or just *churn*, which is the percent of users who quit using your product each year (or month, depending on how you define it).[9] The greater your churn, the faster you lose users.

---

[a] This is just the gross profit earned from selling goods and services to them; recall that gross profit is the sum of the marginal profit earned from each item sold. It doesn't include the CAC.

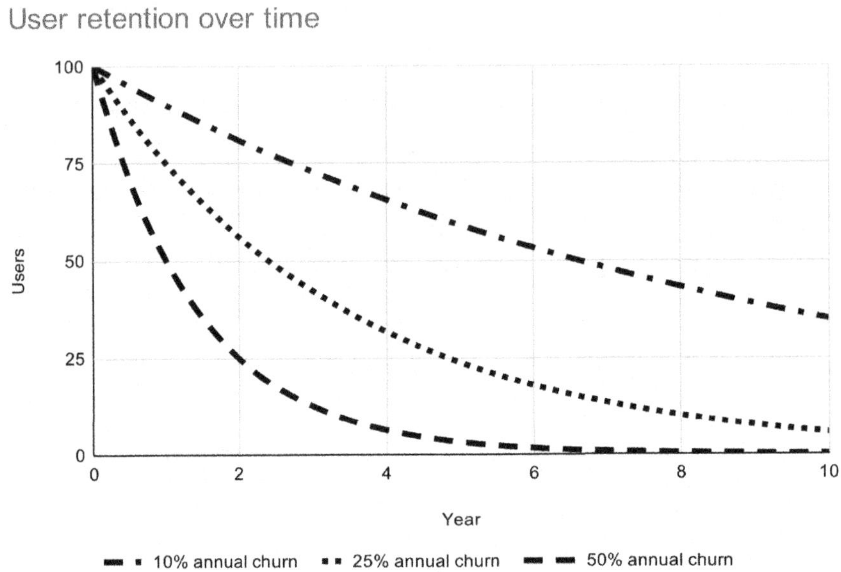

Different churn rates result in very different rates of decay of your user base.

You can compute the average customer lifetime quite easily once you know the churn rate:[10]

Average customer lifetime = 1 / (churn rate)

If your churn is 50% per year, your average user will stick around for 2 years. (Incidentally, this is the same formula that's used to compute the half-lives of nuclear atoms, drugs, and other substances that decay exponentially.[11][b])

Granted, human behavior is never predictable: users' churn rates may not be constant from year to year, users may return to your product after

[b]And they said high school science class would never come in handy!

quitting it the first time, and so on.[12] But this churn rate analysis is a good first step.

Once you have the customer lifetime, you can plug it into this alternate formula for computing LTV:[13]

LTV = (profit per user per year) × (average customer lifetime)

This formula can be used for any business, but it's especially valuable when you're running a subscription business (including *software-as-a-service*, or *SaaS*, businesses), since it's very easy for you to calculate your profit per user per year. Profit per user per year can be framed as:

Average profit per user per year = (average revenue per user per year) × (gross margin %)

Average revenue per user is often abbreviated to *ARPU* in tech circles.[14] The gross margin percent is the same percent we saw in the unit economics section: it's the percent of your marginal revenue that becomes profit (the rest is lost to marginal cost). Digital companies, which often have very low marginal costs, often assume that gross margin is 100% and just report ARPU.[15]

To take an example, GitHub's premium plan for teams costs $4 per user per month, or $48 per user per year. Supposing that the average team has six users, that's $288 per year. If the servers and computing power to support a team costs $8 per year, that's $280 in marginal profit per team per year.

GitHub's pricing page, showing that a premium team plan is $4 per user per month. Source: GitHub[16]

Suppose that paying teams churn at 40% per year — every year, about 40% of them cancel their subscriptions to switch back to GitHub's free tier. Then the average customer lifetime for a paying team is 1/0.4 = 2.5 years. (We don't care how many years these teams spend or have spent in the free tier; all we care about for now is the number of years they stay on the painted tier.)

Putting the numbers together, the LTV is \$280 × 2.5 = \$700.

You can further simplify our math into a one-line equation:

LTV = (Annual ARPU) × (gross margin %) / (churn rate)

To take another example, Facebook's ARPU in the third quarter of 2019 was \$7.26,[17] which means that their annual ARPU was about \$29.04. Because Facebook (like most digital companies) doesn't report the gross margin percent, analysts usually assume it's 100%.[c] Facebook doesn't report its churn rate, but let's guess that it's 10% per year, so the average user will stick around for 10 years.

[c] We would say that a number like 95% is more accurate, but that's just a guess.

Plugging in the numbers, we get that Facebook's LTV is $29.04 × 100% / 10% = $290.40.

Rules of thumb

The rule of thumb is that your LTV should be greater than your CAC. The amount of money you ever make from a customer must be greater than the amount of money you spend to bring them on.

Thinking back to unit economics, LTV is your "marginal revenue" per customer, CAC is your "marginal cost," and the difference is your marginal profit — which, of course, you want to be greater than zero. In this way, customer economics is just a version of unit economics where the "unit" is a customer, so all the rules we talked about in that section apply.

The LTV:CAC ratio is important when analyzing a company or product's financial success, since just looking at the number of users doesn't tell you much about a company's profitability.[18] Anyone can get a ton of users by selling a dollar for ninety cents — this is pretty much what MoviePass, the ill-fated startup that offered unlimited movies for $10 a month,[19] did. The LTV:CAC ratio is much harder to game than the number of users.

You definitely want your LTV to exceed your CAC, but just "breaking even" in this way doesn't let you earn a profit or grow your company. Plus, it's likely that your CAC computation missed some expenditures like employee salaries and office space. So, to ensure tech companies are making a healthy profit, tech analysts and investors prefer for tech companies' LTV:CAC ratios to exceed 3:1.[20d] That is, they expect LTV to be three or more times greater than CAC. This 3:1 ratio is so embedded in the minds of Wall Streeters and Silicon Valleyites that it's often called the *magic number*.[21]

---

[d]This ratio is usually used when speaking about SaaS companies, but it can be applied to companies that offer consumer products as well.

Case study: Amazon's Kindle Fire

You can create some inventive business models once you have a strong grasp of LTV and CAC. A great example comes from Amazon, which sells dirt-cheap Android-based tablets called Kindle Fires for as little as $50.[22] It's widely known that Amazon makes no money on the sale of these devices — in fact, they probably sell each one at a loss.[23] So why does Amazon sell them?

A $50 Kindle Fire tablet from Amazon. Source: Andrew Chen[24]

Simple: each Kindle Fire increases the user's LTV. When someone starts using a Kindle Fire, they get drawn into the Amazon ecosystem. See, Kindle Fires don't actually run Android; they run a spin-off without any Google services, known as Fire OS. Kindle Fire users all have to use

Amazon's app store and services, and Amazon's products (Kindle, Prime Music, the Amazon store, and so on), are shown front-and-center on the homescreen.[25]

Amazon knows that whenever someone starts using a Kindle Fire, they're inclined to use Amazon services more than if they were using any other device. This means that Amazon makes a lot more money off them than before.

In other words, Amazon takes a loss on each Kindle Fire — that's the CAC — because they know that they'll make a lot of money off people who use the tablets — that's the LTV. This LTV exceeds the CAC of actually selling a Kindle Fire, so it's a smart business move for Amazon.

This business model is quite common, in fact. Many hardware sellers use this approach. Google may not make much money selling cheap Chromebooks but knows that getting users to use Google products earns Google a profit in the long run.[26] Xbox and PlayStation lose hundreds of dollars on each gaming console sold[27] but make it up by earning fistfuls of profit from each video game that customers buy.[28] (The common thread here: hardware has bad margins but enables you to make money off complementary software, which has phenomenal margins.)

This model is called the "razor-and-blades" model, named after shaving companies' strategy of selling razors for cheap but making hefty margins on each set of razor blades sold.[29] The same applies to inkjet printers: the printer itself is sold at cost or at a loss, but the ink cartridges (which only work on a specific printer) are sold for a hefty profit.[30]

The same insight underlies gaming consoles, printers, razors, Chromebooks, Kindle Fires, and a vast variety of other products: it's OK to have a high CAC as long as your strategy enables a higher LTV.

Chapter 10

Segmentation

PRODUCTS RARELY COME in just one tier. You can buy print books in cheaper paperback or pricier hardcover editions. You can buy Economy, Business, or First Class airplane tickets (not to mention the million variants of Economy Class). And you can choose from several tiers of service on SaaS products, from Free to Plus to Small-Business to Enterprise (and more).[1]

Giving customers more choice is generally a good thing, but this strategy is actually a savvy move to maximize profits. Economic theory shows how we can understand (and use!) this technique.

Demand curves

This technique comes down to perhaps the most fundamental, and most obvious, concept of economics: more people will buy a product when it's cheaper.[a]

We can draw a graph to represent it, taking video streaming services as an example. The price-vs-quantity graph is known as a *demand curve*, which you might recognize from Econ 101.

---

[a] Yes, the exceptions of Veblen goods (and the mysterious Giffen goods) apply,[2] but we won't cover them here.

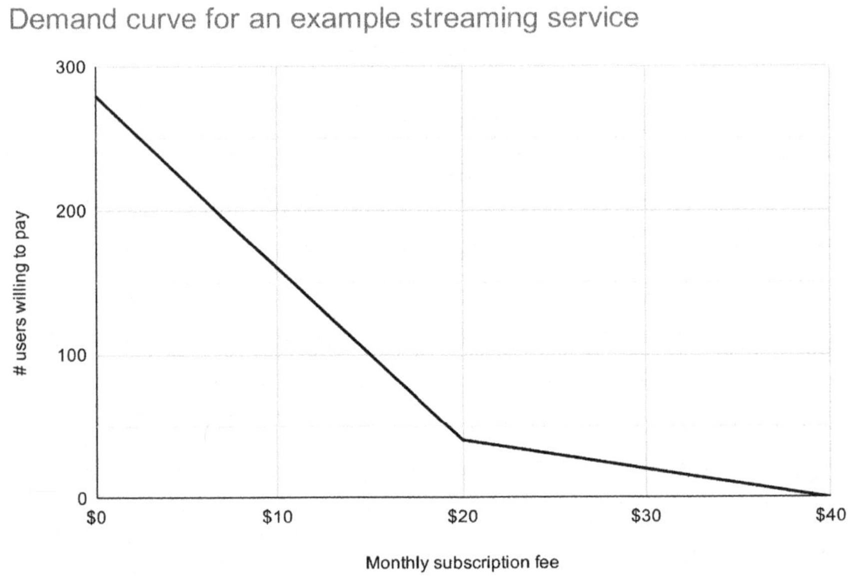

A demand curve for video streaming services.

If we made our streaming service $10 a month, we'd get 160 subscribers; if we made it $20 a month, we'd get 40 subscribers; and so on. This kind of inverse relationship works for all kinds of products: phone charging cables, Fortnite skins, enterprise software subscriptions, and so on.

Revenue maximization

If you price your product too high, nobody will buy it; if you price it too low, you won't get enough money from your many buyers. To maximize revenue, you want to set a "sweet spot" price that gets you enough money from each customer but still attracts enough customers.

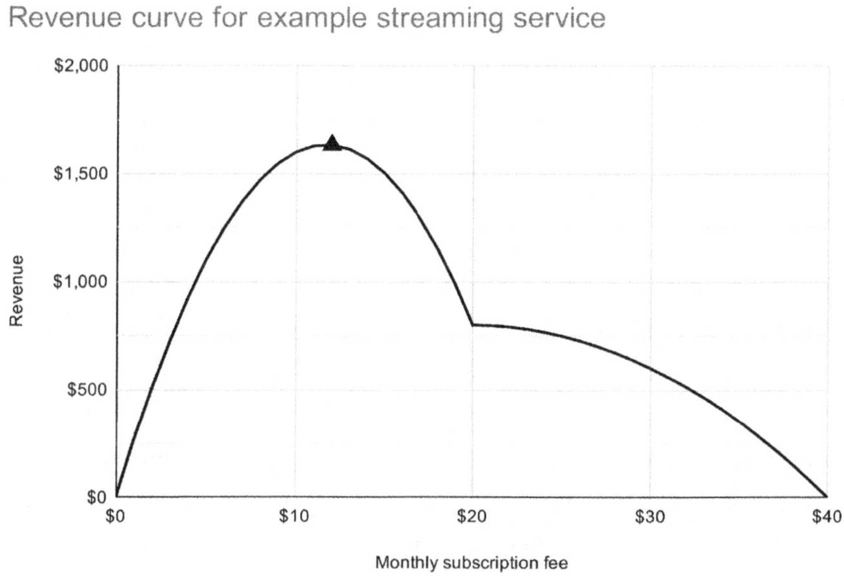

Changing the price of our example streaming service changes our expected revenue.

If we're launching our own streaming service, we'd want to engineer the price to maximize revenue. Looking at the graph, it appears that the best price is $12, which earns you $1,632 in revenue.

🎁 Bonus video

Apple's deep understanding of supply and demand was the key to the success of AirPods — and holds the key to the success of their augmented reality ambitions. Watch this bonus video to learn how Apple puts economics to use.

productalliance.com/videos/apple

User segments

If you treat your users as a monolithic bloc and sell everyone the same product, you won't be able to do any better than the simple curve-maximization analysis we did before. But not all customers are created equal, and not everyone is willing to pay the same amount. If you can carefully split users into *segments* and sell each segment a different product at a different price, you can squeeze some more money out of your market. This is the science of *segmentation*.[3]

Taking our streaming service as an example, suppose you do some market research and figure out that your market is made up of two segments: casual viewers, who are large in number but not willing to pay much, and movie buffs, who are rare but willing to pay a lot. You'll realize that each segment has a slightly different demand curve.

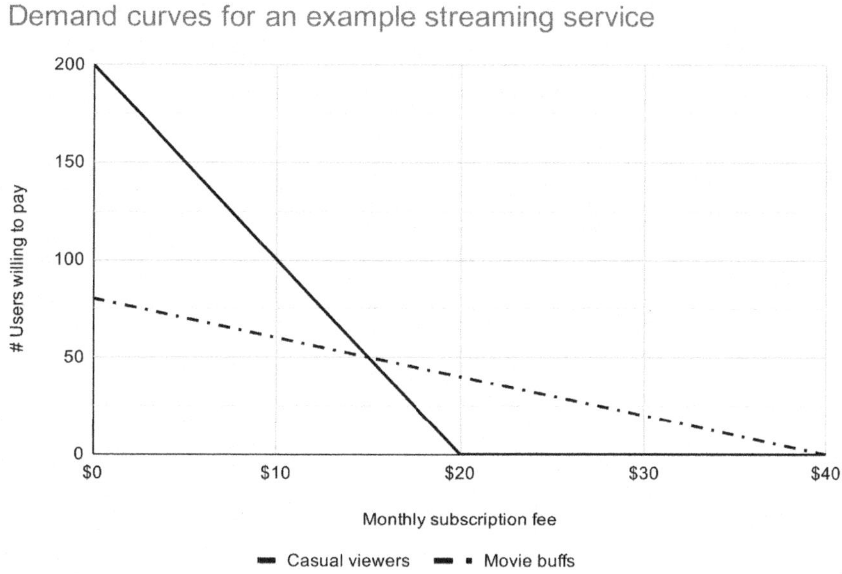

Our original demand curve is actually made of two curves, one for each user segment.

Now we can see why the original demand curve had a bit of a bend: it was the sum of two very different demand curves! The casual viewers are more numerous, but their *willingness to pay* falls off quite quickly; movie buffs are fewer in number but more tolerant of higher prices.

Elasticity

Because casual viewers are more price-sensitive, their demand curve is much steeper. In economics speak, their demand is highly *elastic*: small swings in price generate large swings in quantities sold. Movie buffs' demand curve is shallower, or more *inelastic*: small swings in price generate small swings in quantities sold.

Generally, demand curves are inelastic when buyers are highly-motivated to buy it, when the item is essential, or when there aren't many available substitutes for the product.[4] For instance, the demand curve for Ubers at 2am is highly inelastic: people will take them almost regardless of the price since they need a ride home and, in most cities, don't have the alternative of public transit. Meanwhile, the demand for strawberry yogurt is probably quite elastic: if most yogurt sells for $2 but you raise the price of strawberry yogurt to $4, most buyers would move to a cheaper flavor, since that would be a good-enough substitute and strawberries are hardly essential.

The differing demand elasticity of casual and dedicated users leads to the phenomenon of *whales*: when only a few users will pay, but those users will pay titanic sums.[5] In video gaming, where this phenomenon is very common, casual gamers have extremely steep demand curves: they'll rarely pay even a cent. Meanwhile, hardcore gamers would gladly pay anything from one to hundreds of dollars — in 2016, the average paying user of the mobile title *Game of War* spent $550![6] These rare "whales" are game studios' primary sources of revenue.

Sweet spots

Because casual viewers and movie buffs have different demand curves, it follows that each segment has a different revenue curve, and thus a different sweet spot where revenue is maximized.

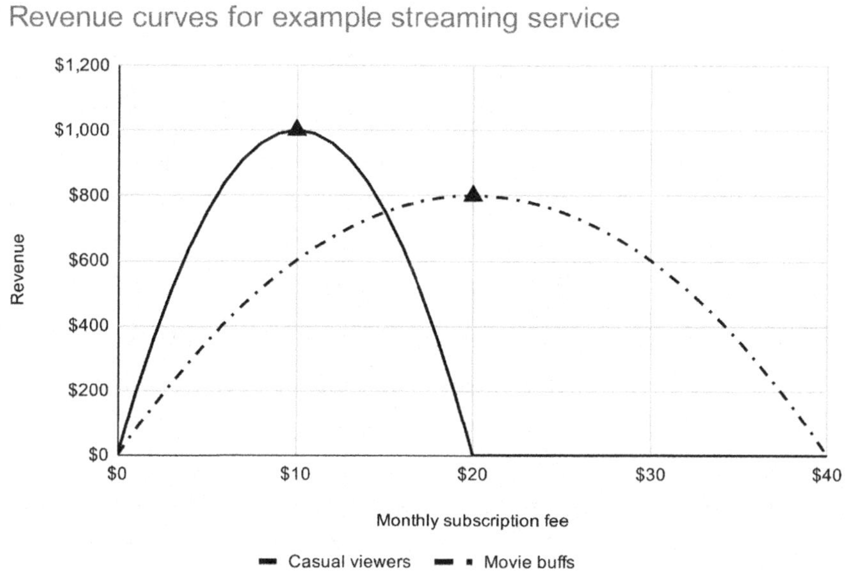

Each user segment has its own "sweet spot" price for maximizing revenue.

From the graph, we find that charging everyone $12 is inefficient: it's at the sweet spot of neither curve. Instead, you'd want to charge casual viewers $10 a month and movie buffs $20 a month. This would earn you $1000+$800 = $1800, a considerable improvement from the $1632 you'd earn from charging everyone a flat $12. This is segmentation in action. (In a perfect world, you'd charge every single customer the maximum amount they'd be willing to pay, a tactic known as *pure price discrimination.*[7] That's usually impossible, though, so breaking people into a few similar segments is the best you can do.)

Tiering

Your first challenge as a product manager, then, is to define the right user segments. This requires a lot of user research and looking through data to find groups. Ultimately, you want everyone within a segment to be similar to each other, while each segment is very different from other segments. This principle is known as *"internally homogeneous, externally heterogeneous"*[8] or *"same within, different between."*

Once you've done that, you have to create a different "tier" of your product for each segment and target them appropriately. In the non-tech world, there are plenty of clever segmentation tricks like this. Airlines have business-class seats for business travelers flying on the company's dime (and thus with more inelastic demand curves) and cheaper economy seats for cost-conscious travelers. Pricey hardcover books come out earlier to grab the hardcore fans, while cheaper paperbacks come out later to sweep up the more price-sensitive readers. Most car makers have standard and luxury brands, often with similar innards but different amenities: the cheaper Toyota and pricier Lexus,[9] the simple Volkswagen and upgraded Audi,[10] and so on.

In the tech world, most subscription services, from Tinder to Trello, have multiple tiers of service, and many have cheaper tiers exclusively for students, who have less disposable income. (Indeed, the whole *freemium* concept is just a version of segmentation.) Hardware is usually sold in tiers: the iPhone comes with normal and Pro lines,[11] while Samsung offers entry-level Galaxy J phones, mid-range Galaxy A phones, and flagship Galaxy S phones.[12]

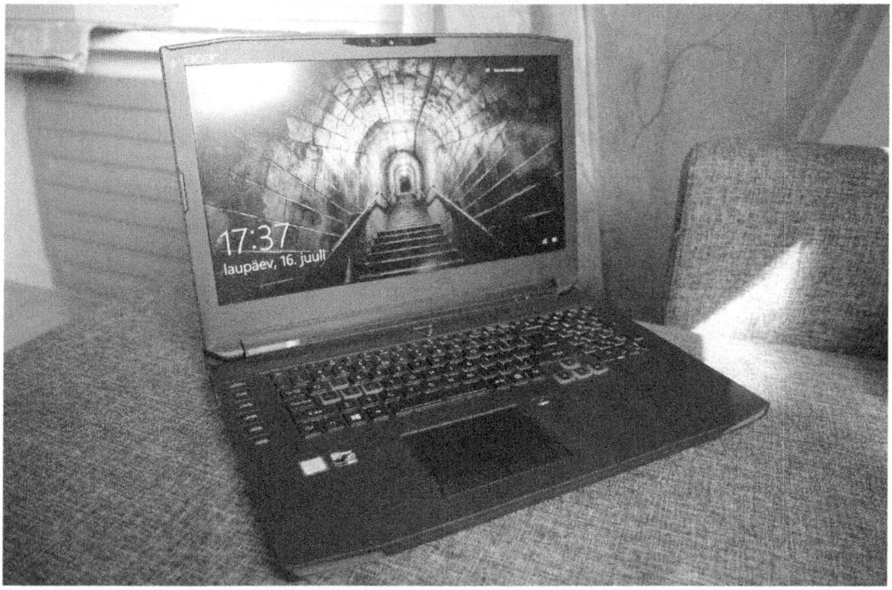

A gaming laptop. These devices are known for being bulky, hot, and powerful, and they often come with brightly-colored keyboards. Source: Andri Koolme[13]

Another instructive example comes from computers. Laptop makers often have separate brands, like Asus's Republic of Gamers, that sell powerful, expensive laptops to hardcore gamers. These gaming laptops are often so huge and vividly colored that stereotypical gamers flock to them but non-gamers avoid them, while non-gaming laptops are so plain that gamers steer clear. The reason? The key to product segmentation is to ensure that customers with a higher willingness to pay, like gamers in this case, don't "leak" to your cheaper tiers.

Case study: AirPods

In 2019, Apple announced a new line of wireless headphones — the AirPods Pro[14] — to complement their original AirPods, released in 2016.[15]

It was a technical innovation, sure, but also an economic one.

The pricier AirPods Pro on the left and the cheaper AirPods on the right. Source: Future[16]

Here, Apple noticed that the market for wireless headphones is made of two user segments: dedicated Apple fans who will pay top dollar for the newest, highest-quality Apple products, and non-loyalists who just want a solid set of headphones for a good price. The former market would gladly scoop up the higher-price (and presumably higher-margin) AirPods Pro, while the latter would be more likely to take the regular AirPods. If Apple only had the regular AirPods, they would have missed the opportunity to get more money from their superfans; if Apple only had the AirPod Pros, they wouldn't have sold anything to the more cost-conscious consumers.

This segmentation strategy, indeed, is classic Apple. For the superfans, Apple offers the latest iPhone (including the Pro, Max, and Plus variants) and MacBook Pro, not to mention the ever-growing catalog of subscription services like Apple Music and Apple Arcade. Meanwhile, non-loyalists and budget-watchers can get older or smaller iPhones and

MacBook Airs — and by offering these lower-end products, Apple ensures they're getting money from people who might otherwise turn to Android phones and Windows PCs.[17]

Apple knows their two segments and how to target them. And with this strategy, the AirPods line became a smashing financial success, pulling in $12 billion in 2019 — more than the revenue of Spotify, Twitter, Snapchat, and Shopify combined.[18]

Chapter 11

Market Failures

MANY THINGS IN OUR LIVES are mediated by markets: supermarkets, financial markets, ridesharing markets, job markets, dating markets,[1] and so on. Any time people are negotiating and making agreements, you have a market. For this reason, knowing how markets work is vitally important for PMs.

When done well, markets can be remarkably effective. But, unfortunately, markets often go wrong. When job markets go wrong, people who lie on their resumes get hired, or maybe the boss hires their unqualified friends and relatives.[2] Once people get property or health insurance, they're more likely to behave recklessly because they're already protected.[3] Without seller accountability or customer education, scams proliferate in economic markets. And so on.

The good news is that markets often fail for very predictable reasons. Economics can show us why markets fail and what we can do to fix them.

Informational asymmetry

In an ideal world, everyone would have *perfect information* available to them, so they'd be well-informed before making any decision. People would know exactly who they're doing business with, buyers would know exactly what they're buying, and so on.[4]

But, as you can tell, that's rarely the case. In truth, one side of a transaction usually has less information than the other, a tendency known as *informational asymmetry*.[5] Buyers usually know less about a product than the seller; employers can't discern all of an applicant's flaws from interviews; voters won't learn a politician's true beliefs until said politician takes office.[a]

Adverse selection

When the side with more information exploits that imbalance to take advantage of the other side, it's known as *adverse selection*.[6] This usually happens when the seller tricks the buyer into spending too much for a flawed product.

For instance, in 1994 a woman named Doree Lynn paid a Washington, DC jeweler $14,500 for a dazzling emerald ring. But a few years later, her expensive gemstone started cracking. It turned out that the stone had been treated with epoxy resin, which jewelry stores often apply to make jewels look better in the display case; the problem is that this treatment leads the stone to crack eventually. The jeweler hadn't disclosed this information to Lynn, which led her to overspend on the ring.[7] And because Lynn wasn't an expert on jewelry — nobody can be expected to be an expert on everything they buy — she wasn't able to find out about the epoxy treatment until it was too late.

Fortunately, your brain will often warn you when you're at risk of getting duped by adverse selection. You've felt this feeling if you've ever seen a suspiciously cheap product on Amazon. If you see a $8 desk lamp amid a sea of $20–$40 lamps,[8] you instantly think there's a catch. That $8 lamp *must* be a piece of junk. You can tell that the seller must know something that they didn't tell you: that the lamp catches fire, falls apart, doesn't turn on, etc.

(Why is it called "adverse selection?" The term comes from a landmark paper that tries to explain why so many used cars are faulty — or,

[a]Sometimes *both* sides lack information about each other. When two people meet on a dating app, neither knows how attractive the other really is in real life. So the information is technically symmetric, but it's far from perfect.

slangily, *lemons*. Car sellers know if a given car is a lemon, while buyers don't. Thus, buyers hesitate to put up a lot of money for cars, which means that used car dealerships don't sell high-value, high-price cars, leaving just cheap lemons on the market. Thus, most of the used cars up for sale are lemons. Information symmetry has an "adverse" effect on the "selection" of used cars.[9])

Brands

Consumers have evolved several defenses against informational asymmetry and adverse selection. Innate skepticism, as we saw with the cheap lamps, is one of them. Another is looking for brands.

There's a reason people buy Apple's $40 Thunderbolt cables[10] over dirt-cheap $10 Thunderbolt cables made by anonymous factories in Asia.[11] People know that Apple makes high-quality products, but they don't know if these anonymous factories are hiding the fact that they're actually selling garbage. Nobody wants to waste $10 on a piece of junk — or worse, risk frying their $1500 laptop with a badly-wired cable.

In other words, brands offer a "known quantity;" they give customers information that puts them on a level playing field with the seller, which helps customers make sure they don't get duped.[12] If you've ever been in a foreign country and gone to a McDonald's because it was the only restaurant you were sure would be decent, you've experienced this phenomenon. Franchises sell predictability, which gives them a big leg up on small-time businesses.[13]

A knockoff USB-C charging cable on the left, with a genuine Apple charging cable on the right. Source: WCCFTech[14] and Imgur[15]

This is why brands matter so much to tech companies. People are more likely to trust Intuit, the maker of finance software TurboTax and QuickBooks, with their finances than some random startup. They trust that Intuit isn't stealing their financial data, but they can't tell if those random other apps are.

Incentives

People respond to incentives, as you know if you've ever filled out a survey for a shot at a $50 gift card or cruise to the Bahamas. When the incentives for all parties in a transaction are aligned, great things can happen. If you refer a friend to join Airbnb, both of you get free travel credits, and Airbnb gets a new user[16] — everyone wins. Quora and StackOverflow users get reputation boosts when they write content that the community enjoys; these forces have driven the creation of truly impressive compendiums of human knowledge.

But when incentives aren't aligned, problems can ensue, and markets can fail.

If you've ever spent lavishly on a business trip because it was on the company card — we won't judge — you've experienced misaligned incentives. You've taken part in the *principal-agent problem*, which says that people acting on behalf of someone else don't always act in the other person's best interests, since the incentives are different.[17] In our example, the company's goal is to save money, but your goal is to have a luxurious experience. Because you aren't penalized for spending lavishly, you don't care about the company's goal and will actively work against it.

The way to fix this would be to bring the incentives back into alignment: if you were paid extra for choosing cheap flights or meals, you'd quickly become as frugal as the company would like you to be.

No receipt? Your burger's on us

A more colorful example of incentive misalignment and realignment comes from the world of fast food. Ever seen a sign at the cash register that says the meal is free if you don't get a receipt? It's not so the chain can brag about how detail-oriented their cashiers are — it's to make the incentives work.[18]

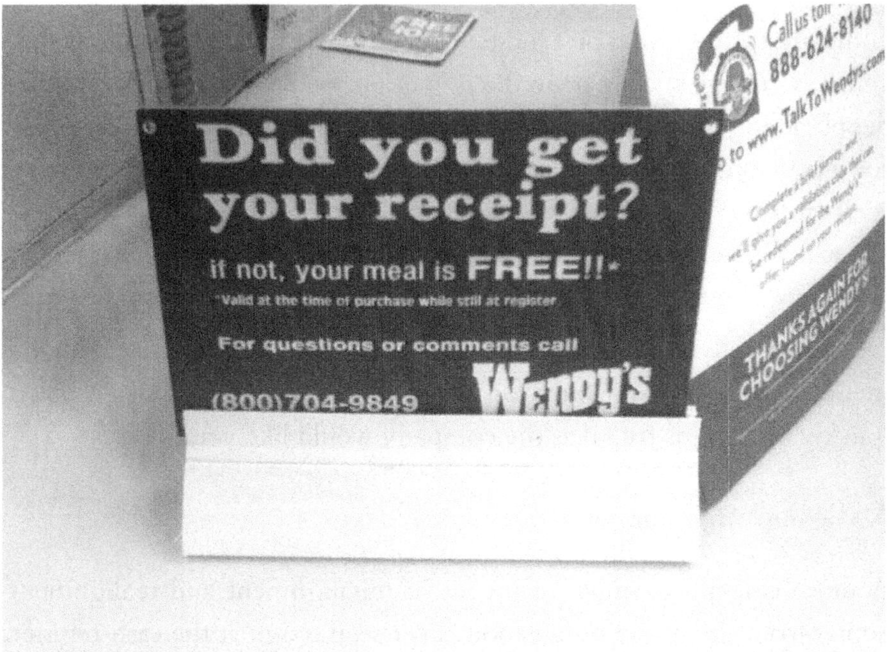

A sign at a Wendy's advertising that your meal is free if the cashier doesn't give you a receipt. Source: Anson W. on Yelp[19]

Think about it: imagine you're a cashier at Burger King, making minimum wage for hours of demanding physical labor. You are strongly incentivized to pocket the money that customers give you for the food instead of putting it in the cash register. You don't particularly care about helping Burger King turn a profit, and indeed, the extra cash could easily double your hourly earnings. This is the principal-agent problem at work: Burger King hires you, the cashier, but you see no reason to work in BK's best interest.

Now imagine you're Burger King. Of course, you don't want cashiers to pocket the money. You could hire people to monitor cashiers or install sophisticated cameras and tracking systems to catch cashiers in the act, but that'd be too expensive. So how do you cheaply align cashiers' incentives with the company's?

Burger King did this by instituting the "free meal if no receipt" policy. With this policy, customers are incentivized to monitor the cashiers for free, eagerly trying to win their free Whopper and fries. Cashiers are now incentivized to put money in the register and give receipts, since they know they'll be caught by hungry customers if they don't.[20] In other words, by giving customers an incentive, Burger King managed to align cashiers' incentives with the company's and thus prevent fraud on the cheap.

Cutting out collusion

It's not just burger joints: incentive misalignments are everywhere on tech platforms like Uber and Airbnb. On these two-sided markets, there are three kinds of players: the company itself, the "sellers" (like drivers and hosts), and the "buyers." The more moving pieces there are, the more likely that the incentives are misaligned, and thus the higher the chance of chaos ensuing.

Sometimes sellers can exploit the platform's weaknesses to fleece buyers and get free money from the company. In 2019, Uber drivers created "Surge Clubs," where multiple drivers would collude to close the app at the same time. This would trick Uber into thinking there was a shortage of drivers, thus triggering surge pricing. This would net the drivers up to $20 extra per ride — without there actually being a genuine "surge."[21]

In other cases, buyers and sellers collude to cut out the platform company, depriving the company of fees. Guests could find Airbnb hosts on the Airbnb website and then contact them off the platform, such as by calling the hosts' personal phones to arrange a stay and paying in cash. This would let both guest and host save the 6–12% service fee that Airbnb charges.[22]

This would be bad for Airbnb's business, of course, since people could use Airbnb's listing and searching features for free without paying them anything. This is why Airbnb has taken drastic steps like censoring any phone numbers listed in Airbnb listings, on guests' profile pages, and in private messages.[23] (It's a leaky solution, though: hosts can just write their phone number on a piece of paper and leave it in the home so that you can arrange stays with them privately when you come back to the area.)

Yet another type of incentive mixup happens when the company is incentivized to exploit its sellers. Uber is notorious for using psychological tricks to get drivers to drive more, which is good for Uber but not always in drivers' best interests. For instance, Uber continuously adds new rides to a driver's queue so the driver always has another ride ready to go — a kind of "autoplay" for driving, which encourages drivers to keep going even when they may not want to.[24]

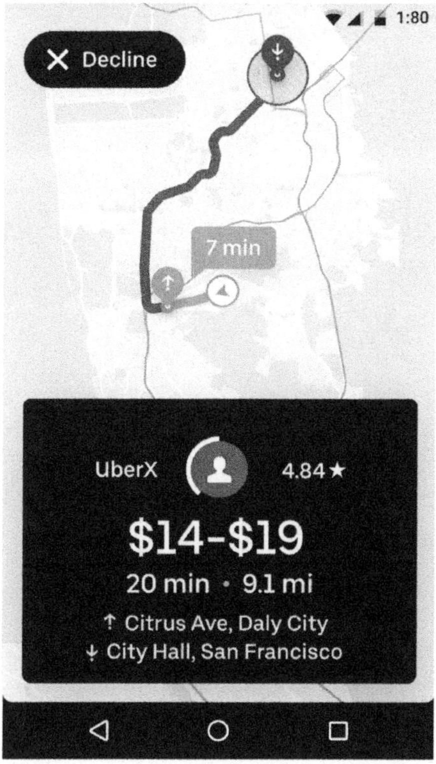

Uber automatically queues up rides for drivers to push them to keep on driving. Source: The Rideshare Guy[25]

The takeaway for product managers is that we have to watch out for misaligned incentives, a problem that becomes increasingly likely when our products involve multiple parties who may not share the same goals (like Uber and Airbnb). We have to design systems like the fast food receipt trick to get everyone's incentives to line up.

Conclusion

IN THE EARLY 2000s, Netflix was starting to pivot away from delivering DVDs via mail and toward online movie streaming.[1] They quickly set up a system that let customers watch unlimited movies — even ones that had just hit theaters — for a low monthly fee.

The subscription service was a hit, and Netflix grew a large and committed user base.[2] By 2007, it was cheaper to stream videos online than to get DVDs in the mail, and watching online was obviously more convenient.[3] Netflix was beating video-rental rivals like Blockbuster on price *and* value — a truly blue-ocean approach.

The problem was that the unit economics weren't in Netflix's favor. Their marginal revenue per customer was just a few dollars per month, but their marginal costs were extremely high, since users only wanted to watch newly-released blockbusters, which cost Netflix a fortune in licensing fees. This service, while popular, was making them lose money for every customer. Forget CAC — Netflix's customer LTV was going to be negative.[4]

If this reminds you of MoviePass, you're on to something. This was the exact same problem that MoviePass was facing: give people cheap, unlimited access to expensive things, and they'll bankrupt you. (The fact that both cases involve movies makes the comparison especially apt.)

But, unlike MoviePass's flailing team, Netflix's product managers realized the economics were against them and sought to build features to subtly reduce their marginal cost per customer. Netflix realized that they could save money by encouraging people to watch older, and thus cheaper, movies.

So Netflix built their now-famous recommendation engine and queue, which let them learn which movies you like and suggest older movies that you'd be interested in from their "back catalog." This perfectly aligned incentives: it was a win for the customer, who could discover new movies and binge their favorite genres even more easily, and a win for Netflix, which got users to *voluntarily* watch movies that cost Netflix less.[5]

With this slick strategy, Netflix turned the business around and made their unit economics work for them. The rest, as they say, is history. Netflix's PM team deserves a lot of credit — as does their understanding of the economic concepts we saw in this chapter. ❦

All QR codes from Part II

In case you skipped over any QR codes from the last few chapters, here's a roundup. Scan them with your phone to watch bonus videos and try interactive demos.

The fourth market entry strategy (and a popular one in emerging markets), minority stake investment:

productalliance.com/videos/emerging-markets

A mock interview about protecting integrity in two-sided markets:

productalliance.com/videos/brainstorming

How Apple's mastery of supply and demand has helped its products achieve runaway success:

productalliance.com/videos/apple

III

Psychology

We first make our habits, and then our habits make us.

— John Dryden, English poet

Introduction

IN 1993, Microsoft launched a massive encyclopedia project called MSN Encarta.[1] Microsoft bought the rights to a trio of well-known encyclopedias and incorporated their contents into Encarta, then hired an army of paid writers and editors to flesh out the rest of the encyclopedia.[2] The CD was given away for free with Windows, thus ensuring millions of people would have access to it.[3]

A CD that contains Microsoft's 1995 version of MSN Encarta. Source: Internet Archive[4]

Eight years later, an entrepreneur named Jimmy Wales launched Wikipedia, a community-created, nonprofit digital encyclopedia. It started pretty much from scratch, and contributors would all be volunteers — nobody would earn a penny from the project.[5]

It looked like it was going to be a blowout. On one side was Bill Gates; on the other side was a small-time businessman nicknamed Jimbo,[6] whose previous job was running an adult entertainment website named Bomis.[7] On one side was one of the wealthiest companies in the world; on the other side was a ragtag band of volunteers.

But you know what really happened. After a burst of growth, Encarta entered a slow decline. Only 60,000 Encarta articles were ever written, and the project folded in 2009.[8] Wikipedia became one of the most popular websites in the world,[9] with over 50 million articles.[10] Wikipedia has even become a legitimate source for supreme courts around the world.[11]

How did Wikipedia pull it off? Wales, it turned out, knew something about human psychology that everyone else had missed: it's expensive to pay people to work for you, but if you can appeal to the right emotions and drives in people's heads, you can get them to eagerly work for you for free.

Wikipedia was a product that understood and worked with human psychology; Encarta was not. Understanding how human psychology works — and how to put it to use in your products — is one of the most underrated skills in a PM's toolbox.

Chapter 12

Pricing Psychology

One of a PM's most important jobs is to bring in revenue, and this means knowing how to convince buyers to spend more money. Fortunately for you, people aren't hyper-rational robots — they take mental shortcuts to save energy, and if you know these shortcuts, you can get buyers to spend more.

Three theories of price

If you want to buy a domain name for your website, you'll probably head to a site like GoDaddy, Squarespace or Namecheap. One thing you'll quickly notice is that each website has a very different approach to pricing. GoDaddy's prices will remind you of Walmart or other big-box stores, with "99" endings like \$2.99 or \$11.99. Squarespace's prices will be elegant round numbers with no cents to speak of, like \$20 or \$30. And then Namecheap chooses totally random-looking prices like \$1.67 or \$4.88.

Why do you get such differences? It's because each vendor subscribes to a different *theory of price*; each uses a different strategy of setting prices to attract customers. Chances are that you'll use one of these three theories when trying to set prices for your products, so it's worth knowing their logical underpinnings and strengths and weaknesses.

Charm pricing

GoDaddy uses one of the best-known pricing strategies: making prices just short of a round number. Setting prices that end in 95, 98, 99, 89, 49, etc. like this is known as *charm pricing*.[1] You see this pattern everywhere, from convenience stores ($3.99 for a bag of chips) to video streaming services ($15.99 per month[2]) to smartphones ($849 for an iPhone[3]).

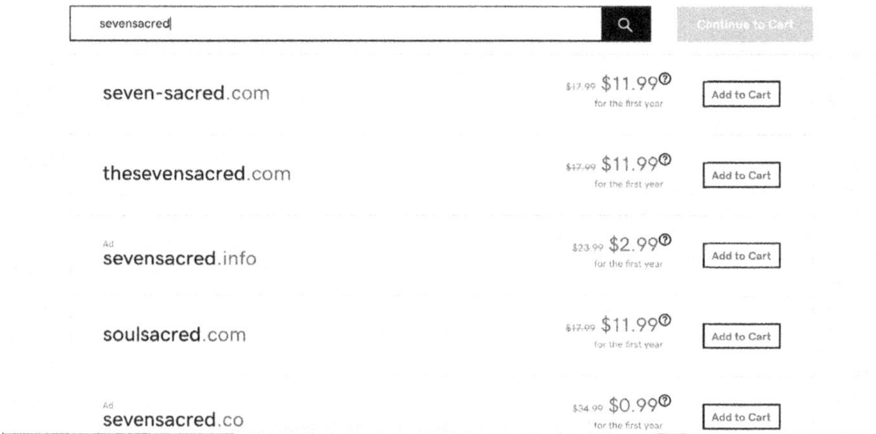

Domain name pricing on GoDaddy. Source: GoDaddy[4]

The logic here is simple: people read from left to right, so they pay more attention to the first digit or two of the price. Marking something as $2.99 thus makes people read it as $2 rather than $3, which makes them more inclined to buy.[5]

There's more to it than lazy rounding, though; there's something about the number 9 that's unusually appealing to human minds. For instance, one study found that people were more likely to buy a dress if it was priced at $39 rather than $40. No surprise there. But that same study found that people were more likely to buy the dress if it was priced at $39 than at $34.[6] That's right, people were more likely to buy when the price went up! The exact psychological mechanism here is unclear, but it seems like the number 9 equates to "sale" or "good deal" in people's minds.[7]

Because "9" or "99" endings are so frequently used at lower-end stores like Walmart, they've become associated with cheap or discounted goods. This can be a marketing asset if your company's brand centers around cheapness. GoDaddy advertises itself as a cheap, no-frills domain shop for non-technical people; GoDaddy's old ads featured supermodels, indicating that they were targeting average people rather than IT admins or CEOs.[8] GoDaddy's "99" pricing thus plays perfectly into its brand as the "Walmart of domain name vendors."

Being associated with cheapness isn't always a good thing, though. Starbucks prides itself on being a premium brand, with imported coffees, sleek interiors, and the vibe of a European coffee house.[9] Using 9's for its prices would just make it look like Dunkin' Donuts.[a]

This is why Starbucks prefers to end its prices with classier 5's, like $4.95.[10] For instance, consider the prices of cold coffees at one Pennsylvania university:[11]

Drink	Grande	Venti
Iced Caffe Latte	$4.65	$4.95
Iced Caffe Americano	$2.65	$3.15
Iced Caramel Macchiato	$4.65	$4.95
Iced Flavor Latte	$4.45	$4.95
Iced Coffee	$2.65	$2.95
Iced Coffee w/ Milk	$2.65	$2.95

Prestige pricing

The opposite of charm pricing is *prestige pricing*: purposely setting your prices to round numbers to show that you aren't trying to offer sales or

[a] No offense intended; Dunkin's donuts are delicious.

discounts.

Prestige pricing is, as the name implies, popular among luxury products[12] that want to avoid any association with the Walmarts and GoDaddys of the world. Ferraris' price tags use numbers like $625,000[13] rather than, say, $599,999 or even $599,000. Michelin-starred restaurants charge $355 rather than $349.99,[14] while even somewhat-nice restaurants put $25 or $35 on the menu rather than their charm-priced equivalents.[b]

Domain name pricing on SquareSpace. Source: Squarespace[15]

Squarespace, as we saw before, uses prestige pricing, charging amounts like $20 or $30, with no cents even mentioned. This fits into Squarespace's brand as a stylish, creative service for sophisticated customers. Squarespace is trying to be the anti-GoDaddy, and the pricing strategy plays right into it.

Prestige pricing works for more reasons than just signaling sophistication. Round numbers are pleasant to look at and easy to comprehend;

[b] We're surprised that Apple doesn't use prestige pricing, even on their priciest products.

to use an analogy, a \$80 price tastes like a smooth syrup, while \$78.49 tastes like a chunky soup. Because round prices are easier to comprehend, they engage the emotional parts of people's minds rather than the rational parts — leading people to make decisions based on feelings rather than facts. Since luxury products cater to people's emotions more than their wallets, round prices should help sell these products. The science bears this out: one study found that champagne sold better if it was priced at \$40 than at \$39.72 or \$40.28.[16]

Quirky pricing

The third theory of pricing is a little stranger: it suggests that you choose bizarre prices like \$4.77 or \$6.32. You won't see this strategy used very often, though some discount stores might employ it. For instance, the hyper-efficient, no-frills grocery chain Aldi, which is popular across Europe and parts of the US,[17] has many strange prices on its shelves. Though many Aldi items are charm-priced, it's not unusual to see bananas for \$0.44 a pop, a dozen eggs for \$1.18, or a box of cookies for \$1.35.[18c]

Using these quirky prices sends a clear message: "we aren't trying to be clever by playing around with prices; we're giving you the lowest price we can possibly offer." It shows that you're always trying to slash prices for customers rather than giving yourself meaty margins.

[c] If you're used to shopping at Whole Foods, you may need to pick your jaw up off the floor now.

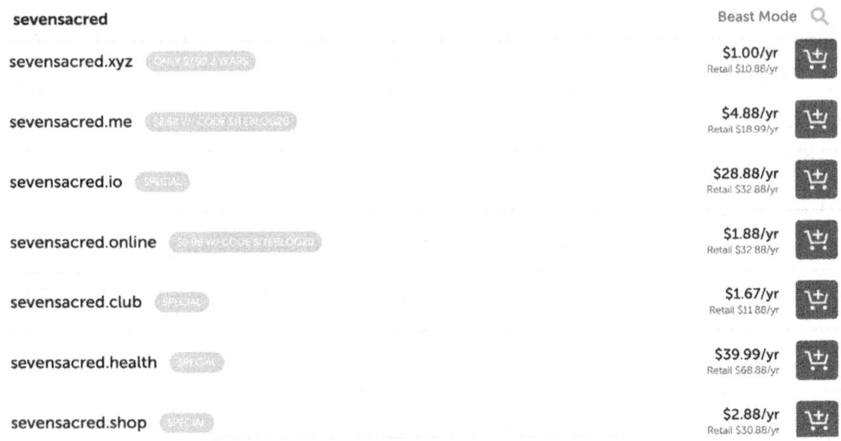

Domain name pricing on Namecheap. Yearly costs of $1.67 or $28.88 are common here. Source: Namecheap[19]

This works well for Aldi, which is serious about cutting costs: it employs a fraction of the employees of the usual grocery store, it doesn't give you free bags, it has minimal decor in stores, and it has severely limited hours.[20] It also works well for Namecheap, whose brand is all about getting you websites at bargain-basement prices. It's right there in the name: get your domain *names* for *cheap*.

Your products can use quirky pricing, but you have to be serious about cutting costs, like Aldi and Namecheap. The customer has to realize that you're earning almost zero margin. As a result, this doesn't work well for software products, which by definition have almost no marginal costs and thus have terrific margins; nobody will be fooled if you make your subscription service $4.37 per month. The approach might work, though, if you're selling hardware products or are trying to charge minimal fees for your gig-economy startup.

Herding

When you're trying to set a price for your product, the three theories of pricing are just a starting point. Your product doesn't exist in a vacuum; you have to look at what others are doing.

Specifically, you might have noticed that many products in the same category fall in the same narrow price band. There seems to be a go-to price for movie subscription products, enterprise software, video games, and so on.

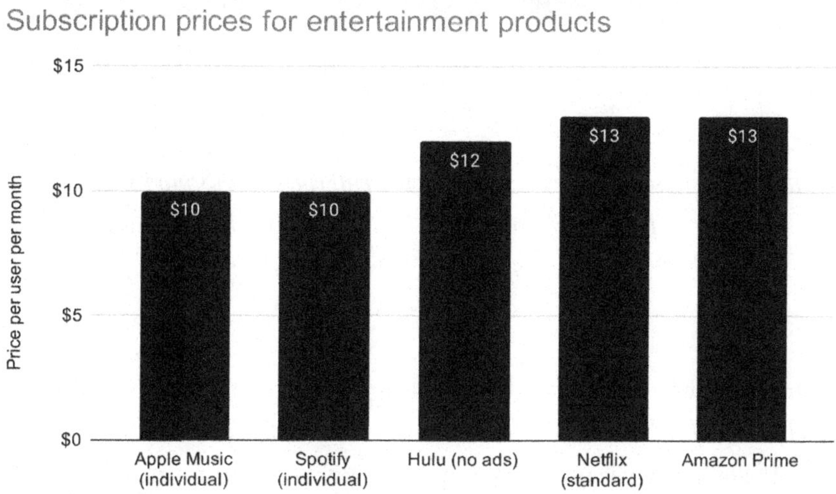

The monthly subscription prices of selected entertainment products. Sources: Apple,[21] Spotify,[22] Hulu,[23] Netflix,[24] Amazon[25]

This hunch is right! Enterprise productivity software, from to-do apps to file storage, all seem to cost in the neighborhood of $10 per month. Entertainment subscriptions seem to have "herded" around $12, as of the time of writing. And console video games are almost always sold for about $60.[26]

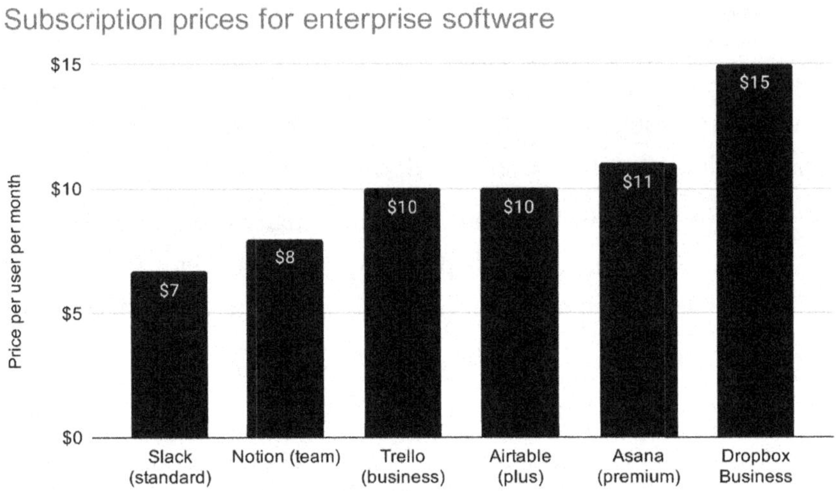

The monthly subscription prices of selected enterprise SaaS products. Sources: Asana,[27] *Trello,*[28] *Dropbox,*[29] *Notion,*[30] *Airtable,*[31] *Slack*[32]

One of the reasons for this herding of prices is our cognitive bias of *anchoring*: our idea of a good price depends on expectations and context.[33] If a customer is used to paying $10 per user per month for all their enterprise software, they've *anchored* on $10 as a reasonable price. They'll think a price of $20 per user per month is ridiculous — even if the software is objectively twice as good as the rest. And any lower price will feel amateur. The PMs creating these enterprise products surely knew this and thus kept their prices within the "acceptable" band.

You might have experienced this same effect in your daily life if you've moved between cities. Researchers have found that people who move tend to pay the same amount for an apartment before and after the move, even though the cities might have vastly different costs of living.[34] If all the apartments you looked at in San Francisco cost $2000 a month, that becomes ingrained in your head as a "reasonable" rent, and thus you go looking for $2000 apartments when you move to Pittsburgh, even though that might well get you a mansion.

Changing prices

Once you've set a price, you'll probably have to start thinking about whether you should change it.

First off, note that price cuts work, but only if they draw the buyer's attention. Silently slashing prices won't make people jump to buy your product. But if you boldly cross out the old price and highlight the new price with big text and bright colors, people will jump on your discount — even if it's not much of a better deal.[35] If you're going to reduce prices, make sure you make it obvious, since it's the excitement about the change — not the raw change in the dollar figure — that motivates people to buy.

But while it's easy (and popular) to cut prices, it's much harder to raise prices without customers complaining. Thus, if you aren't sure, it's better to err on the side of setting your price too high.[36]

While setting prices too high might sacrifice your market share in the short term, the tactic gives you more flexibility in the long term. And the value of high prices is underrated in general. Higher prices make people enjoy products more; brain scans have shown that people literally enjoy wine more when the bottle's sticker price is higher.[37] And higher prices let your brand come across as premium, another reason why Starbucks purposely has such expensive coffee.[38]

▸ Watch this

Should you raise prices if it means you might lose customers? It depends on how sensitive customers are to price changes! Neel, one of your humble authors, worked through this puzzle in a mock interview to figure out if Spotify should increase its monthly price from $9.99 to $11.99.

productalliance.com/videos/product-pricing

Veblen goods

For some luxury goods, in fact, higher prices often make products more desirable. This category is called *Veblen goods*, and it includes sports cars, expensive watches, diamonds, [39] and (depending on who you ask) iPhones.[40] These products are appealing in part because they're exclusive; having these goods signals to others that you're rich. The more expensive these goods are, the harder they are to get, and thus the more powerful status symbols they are. You might have heard of the popular term for this trend: *conspicuous consumption.*[41]

A collection of watches on Rolex's website. They start at $14,800.[42] *Source: Rolex*[43]

The other half of the Veblen goods theory is that people associate high prices with high quality,[44] so raising prices can make your products more desirable. (If you've ever avoided a cheap item on Amazon, fearing that it would be low quality, and gone toward a more expensive item instead, you'll know what we mean here.)

One fun anecdote: a jewelry store owner in a touristy beach town had trouble selling jewelry in one particular case. She told her assistant to cut prices in that box in half, but the assistant misinterpreted and accidentally doubled prices — and the jewelry in that case sold out immediately. The wealthy vacationers who stopped by the store certainly weren't jewelry experts, but when they saw high-priced jewelry, they figured it was high-quality and thus worth buying.[45]

Salvaging a low price

As we've mentioned, your best bet is to start off with a high price and gradually cut it down to size if you aren't getting enough demand. But what if it's too late to start with a higher price? What if your prices started out too low and are too "sticky" for you to increase them?

You can take a page from the food industry, which has long faced this problem. The makers of Skippy peanut butter once observed that their margins were falling, but their marketing team knew better than to raise prices. Instead, they added an indented bottom to their jars, which reduced the amount of peanut butter in the jar by 10%, all while keeping the jar size and price the same. This strategy, often called "shrinkflation," gave Skippy a free 10% margin boost without tipping off customers.[46]

The indented bottom of a Skippy peanut butter jar. Source: MetaFilter[47]

If you've ever opened a bag of chips and discovered, to your dismay, that the bag was mostly filled with air, you've fallen victim to shrinkflation as well.[48] (Food companies say the air prevents chip breakage,[49] but it's not like there are many chips to break in the bag to begin with!)

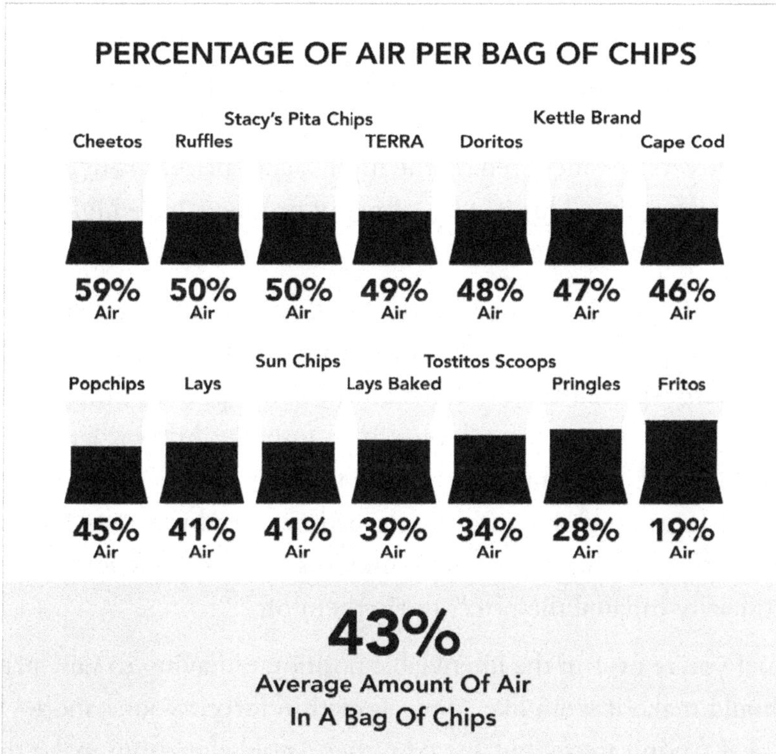

The percent of air in the bags of various popular chip brands. Cheetos are the worst offenders, with 59% air, while the humble Fritos are the best, with just 19% air. Source: Kitchen Cabinet Kings [50]

You can't pull this exact same trick in tech products, of course. In theory, you could slowly roll back features and benefits while keeping the price the same, but users tend to notice when features get cut. For instance, Evernote users were furious when the company restricted the free tier to syncing on two devices,[51] leading many users to jump ship to competitors like OneNote.[52]

So your only option is to increase revenue while keeping functionality the same. But instead of raising prices, you can just reduce the discount. If your product's sticker price is $99 and is permanently discounted to $69, you can just quietly reduce the discount to $79.[53] Customers probably won't notice, and since the price is still discounted, they'll still happily buy the product. (This is another example of anchoring: buyers get anchored on the high sticker price, so anything less looks like a bargain. This is why so many products have high MSRPs but are permanently "discounted."[54])

Finally, if you *do* have to raise prices, it's important to make the increase look fair. One Uber economist explained that users are more likely to take a surge-priced Uber ride when the surge pricing is 2.1x than if it's 2.0x. Why? The 2.1x multiplier is so unnatural that riders assume that an impartial algorithm spat out the number. Riders figure the ride is worth 2.1x as much because the algorithm priced it at 2.1x as much. But the 2.0x multiplier is a round number, so riders think some human has artificially inflated the prices to rip them off.[55]

So, if you're ever in the unenviable position of having to raise prices, you should make it seem like some algorithm forced your hand — nobody likes paying more, but they'd rather a cold algorithm make them pay more than a scheming human.

Everything's relative

You probably aren't just setting a single price, though. You probably have a portfolio of products to price, and while this poses new challenges, it also opens up a whole new toolkit of psychological tactics.

Arbitrary cohesion

We humans might *think* we know how much things are worth and how much we're willing to pay for them, but we really don't. We look for context clues to figure out if something is a good deal, and it's surprising how strongly we follow them. When a pilot is landing in the dark, she needs runway lights so she knows where to land the plane.[56] We humans often operate in the dark when buying products, so we lock onto any "runway lights" we find.

This phenomenon — where people fixate on a certain price with no rational reason for doing so — is known as *arbitrary cohesion.*[57] The famous psychologist Dan Ariely showcased the principle with an experiment. He had MIT students bid on chocolate, wine, books, and other goods. But there was a twist: he had each student write down the last two digits of their Social Security Numbers (thereby having them choose effectively random numbers from 0 to 99) before starting the auctions.[58]

These numbers are irrelevant to the values of the items being offered, so this twist shouldn't have impacted students' bids. But it did. Students who wrote down numbers from 0–19 bid an average of $8.64 for the wine, but students who wrote down numbers from 80–99 bid an average of $27.91.[59] Ariely got people to triple their bids just by getting them to think of a bigger number!

As Ariely's experiment shows, it's surprisingly easy to nudge people toward a given price. As a PM, you can strategically align these "runway lights" to guide potential customers toward a profitable outcome.

Anchoring

Anchoring, which we saw earlier, is one type of arbitrary cohesion. When unveiling the iPad, Steve Jobs knew that potential buyers would have no idea what the price of the iPad should be, since it was the first product of its kind. So he knew he could easily get people to anchor on a high price, then show a lower price to make the iPad look like a good deal. This is exactly what he did: he showed a $999 price tag on screen for several minutes, then dramatically showed it being crushed by a $499 falling in from the top.[60]

If you're selling a suite of products, you can use anchoring to raise your prices. A $12 slice of pizza might normally seem outrageous, but if other slices on the menu are $18, $20, and $22, it'll look like a steal.

In other words, people compare prices to other nearby prices, not some objective dataset about reasonable prices in their heads.[61] So if you're selling a line of phones, you shouldn't just raise the prices of a few phones — you should raise the prices of *all* phones in tandem so they all look reasonably priced.

Another trick is to *prime* users by showing them higher prices before introducing them to your (relatively reasonably-priced) goods. In one experiment, researchers set up a CD store next to a sweatshirt stop. When the sweatshirt vendor raised prices, people were willing to spend more at the CD vendor — even though the CD vendor hadn't changed a thing.[62] Getting users anchored on a higher price helped justify future high prices.

Decoy effect

Built on anchoring is a second key type of arbitrary cohesion: the *decoy effect*, where you add an irrelevant product option to steer people toward the product you actually want to sell.[63]

The most famous example of the decoy effect came when Dan Ariely found a surprising offer on the Economist's website: you could get a web-only subscription for $59 a year, a print-only subscription for $125 a year, or a web and print subscription for $125 a year.[64]

The print-only subscription seems like a waste: who would buy it when the web-and-print subscription offered more for the same price? Ariely wondered why the Economist offered it in the first place.

So Ariely, the psychology professor that he was, decided to put this question to the test. He showed modified versions of the Economist's pricing table to two sets of students. He showed only the web and web-and-print options to the first set, while he showed all three options to the second set. The second set saw the print-only option, while the first set didn't.

Because the print-only option would never be chosen, Ariely figured students' behavior would be the same. He thought both sets of students would choose the web-only and web-and-print options at the same frequency.[65]

But that's not at all what happened:[66]

Option	When two options shown	When three options shown
Web only ($59)	68%	16%
Print only ($125)	*Not shown*	0%
Web & print ($125)	32%	84%

Simply adding the print-only option, which was supposed to be irrelevant, completely changed students' behavior. While only a third of students chose the web-and-print subscription in the 2-option test, that number jumped to over four-fifths once the print-only option was introduced.

Ariely realized that the Economist never intended for anyone to buy the print-only subscription. Instead, the print-only subscription made the web-and-print bundle look like an amazing deal, thus pushing buyers toward it.[67]

Normally, when you're comparing products, you have to trade off between two aspects, such as price and quality. You can get a higher-quality product or a lower price, but usually not both. It's not clear which one is better, since each has advantages over the other.

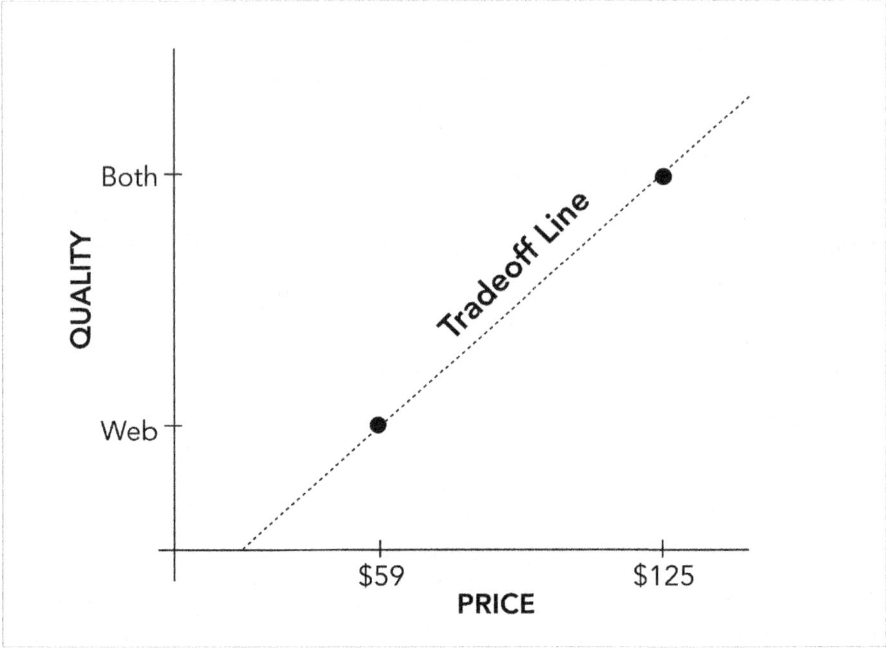

The Economist's web-only and web-and-print offerings had a clear tradeoff: the more access you want, the more you'll have to pay. Thus, both lie on a tradeoff line.

You can then add a *decoy*, which is similar to but worse than the option that you want people to buy, which is called the *target*.[68] In the Economist case, the print-only version was a decoy. Note that the decoy lies below the tradeoff line, meaning that you'd rarely choose it since there are better options available.

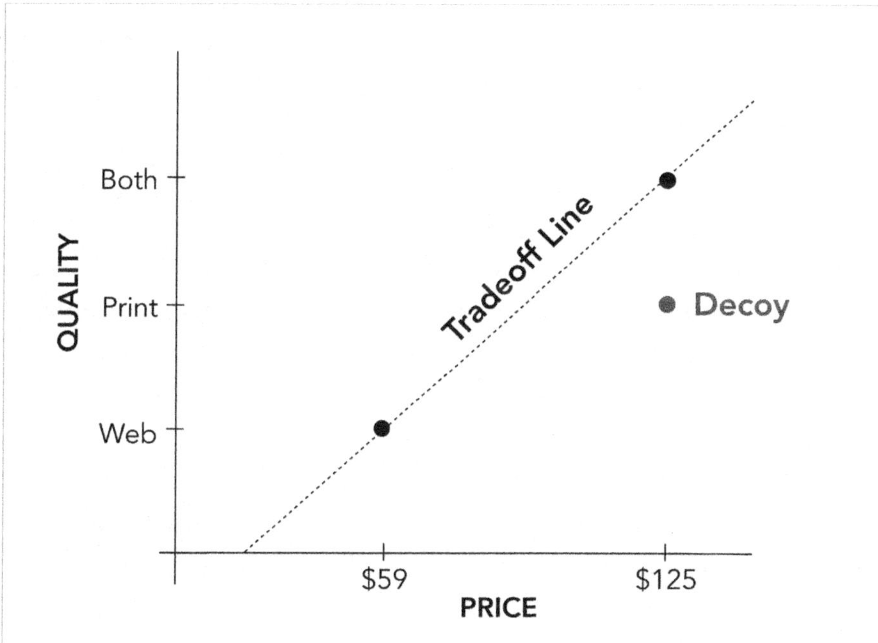

The Economist's print-only offering was strictly worse than the web-and-print deal: less access for the same price. Thus, the print-only offering fell below the tradeoff line and was a decoy.

This situation is known as *asymmetric domination*: the decoy is thoroughly beaten by the target, whereas the target and the other option (the *competitor)* are closely matched.[69]

One of the core tenets of arbitrary cohesion theory is that people try to compare similar things, since comparing apples to oranges is too hard. If you have three used-car options — two Mustangs and a Camaro — you're probably going to compare the two Mustangs and choose the one with, say, fewer miles on it.[70]

This means that, when given a choice between the target, the decoy, and the competitor, buyers will ignore the competitor and focus on the easily-comparable target and decoy. (Choosing the target over the decoy becomes easy to justify — "I found something that's easily better than the alternative" — and humans love making easily-defensible choices.[71])

Since the decoy is strategically designed to be slightly worse than the target, buyers will flock toward the target — thus buying the product you wanted them to buy all along.

To put it into practice, consider the classic example of the movies. Suppose the theater offers a lower-margin small size for $3 and a higher-margin large size for $7. These two choices fall roughly on the tradeoff line, so buyers probably won't significantly prefer one over the other. But if the theater introduces a $6 medium size, buyers will figure that the large size lets them get extra soda for just $1 more and thus prefer the large. The medium is close to the large but falls below the tradeoff line, so the theory confirms that buyers will go toward the large.[72] (If the theater wanted to boost sales of the small, they could introduce, say, a $2 extra-small size.)

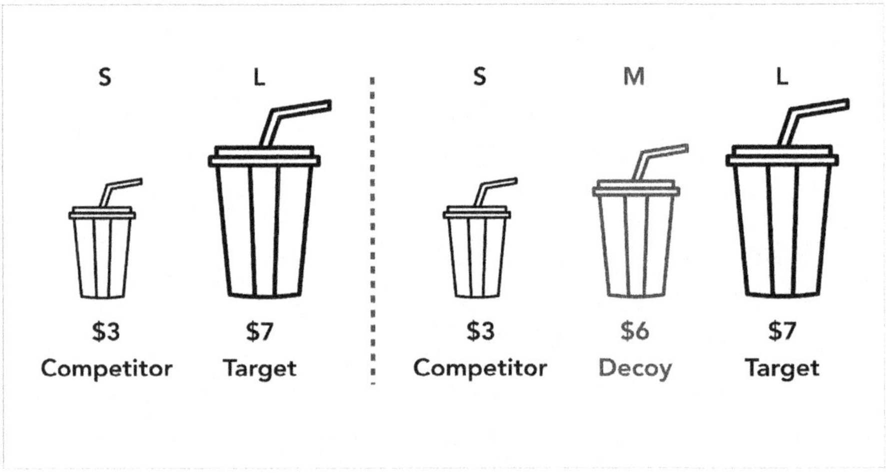

Here, the medium-sized soda is a decoy: it's clearly worse than the large soda. This will nudge moviegoers toward the large.

Let's take a more nuanced example from the world of tech. Suppose you want to buy a powerful Mac Pro desktop computer. You can get a machine with eight CPU cores for $6000, 12 cores for $7000, and 16 cores for $8000.[73]

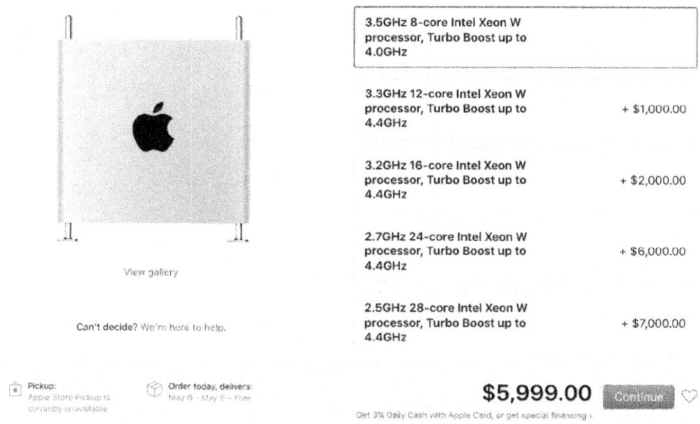

Apple's Mac Pro customization page, offering a $6000 machine with four possible upgrade paths. Source: Apple[74]

Each additional core beyond the 8th is $250. This is a hard tradeoff between price and power: how much is a core worth to you? How many do you need? What's a good balance to strike? You might decide to split the difference and go for the $7000 model, or *SKU*.

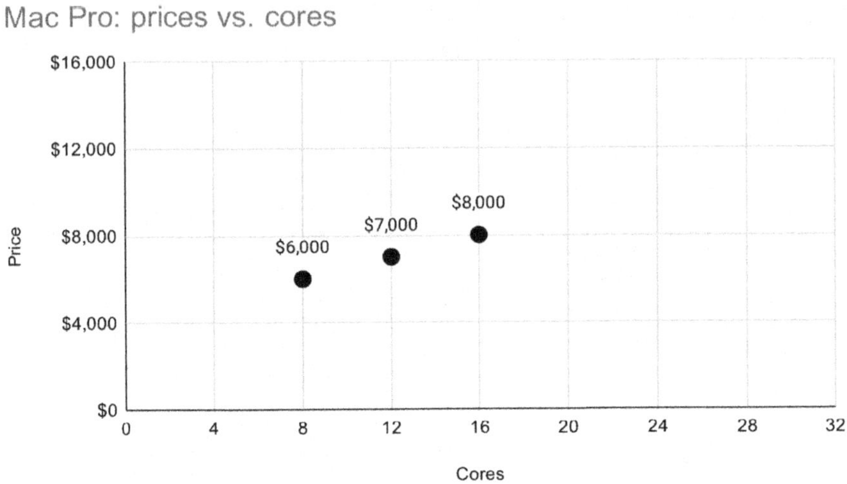

Three possible Mac Pro configurations that you can buy. Source: Apple[75]

But Apple offers more than those three SKUs. They actually offer five.

If you look carefully at the graph, you'll notice that there's a huge gap between the 16- and 24-core SKUs. The 16th through 24th cores cost $500 each instead of the usual $250.

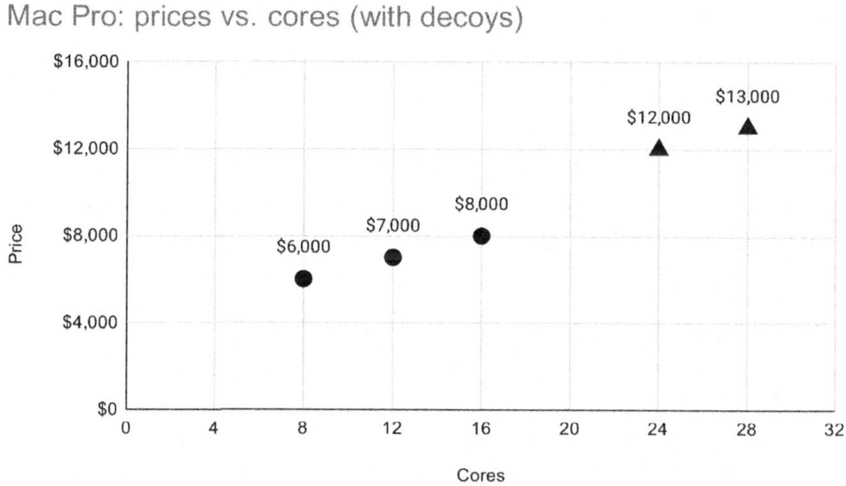

All five Mac Pro configurations. The two triangles mark the pricier decoys. Source: Apple[76]

All of a sudden, the $8000 SKU looks a lot more appealing. You get a good core-per-dollar value before the tradeoff becomes excessive. And, thus, Apple has convinced you to buy a more expensive computer — just by adding a few badly-priced SKUs that you probably wouldn't have bought regardless!

Compromise effect

Similar to the decoy effect is the *compromise effect*, where people usually prefer buying the middle-priced, middle-quality item since it's easier to justify than one of the extremes.[77] (Notice that we humans feel a strong need to justify our decisions[78] — so you, as a PM, should make your most profitable products the easiest purchases to defend.)

For instance, consider a study where experimenters offered buyers a few cameras to buy. When only two cameras were shown, buyers were evenly split between the two. But when experimenters added a third, more expensive, camera option, more people sprang for the mid-priced camera, with the rest splitting evenly between the cheaper and pricier option.[79]

Camera	When two options shown	When three options shown
Camera A ($170)	50%	22%
Camera B ($240)	50%	57%
Camera C ($470)	*Not shown*	21%

In this example, you can imagine that the average person isn't an expert at cameras and has no concept of what a fair price for a camera should be — and they probably can't even evaluate what makes a camera good. Thus, people fall back to their *heuristics*, or mental shortcuts: pricier things are usually higher quality than cheaper things, and the safest bet is to go down the middle.

Or consider Starbucks: their menus used to show the short, tall, and grande sizes. But later they added the extra-large venti size to the menu and hid the short option.[80] Why? They knew people would prefer to go right down the middle; such customers bought talls before change but bought (more profitable) grandes after the change.[81]

💼 Interview tip

The compromise effect and decoy effect are commonly used when pricing consumer hardware, so make sure you cite them if you're interviewing at a company that sells such products. For instance, Google's high-end Pixel phones rarely sell more than a few million units[82], but they're still strategically useful because they nudge users into buying more expensive Android phones by other manufacturers.

The compromise effect can sometimes reinforce the decoy effect. Remember the Mac Pro example from earlier: Apple steered buyers to the 16-core SKU, which was boosted both by the presence of the decoy 24-core SKU and the fact that it was the middle of five SKU options. Sometimes the two effects are at odds, though; the middle of three options is often made the decoy, but the compromise effect naturally steers people toward the middle option. So when you're designing your portfolio of products, make sure you think about ways that the two effects could help — or hurt — each other.

Interview tip

If you're asked about pricing a line of products (a question that becomes especially common once you hit senior PM and above), make sure you call out the potential conflicts between the decoy effect and the compromise effect. Ideally, you'll be able to set up your pricing so that the decoy effect overlaps perfectly with the compromise effect. If the compromise effect steers customers toward the middle option, make sure the decoy effect steers people toward that same option.

Designing a pricing table

It's time to put all these tricks together and design a table of the products you're going to offer and the prices of each.

First, make sure you know how many choices to offer. Humans seem to have an affinity for the number three — there are over a dozen "rules of three" on Wikipedia[83] — and, as such, it's no surprise that so many menus and product lines have three options. There's small, medium, and large at restaurants; BMWs come in 3-, 5-, and 7-series; gas comes in three octane levels; and so on. Humans don't like being forced into just one option, but they get overwhelmed by too many options (ever tried choosing from among twenty ice cream flavors?)[84] Three options is the sweet spot, so you should lean toward offering three price options for your products too.[85]

Now comes arranging your products. People's eyes are naturally drawn to the middle of a set, and people prefer things that they look at more — so you should put your most profitable items in the center of the page.[86] (This is the same reason why the most profitable items for a supermarket are on the eye-level shelves.[87]) This trick may apply more to horizontal lists, though,[88] since people tend to look more at the top item of a vertical list.[89]

This is why it's so common for subscription services to offer three tiers of service, with the middle one highlighted as "recommended" or "best value." Enterprise software products, entertainment products, and even magazines use this tactic a lot.

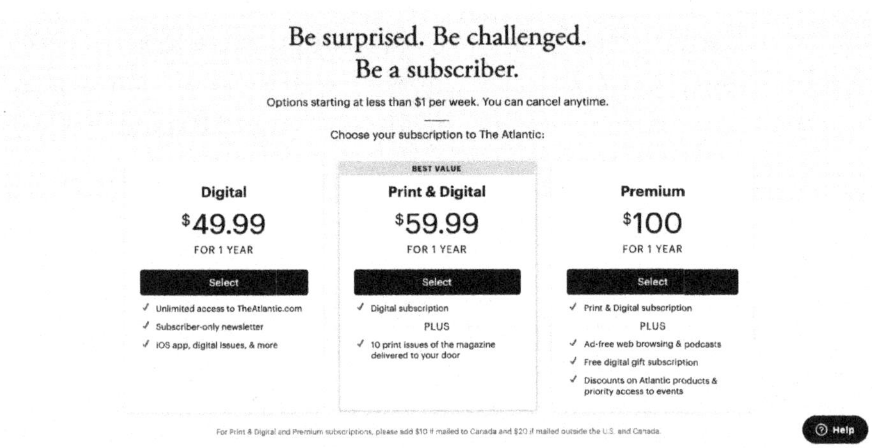

Print and Digital subscription offerings from The Atlantic. The middle one is labeled as "best value." Source: The Atlantic[90]

You might also notice that expensive restaurants don't put dollar signs next to their menu items. This is for a reason: seeing dollar signs makes people start thinking about money and how to minimize their monetary loss. Thus, they'll gravitate toward the cheapest options, which are usually the least profitable for the restaurant. By getting rid of dollar signs, restaurants get buyers thinking about quality — so they'll choose the items they want the most and only think about the price after they've chosen their item.[91] We don't see tech products using this hidden-dollar-sign trick that often, but it's worth considering.

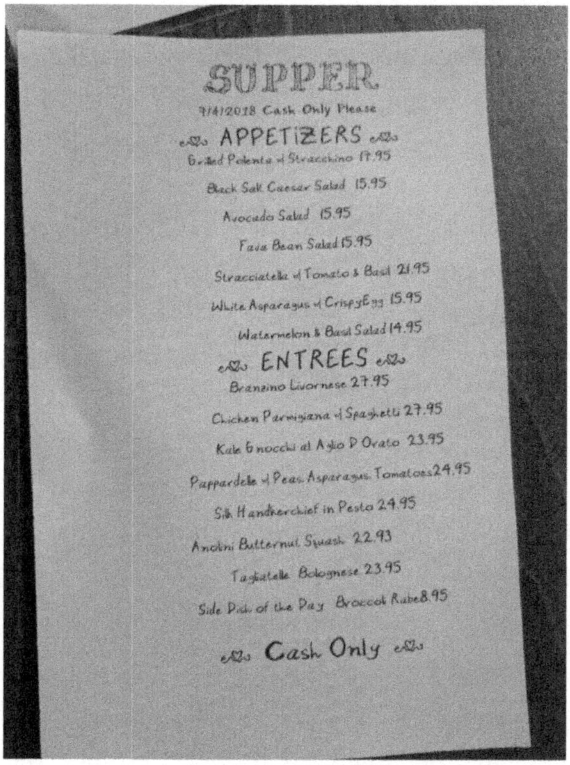

This restaurant menu doesn't align the prices, making it harder for customers to scan the menu looking for the cheapest price. Source: Yelp[92]

You also don't want to encourage people to compare prices, since that will also get them to hunt for the lowest price. This is why many fancy restaurants center-align menu items as well, so that the item names are down the middle of the page and the prices aren't aligned. This makes it harder for customers to scan the list of prices and thus less likely that they'll hunt for the cheapest item.

Discounts and bonuses

Finally, let's discuss how to sweeten the deal for your customers through discounts and bonuses.

Loss aversion

The first thing to understand is the concept of *loss aversion*: people hate painful experiences like losing, and the pain of losing usually outweighs the pleasure of gaining an equal amount. Take behavioral scientist Amos Tversky's coin flip experiment: would you take a coin-flip bet that gives you $10 if the coin lands "heads" and takes $10 from you if the coin lands "tails"?[93] Over enough games, you would end up with exactly as much money as you started out with. In other words, the *expected value* of the game is zero dollars.[94] So study participants wouldn't really have cared about the game.

Tversky then changed the game to give people $11 if they won and take $10 if they lost. Thus, if you played the game 100 times, you'd be expected to win $550 (50 wins times $11) and lose $500 (50 losses times $10) for an expected profit of $50, or 50¢ per game. A rational person would gladly have played this game an unlimited number of times.

But that's not what Tversky's participants did. Few people chose to play the $11/$10 game. Tversky had to keep increasing the reward for a win. Tversky finally got a majority of the class to play the game when he increased the reward to $22.50 for a win versus a penalty of $10 for a loss. This means that, for his students, the pain of a loss was 2.25 times as strong as the pleasure of a win. This gambling example is a bit of an outlier — averaged across many situations, a loss feels about 1.31 times as bad as a win feels good — but it demonstrates the point well.[95]

This is important because the two ways you can sweeten the deal for a customer is to discount the price or add a bonus — reducing the cost or increasing the benefit. Because of loss aversion, discounts are usually more effective than bonuses, since taking away a loss is more powerful than adding an equivalent gain.[96] People would rather avoid a $5 loss than find a $5 gain, even though they're economically the same.

The twist to loss aversion is that there are diminishing returns to the emotional impact of a gain or loss.[97] Winning $10 isn't twice as pleasurable as winning $5. The exact shape of this "diminishing sensitivity" graph isn't scientifically determined, but we can approximate it by saying that the emotional impact is proportional to the square root of the change in dollars. For instance, quadrupling the amount of money you earn will make you twice as happy.

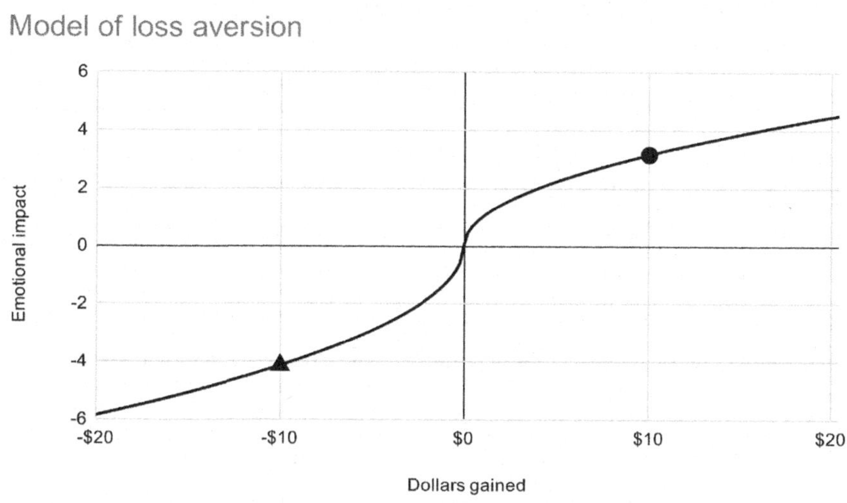

There are diminishing returns to losses and gains, shown in the concavity of the graph. Notice, too, that the emotional impact of a loss is greater than that of a gain: a gain of $10 has an impact of about 3, while a loss of $10 has an impact of about -4.

So, to maximize user happiness, you want to break their wins into as many chunks as possible and sweep all their losses into one big bucket.[98] By our model, winning $5 four times is about twice as pleasurable as winning $20 once. (This is why infomercials and car dealerships throw in lots of small bonuses — "buy now and we'll add X, Y, and Z for free!") So if you're going to offer users a free gift, throw in many small bonuses — say, a tote bag plus a sticker plus a free month — rather than one big bonus.

On the flip side, paying $5 four times is four times more painful than paying $20 once, per our model. In other words, people hate the idea of paying for marginal goods; they'd rather pay for everything up front. This is why people love buffets and "all-inclusive" travel packages instead of à la carte options, and why many people would rather pay thousands of dollars for a car they rarely use rather than having to pay $15 for each Uber ride to the store.[99]

This insight might be why subscription services like Netflix and Spotify have done so well, beating out the old iTunes model of buying each song or movie as you went. It feels much better to make one upfront payment each month (something you'll probably forget about, anyway) and get each subsequent movie/song for free instead of having to reach into your wallet each and every time you want more entertainment. (Spotify, in other words, is a "buffet" for music, and humans love buffets.)

Cut stacking

Finally, if you're going to discount your products, you should remember that people are bad with percents.[100] Try the math yourself: if a product is discounted by 20% and then discounted again by 25%, what's the final discount percent?

You might have jumped to say 45%. But the true discount is only 40%. The math to get the real amount is hard: $1-(1-0.2)(1-0.25) = 0.40$. The average person isn't going to do that math in their head because just adding the discounts, while wrong, is so much easier.

So if you're discounting your products, you should consider stacking discounts to make the overall discount seem bigger than it really is. A

20% discount stacked with a 25% discount *looks* like a 45% discount, but it's only a 40% discount, so it looks good for the customer while not hurting your bottom line as much as just advertising a 45% discount.

Permanent discounting

Though discounts are often applied once your pricing strategy is set in stone, you can actually make discounts part of your pricing strategy from the get-go. If you decide to set a semi-charmed price of $11.95 per month for your subscription service, you don't have to make $11.95 the sticker price. You can instead make the "original" price $20 and make the product seem permanently discounted to $11.95 — "over 40% off!"

This takes us back, full-circle, to the strategies of setting your opening price: herding, the three pricing theories, and the like. If you can incorporate permanent discounting at this early stage, you'll be setting yourself up for success from day one: you'll attract customers with a discount, get people to anchor on the sticker price so your new price looks better, and give yourself the flexibility to raise prices by reducing the discount.

Chapter 13

Motivation

NOW IT'S TIME to turn toward using psychology to get people to use your product. It's a three-step process: understanding users' motivations for using your product, convincing them to buy and sign up, and getting them to stick around once they've taken the plunge. That's what we'll focus on in this chapter. But let's start by understanding how to get people to want to use your product in the first place.

Intrinsic and extrinsic

The first thing to know about motivation is that it comes in two major flavors: *intrinsic* and *extrinsic*. Extrinsic motivation involves giving people external incentives — money — to do something, while people who do things voluntarily are driven by intrinsic motivation.

The best example of the tension between intrinsic and extrinsic motivation comes from the famous Israeli daycare experiment. At one daycare, about a third of parents came late to pick up their kids, causing inconvenience to the staffers. To cut this tardiness rate, the daycare started fining parents $2.70 if they were ten or more minutes late. But this didn't help the problem at all. In fact, the fraction of parents who were late doubled![1]

Why? Before the change, parents came on time because they would feel guilty or shameful if they were late, since they knew they were inconveniencing the teachers. This was intrinsic motivation: nobody wants to feel guilt, and they'll go out of their way to avoid it. But when the fine was instituted, parents started feeling only extrinsic reasons (money) to come on time. Parents quickly did the math and figured that extra time was worth the money; all of a sudden, guilt no longer motivated them.

This is a powerful point: intrinsic motivation is far more powerful than extrinsic motivation,[2] but extrinsic motivation tends to "crowd out" intrinsic motivation.[3] Once extrinsic motivators — in the daycare's case, money, or *market norms* — are introduced, people's intrinsic motivation — in this case, *social norms* — are thrown out the window and can't be restored.[4]

More fundamentally, everyone does tasks for a reason. When a monetary reward is introduced, people lose any innate interest in the task and only do it as a means of getting the money. The task loses its attractiveness, and once the reward is gone, nobody finds the task interesting anymore.[5]

This is why people love doing hobbies for free, but that motivation vanishes once they start getting paid for it. This quote from an artist explains it pretty well:[6]

> *Not always, but a lot of the time, when you are doing a piece for someone else it becomes more "work" than joy. When I work for myself there is the pure joy of creating and I can work through the night and not even know it. On a commissioned piece you have to check yourself — be careful to do what the client wants.*

Case study: Quora, Yelp, and open-source software

In 2007, a startup called Mahalo introduced a question-and-answer website where people could earn real money for answering community-submitted questions correctly.[7] A few years later, the Q&A website Quora launched; it was the exact same idea, but contributors weren't paid a penny.[8] Which one won out?

As you know, the answer is Quora. Mahalo never got more than 15 million users,[9] and the app fizzled out in 2014.[10] Quora, meanwhile, was valued at $900 million in 2014[11] and surpassed a $2 billion valuation in 2019.[12]

Quora realized it would succeed by drawing intelligent,[13] well-respected "thought leaders" to the platform,[14] and the founders probably knew that such contributors would demand top dollar if they were to be paid to contribute. Instead, the founders must have realized that these talented contributors would contribute for free if the intrinsic motivation of gaining internet fame, contributing to the community, and feeling like you helped people wasn't crowded out by narrow monetary concerns.

This is, in many ways, similar to lawyers who do pro bono work. In one case, lawyers weren't willing to work for elderly clients for $30 an hour, but they were perfectly willing to do it for free. Why? When the work was framed as volunteer work, the lawyers would happily contribute, but the moment a price tag was attached to it, the lawyers started comparing it to their regular cases, which paid far more than $30 an hour.[15]

Generally, highly-skilled people would demand such a high price tag for their work that you're much better served by appealing to their intrinsic motivations like altruism. People are willing to work for you for free, but only if the work feels meaningful or otherwise appeals to people's intrinsic drives. (The inverse is digital "drudge work" platforms like Amazon's Mechanical Turk: most people wouldn't get any intrinsic pleasure from doing these menial tasks for a faceless business, so extrinsic motivators — money — are the only way to motivate them. People might probably volunteer to do those same tasks, though, if they were for science.[16])

More generally, this strategy of appealing to intrinsic motivation is very powerful for platforms that live and die off *user-generated content*, from Quora to Yelp to Twitter. Bear in mind that these platforms sometimes also offer extrinsic rewards, but not in the form of money. For instance, Foodies love reviewing restaurants on Yelp because it makes them feel sophisticated and influential (intrinsic motivations) — but the top reviewers are also added to the "Yelp Elite" club, which gives them bragging rights and access to exclusive dinners and parties (extrinsic motivations).[17] Still, these extrinsic motivators are icing on the cake, not the cake itself; few people would spend thousands of dollars eating out and writing hundreds of Yelp reviews just for the free drinks.

Finally, intrinsic motivation is the reason why *open-source software* works so well. Open-source projects, such as the Firefox web browser, the Linux kernel that underpins operating systems like Android, and famous developer tools like D3 and Bootstrap,[18] are created and maintained mostly by volunteers, and anyone can see and contribute to their code.[a] People are happy to contribute to these community-driven projects for the same reason that lawyers are happy to do pro bono work; if money were brought into the equation, these highly-skilled developers might lose their appetite unless paid huge sums.[19]

Self-determination theory

So what gets people to be intrinsically motivated in the first place? There are many frameworks here, but one of the most powerful ones is *self-determination theory*, or *SDT*. SDT explains that people want to fulfill three innate desires: competence (feeling like you're good at something), autonomy (having control over your destiny), and relatedness (feeling connected to others).[20] For a task to intrinsically motivate someone, it must appeal to one or more of those desires.

[a] There's also a category of pseudo-open-source software, which is developed by a for-profit company but publishes its code and plans online. These include Google Chrome and Facebook's React. It takes a very wealthy company to bankroll projects like these; it's remarkable how far open-source projects with far smaller budgets have gotten.

People feel competent when they can be confident, gain skill, and impact their environment. It's especially important that people's challenges match their skill level.[21] This last bit is why humans perform so well when they enter the famous *flow state*,[22] where people can spend endless hours on a task when the difficulty is perfectly matched to their skill level.[23]

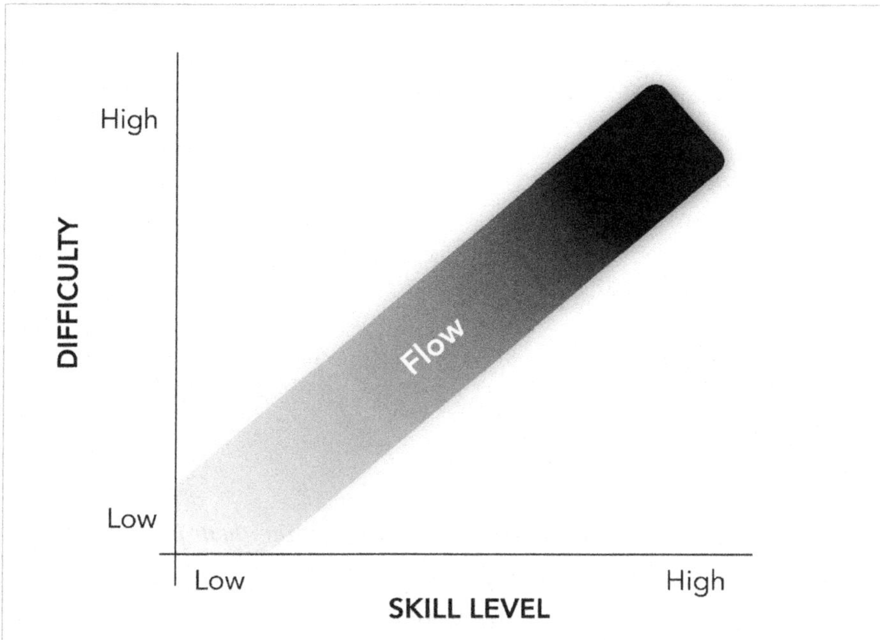

The flow state happens when the difficulty of a task closely matches your skill level.

If your product can get people feeling a sense of flow, they'll fall in love with it. Video games are so addictive precisely because they tap into flow state: successful games will always throw you a new challenge that matches your skill level and keep pushing you as you improve.[24]

Autonomy is about feeling independent and being able to take actions that match your desires.[25] Products that do well on autonomy let users control how they use the product and how they progress.[26] A good example of this is Khan Academy, which lets you jump around freely between lessons, while a traditional online course would normally make you go through lessons in order.

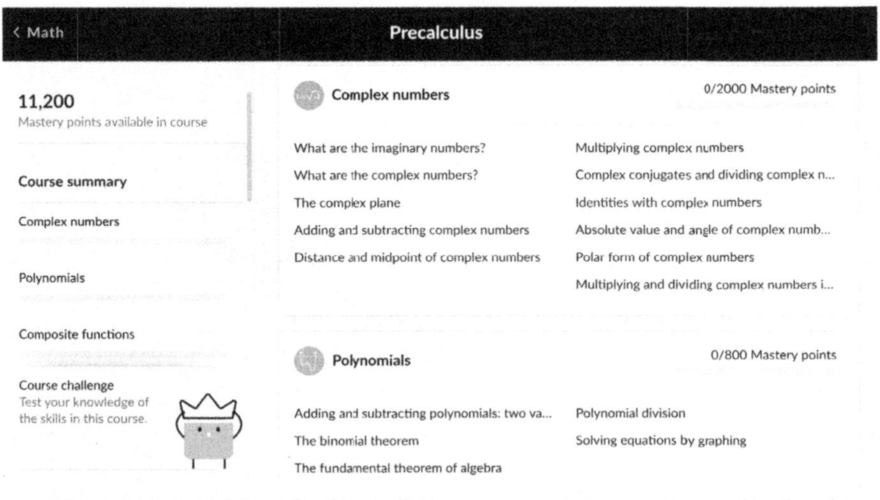

Khan Academy gives users a lot of autonomy by letting them proceed through lessons at any rate — and in any order — that they like. Source: Khan Academy[27]

The general product advice here is to set up a well-defined world and then give users free reign over it.[28] Khan Academy, Wikipedia, and most blogs let you learn anything in the library at any time; many digital courses give you a strict structure to follow. Freelancing platforms like Fiverr let you decide which tasks to take on; apps like Uber essentially force drivers to go wherever the company wants them to go.

Relatedness is about feeling a sense of belonging and connectedness with others. Tech products touch less on this area, but it's the reason that users form such strong bonds with social media apps.[29]

Case study: Twitter

Many successful apps can fulfill all three pillars of self-determination theory. Twitter is a great example. You can measure the growth in your Twitter skills as you rack up ever-more followers, likes, and retweets and craft the perfect list of lists and people you're following. You can decide exactly what you want to tweet about and who to follow; anyone can write for the public's consumption. And you can engage with friends, family, and all kinds of interesting public figures.

People love contributing to Wikipedia, forums, or open-source software because they hit those pillars as well. You can slowly grow your following and be proud of the work you've put out; you can contribute in any way you see fit; and you can meet like-minded people and maybe even become semi-famous.

Employee motivation

An interesting aside is that this same theory is key to assembling a great team at your company. Employees flourish when they can be autonomous: one Cornell study found that businesses that gave employees autonomy grew four times faster than companies that relied on top-down leadership and had three times less employee turnover.[30]

The classic example of this is Google's *20% time*, where employees are allowed to spend part of their work hours working on independent projects for the company. Such famous products as AdSense, Gmail, and Google News have come out of this time.[31] (Fun fact: Google didn't invent this approach. In the 1940s, 3M started letting employees spend 15% of their time on projects of their choosing.[32] The Post-It Note was invented through an employee's spare time through this program![33])

Motivation 3.0

There are many spins on the core of self-determination theory. A similar theory, called *Motivation 3.0*, was put forward by Daniel Pink. It says that people need to feel mastery (like competence), autonomy, and purpose, and appealing to those desires can help you motivate people to act.[34] The last part — purpose — explains why people love volunteering. (It's called Motivation 3.0 because it succeeds Motivation 1.0, where ancient people were allowed to do whatever they wanted, and Motivation 2.0, where people were motivated with crude extrinsic rewards and punishments, known as *carrots and sticks.*[35])

The four organs

We've seen several ways to categorize rewards so far. Intrinsic and extrinsic rewards appeal to different elements of our psyche; self-determination theory's trio of competence, autonomy, and relatedness help us feel like more complete human beings. The last, and perhaps most concrete, way to think about rewards comes from a framework made popular by NYU professor Scott Galloway.

Galloway argues that products can reward one of four organs, metaphorically speaking: the brain (knowledge), the heart (love), the stomach (consumption), and the genitals (sex appeal).[36] To be happy, people need to satisfy all four organs — so you should target your product's rewards at one of the four.

The brain

Starting at the top of the body, the first organ that needs to be satisfied is the brain. The brain seeks to learn, to understand, and to grow. Google Search is the classic example of a product that feeds the brain: each time you get search results, you feel a little smarter and more powerful. Just the act of searching feels like you're plugging your brain into some miracle machine that can hunt down any piece of information in the galaxy.[37]

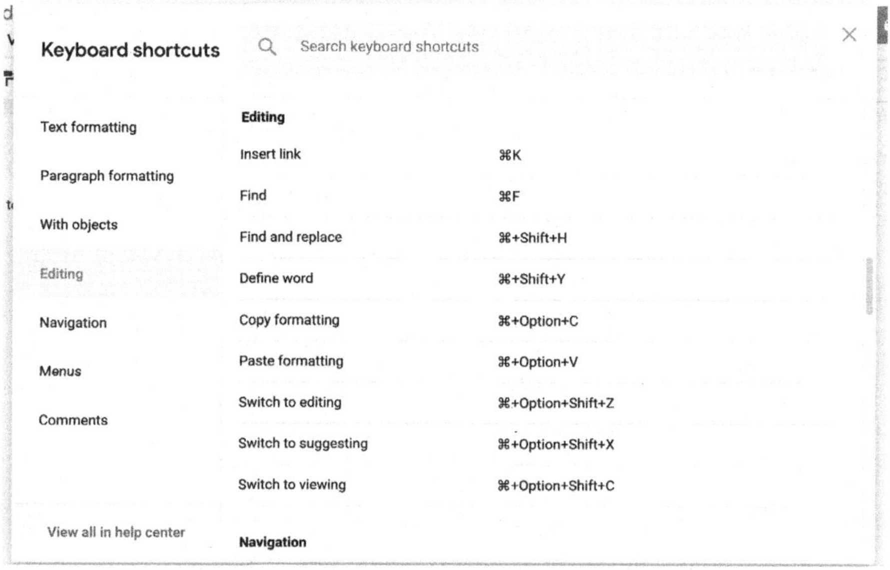

Google Docs offers an impressive array of keyboard shortcuts; learning them makes you feel like a wizard who can make magic with a keyboard. Source: Google Docs

We'd add that, when a product makes you feel like you've learned something or gained a new skill, it's rewarding your brain. This is why products with learning curves are often hard-to-use at the beginning but very rewarding to use once you've mastered them. Whether you're getting good at Spanish on Duolingo, learning how to make incredible Photoshop creations, or just figuring out how to use obscure commands in Excel, this process of learning is very rewarding. You feel like your brain is growing and you're able to do things you could never do before.

The heart

Moving down the body, we come to the heart, which needs to be fed with love, friendship, happiness, and human connection. Facebook is the master of this organ, since its products are among the most popular ways for us to stay in touch with loved ones, reconnect with old friends, feel social validation (via likes on our posts), and be part of social groups (via groups or group messages).[38]

More broadly, anything that lets users feel popular, loved, well-connected, accepted, or high-status[39] rewards to the heart. Social media apps obviously help users feel these feelings — who hasn't gotten a rush from getting a lot of likes and comments on their new Instagram picture? Online forums and communication platforms like Reddit, Quora, and StackOverflow also help people feel like they're part of a community, which is a big reason for the enduring popularity of these platforms.

Email also taps into this need for social validation, since there's an unspoken social obligation to respond to emails. Answering your emails also makes you feel like you're being a good person and helping others out.[40]

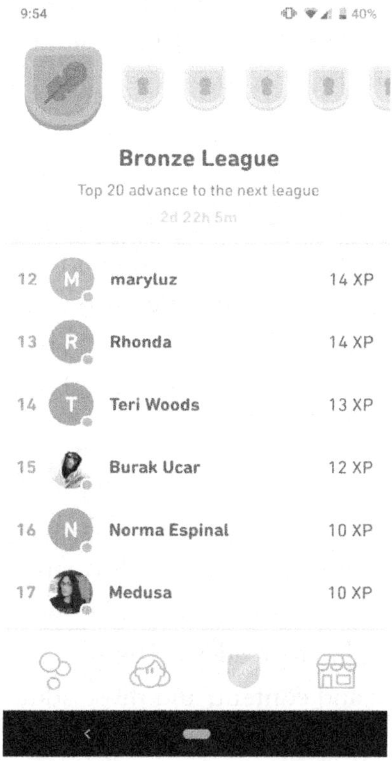

Duolingo lets you compete against friends and strangers in weekly "leagues;" win a league and you can enter a more competitive one. Source: Duolingo

A bit of friendly competition doesn't hurt, either. Playing against your friends in apps like Duolingo, which lets you compete against friends to learn new languages, helps you stay close with these friends (heart rewards) while also feeling a sense of growth and accomplishment (brain rewards). Plus, feeling smarter than your friends is always a nice feeling.

The stomach

Moving down the body further still, we reach the stomach: the organ obsessed with consumption. The gluttonous stomach wants to obtain and eat as much stuff as possible. Amazon, which lets us get any product our heart desires in just two days, quite literally feeds our hungry stomachs.[41]

We can break down this notion of "stuff" into resources, information, and money. Big eaters, pack rats, and compulsive hoarders[42] love gathering physical resources like food and tangible goods. This impulse makes sense: we humans evolved in an environment of scarcity, where starvation was always around the corner. There was no downside to gathering as much food, and as many tools and other goodies, as possible.[43]

Tech products sometimes serve this need for physical resources; the best examples are ecommerce businesses. It's more common, though, for tech products to satiate our need for information. Tech products are more likely to help people hoard information, though. Newsletters that offer free tips and insights to readers, Twitter and Pinterest's infinite-scrolling lists of stories and content, and those addictive *listicles* on Buzzfeed all tap into our desire to gather information.[44]

Like with physical resources, there's a good reason why we like devouring information: information helped our ancestors stave off death. Knowing how to tell a poisonous berry from a tasty one, or knowing what an oncoming cheetah sounds like, was instrumental in survival.[b]

The last kind of stomach reward, and the most self-evident, is money. Discounts on ecommerce websites, sign-up bonuses, incentives to invite friends, and "buy two, get one free" deals all tap into this deep desire to hoard money.

Sex appeal

The last organ down the body is the genitals. All life needs to reproduce, so we humans are deeply drawn to anything that might increase our

[b]Modern humans now suffer from the opposite problem: instead of being starved of food, resources, and information, we're overwhelmed with too much of it.

sex appeal. Galloway argues that Apple is the master of this: their shiny, high-end, luxury products help you signal your wealth and sophistication to potential mates.[45] Apple's variety of gadgets gives you plenty of ways to showcase your wealth: on your head (AirPods), on your wrist (Apple Watch), and in your hand (iPhone or Apple Card).

Luxury products and dating apps offer clear rewards to your real (or perceived) sex appeal, but plenty of other products feed this need in more subtle ways. Social media apps let you showcase your popularity to potential mates; photo filters in Instagram help you look more attractive; stylish Airbnbs let you brag about your cool vacations at parties; and so on.

💼 Interview tip

One insight from the four organs framework isn't particularly relevant to psychology but is interesting nonetheless: your profit margins tend to get better as you move down the body. People will pay a lot more for food and sex than they will for information.[46]

Apple realized this during its troubled 1980s and 1990s. Back then, the company spoke to consumers' brains, offering computers with better interfaces and specs than the competitors. Geeks loved it, but it was hardly sexy. But with the advent of the iPod in the 2000s, Apple started selling luxury gadgets that would help you show off your wealth on the go. Thus, Apple pivoted to focus on sex appeal, which helped the company grow its margins and thus become an immensely-profitable juggernaut through the 2000s and 2010s.[47]

Combining the rewards

Products aren't caricatured into serving just one organ, though. They can reward users by serving multiple organs at once.

A good example is Google Photos, which lets users store an unlimited number of photos, create albums and scrapbooks, and share pictures with their friends. Google Photos hits all four organs.

First, the brain. Google Photos lets us easily remember our past vacations and pull up our favorite memories in an instant (you can search for "bar" and it'll automatically pull out every picture you've taken at a bar). This lets us have a second brain for memories, which gives a similar rush of power as Google Search. Plus, having unlimited photo storage appeals to the logical part of our brains, since we no longer have to spend money on cloud storage or external hard drives.

Google Photos lets you print your favorite photos as photo books. These make great gifts. Source: Google Photos[48]

Google Photos is even better for the heart. The app automatically tags people in your photos and then lets you automatically create albums containing every photo you've ever taken with a particular friend or family member. These albums are wonderful ways to relive your fondest moments or just find a good picture to send to your friends on their birthdays. Plus, you can print photo books and canvases straight from the app;[49] these make great gifts for important people in your life.

The unlimited free storage makes Google Photos great for your stomach: it gives you the freedom to take literally as many photos as you can. It thus lets you hoard memories without ever worrying about the downsides. The allure of "unlimited" never fails to make users happy. (Just ask Neel, who has over 100,000 pictures in his Google Photos.)

And finally, Google Photos does its part to help with sex appeal. The app gives you a wide range of editing tools, from cropping to adjusting lighting to applying over a dozen filters.[50] These help you make impressively attractive profile photos right in the app. Google Photos can also automatically enhance your photos — often without you even needing to tell it to — which helps you look great without having to put in any work at all.[51]

Put it together and you have a product that can reward all four organs — a surefire recipe for getting users to spend a lot of time and energy with the product.

Chapter 14

Getting the Click

Once you understand why people might want to use your product, the next step is to get them to sign up, buy, enter their email address or credit card information, or otherwise take action. This is a game of persuasion, and there's a huge book of psychological tactics you can use to get that fateful click.

The scarcest resource

We've talked about how to get people to want to use your product. But motivation alone isn't enough. No matter how much you might want to sign up for Disney's streaming service, Disney+, you won't do so if you don't have the money. Even if you're in love with a Michelin-starred restaurant in your town, you won't go if you can't get a reservation.

To get someone to use your product, in other words, you have to make sure they're able to.[1] People are able to do something when they have enough of four key resources: time, money, physical energy, and mental energy. If they lack even one of these, they won't take action.[2] People might really want to download your free app, but if they can't find it on their default app store, it'll take too much mental energy to find it — so many will drop off.

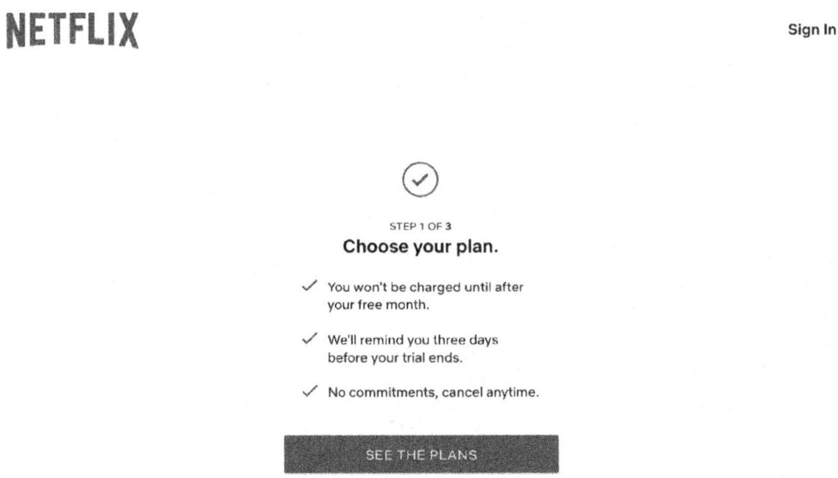

Netflix's signup form emphasizes that there's no monetary risk. Source: Netflix[3]

Thus, if someone isn't taking your desired action, you need to reduce your usage of their scarcest resource at the moment.[4]

Netflix's free trial

Consider Netflix's goal of getting people to sign up for a paid subscription. Signing up only takes a minute, so time isn't an issue. You can sign up on pretty much any device, so looking around your house — a relatively high use of physical energy — isn't a problem either. And the signup form is pretty easy to fill out; you only have to provide basic information like your email address and credit card number, some of which your browser might be able to autofill for you. Thus, mental energy isn't a problem either.

People's scarcest resource, rather, is money, given that Netflix costs a not-insignificant amount of money each month. Potential buyers might be hesitant to throw money after a product they don't like. This is why

Netflix goes out of its way to offer a free trial and remind you that there's zero monetary risk to signing up: "cancel online anytime, 24 hours a day," "you can easily cancel your account online in two clicks," "there are no cancellation fees," and so on.[5]

These tactics reduce potential customers' anxiety about money, which is their scarcest resource in this context. Now, there's very little *friction* stopping people from signing up — which is great news for Netflix.

Google My Business's anti-abuse feature

You can also apply this principle in reverse: to discourage users from doing things you don't want them to do.

For instance, consider Google My Business, a tool that lets business owners create a Google Maps listing and thus make edits, add photos and hours, and interact with customers. Owners can also "claim" auto-generated listing as their own.

Naturally, the real owner of a given business is highly-motivated to claim it, but so are their competitors. An unscrupulous pizzeria owner might be tempted to fraudulently claim a competitor's listing so they could set fake hours, post pictures of unappetizing pizzas, and otherwise sabotage their business. The question becomes: how can Google let legitimate owners claim their businesses while making fraudulent owners not want to?

The answer lies in the resources for action. Creating or claiming a listing is free, so there's no monetary restriction. The form takes about five minutes to fill out and asks easy questions like your business's name and phone number,[6] so time and mental energy aren't problems either.

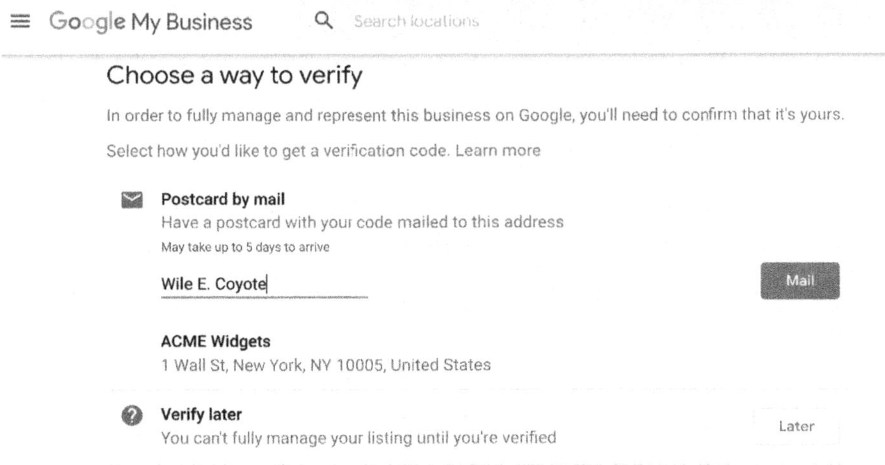

Google My Business makes you verify your business's identity and address by mailing you a postcard containing a special code. Source: Google[7]

So Google decided to make the process take a lot of physical energy: it will mail a postcard to your business's address. You can only take over the business's listing if you type in a code found on that postcard. The postcard can take days, if not weeks, to arrive and requires you to monitor your mail, so it's a significant tax on users' physical energy (and time, in a way).[8]

Adding all this friction makes it hard for legitimate business owners to claim their business; you'd think some enterprising Google PM would do away with the postcard requirement to encourage more business owners to claim listings. But the friction added here is essential: while it taxes legitimate business owners' physical energy, it taxes fraudulent owners' energy *even more*. If you don't actually own the restaurant, it becomes a lot harder to find a way to redirect the postcard to you. It's not impossible, but it becomes such a hurdle that you won't bother.

So while it's usually a good thing to reduce the amount of time, money, mental energy, and physical energy that you require from users, increasing your demands can sometimes be useful to ward off bad actors.

The power of defaults

If you can get people motivated to use your product and eliminate the resource barriers that would stop them from using it, you stand a good chance of winning them over. With enough elbow grease, persuasion works.

But the easiest way to win customers over is to not have to persuade them at all! People have a strong tendency to stick with the default choice, so if you set people's default choice to the one that benefits you the most, you won't have to actively persuade them at all.

The most famous case study of this was in Europe, where some countries let residents opt in to donating their organs when they died, while other countries defaulted to making residents donate their organs.[9] The second group of countries made organ donation the default and made it fairly hard to opt out.[10] The result? Opt-in countries saw just 15-20% of residents opt in, while opt-out countries saw almost no residents opt out, resulting in a near-100% consent rate.[11]

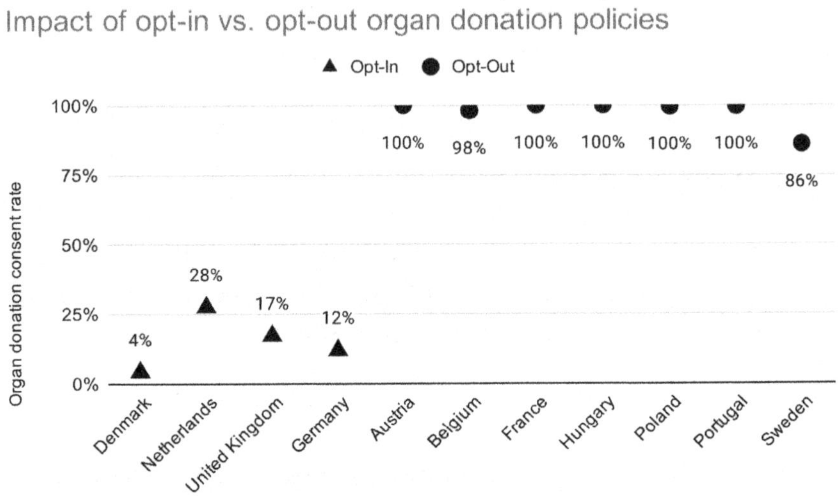

Making organ donation the default (opt-out) greatly increases donation rates compared to the standard opt-in model: Source: Dan Goldstein[12]

Examples of this pattern abound. The financial services firm Vanguard found that 91% of new hires put money into 401(k) retirement plans when they were opted into these plans by default, while just 42% put money into 401(k)s when that action wasn't the default.[13] Disney World's restaurants found that kids in the park "consumed 21% fewer calories and 40% less fat and sodium" when the default choices in kids meals were changed from soda and french fries to juice and vegetables.[14]

Why does this work? People like mental shortcuts, and offering a default gives people one less decision to make.[15] People also figure that the person who set the default knew what they were doing, and they're inclined to trust that choice — especially when people are dealing with unfamiliar or complicated areas.

For PMs, one common trick is to pre-check checkboxes that users might otherwise not care enough to opt into. This trick is very common in privacy settings pages and onboarding flows; many products will make users give away large amounts of data by default.[16] And virtually all online services automatically opt new users into their mailing lists. You have to be very careful using this tactic, though, since users have learned about this trick and distrust products that use it excessively.[17]

The power of defaults can also help you prop up less-successful products. Apple Maps has long been the default on iOS, which led to it being three times more popular than Google Maps — which most people thought of as better — as late as 2015.[18] Again, be careful with this tactic. Microsoft made Internet Explorer the default Windows web browser for decades, which boosted the browser's popularity but got Microsoft in hot water with European antitrust regulators in 2009.[19]

Framing

Would you use a credit card that gives less cash back than most competing cards, doesn't let you pay your bills on the web,[20] and doesn't even show you the card number?[21] Maybe not. But would you use a sleek titanium card with no annual fee, an easy-to-use app, remarkable security features, and a promise to keep your financial data private?[22] Probably!

You might have guessed that we were talking about the same card in both cases: the Apple Card, which debuted in 2019.[23a] It goes to show that the way you talk about a product is just as important as the product itself; the exact same thing can seem great or terrible depending on how you talk about it.

This is the psychological concept of *framing*: the lens through which people view something has a big impact on how they perceive it.[24] There's no such thing as a neutral, impartial observer; everyone's viewpoint is colored by the context in which they see something.[25] A surgery

[a] The card has overcome some of the flaws it was criticized for back in 2019.

with a 10% chance of failure feels a lot worse than a surgery with a 90% chance of success, but they're really the same thing.

If you're savvy about framing, you can control the lens through which potential customers view your product, which can go a long way toward making your product look a lot more attractive.

Negativity biases

One practical application of this theory is in writing text for websites' *landing pages* and call-to-action buttons. Remember loss aversion: losing feels more painful than winning feels pleasurable. This means that it's more effective to frame your product as something that removes losses than as something that adds gains. For instance, suppose you're selling a product that helps ecommerce companies increase the percent of users who buy on their site (i.e. you're increasing the *conversion rate*). Saying "stop losing customers!" will pack more of a punch than "get more customers!", since the pain of loss exceeds the pleasure of gain.[26]

Similarly, people weigh negative emotions more than positive ones.[27] This is why so many products advertise themselves as resolving users' *pain points*.[28] It's not "be more entertained;" it's "be less bored." It's not "get ahead"; it's "stop falling behind." And so on.

Percents

People also tend to find big numbers more persuasive than small numbers, and they generally overemphasize the negative things they hear about products. This is why a "99% fat free" yogurt sells better than a "1% fat" yogurt: it's better to advertise a big number than a small one, and it's better to emphasize the good than the bad.[29]

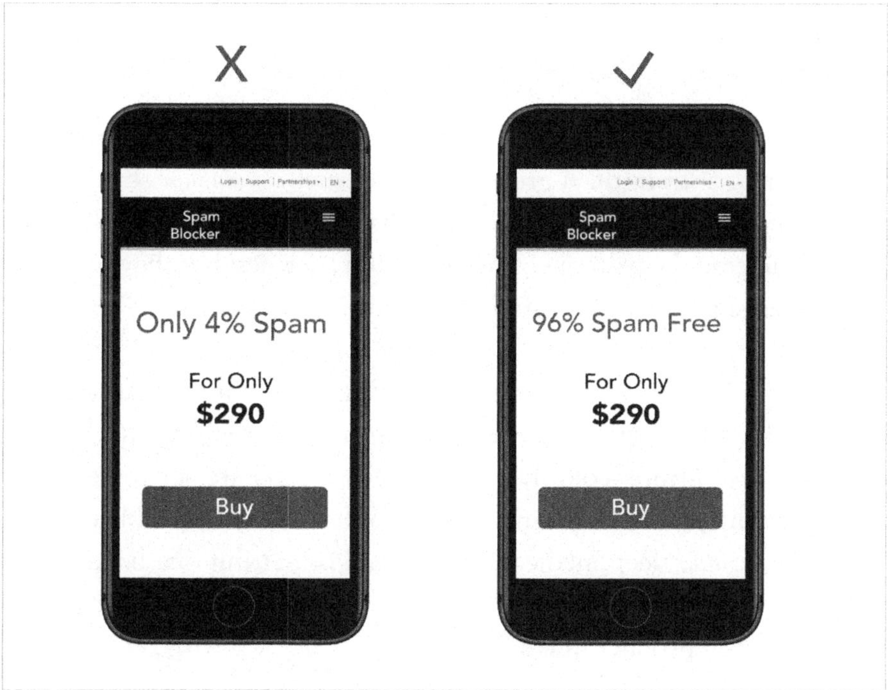

An email spam-blocker might catch 96% of spam but only let 4% through. The principle of framing says that you should emphasize the positive (96% blocked) rather than the negative (4% allowed). Source: MobileSpoon[30]

Another example of framing percentages: suppose a subscription for your product was originally $60 for 12 months but you cut it to $40 for 12 months (or, equivalently, $60 for 18 months). You could frame this as a 33% price cut (from $60 to $40) or a 50% longer subscription (from 12 to 18 months). Because people think bigger percentages are better,[31] you'd be better served emphasizing the "50% more time" than the "33% off."

Turning weaknesses to strengths

Framing is so powerful, in fact, that you can use it to turn a product's weakness into a strength. A great example of such a *judo move*[32] is nighttime cold medicine. Medications like Nyquil[33] and Tylenol PM[34] are designed to ease the pain of colds, fevers, and allergies, but they have the unintended side effect of causing drowsiness.

This would normally be considered a weakness, but the marketers of these products have turned it into a strength by advertising these medications as "nighttime cold meds." These products are supposed to be taken at night (hence "Ny" and "PM"), so they now do double duty as pain relievers *and* sleep medications. Instead of getting one benefit and one side effect, now you're getting two benefits! Clever framing thus turned a flawed product into a hit.

You can apply the same principle to your products, too. You aren't missing a feature; you've purposely left it out so you can focus on the more important things. You aren't lacking support for a particular operating system; you're building a custom, tailor-made experience for people on the OSes that you do support.

Google's Chromebooks are great at spinning weaknesses into strengths. The laptops don't let you do much work on local apps, instead making you do most of your work on the cloud. This could be seen as a weakness compared to Windows or macOS, but Google turns this fact around to argue that Chromebooks are great for students, who can jump around between devices without worrying that some important file will be left on one particular device.[35] Similarly, Chrome OS's inability to run desktop apps like Microsoft Word or Photoshop could be seen as a huge disadvantage — but it also lets Google boast that Chromebooks don't need antivirus, since nothing dangerous can get installed in the first place.[36]

Free!

The word "free" has been called one of the five most powerful words in the English language.[37b] People love free stuff, and they react irrationally whenever they see the word "free." Dan Ariely calls it an "emotional hot button" that never fails to attract customers' attention.[38]

People act irrationally in the presence of free stuff. Students in one experiment were offered a choice of a $20 gift card for $7 or a $10 gift card for free. The $20 offer was better, since you'd gain a net of $13, but most students went for the free $10 gift card.[39] The ice cream chain Ben & Jerry's gives out free ice cream every April 9th,[40] which leads people to form lines out the door and around the block. It doesn't make any rational sense to spend that much time in line for a cone that normally costs a few dollars, but people love getting free stuff so much that they'll gladly do it.

Why does "free" work so well? It's because of loss aversion: free stuff has literally zero cost, so there's zero downside. This means that free things are all upside, which short-circuits our brains into desiring as much free stuff as possible.[41]

---

[b] The others being "you," "because," "instantly," and "new."

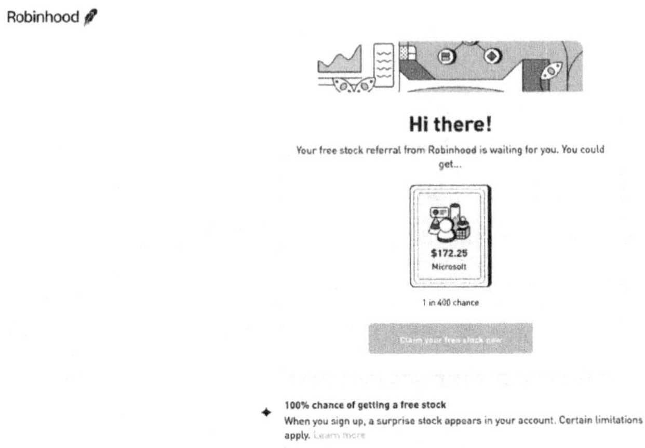

Robinhood offers a free stock for signing up, a powerful motivator. Source: Robinhood[42]

Free thresholds

You know by now how powerful free trials are, but one other interesting tactic is to dangle "free" stuff in front of users to incentivize them to behave in ways you want. For instance, in the late 1990s Amazon started offering free shipping on purchases over a certain amount. People around the world added things they didn't need to their cart to get over that threshold and get the sought-after free shipping. This trend held everywhere except France, where average order values didn't increase. The difference came because France made shipping about 20¢ instead of free — but even that tiny charge was enough to turn off people's "free" radars. Once France made shipping free over the threshold, customers fell in line with the rest of the world.[43]

This tactic has kept working since then: a free shipping threshold increased the average order value for one ecommerce startup by over 7%.[44] And it works outside ecommerce, too. Kickstarter projects, for instance, often give out free goodies — stickers, certificates, conversations with founders, and so on — to people who donate above a certain threshold.[45] It's worth thinking about how your product can use this tactic to encourage the behavior you want.

Incrementally free

We mentioned before that there's a diminishing return to the pain caused by losing money. In our model, quadrupling the amount of money you spend will only double the amount of pain you feel. This means that people love the "buffet" model, where they pay a large fee up front but get everything afterward for free. The blunted pain of that large cost is less than the combined pricks of many small payments. This, in turn, explains the success of subscription-based, "all-you-can-eat" products like Netflix.[46]

This model of *incrementally free* goods works even better because of people's unusually strong responses to free things. We'd argue that this is because most purchases come with an inherent sense of guilt: you're always wondering in the back of your head whether those dollars were worth it. This is the reason we get *buyer's remorse*, after all.[47]

But when you get incrementally free goods and services, that downside never shows up, since you aren't spending money at that moment. Incrementally free goods thus liberate you from the guilt of buyer's remorse. Being absolved of guilt is an addictive feeling that keeps people coming back. There's a reason that people go crazy for things as big as all-inclusive cruises or as small as unlimited soda refills at fast food joints. Thus, creating all-you-can-eat business models isn't just a great way to get users to subscribe — it's a powerful way to boost user satisfaction.

The downside of free trials

Free stuff can be *too* alluring, though. Since there's no downside to taking free stuff, people who aren't interested in the product at all will take it. This means that people who have no real interest in buying broccoli dip will still gobble up free samples of it at Costco — and, more ominously for tech products, people who have no intention of signing up for the paid version of a product will sign up for the free trial.

This is especially problematic for enterprise software startups, which try to follow up with most (if not all) free trial customers to upsell them to the paid version. If everyone and their dog signs up for a free trial, your sales team will waste a lot of time chasing down leads who'll never become paying customers.

For this reason, it's often helpful to add a slight bit of friction to the free trial signup flow to drive off people who don't really need the free trial.[48] Making people input their credit card details up front is a good way to do this.[c]

[c] It also makes people more likely to stick around once the trial ends, since their credit card details will be in by default, and they may not feel like overcoming the inertia to change that.

Chapter 15

Stickiness

ONCE YOU'VE GOTTEN SOMEONE to sign up for your product, you need to keep them there. This is the science of *stickiness*: it's how to keep people coming back day after day. And tech products are extraordinarily sticky: we check out phones almost 100 times a day[1] — that's once every ten minutes we're awake — and 61% of us check our phones within five minutes of waking up.[2] You surely know how easy it is to get addicted to Twitter, Instagram, and other such products. So how do they do it — and how can you get users coming back like they do?

Building habits

One of the most powerful ways to keep users coming back is to make the product part of the user's daily habits. Products that are used frequently and have high utility are more likely to be habit-forming, but you can habit-ify a low-utility action as long as it happens frequently enough.[3]

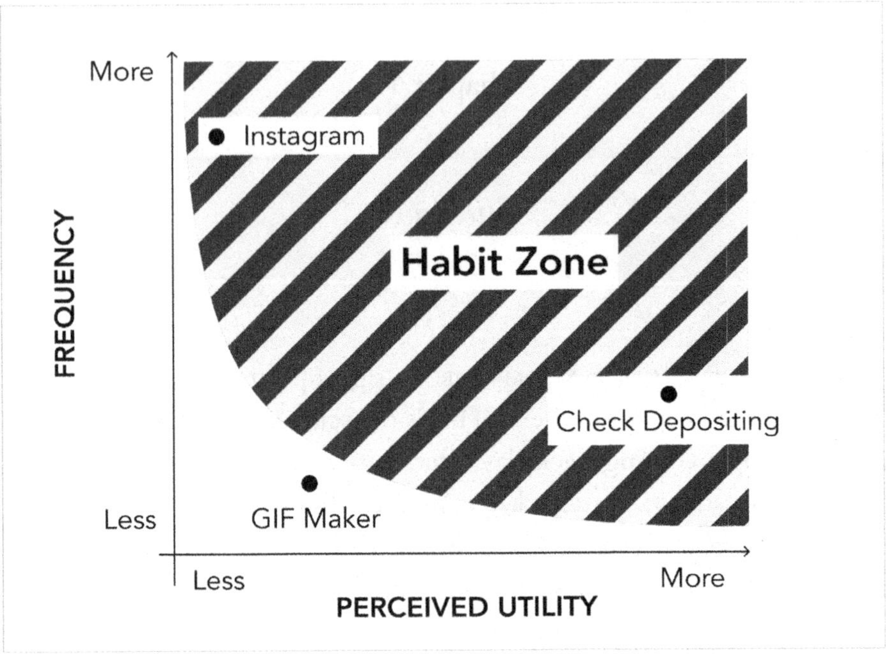

In order for an action to become a habit, it has to occur frequently enough and have high enough utility. Products that are neither useful nor used very often are probably not going to be habit-forming. Source: Sumit Garg[4]

The popular *Hooked model* explains how you can create habits. You start by using *external triggers* to get someone to visit your product.[5] These include paid advertising (*paid triggers*), favorable mentions in the press (*earned triggers*), word-of-mouth (*relationship triggers*), and push notifications (*owned triggers*).[6] One of these things will prompt a user to download or open your app.

The goal is to stop relying on external triggers, which get expensive, and make users open the app because of *internal triggers* — in other words, people start using your product out of habit.[7] To get them there, you take the user through multiple cycles of use, each time making the habit a little stronger. In each cycle, you give the user some reward for taking an action (like opening the app) and make them invest in the product. This investment sets up the next round of triggers, thus drawing the user back.[8] Eventually, users stop needing external triggers and come back to the app because it appeals to one of their internal motivators (recall the frameworks from the motivation chapter). They visit Netflix anytime they're bored, Facebook any time they're lonely, or Twitter any time they feel behind the curve.[9]

A good example of this model is a messaging app like WhatsApp or Snapchat: users download the app (action) because due to word-of-mouth from their friends (an external trigger), see if anyone has written to them (reward), and send a message (investment). When a friend writes back, that makes a push notification (external trigger), which draws users back into the cycle, but this time a little deeper. Eventually, the messaging app becomes a habit: people instinctively open it anytime they have something to share with friends.

The idea is that each round of rewards makes users feel more positively about the product, and each round of investment makes users more likely to stick with it — people like consistency, so they aren't likely to leave a product they've spent a lot of time and energy with.[10]

Variable rewards

The secret to making this Hooked loop work is in *variable rewards*. Science shows that humans don't get pleasure from getting rewards — they get pleasure from the *anticipation* of rewards. Scientifically speaking, the release of dopamine (nicknamed the "happy hormone"[11]) spikes right before you get a reward.[12]

What really gets your dopamine going, though, is randomness. We humans love finding patterns in things, and dopamine is evolutionarily designed to draw our attention to new things that we haven't matched to a pattern yet.[13] Randomness is, by definition, impossible to fit to a pattern, so random rewards will always keep our dopamine flowing. Dopamine is a big reason why we get addicted, therefore randomness makes us addicted. This is why slot machines, which pull in over $45 billion a year in the US (that's three-quarters of all casino revenue!),[14] are so addictive.

This means that products can't give out the same rewards — information, updates, job opportunities, messages, and so on — every day. Those will quickly get boring. Instead, they have to keep users entertained by giving out new rewards every single time the user opens the app. Social media is great at this; there are always new updates, and you never know how many likes and comments your posts are going to get. YouTube, Netflix, Spotify's autoplaying videos and recommendations are also a form of variable rewards, since you can never be quite sure what you're going to get.

The infinitely-scrolling lists of Twitter, Pinterest, and Reddit also provide variable rewards. Each scroll is like reaching your hand into the digital cookie jar — you never know what you're going to get, but you know it's going to be new and exciting. Infinite scrolling has even been called "the internet's slot machine."[15]

Variable rewards work great for entertainment apps, but they're less appropriate for tools. You want tools like your bank app to give you the same no-nonsense information every time instead of playing distracting games. Similarly, if Uber randomly gave you a 10% discount or a 10% markup, you'd probably just get annoyed. But apps like these can still subtly work in some randomness atop the app, like if Uber gave you a 5% chance of getting a discount card for the week or if your bank app randomly found useful credit card deals for you.

While variable rewards are powerful, users have wisened up to them; people can now spot products designed to be addictive. People know that social media can be unhealthy and the toolkit that those PMs use.[16]

This knowledge has reached even Congress: a bill introduced in 2019 aimed to stop the addictive autoplay and infinite-scroll features of social media websites.[17]

Bonus video

Snapchat is one of the world's most addictive apps, with over three billion Snaps sent per day.[18] Watch this video to discover the psychological playbook that has fueled Snapchat's success.

productalliance.com/videos/snapchat

Switching costs

Another way to keep users around is to make it hard to leave — in other words, raising the *switching costs*. The reasons users hesitate to switch fall into three major buckets: a lack of portability, a high upfront cost, and social pressure.

Portability

The biggest bucket is the lack of portability, whether that be of people, data, or ecosystems. Influencers hesitate to switch social networks because it's hard to carry your list of followers from network to network, and everyday users might hesitate to jump from a messaging app that 90% of their friends are on to one that just 10% of their friends are on.[19] Other kinds of data are also hard to transfer: your Spotify playlists, Gmail emails, Instagram photos, and Netflix profile are hard to move to competitors.

It's worth calling out the last one in particular. User-visible data like photos, messages, and to-do lists can be moved with enough effort; you can always manually save all your Instagram photos to your camera roll if you really want to. But sophisticated user models created by machine learning, such as Netflix's detailed profile of your tastes, are invisible to the user and thus literally impossible to move.

Plus, a lot of utility comes from having access to other people's data; Netflix's *collaborative filtering* algorithms, which recommend movies based on what similar users have watched before, are a prime example. Since you can't move other people's data to a new app, the utility of these algorithms can't be ported over either.

Another example is Facebook's *look-alike audiences* feature, which predicts which Facebook users behave like customers whose data you've uploaded and lets you target ads at those users.[20] The raw data is hidden from advertisers, so they can't export it. Models like Netflix's and Facebook's are therefore much more powerful "barriers to exit" than user-visible data.

Ecosystems are the last component of portability; there are often large ecosystems built around a product that don't easily transfer to others. Banks and other financial institutions live and die off Excel, and there's a huge ecosystem of Excel add-ons specially made for their use case.[21] Moving to a competitor like Google Sheets becomes that much harder. Trying to launch a new operating system is hard because nobody's built any apps for it yet, trying to launch a new browser without any addons is tough, and so on.

The set of products you use is also a sort of ecosystem, and substituting a new product that's less compatible with the other products might make your life harder. Microsoft Office tools are very well-integrated with each other, so if your company is an all-Microsoft shop, leaving Outlook for Gmail or Teams for Slack would be hard since you'd lose many of those integrations.[22]

Upfront costs

Another reason people don't switch is just that it would take too much time and effort to learn or set up a new product.

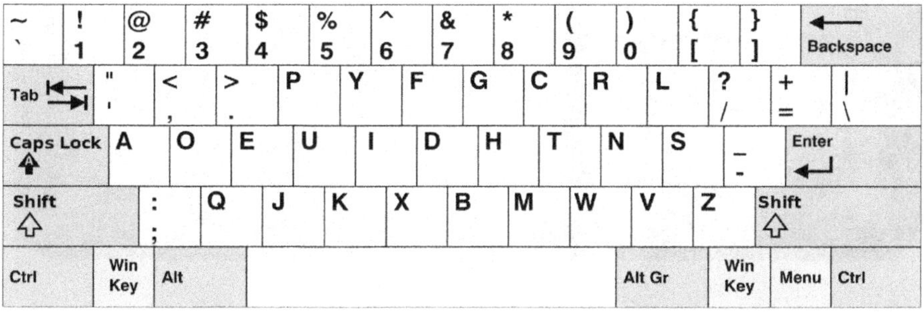

A keyboard with the Dvorak layout. Unlike QWERTY, it tries to help typists keep their fingers on the middle row as much as possible. Source: Wikimedia[23]

The classic example is the Dvorak keyboard, a QWERTY competitor created in the 1930s[24] to speed up typing by putting more keys on the "home row," which is the middle row where your fingers usually sit. Dvorak claims to increase typing speeds by up to 70% and reduce the distance your fingers travel fifteen fold.[25]

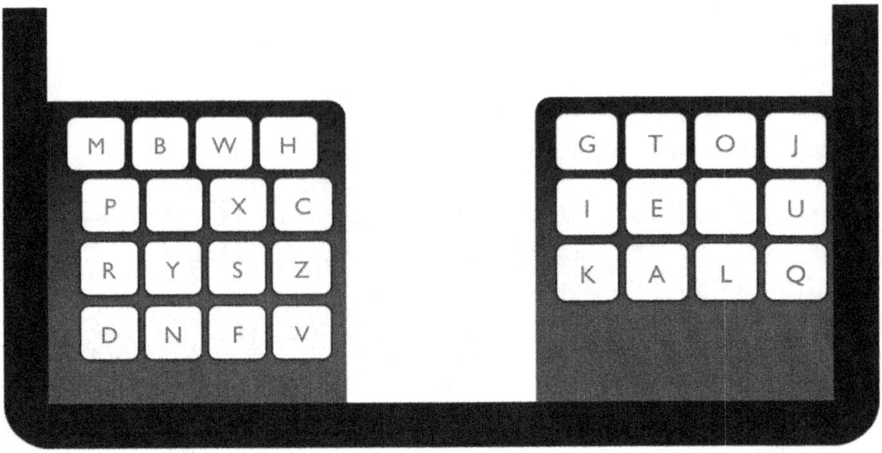

The KALQ keyboard layout, introduced in 2013, puts keys on the sides of the screen so it's easier to type with your thumbs. Source: New Atlas[26]

And then there's KALQ, a lesser-known keyboard variant that's optimized for touchscreens. KALQ splits the keyboard into two halves near the edges of the screen, which makes it much easier to use when typing with your thumbs than the full-width QWERTY keyboard.[27] Studies show that KALQ increases typing speed on phones by 34% over QWERTY.[28]

As you can probably tell, though, neither of these keyboard layouts has gained much mass adoption. While both layouts handily beat QWERTY, the weeks of training it takes to learn them isn't worth it for most people[29] — not to mention that all your training would be worthless anytime you picked up a device that only supported QWERTY. The widespread educational and technical infrastructure behind QWERTY makes it practically impossible for our society to move off it.

This problem is also quite common in enterprise technology, where dominant players are entrenched. For example, generations of employees have grown up using Microsoft Office and Windows, and switching to a competitor like Google Docs would force companies to retrain their staff — something many of them are hesitant to do.

Sometimes switching just takes too much time and energy. Consider cloud computing platforms: you can move all your customer data and backend servers from, say, Amazon Web Services to Microsoft's Azure, but trying to migrate everything is too risky. Shutting servers down to move them over could make your service unavailable to customers, and it's hard to be completely sure that everything will work fine on the new provider. Add to this the fact that cloud providers' data is often in incompatible formats (a portability issue) and you see why cloud *vendor lock-in* is such a problem.[30]

This happens in consumer tech too. For instance, we love Intuit's financial tool Mint, which gathers all your financial data — bank accounts, credit cards, bills, etc. — in one convenient interface. A rival product called Personal Capital offers many of the same features[31] and, in 2018, even offered $100 to customers referred by a friend if they linked a bank account.[32] We wanted to try this product, but the pain of importing all our financial accounts again was too high to make it worth it.

This is the reason for the popular Silicon Valley saying that new products must be "10x" better than the competition to take off.[33] Anything less and users won't go through the hassle of switching.

Social pressure

Finally, it's often hard to leave powerful brands because they've created a kind of peer pressure to stick with them or given the competition a bad reputation.

For an example of peer pressure, look no further than Apple's iMessage, which gives fellow iPhone users pleasant blue bubbles but Android users gaudy green bubbles.[34] Getting an ugly-colored bubble is bad enough, but the color distinction also lets iPhone users identify and shame Android users who haven't gotten on the iPhone train.

Legacy tech companies have done well for decades by making the upstart competition look bad. Intel has long been the gold standard for computer chips,[35] and the company has managed to sow doubt in customers' minds around competing chipmakers like ARM[36] and AMD.[37] Even when the competition makes flat-out better chips,[38] you'll feel bad buying anything but Intel.

Incumbents are especially powerful in risk-averse big businesses. You might have heard the late-20th-century saying, "nobody ever got fired for buying IBM."[39] People buying on behalf of their companies usually try to pick the lowest-risk option, and the perceived safety of big brands plays right into this mindset.[40]

Case study: Bloomberg Terminal

In finance, almost every investor uses the Bloomberg Terminal, a hardware/software suite designed by billionaire Michael Bloomberg. The computer lets you pull up data on almost any company under the sun, talk to traders around the world, and get breaking financial news. It comes with a colorful custom keyboard with handy shortcuts for common financial tasks, such as looking up mortgage data or pulling a company's stock price.[41]

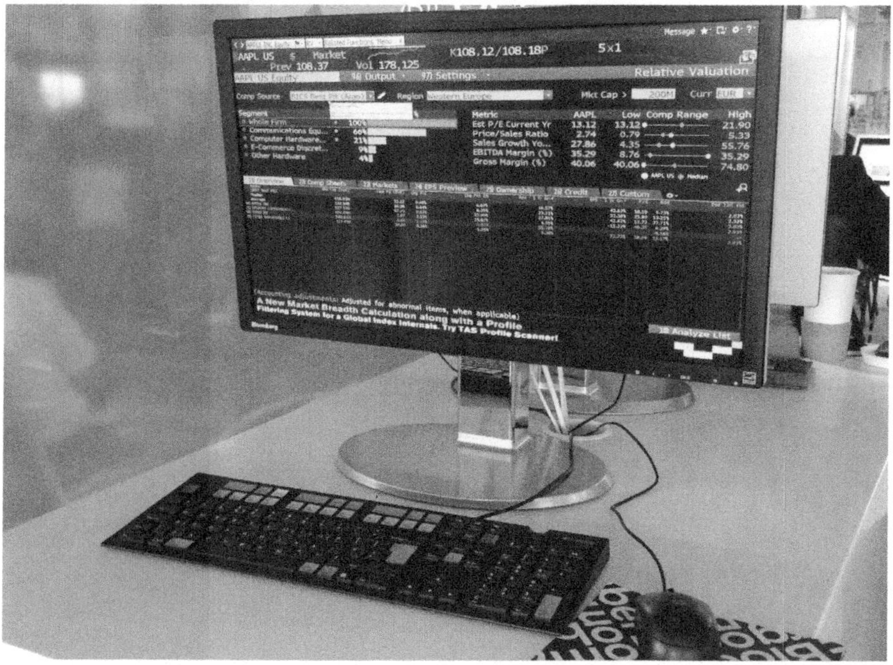

A Bloomberg Terminal, which is popular among traders on Wall Street. Source: Wikimedia[42]

The keyboard on a Bloomberg Terminal. The top two rows of keys are customized; they're shortcuts for things like government news and getting quotes for stock prices. Source: Travis Wise[43]

However, each Bloomberg Terminal machine costs $20,000 a year,[44] is locked to Windows,[45] and has, by all accounts, a somewhat dated user interface.[46] Countless startups have offered a cheaper and fresher experience,[47] but Bloomberg Terminal remains a dominant player.

Bloomberg Terminal has used all three buckets of switching costs to make it hard for customers to jump. One of Terminal's most popular features[48] is a social network of sorts that lets bankers and traders communicate with other Terminal users around the world.[49] This network of people, or the *social graph*, isn't easy to port over; leave Terminal and you lose easy access to colleagues.[50] These *network effects* are a major type of portability problem.

There are also large upfront costs to leaving Bloomberg Terminal: the software and even the keyboard are highly-specialized, and finance workers have trained on them for years. Installing new hardware and retraining employees would be a heavy burden to bear, and it could be risky, since putting traders out of commission for days or weeks could make you miss a profitable trading opportunity.

And, finally, there's social pressure to stay on Bloomberg Terminal. Finance employees are used to Terminal, and many of them are fond of it (what other financial tool includes a high-end version of Yelp and a system for shopping for luxury goods?)[51] To many people, being on Wall Street equals using Bloomberg Terminal;[52] any shop without Bloomberg Terminal is thus prone to looking amateur.

Sunk-cost fallacy

The psychological reason switching costs are so powerful is the *sunk cost fallacy*, which describes people's tendency to stick with something subpar because they've already invested so much time and energy into it and would feel bad throwing all that away if they left it. It's a fallacy because you've already made those investments and there's no way to get them back (it's a sunk cost), so sticking with the subpar thing doesn't really save you any time or energy.[53]

A specific, and relevant, version of the sunk cost fallacy is the *endowment effect*, which explains how people irrationally overvalue things they already have.[54] For instance, some participants in a study were given a chocolate bar to hold on to for thirty minutes; at the end, they were asked how much they'd sell the bar for. This group named an average price of $1.72. But other participants weren't given chocolate bars; they were just shown the bars at the end of the study and asked how much they'd sell them for. This group named an average price of just $1.35. That is, people thought the same chocolate bars were 37¢ (or 27%) more valuable just because they possessed them![55]

This means that free trials are especially powerful: once someone has made a product part of their habits and workflows, they're unlikely to give it up even once the trial is over. Because they feel like the product is "theirs," they value it far more than a new customer who hasn't done the trial.

More specific still is the *IKEA effect*, which explains that we overvalue things that we created ourselves, such as IKEA furniture.[56] One study found that, when participants were asked to make origami, they valued their own creations at 19¢ but other participants' creations at just 5¢.[57] PMs can thus get users to stick around by letting them customize and configure their products,[58] such as by installing Slack bots, building out Trello boards, or curating a list of Twitterers to follow.

Generally speaking, the more people invest in your product, the more they'll like it (much like people love their tricked-out cars), so give people every opportunity to make the product their own.

Getting over switching costs

This all isn't to say that switching costs can't be overcome. They can — so you should adopt these tactics in your products and make it hard for competing products to use them.

To get over the problem of upfront costs, you can use *staged rollouts*:

letting users slowly migrate to your new solution instead of forcing them to move over all at once. This smooths out the cost of moving and reduces the risk.

For instance, when Adi worked on Microsoft Azure, he found that many companies weren't migrating their *on-premises* data centers to the cloud. Many companies took up to a decade to just upgrade their Windows Server software on their "on-prem" servers![59] It turned out that companies were hesitant to move everything over to the cloud since they wanted particular workloads, such as those that had to run with minimum *latency*, to always be done on-site.[60]

So Adi's team created a *hyper-converged hybrid cloud* system that lets customers slowly move workloads from on-prem to Azure while keeping the essentials local.[61][62] The strategy worked: previously hesitant customers started using the hybrid system, and Microsoft CEO Satya Nadella named this strategy a major contributor to Azure's breakneck growth.[63]

To get over the lack of portability, one easy move is to build tools that let users import data from competing tools to yours. The task management tool Asana, for instance, lets you import data from competing products like Trello, Airtable, Monday.com, Smartsheet, and even Google Sheets with just a few clicks.[64]

You can also "import" users' muscle memory: Google Sheets has implemented most of the same functions, shortcuts, and features as Excel,[65] thus making it easier for users to switch over. (Granted, Google Sheets misses many advanced features from Excel, but Google Sheets has enough similarity for the average user.[66])

Gamification

Self-determination theory tells us that people like feeling autonomous and competent, and common sense tells us that people like to have fun.

Games let us experience all those feelings, which is a big reason why we love sports, board games, video games, and other games so much. You can make your product more lovable — and thus more sticky — by adding *gamification*, or importing game mechanics and design principles into your product.

The seven parts of gamification

Gamification isn't about making your product into a game; turning your to-do list into a Pac-Man game is a fun diversion but doesn't give users a deep feeling of satisfaction. Instead, you have to incorporate the seven key mechanics of successful games into your product's core design.[67]

First, users (and players) need to have goals. We humans have a psychological need to find purpose and direction in life, and goals give us something concrete to strive toward,[68] whether that's mastering your curveball, beating the final boss, or just learning how to hold a conversation in Spanish. Completing the goal helps us feel pleasure and gives us a rush of emotion.[69]

Games are structured as a series of overlapping goals: finish the level, get the Pokémon badge, win the game, etc. When you're trying to add gamification to your product, think about the goals users might have. Do they want to be productive? Do they want to learn something? Do they want to get a job?

Once you've found a user's goal, you need to give them rules for how they can move toward the goal.[70] How exactly do they get closer to winning? In tennis, the goal is to win a match and the rules include how to score and how to serve. In the email technique of Inbox Zero, the goal is to clear your inbox, and the rules are to either answer, delete, snooze, or delegate every email (you can't just ignore it).[71] The rules have to be clear; a game where it's impossible to know how to win isn't a fun one at all.

Third is feedback: users (and players) need to be able to easily measure their progress to their goal. These include progress bars, points,[72] and other metrics. Most games are pretty good at this: winning or losing the game is a crystal-clear piece of feedback, and intermediate points like scoring goals or getting a KO can tell you how you're doing during the game. Other things in life have much murkier feedback: how do you measure if you're successfully learning a language, being a good friend, or succeeding in your career? Gamification tries to attach concrete, measurable feedback to these murkier topics.

One important part of feedback is that players hate the idea of losing progress. Our mental model is that you can only ever move forward in a game; getting pushed backwards is thus very frustrating. (This is why people hate getting hit with Mario Kart's blue shells so much.[73]) So, for instance, you should generally avoid taking away points or shortening progress bars unless the user opts in.

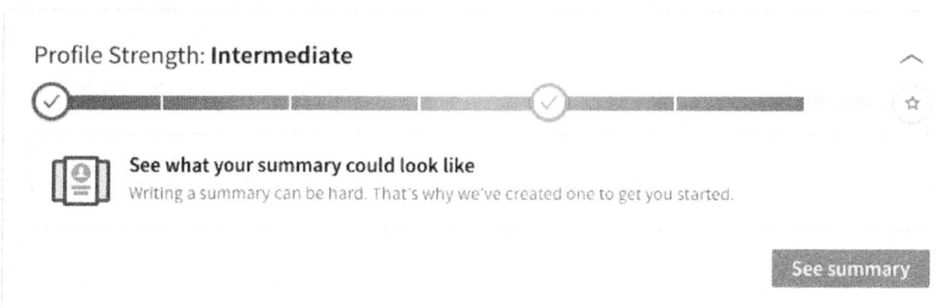

LinkedIn's progress bar for filling in your profile. This gamifies the process of adding data to your profile. Source: Pointzi[74]

The fourth and most famous part of gamification is the rewards:[75] the intrinsic and extrinsic prizes for achieving your goal, which give you a reason to work toward the goal in the first place. The reward in most games is intrinsic, but wagering on games makes the rewards extrinsic. In product gamification, the most common form of rewards are points, badges, and leaderboards,[76] which go together so frequently that they're often called the *PBLs*.[77][78]

But people won't do things just for the points, badges, and leaderboards; people value PBLs because they're proof of their accomplishments, not because the PBLs are inherently valuable. You can't expect people to do menial tasks just because there's a badge attached. Instead of thinking about PBLs first, think about the kinds of achievements you want to praise. For instance, users won't fill out their LinkedIn profile because they like seeing the progress bar fill up. They do it because they love the thrill of completing something — games are one of the few places in life where you can be 100% done.[79] Completing their profile gives people a sense of mastery, and that's the real reward, not the points on screen.

Note that the right type of reward depends on the product. Loyalty programs like Starbucks and airline frequent flyer miles are a sort of gamification, and because you have to pay to "win" these games, customers expect monetary rewards like free flights and free coffee. Starbucks customers probably wouldn't be satisfied if they just got a virtual badge for drinking the most coffee. Meanwhile, users don't expect monetary payment for doing free things like rating stores on Google Maps; they're content getting a feeling of altruism and accomplishment, and giving them something as simple as giving them free socks will delight them.[80]

In other words, the rewards have to be tied to users' motivations, which is the fifth part of gamification.[81] If people want to make money or find deals (stomach rewards), give them that. If they want to feel like they're making a difference in the world, design your system so they get bigger rewards as their social impact becomes bigger.

The last two parts are the *freedom of choice* and the *freedom to fail*. Games are no fun if players are forced into it or if they're severely punished if they get something wrong.[82] The freedom of choice means that your gamification should always be an add-on to the product, not the core of it; users should feel free to ignore the gamification if they don't like it. Don't hide key features behind achieving a certain "level," for instance. And the freedom to fail means users should always be able to try again. Limited-time "quests" with rewards that you can never get elsewhere are thus risky to implement, though they're more OK if you have a recurring series of them.

Case study: Robinhood's tapping game

The fee-free investment app Robinhood provides a textbook example of gamification done well. In 2019, Robinhood announced that it was launching a new debit card and created a waiting list to get a card.[83]

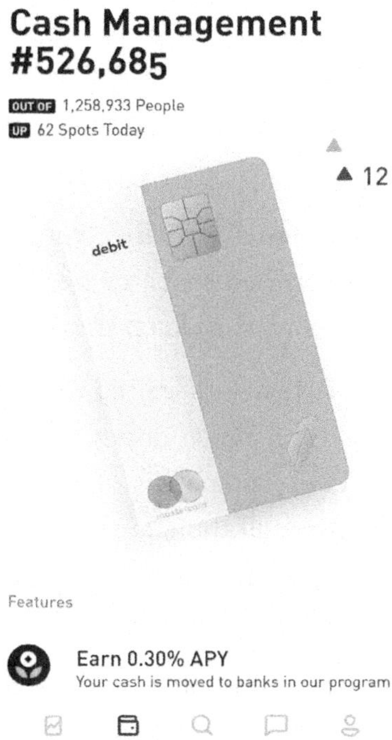

A user halfway through tapping on the debit card picture to move up the waitlist for Robinhood's debit card, known as Cash Management. Over 1.25 million people appear to be in line.

This was no ordinary waitlist, though; you couldn't just drop in your email address and wait to get the invitation. Robinhood, instead, made it into a competition. Everyone on the waitlist was allowed to tap an image of a debit card up to one thousand times per day; people with more clicks would move up. Robinhood even showed you your position in real time and showed how far you moved up with every successive tap — the digits in the counter would scroll like an old-fashioned car odometer.[84]

The icing on the cake, though, was that Robinhood let you jump ahead in line by inviting friends to join the waitlist. Given how dedicated "players" at the top of the waitlist were, you couldn't move beyond a certain point just by tapping. Inviting friends was the only way to keep winning the game.[85]

The game was a viral hit: as you can see from the picture, the waitlist regularly exceeded a million people long. This is because the game did fairly well on most of the seven parts of gamification.

The first part, the player goal, was relatively clear: get high enough on the list that you'd get an invitation. However, Robinhood never told you exactly how high up you had to be to get an invitation; this was probably intentional to get players to keep striving to hit #1.

The rules, the second part, were clear as well. You'd move up with enough clicks and referrals and move down if you couldn't keep pace with your competitors. There was a bit of weirdness around the top of the list, where people using all their taps and referrals could still fall backward due to some strange mechanic.[86] But for most people, it was pretty clear.

Part three, feedback, was excellent. You'd see how far you'd moved up every single time you tapped the debit card. The fourth part, rewards, was also good; everyone knew that they were in it for the debit card. (Again, though, it wasn't clear if you actually had to play the game to get the card; Robinhood never published a cutoff.[87])

Part five is user motivations, and here the game felt a little silly. People wanted to get a debit card, so why were they playing a glorified clicking game? It felt like a cheesy way for Robinhood to suck up people's time and go viral. Still, it worked.

Part six, the freedom to fail, was handled well. You certainly didn't have to play the game to use Robinhood's other features, which was good, though Robinhood didn't make it clear if you'd ever be able to get the card without playing. Part seven, the freedom to fail, was a little weaker, since you could fall backward if you didn't play for even one day. Fortunately, moving back up wasn't impossible.

We can then give Robinhood's game a subjective score for each part of the gamification process:

Nº	**Part**	**Grade**
1	Goals	B+
2	Rules	A
3	Feedback	A+
4	Rewards	A
5	Motivations	C
6	Freedom of Choice	A-
7	Freedom to Fail	B+

Overall, pretty good — and remarkably effective.

Case study: Todoist

Sometimes the goal of gamification is easy: in Robinhood's case, it was to maximize the size of the waitlist. Trying to maximize your company's revenue through gamification is straightforward as well.

But sometimes your gamification is intended to help users achieve *their* goals rather than yours. This is common in self-improvement apps that aim to help people improve their wellness, learn new skills, or become more productive. In this case, it's harder to nail down the thing you should be optimizing for, since users' goals are tremendously diverse. Getting gamification right, as a result, is a lot harder.

The productivity app Todoist is a great example of a self-improvement product that got gamification right. At its surface, it's a to-do list app, so users' immediate goals are fairly clear: achieve the things on their to-do lists. But when you look deeper, it becomes murkier. *Why* are people using a to-do list app in the first place?

Todoist realized that people want to make systematic changes to their lives. They don't just want to remember to reschedule their dentist appointment. They want to become more productive people with better habits and better time-management skills.

So Todoist implemented a gamification system that rewards long-term consistency in achieving to-dos and helps people work toward becoming more productive and on top of their goals.

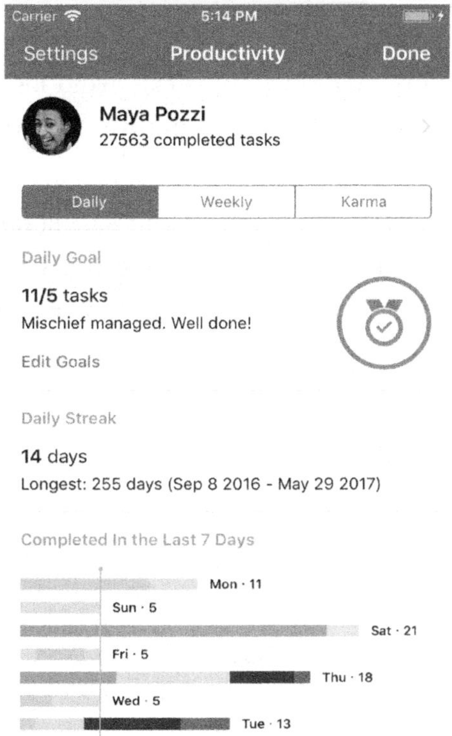

A user's Todoist dashboard, showing her progress toward her goals. Source: Todoist[88]

Todoist did this by building a "karma" system that tracks your progress over time. You gain karma by achieving tasks consistently and hitting your milestones, while you can lose karma if you fall short.[89] These points are sort of scoreboard for your life, showing you how far you are on your quest to self-improvement.

The karma system's rules dictate how you gain or lose karma, thus giving users clear rules on how to behave. You gain karma by adding tasks, completing tasks on time, meeting your daily and weekly targets, and getting "streaks" by meeting your targets several times in a row. You can even *lose* karma if your tasks are more than four days overdue! (This is one of the rare instances where it's OK to take away users' points — this harsh feature is optional since users can avoid losing points by just not setting due dates on tasks, or they can turn off karma entirely.)[90]

These rules tell users how to "win" the game and thus change their behavior. If I'm frustrated that I keep losing karma for having overdue tasks, I'll learn how to be more realistic and not set overly-optimistic due dates — thus letting me do better in the game and become a more productive person. Gamification works when success in the game equals success toward the user's goals.

Latest updates

8 hours ago	**4600**	-12
19 hours ago	**4612**	+16
21 hours ago	**4596**	+24
1 day ago	**4572**	-12
2 days ago	**4584**	+8 -12
3 days ago	**4588**	-9
3 days ago	**4597**	+8

Todoist's karma system awards you points for meeting your goals and takes away points when you fall short.

The karma system gives users clear feedback, and a dashboard tells you every time you gained or lost karma. Karma is the reward, of course, and it's all intrinsic. You can also "level up" by accumulating enough Karma. Get 10,000 karma and you become a Master; get 50,000 and you become Enlightened. You can even brag about leveling up on social media — a sort of extrinsic reward.[91]

You are an **intermediate**. Your karma is **4600**.

Karma	Level	
0→499	**Beginner**	
500→2499	**Novice**	
2500→4999	**Intermediate**	Your current level
5000→7499	**Professional**	
7500→9999	**Expert**	
10000→19999	**Master**	
20000→49999	**Grand Master**	
50000++	**Enlightened**	

Todoist's karma system has "levels" that you can unlock for gaining progressively higher amounts of karma.

Todoist gives you freedom of choice, since you can opt in or out of the karma system at any time, and even if you're in the karma system, it's not like having low karma will stop you from using the tool effectively. Todoist does lack some of the freedom to fail; step away from Todoist for long enough and all your karma will have drained away, which makes coming back to the app somewhat demotivating. Perhaps to soften the blow, Todoist lets you go into vacation mode, which freezes your streaks and karma while you're away (as long as you remember to turn it on).[92]

Why gamification fails

Contrary to popular belief, gamification isn't a silver bullet. An estimated 80% of gamification efforts fail,[93] in large part because most PMs don't know when gamification is appropriate. You can't just bolt points and badges onto an app and expect it to work.

Gamification can fail if you choose the wrong rewards. For instance, Zappos once started giving away badges and virtual points to shoppers[94] for doing things like "favoriting" a shoe and buying multiple pairs of shoes. Users found it bizarre and somewhat unfair: they were spending *real* money, and Zappos only gave them virtual prizes?[95] Users, conditioned by years of frequent flyer programs giving them free flights and hotel loyalty programs giving them free nights, expected money out of an ecommerce rewards system. Zappos ultimately shuttered the effort[96] because it was hurting their brand image.[97]

Gamification can also fail if the rules aren't clear. Consider Klout, the mid-2010s service that gave you a score measuring how important and popular you were across social media platforms. Klout's rewards and feedback system were clear: you'd get a score from 1 to 100,[98] and you could brag about this number to friends and colleagues.

The trouble was that the scoring system was totally unintuitive. People found their scores going *down* when they connected new accounts, so to boost their score they'd just disconnect certain accounts. Klout later added a way for you to give "+K" praise to others on the platform, but oddly enough, that didn't influence your score. Klout's scoring system was both confounding and easy to game — which made the experience annoying and frustrating, not fun.[99]

You also want to make sure that your gameplay isn't so deep and complex that it overshadows the actual goal of your product. You want it to be a product with gaming tacked on, not a game with some utility tacked on.

Consider the habit-tracking app Habitica, which lets you role-play a fantasy character and level up, fight bosses, and collect items as you track and improve your habits. It's a very fun app, but it's so complicated — there are pets, guilds, healing potions, foods, etc.[100] — that learning the game takes longer than just learning how to track your habits.

After a while, you find yourself looking for ways to optimize your character's loadout of equipment (there are over a hundred swords, staves, shields, robes, and the like[101]) and collect all the pets (there are well over 200 varieties[102]) rather than trying to get better at your habits.

This happened to Neel, who was an avid user for over a year — but when he realized he was spending hours searching for a rare sword rather than getting better at going to the gym, he realized that the game had taken over the app for him. Because the game was so complex and immersive, it had become distracting. The gamification, in other words, had gone too far.

Conclusion

THE SHORT-FORM VIDEO APP TikTok burst onto the tech scene in 2018 and 2019, racking up almost 700 million downloads in the second year — good enough for second place in the app store rankings, behind only WhatsApp.[1] Anyone who's ever used TikTok can attest that it's incredibly addictive, with sociologists calling it "digital crack cocaine."[2] How does it grab such a firm hold on our attention the minute we open the app and never let go?

The answer lies, in part, in TikTok's deep understanding of human psychology. First is user motivation. TikTok knew that youth, its target demographic, desired entertainment and social validation but weren't getting that on conventional social media apps like Instagram or Facebook.[3]

Those apps are all about staying in touch with people you know or admire. Any entertainment value is incidental; you as a user have to hunt down entertaining accounts to follow or groups to join. TikTok is different. The homepage doesn't show a list of what your friends posted but rather a machine-gathered list of the most viral and entertaining content from around TikTok, no matter who posted it. It's like if the "explore" tab of Instagram or Twitter, and not the feed of stuff from people you follow, was center stage. Users come to TikTok seeking entertainment — filling their bellies, per Galloway's framework, with tasty videos — and TikTok delivers.[4]

TikTok also realizes that youth, especially teens, crave social validation, which gives them *rewards of the heart* and also *self-determination theory's* feeling of competence. For these Gen Z-ers, validation online usually comes from strangers liking their creations; in other words, validation comes from being an influencer. But on social networks like Instagram, becoming an influencer is hard. It takes a long time (and a lot of posts) to cultivate a huge list of followers, and you have to know how to market yourself to reach new people. But TikTok makes attaining fame (albeit fleeting) so much easier: anyone who makes an especially entertaining video will automatically get seen by millions of people.[56] No need to build a follower list; make something good and you automatically have a chance at digital "riches." This combination of instant feedback and random chance makes becoming famous on TikTok an addictive game rather than a tedious job.

TikTok also knows how to get over the *switching costs* that might hold people back. Twitter and Instagram are only useful once you've picked a set of people to follow, and many newcomers to social media might not know what they like off the top of their head. Meanwhile, TikTok (like YouTube) plunges you into an endless sea of videos right out of the box. You don't have to tell TikTok what you like; TikTok will just show you loads of entertaining stuff and learn what you like.[7] Because TikTok isn't really a social network, users don't mind as much if their friends aren't on it, which helps the app sidestep the *network effects* that make it hard for so many products to take off.

Finally, TikTok knows better than anyone how to make users stick. TikTok runs the *Hooked model* loop on autopilot: each time you open the app and watch videos, TikTok learns what you like, automatically tailoring the app a little better to your tastes. This makes you more likely to come back the next time, which will improve the algorithm again, and so on.[8] TikTok has also mastered *variable rewards*. On conventional social media apps, you can roughly predict what you're going to see on your feed, since you choose who you follow. But each scroll on TikTok gives you a random burst of entertainment. That utter unpredictability keeps TikTok incredibly surprising, and surprise triggers dopamine, so TikTok is basically a waterfall of dopamine.[9]

We could go on and on, but you get the point. Knowing human psychology has helped TikTok become one of the most explosive, addictive, and viral apps in history — and you too can use this knowledge in your own products. ❦

All QR codes from Part III

In case you skipped over any QR codes from the last few chapters, here's a roundup. Scan them with your phone to watch bonus videos and try interactive demos.

A mock interview where Neel, one of your authors, applies pricing psychology to analyze Spotify's pricing strategy:

productalliance.com/videos/product-pricing

The psychological tricks that have fueled Snapchat's success:

productalliance.com/videos/snapchat

IV

User Experience

Design needs to be plugged into human behavior. Design dissolves in behavior.

— Naoto Fukusawa, professor of industrial design

Introduction

CT SCAN MACHINES are one of the marvels of modern medicine. They let doctors see through your body to quickly diagnose diseases, identify injuries, and plan for treatments and surgeries. And, while they use ionizing radiation, they're safe enough to use on small children.[1]

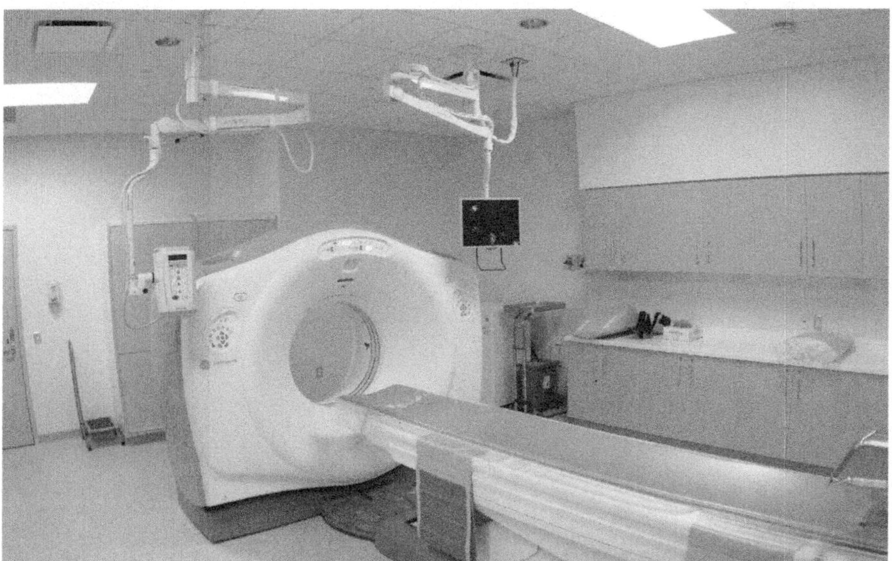

A normal CT scan machine. Source: Wikimedia[2]

The problem is that small children are often afraid to slide themselves into the middle of a giant, cold, unfriendly-looking machine. It's often dark inside, with strange lights and noises. Most children are too scared to lie still enough for the CT scan to work — to the point where 80% of children have to be drugged to sleep before going into the machine.[3]

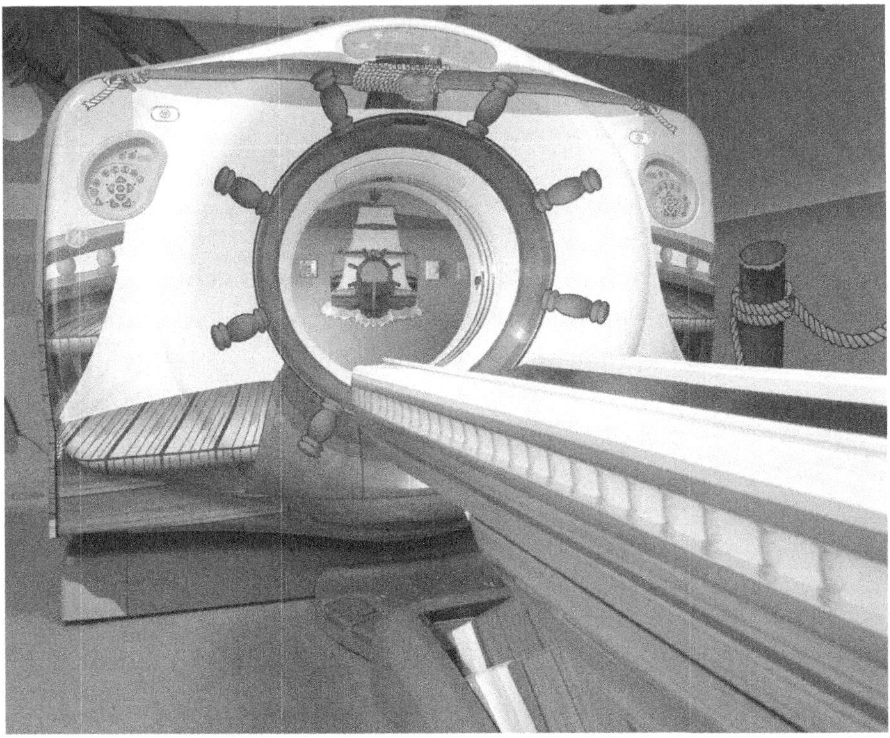

The redesigned CT scan machine, which looks like a pirate ship! Source: Slate[4]

So a team working for a pediatric hospital decided to redesign the CT scan machine. Instead of being an unfriendly, pale robot, the machine became a pirate ship — complete with a deck, mast, and captain's steering wheel. Kids going into the machine are told they'll be sailing on a pirate ship and need to stay completely still while on the boat, presumably so they don't get seasick. At the end of their "voyage," they can pick a "treasure" from a pirate's chest.[5]

The machine itself didn't change, but the kids' reactions sure did.

Before, kids were wracked with anxiety and worry at the thought of going into the cold, intimidating machine. Now, one six-year-old girl who went into the pirate-themed machine tugged on her mother's skirt, asking, "Mommy, can we come back again tomorrow?" The team no longer needed to sedate the kids; patient satisfaction scores went up 90%. The redesign was so effective, in fact, that the hospital redesigned nine different machines to follow the theme of "adventure machines."[6]

It goes to show that it's not enough to create a functional product. To make users happy, you have to craft experiences that play to what they enjoy but avoid what they dislike. If you understand this, you're on your way to creating great *user experiences* (*UX*) for your products.

Note that it's important to differentiate between UX and the *user interface*. or *UI*. While UX is about a user's holistic experience interacting with your company or product, UI is more narrowly focused on making the interface elements on your screen as attractive, intuitive, and functional.[7]

UX is all about understanding user journeys and solving user problems, so it's more in a PM's wheelhouse, while UI leans more toward branding and visual design. Thus, we'll primarily cover UX in this part of the book, but we'll touch on related UI topics occasionally. After all, you need to have both: good UX with bad UI is a tasty cake that looks like a pile of goop, while good UI with bad UX is a beautifully-iced cake that tastes like rotten eggs.[8] UX makes a product useful and enjoyable, while UI makes it intuitive and good-looking.[9]

Chapter 16

Cognition

IT'S SHOCKING how catastrophic removing a button can be. When Microsoft launched Windows 8 in 2012,[1] its product managers decided to rethink the entire Windows experience from the ground up.[2]

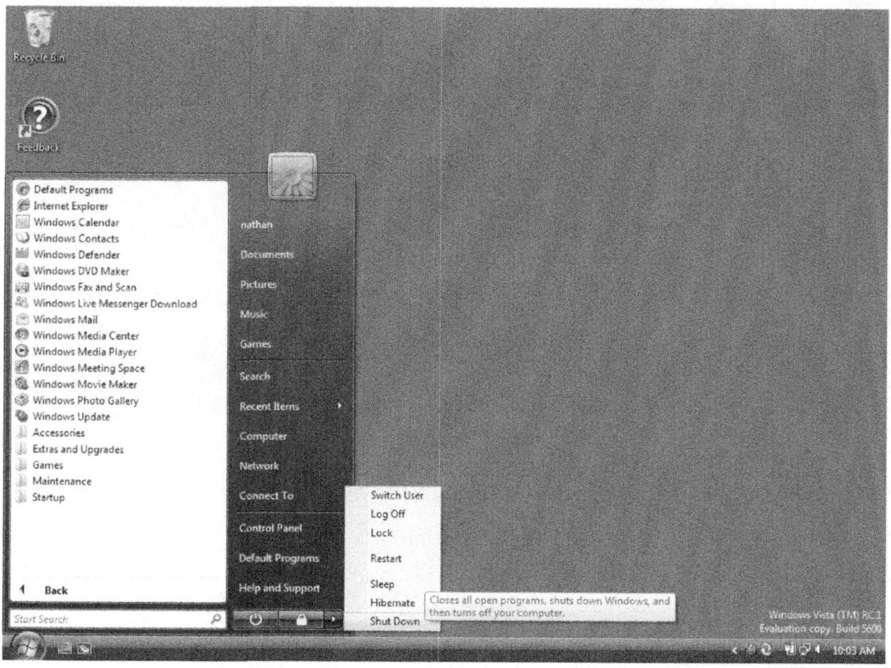

The Start menu in Windows Vista. Source: ToastyTech[3]

The most infamous of those changes was a decision to remove the Start button, a widget that had graced Windows since 1995 and become the operating system's most iconic feature — and, in some eyes, Microsoft's most famous product.[4] A Windows PM claimed that user data showed that people were increasingly pinning apps to their taskbars at the bottom of the screen instead of searching for apps in the Start menu, and so the Start button got the axe.[5]

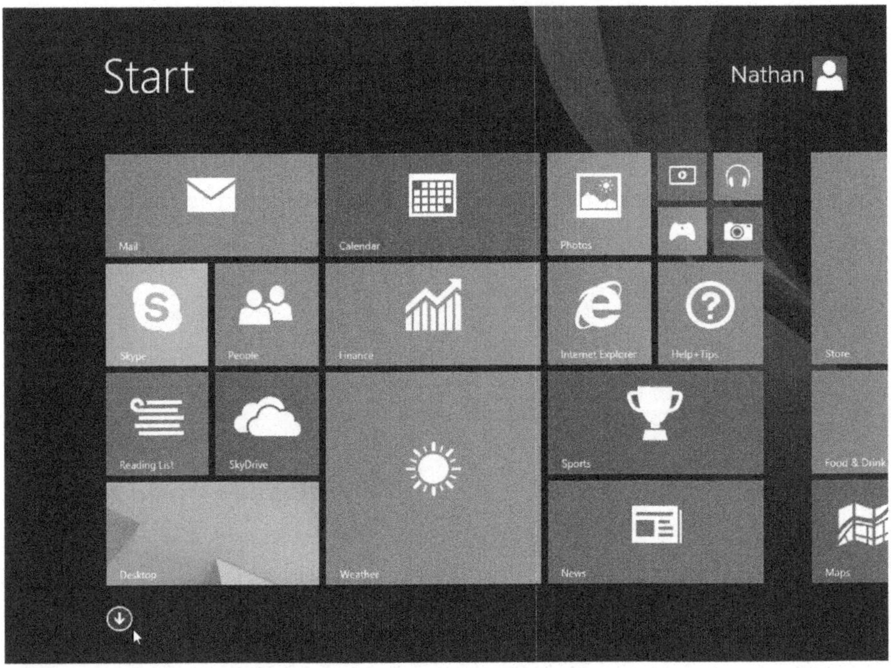

Windows 8's Metro UI, which has tiles on the homescreen but no Start button. Source: ToastyTech[6]

Complaints were swift — and brutal.[7] The removal of the Start button was the most common complaint against Windows 8.[8] The Start button was replaced with a "Start screen" where apps were shown on colorful tiles;[a] this offered much the same functionality as the Start but-

[a] You could actually still access the Start menu by moving your mouse to the bottom left corner of the screen... but that feature was very hard to discover.

ton, but reviewers and users alike griped about having to re-learn how to launch apps and navigate around their operating system.[9] The Start screen was likened to a hard-to-navigate "maze of flashing lights," and few people could figure out all the shortcuts you had to learn to use the screen effectively (such as typing an app's name to search for it).[10]

This frustrating and disorienting experience was surely one of Windows 8's biggest woes. The new version of Windows never really took off: even when Windows 8's market share peaked at 8% in September 2013, Windows 7 still controlled 46% of all PCs. (Windows 7's market penetration actually *increased* to 61% in the years after!)[11] Feeling the pain from losing out on an entire upgrade cycle (and thus a lot of OS and PC sales dollars), Windows put the old-school Start button back in Windows 10 in 2015.[12]

Windows 10 brought the old Start button back. Source: ToastyTech[13]

Windows users had a very specific *mental model* of what using a Windows PC was like, and that model centered on the Start button. They'd been trained to use the Start button for almost two decades. When Windows 8 took that away, all the users' mental shortcuts, accumulated knowledge, and "feel" for the product were thrown out.

When you're trying to design a great user experience, you have to start by understanding how people's brains make sense of technology. We didn't evolve to use computers, phones, smart watches, and the like, so our brain has to develop a complicated series of tools to help us make sense of them. Only by understanding these brain patterns can you avoid creating the frustration and confusion that Windows 8 brought.

Mental models

This understanding of user cognition starts with mental models: people's intuitions for how something works.[14] When you pick up a pen, your brain instantly knows how to use it (or, at least, how it thinks you should use it): if it has a button at the end, press it, or if it has a cap, remove it. This is based on your experience with the thousands of pens you're likely to have interacted with in your life, and it lets you pick up and use almost any new pen without even having to think about it.

Neel once had one of these erasable pens. It confused all his friends because they'd all see the nub at the top of the pen and push down, expecting the tip to slide out, but nothing would happen. Turns out that the nub was actually the eraser, and the way to bring the tip out was to press the clip on the left side of the pen. This pen is great, but it shatters people's mental models of how to use a pen, leading to a confusing user experience for the uninitiated. Source: Pens and Pencils[15]

We have mental models for everything, and when they're broken we get confused. Western readers know that the way to read a book is to position the spine to your left, use your right hand to open to the first page, and turn pages on the right-hand-side to move forward. When Westerners are handed a Japanese book, which is read the opposite direction,[16] they're often confused: they open to what they think is the first page and find that it's actually the end of the book, and realize that they have to read in a direction that feels like "back-to-front' for them.

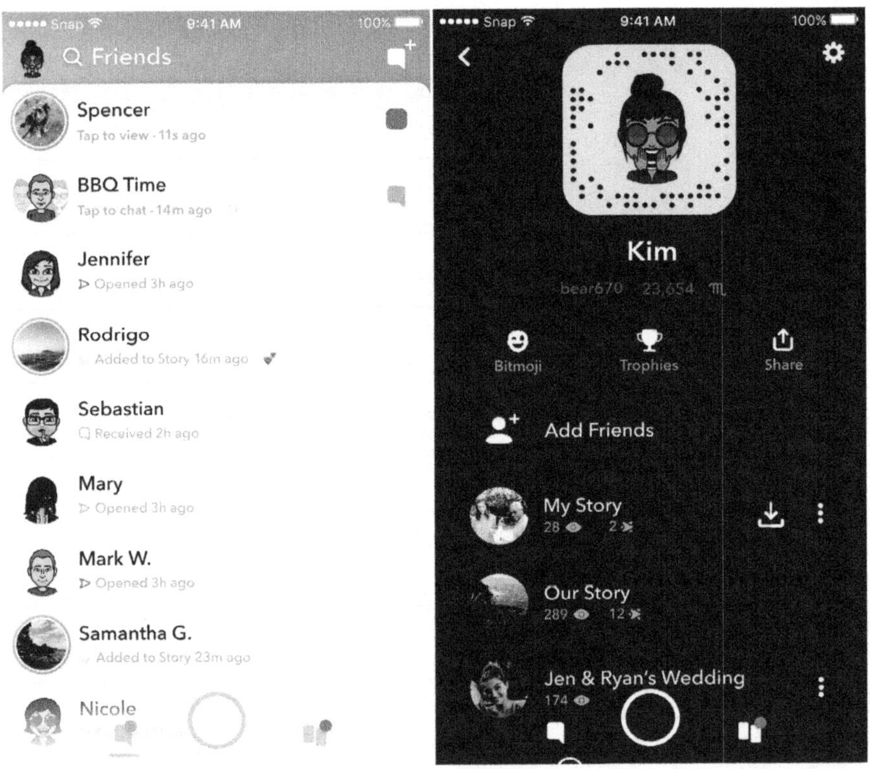

Snapchat's controversial 2018 redesign merged the friends list with the stories page, which confused and angered many users. Source: Business Insider[17]

These same confusions happen with tech products too. You've seen the example of Windows 8. Another example comes from Snapchat: for many years, Snapchat users grew used to a simple three-screen layout for the app: a list of recent messages on the left, a recording screen in the middle, and a list of friends' stories on the right. But, in 2018, Snapchat rolled out a controversial redesign[18] that moved stories into the messages screen, resulting in a confusing and cluttered interface.[19] People's expectations had been shattered, and they made their displeasure known: 1.2 million people signed a petition asking Snapchat to revert to the old design,[20] and Snapchat's user sentiment score dropped by 73% almost instantly.[21] Snapchat stock plunged almost 20% in a day following the redesign.[22]

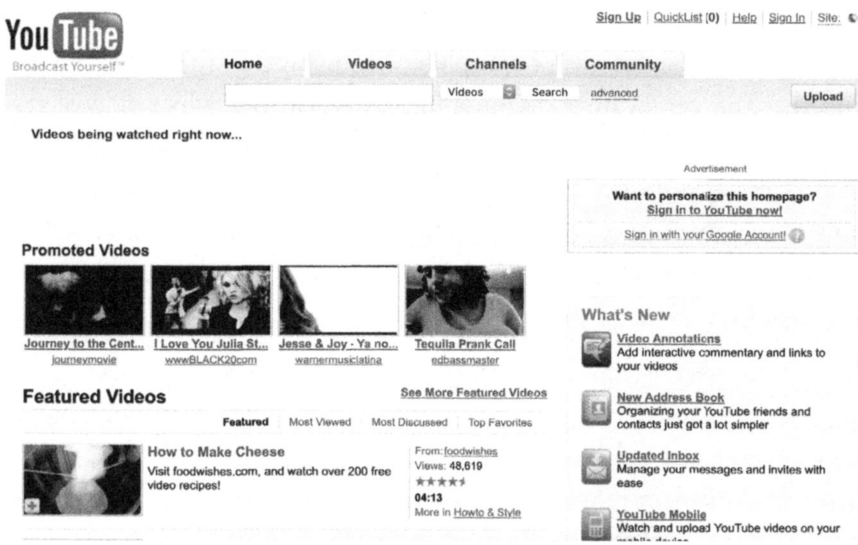

YouTube's homepage from 2008. A lot has changed since then, but familiar elements like the video list and search bar are still there. Source: Internet Archive[23]

That's not to say that redesigns are all bad: ones that preserve or gently update users' mental models can succeed. YouTube, for all its redesigns over the years, has preserved its core mechanics — search for a video with the top search bar, create playlists, subscribe to creators, etc. — enough that the same mental models would apply.[24] Someone who last used YouTube in 2008 wouldn't have too hard a time with more modern versions. (As a bonus, apps like YouTube[25] and Facebook[26] let users opt into redesigns so they can gently transition to new mental models without having to immediately throw out the old ones.)

Another potential source for frustration (and even danger) comes from users not knowing what mental model to apply. In 2016, a Tesla enthusiast named Joshua Brown was driving his Tesla in Autopilot mode on a Florida highway. A tractor trailer suddenly turned in front of his car. Neither Joshua nor his supposedly self-driving car noticed the truck. The car ran ran straight into the truck, killing Brown instantly.[27]

Tesla's technology wasn't completely ready at the time; one analysis found that the car's cameras couldn't distinguish the white side of the truck from the bright sky behind it. But another factor to blame was that Brown ignored the car's repeated warnings to put his hands back on the wheel; it's rumored that he was actually watching a movie while the fatal crash occurred.[28]

Brown should have been more careful, but Tesla's confusing user experience contributed to his actions. We humans have developed good mental models for driving a car (you're always alert, with your hands on the wheel) and riding in a car (you're disengaged and can sit back and relax). But Autopilot in 2016 demanded that users be in a strange hybrid mode: they could sort of let the car drive itself, but they also had to always be alert and ready to take control back.[29]

Brown, like most Tesla users, didn't have a mental model for being a hybrid rider-driver. Because the product was called "Autopilot," he likely assumed that it was fine to apply the rider model.[30] He chose the wrong mental model, and so he wasn't careful enough to avoid the disaster. Again, Brown deserved some blame, but so did Tesla for misleading him into choosing the wrong mental model.

Hopefully you won't be working in such life-and-death domains, but the point stands: if your users can't find the right mental model to use your product, they're in for an unpleasant experience.

Reusing mental models

We've established that forcing new mental models onto users, or disrupting their cherished old ones, can lead to frustration and, in the worst cases, danger. It follows, then, that when you're building a new product, the simplest and easiest way out is to just reuse people's existing mental models. This is known in UX circles as *Jakob's law*: users spend most of their time on products besides your own, so they prefer if your product behaves like the ones they're used to.[31]

For instance, virtually every ecommerce website, from Amazon to obscure dropshipping stores,[32] puts the cart in the top right of the screen. There's no specific reason why it has to be there, of all places, but it's become convention, and any website that strays from that will just confuse users who've gotten trained to look to the top right for their cart. Similarly, search bars tend to be at the top center, user login buttons tend to be toward the top right, and company logos (which usually lead you to the homepage) tend to be in the top left. You'll see this same pattern across countless websites, to the point where web development toolkits just assume that you're going to use this pattern and don't support alternatives.[33]

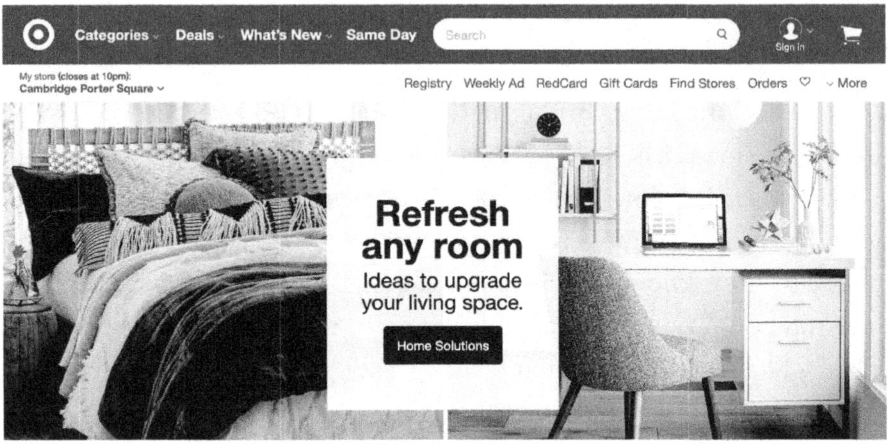

Target's website follows the same design patterns as almost all ecommerce websites: cart in the top right, account next to it, search bar in the top center, home button in the top left, etc. This is because users have a definite mental model for how an ecommerce site works, and anything else would confuse them. Source: Target[34]

When you're launching a new product, following existing mental models is a key way to ensure users aren't afraid to switch to your product. Google Docs and Sheets, for instance, explicitly targeted Microsoft Word and Excel users, so they copied major patterns from those apps' user interfaces. Docs borrowed Word's familiar bold-italic-underline trio of formatting buttons, its File-Edit-View-Insert-Format-Tools menus, and so on. Google Sheets, meanwhile, reused most of Excel's formulas.[35] This meant that mental models for using Word and Excel could be pretty easily imported to Docs and Sheets, thus making it easier for people to switch.

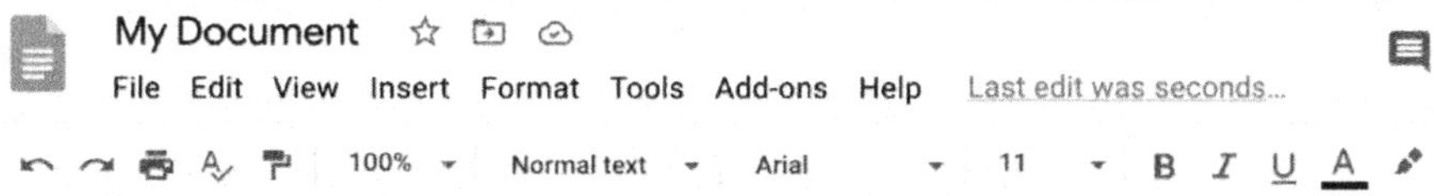

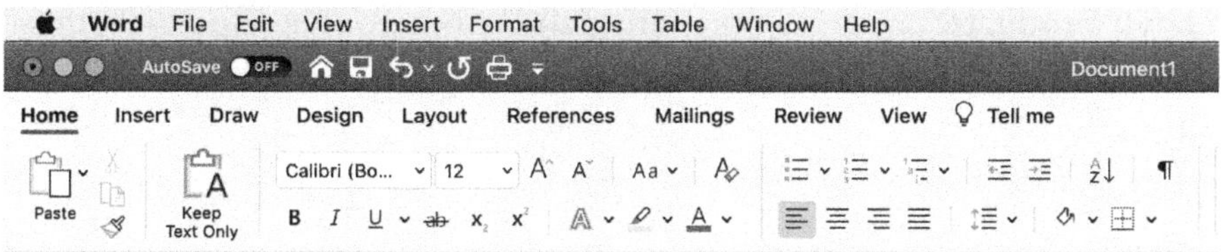

By keeping roughly the same toolbar and menu structure as Word, Google made it easy for people with mental models for using Word to pick up Google Docs.

Indeed, nowadays most consumer apps look pretty similar: sans-serif fonts, pastel colors, plentiful whitespace. By staying in line with users' expectations, the makers of these products can minimize user confusion and, more importantly, direct their energy toward creating the features and experiences that really make their product unique. It's similar to how Barack Obama and Steve Jobs famously wore pretty much the same outfit every day: it freed up their mental energy to focus on more important decisions.[36]

Interview tip

If you're drawing a user interface for a new product on a whiteboard, you can (and should) lean heavily on established mental models and *design patterns.* You don't have to sketch out how a sidebar menu works if you just say that you're going to reuse the slide-out *hamburger menu* pattern that many Google apps use.[37]

The same guidance applies when you're trying to design new features. If you're adding a social networking feature to an app, for instance, you can just say that you're going to borrow the Twitter model. This lets you easily add the concepts of followers, threads, likes, re-posts, etc. without having to "re-derive" them yourself. By referencing well-known products' patterns, you can make it much easier for the interviewer to visualize your ideas without you having to explain every detail.

Cultural diversity

Mental models are closely tied to people's cultures, histories, and geography, so it's no surprise that mental models vary across the world. One of the clearest examples of this is the varying connotations of colors in different cultures. Red signifies danger in many Western cultures but symbolizes happiness and good luck in many Asian cultures, while white is associated with purity and peace in the West but death and bad luck in China.[38] (Incidentally, the color blue has a positive connotation in many cultures — peace and trust in the West, repelling evil in many Middle Eastern areas, and immortality in East Asia[39] — which is probably a big reason why so many app icons use blue.[40])

This diversity extends to people's mental models. People's history with technology has a huge effect on the mental models they hold today. For instance, people in the United States and Europe grew up with desktop computers, which implanted a particular mental model for using tech on their culture: apps in windows, lots of typing, clicking through menus, primarily mouse- and touch-based interaction, and so on. This interaction regime is sometimes called *WIMP*, after its four main components: windows, icons, menus, and pointers.[41] Smartphones look quite different than old-school PCs, but Westerners still use them in a pretty WIMPy way: apps, windows, icons, typing, menus, and the like. Even the way Westerners hold cell phones when they're talking is similar to how they used to talk on landlines: up against the sides of their faces.

Meanwhile, one American tech executive visiting China in 2012 was surprised by how people in China interacted with their phones. They held phones in front of their faces and talked directly into them, using voice more than tapping through menus to get things done.[42]

Why the difference? Part of it, perhaps, came from culture, but a lot came from people's differing histories with technology. In the West, people mostly adapted their mental models for computers (use your fingers to interact with a screen held in front of your eyes) to phones. (Indeed, Microsoft's first phones, launched in the 2000s, looked a lot like mini versions of Windows XP, since that was the computing paradigm people were used to.[43]) But outside the West, many people have never experienced digital technology before phones came around, so they created phone-centric mental models that resulted in the behavior that the tech executive saw.

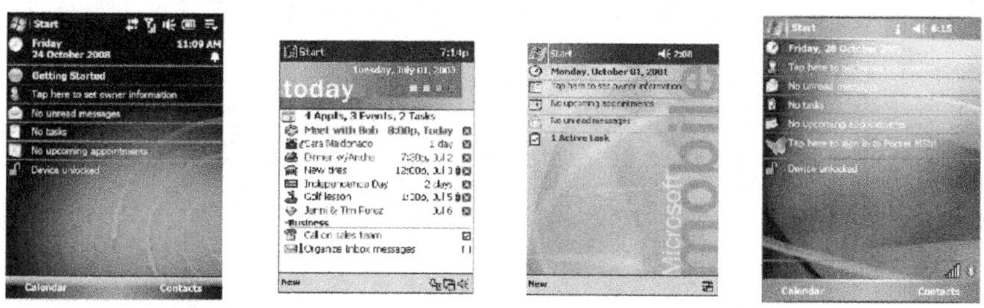

Screens from a Windows Mobile phone from the 2000s. Source: Wikimedia[44]

The difference in mental models runs a lot deeper than just how you hold your phone. The Western mental model of apps on mobile operating systems — an inheritance from the days of desktop OSes — doesn't really apply in China, where most people just use a single app, WeChat, to do everything from sending money to playing games to hailing taxis.[45] It's hardly an exaggeration to say that WeChat *is* the operating system in China.

In fact, skipping desktop and jumping straight into phones helped some regions of the world think of new technology before the West did. The idea of sending money with your phone came naturally to people in Africa, for whom the phone has always been their "everything" device. MPesa, a popular African payment system that lets people pay each other through feature phones, launched back in 2007,[46] a full two years before Venmo launched in the United States.[47]

Similarly, credit cards have traditionally been the highest-tech way to buy things in the West, but that legacy was nowhere near as strong in China. So people in China jumped straight from cash to digital payments with products like WePay and AliPay, to the point where credit cards are hardly used anymore in China.[48] Instead, you pay everyone from merchants to street performers to beggars by scanning a QR code and paying with an app.[49] (In the States, it's common to see friends fighting to put down their credit card to pay for a meal at a restaurant — but at a speakeasy in Shanghai, Parth saw a group of friends fighting to scan the QR code!)

A fruit merchant in China accepts payments via QR code. Source: CGTN[50]

Metaphors

So, how do people create mental models, anyway? One key building block is *metaphors,* which let us comprehend new things by comparing them to things we already understand. You might not know how the sport of Ultimate Frisbee works, but if someone explains it to you as "kind of like soccer, but with a Frisbee," you'll get a decent grasp of the game.[51][b]

Metaphors are especially important for understanding modern technology, which is often abstract and hard to visualize. It's one thing to understand how a toaster works — you can always take it apart and look

[b]Our Ultimate-playing friends would tell you that the sport has many differences from soccer, but soccer isn't a bad comparison for newcomers.

at the internals — but you can't do that very easily for something like the internet, the inner workings of a tablet, or Amazon Web Services. Even tech-savvy people need metaphors to understand these things.

Metaphors are especially valuable early in a technology's lifespan, before people have built up strong mental models. Most people these days know how a computer operates, but when the team at Xerox PARC was creating the first *graphical user interface*, or *GUI*, for a PC in the 1970s, they needed a convenient metaphor to explain to people how they might operate this newfangled technology.[52]

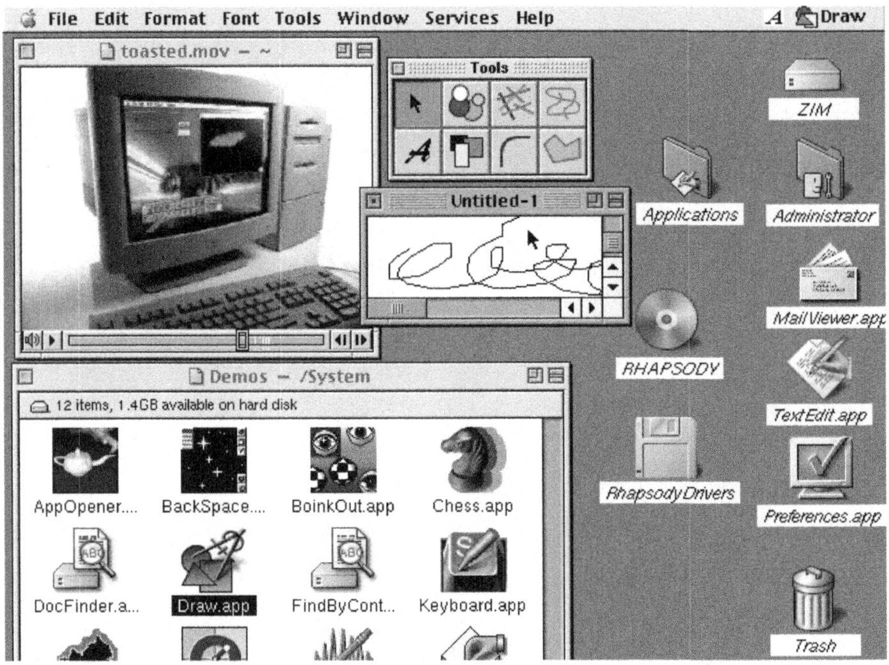

The GUI from a prototype version of macOS in the late 1990s, showcasing the desktop metaphor. Source: ToastyTech[53]

They settled on the *desktop metaphor*, comparing a PC to a physical desk. The main UI was an empty canvas with various apps and "files" scattered around it, which is quite similar to how you might have papers, calculators, and sticky notes scattered around your desk. You'd "grab" one of these items by moving your mouse (represented by a tiny hand) and clicking. Your information would be stored in "files," which would in turn be stored in "folders;" files you no longer needed would go to the "trash." And many of your apps were basically digital versions of the tools an office worker of the time might use: a calculator, a notepad, a Rolodex for storing phone numbers, a binder for organizing files, a typewriter of sorts, and even (if you were bored) a chess set.[54]

This all seems trivial to us today, but it was a huge breakthrough back then: office workers finally understood what this boxy, low-resolution screen, weird plastic mouse, and clunky keyboard could do for them.[55]

We don't take the desktop metaphor all that literally today, but some of the underlying ideas are still around, even in the most modern of phones: files, trash cans, dragging things around with a finger, and symbols for tools (from Netflix to Google Maps) laid out on an otherwise-blank home screen.

Modern apps, when you look closely, are also full of metaphors. Tinder styles itself as a card game where you "swipe" cards of potential romantic interests into a "like" pile to your right and a "pass" pile to your left. This metaphor has been so addictive that pretty much all mainstream dating apps these days have adopted it.[56]

The *kanban* metaphor of moving index cards (complete with colored labels and attachments) between parts of a table is a powerful way to organize tasks and manage projects, and it was a big reason for the success of apps like Trello. And while products like Google Drive and OneDrive keep cloud file storage abstract, Dropbox's very name embraces the metaphor of "dropping" all your stuff in a "box" so you never lose it.

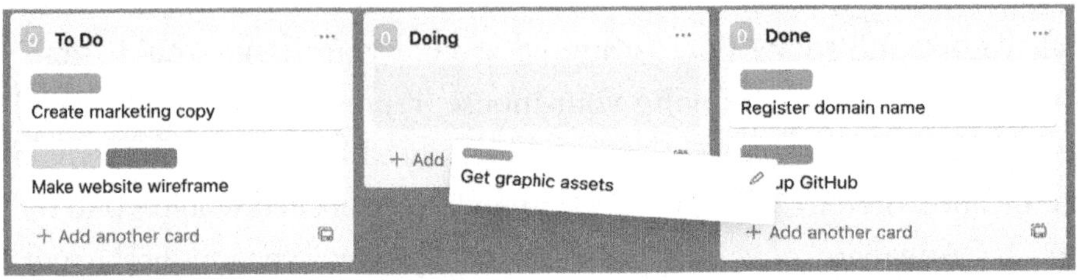

Trello lets you drag cards around as if you were moving sticky notes on a whiteboard. This creates a powerful metaphor that might remind you of exciting brainstorming sessions, which makes Trello a lot more fun to use than an ordinary to-do app. Source: Trello

UI metaphors

Metaphors are especially prevalent when you're creating user interfaces. When users are dragging, swiping, tapping, pressing buttons, and otherwise interacting with their devices, they expect them to behave like similar objects in the real world might. Buttons should look "pushed in" when you press them, things should get smaller when you zoom out, items should slide smoothly when you flick them, and so on.

So, to make UIs easy to understand, many design frameworks explicitly adopt a physical metaphor. The most famous of these is Google's Material Design, which treats all UI elements as pieces of paper, which can be touched, layered, shuffled, and so on.[57] Material treats a screen as a sort of stage covered in pieces of colored paper; a light is shone on the stage from above, so the varying layers and movement of paper cause different patterns of light and shadow.[58] Without getting too much into the design philosophy, the idea is to make users think they're interacting with construction paper — which they have mental models for — rather than a jumble of hard-to-predict pixels.

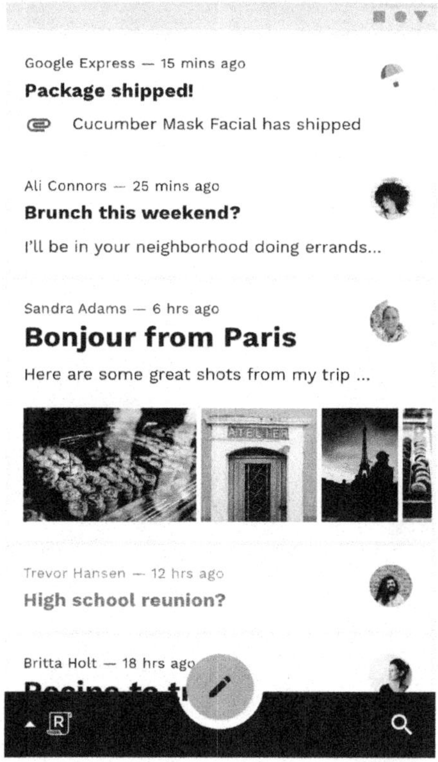

A demo app built with Google's Material Design, with its famous floating buttons, solid colors, and geometric shapes. Source: Material[59]

Color schemes often use metaphors, too. In the 2000s, Steve Jobs summed up his desired "look and feel" of Apple products: "buttons so good you'll want to lick them."[60] His UI framework, called Aqua, featured buttons that looked like they were filled with gel and were given bright, candy-like colors like red, yellow, and green. The macOS dock looked like it was made of brushed metal or frosted glass; items dragged off the dock disappeared in a puff of smoke; widgets dropped on a dashboard would cause a pond-like ripple.[61] Jobs, according to legend, reminded Apple designers about this metaphor by taping Lifesaver candies to their computer monitors.[62]

MacOS 10.8 in 2013, showing its glossy, colorful, and shiny Aqua UI.

(As you might remember, this luxurious, "maximalist" metaphor faded away after 2013, when Apple announced it was switching to a "flat design" for iOS 7. Fortunately for design lovers, iOS's new metaphor still evoked a feeling of frosted glass, what with its plentiful use of blurring and lighting.[63])

New and old

As the desktop metaphor shows, metaphors are most important for new product lines that people haven't yet been able to wrap their heads around. But as these technologies mature, people's mental models get strong enough that they no longer need the explicit metaphors; continuing to use the metaphors can make you seem out of touch.

For instance, when the internet was first created, it was hard to explain how it worked to the average user. Popular press didn't know how to write about it: one TIME cover, filled with menacing red screens flying toward a dark, mountainous landscape, proclaimed, “The Strange New World of the Internet: Battles on the Frontiers of Cyberspace.”[64]

To make sense of this bizarre new technology, people invented a bunch of metaphors: a spider’s “web” of “linked” pages, an “information superhighway,”[65] or a vast ocean of content you could “surf.”[66] The “surfing” metaphor was particularly apt; one early way to describe the sheer amount of information available on the internet was to compare it to TV, except with 5,000 channels.[67]

A circa-2000 book that used the “surfing” metaphor to try to explain the internet to kids. Source: DevRant[68]

But, of course, most technologists today wouldn’t be caught dead using those metaphors. That’s because the culture now has a baseline set of mental models around how computers and the internet work and have thus outgrown the metaphors. In fact, computers and the internet are now understood well enough that they're being used as metaphors to explain even newer concepts: the early iPhone was described as a "computer in your pocket,"[69] and the internet is now used to explain newer technology like blockchains.[70]

As we've mentioned, the degree to which people need metaphors to understand new technology depends on how hard it is to visualize. AR, VR, wearables, and the like are fairly easy to understand, since you can see exactly what they're doing and, in some cases, physically touch them. But technologies like neural networks[71] and cloud computing are harder to virtualize and thus need more metaphors: consider how people use nouns like "stacks," "containers," "firewalls," and "clusters" to explain how cloud computing works.

To take containers as an example, most people's eyes would glaze over if you said this:

> *A container is a standard unit of software that packages up code and all its dependencies so the application runs quickly and reliably from one computing environment to another.*[72]

But if you said you could package an app into a self-contained "shipping container" that could be sent to any "port" or "harbor" in the world, with no outside stuff needed, it would probably click. Indeed, the success of companies like Docker — which really leans into this shipping metaphor — owes a lot to the use of metaphors that help potential customers "get" what they're about.

Skeuomorphism

As we've seen, one way to make a new technology easy for people to understand is to reuse their existing mental models. Or you can use an older technology as the base for a metaphor: "X is like Y, except for Z."

Put these together and you get the infamous UX trend known as *skeuomorphism*, where a new technology copies design elements from an older technology to make it more palatable and understandable to people comfortable with the old technology.[73]

Skeuomorphism has been with us for a long time. In Victorian England, one popular style of horse-drawn carriage was the brougham.[74]

A modern-day horse-drawn brougham carriage. These were popular in the 1800s. Source: Wikimedia[75]

When the first motor cars came out around 1900, they copied many of the design elements of horse-drawn carriages to make them seem like more of a drop-in replacement. For instance, a popular 1899 design was actually called a brougham and looked almost the same as the horse-drawn analogue.

An 1899 car called a brougham, which looked just like older horse-drawn carriages. It's a textbook example of skeuomorphism. Source: Wikimedia[76]

(Interestingly, cars' fundamental design hasn't changed all that much since 1900. The driver's seat has been moved inside, but the core ideas of an enclosed compartment with windows and a motor in the front to simulate horses leading the car are still around. Even our concept of "horsepower" for cars is a relic of the days of carriages.[77])

All kinds of modern-day objects are skeuomorphs, as well. Imitation leather, LED-powered lights that look like wax candles, and cheap plastic drinking glasses that look like crystal goblets[78] are all examples.

LED-powered tea lights that look just like conventional candles, presumably so you can swap them in without too much confusion. Source: Northern Lights and Trees[79]

But the context in which you've probably heard of skeuomorphism the most is in the design of digital interfaces: like we saw with the desktop metaphor, in the earlier days of computing, it was common for the UIs of digital apps to closely resemble their real-world counterparts.[80] Apple was famous for this before around 2013: the Game Center app's UI used green felt and lacquered wood to look like a casino table, the Notes app actually looked like a yellow lined notepad, the contacts list looked like a leather-bound phone book, the Voice Memos app looked just like a real gray microphone, iBooks had a wooden shelf filled with paperback books, and so on.[81]

MacOS's calendar used to look quite like a real calendar, with a bound-leather top and "tearable" sheets of paper. Source: MadeByMany[82]

These skeuomorphisms weren't limited to app UIs: the camera app's "click" sound when you took a photo was an auditory skeuomorph of physical cameras, and ebook readers' "swipe" interaction to flip between pages is an interactive skeuomorph of real books.[83] And iTunes's logo famously included a CD, presumably to remind people what the app could do for them.[84]

iTunes's logo from 2006 to 2010, featuring a prominent CD. Source: Logos Fandom[85]

The value of skeuomorphs

These skeuomorphic designs have been called "hideous,"[86] "tacky,"[87] and "lying" pieces of "kitsch."[88] And, to modern eyes, they are! But they served a valuable purpose earlier in tech's life. By making digital tools look familiar, designers could ease users into modern computing without making them throw out their old mental models.[89] Making a calculator app have the same button layout as a physical four-function calculator improved usability, as did making a calendar app look and feel a lot like your fridge calendar.[90]

Skeuomorphism also helped people figure out how to interact with digital UIs they weren't quite familiar with. A "Deleted Digital Objects Sector" on your computer would be quite hard to make sense of, especially if you were new to computing, but a trash can icon was a useful metaphor that instantly made sense.

The use of file, folder, and trash can icons also helped users find the *affordances*, or the ways you can interact with an object. Users realized they could drag files between folders and the trash can (an affordance that wouldn't otherwise be discoverable) because that mimicked how they could move papers with their hands in real life. Dragging a file to the trash can felt as natural as using your hand to toss a piece of paper in a real trash can.[91]

Flat design

But around the 2010s, skeuomorphism started dying out.[92] Apple replaced its tacky faux materials with simple, abstract designs in iOS 7 in 2013[93] and macOS Yosemite in 2014.[94] At the same time, Apple abandoned its glossy, "lickable" Aqua UI in favor of *flat design*, where gradients and gloss were replaced with simple colors and gentle shadows.[95] These changes had to be made at the same time, since skeuomorphic UIs would look weird in a world of flat designs, and flat designs wouldn't work if they had to simulate complicated physical objects.

iOS 6 on the left and iOS 7 on the right. The transition from glossy to flat design was perhaps the biggest in iOS's history. Source: Reddit[96]

And Apple wasn't alone in going flat: Google adopted Material Design in 2014,[97] and Windows ditched its glassy Aero design from Windows 7 in favor of Windows 8's flat "Metro UI" in 2012.[98]

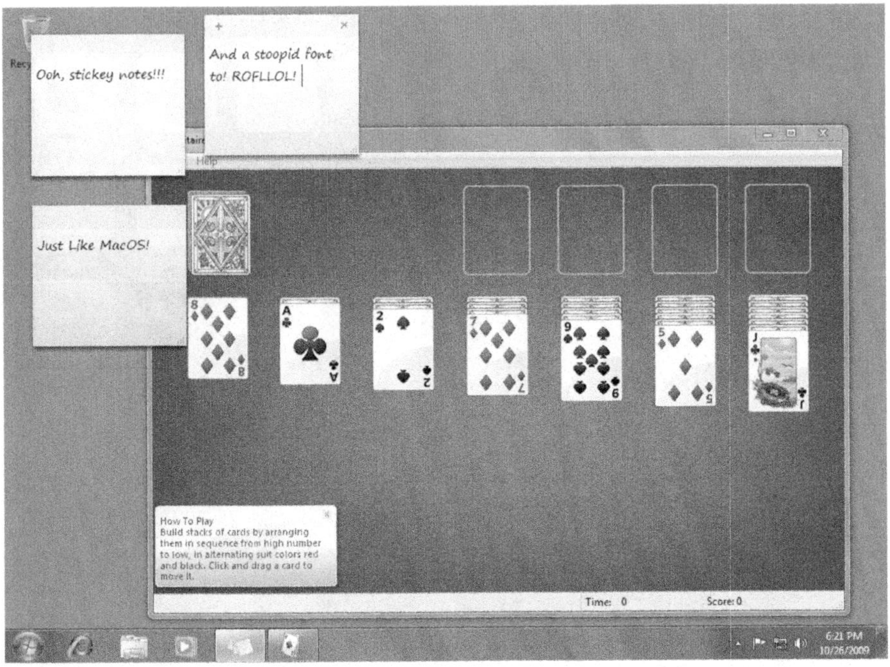

Windows 7's glassy Aero design. Source: ToastyTech[99]

This flatness trend wasn't just a fad: skeuomorphism had outlived its usefulness. As people grew used to computers and phones, they built up enough mental models that they no longer needed the "crutch" of skeuomorphic designs.[100] At a certain point, skeuomorphism was no longer helpful and instead was just unnecessary clutter.[101] Skeuomorphism trains people to adopt new mental models, but after that it's no longer necessary.

Cycles of skeuomorphism

This skeuomorphism cycle repeats itself for many new technologies. We've seen the cycle for personal computing in detail. The same applies for cars: early cars looked just like the horse-drawn carriages they replaced, but over the decades cars became free to adopt their own design senses (though some relics stuck around).

The same cycle has happened with newer technologies, as well. Many smartwatches emulate old-school watches by having a circular face, clock hands pointing to numbers, and a "crown" on the side that you can use to control the device.[102] Watches like the Apple Watch don't have all these design flourishes, but the very fact that it's called a "watch" and not an "iBand" or something is a little bit of skeuomorphism.[c]

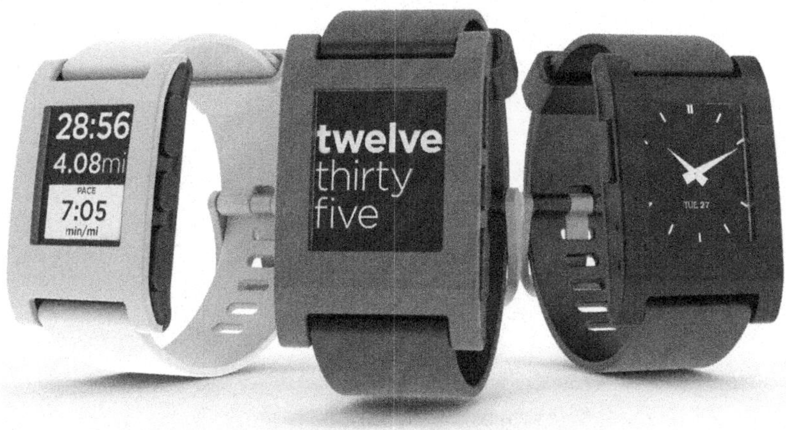

Early smartwatches, which closely resembled traditional watches. Source: Pebble[103]

Another example, while not strictly "skeuomorphism" in the design sense, comes from cryptocurrencies. They're quite different from traditional stocks and bonds, but many popular trading apps let you buy, sell, and track cryptocurrencies just like you would stocks. Cryptocurrencies

[c]Compare this to something like AirPods, which don't even try to compare themselves to a non-digital object.

show up on the same dashboards and get the same kinds of graphs and statistics.[104] While this approach hides a lot of the interesting complexity behind cryptocurrencies (blocks, addresses, rewards, halvings, etc.), it makes this newer financial product a lot easier for traders to understand.

Chapter 17

UX Principles

On March 28th, 1979, at a nuclear reactor in south-central Pennsylvania, some water pumps used to cool radioactive fuel malfunctioned.[1] A valve was stuck open, and the cooling water was spewing out, thus leaving insufficient water to cool the fuel rods. The plant's staff was blissfully unaware of the problem.[2] But eventually, the metal rods overheated so much that they melted straight through their metal containers, sending a plume of smoke filled with radioactive gases into the surrounding countryside.[3] Over 140,000 people had to be evacuated to escape the dangerous xenon and krypton gases.[4]

The meltdown at Three Mile Island wasn't all the employees' fault. The problem came down to a particular light on their control panel. The employees assumed that the light would turn on whenever the valve was open and turn off whenever the valve was properly closed. But they were wrong: the light turned off as soon as the *command* to close the valve was sent, not when the valve was actually closed. That would normally not have been a big deal, but in this case, the valve was told to close but got stuck — so the light turned off while the valve stayed open. The employees thus didn't think anything was amiss until they noticed the core melting down.[5] (It didn't help that the control panel had no gauge to measure whether the fuel rods were adequately covered in water![6])

A confusing user experience, in other words, can literally cause meltdowns. And it doesn't just apply to nuclear reactors: tech products with bad UX can frustrate users, draw bad reviews, and make products flop.[7]

So what makes a product have good UX, anyway? Entire libraries can be filled with books on that topic, but we'll simplify it to a model with four key principles. A good UX is discoverable, gives feedback, is forgiving, and is intuitive. Keep all four of these in mind as you design your products.

Principle 1: Discoverability

The legendary designer Don Norman liked to make an example of some of the most common and badly-designed things in our lives: doors. It's often impossible to know whether a door should be pushed or pulled, especially if they have those metal bars common in so many office buildings.[8] And many doors that look like they should be pushed must actually be pulled, and vice versa.[9] Once you've shoulder-slammed into enough "pull" doors and tugged helplessly at enough "push" doors, you'll agree that such simple things shouldn't be made so confusing.

An example of a badly-designed door: there's no way to know whether you should push or pull. Source: Sam Danner[10]

Norman called these *Norman doors*: objects whose designs tell you to do the opposite of what you're supposed to do. One easy way out is to label the doors "push" or "pull," but Norman argued that doors' functionality should be obvious: if you have to label your door, you've already lost.[11]

We shouldn't be using door handle designs so confusing that they need labels. Source: Neil Pasricha[12]

Finding features

Norman doors lead us to our first principle: that of *discoverability*. When you look at an object, it should tell you exactly what you can do with it and how you interact with it.[13] More formally, the affordances — the buttons, sliders, door handles, and other items you use to interact with an object — should be easy to find and easy to understand.[14]

Norman doors are complete failures of discoverability. Most computer cables, meanwhile, are pretty discoverable. When you see the distinctively-shaped head of an HDMI cable, you know exactly what kind of port to look for on your computer or monitor. (Rectangular-headed USB cables are the exception: it's impossible to know which way to insert them. It feels like you have to flip it over every single time![15])

Norman also cites the humble tape dispenser as an easily-discoverable product. The dispenser's most obvious, or *salient*, feature is the sharp metal blade where a strip of tape usually sits. Once you see it, it's self-evident how you use it: pull the strip of tape and use the blade to cut it.[16]

Meanwhile, laptop touchpads, while slick, aren't very discoverable: just by looking at it, it's not immediately obvious whether you should wave your hand over it, slide your finger, tap, etc.[17] We learn the rough functionality with enough practice, but even then a lot of the more complicated features, like three-finger swipes or two-finger clicks, are hard to figure out unless you read a guide. (Did you know that you can show your available apps on a MacBook by pinching your thumb and three fingers in?)[18]

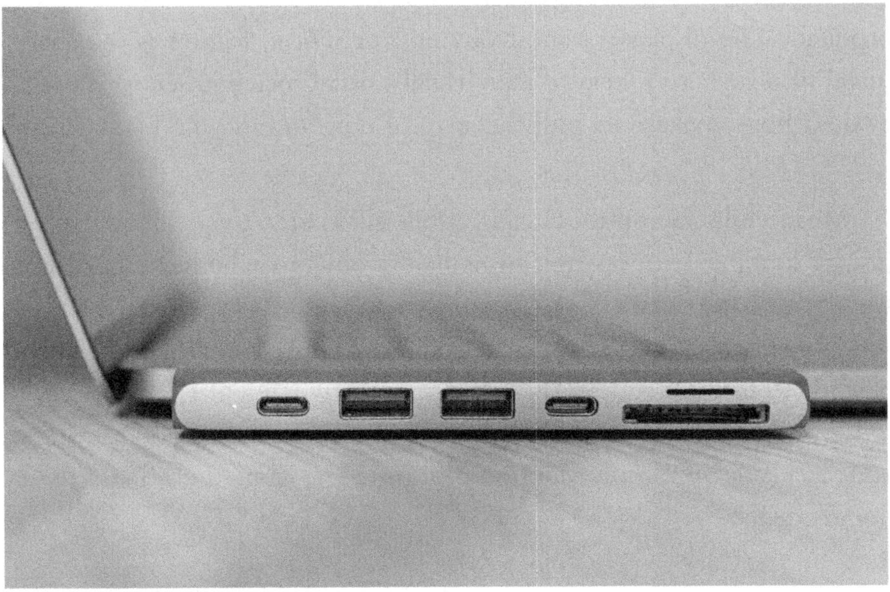

Computer docks are fairly intuitive: you know the oval USB-C cables have to go into the oval holes, thin microSD cards have to go into the thin rectangular holes, and boxy USB-A cables have to go in the boxy holes. The only unintuitive thing is which way to plug the USB-A cable in. Source: Karolina Grabowska[19]

It's not just about making affordances easy to find, though: they have to behave in the way you might expect. (It has to fit your mental models!) The EpiPen, for instance, is commonly used to inject antihistamines into someone experiencing a severe allergic attack. This life-saving device, unfortunately, has a misleading "interface." The very name "pen" leads people to believe that the needle is hidden underneath the removable plastic cap. But actually, the cap is a safety release. When it's removed, the needle comes out of the *opposite* side, leading many people trying to help a patient to accidentally stick themselves.[20]

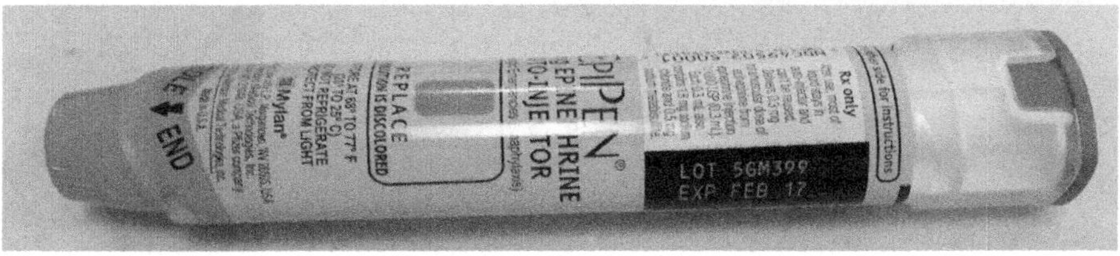

An EpiPen, used to inject epinephrine when people have severe allergic shocks. Source: Wikimedia[21]

When you apply these rules, you can start figuring out how to ensure your affordances are discoverable. Norman suggested that "push" doors be equipped with metal plates and "pull" doors be equipped with handles like the ones on cars. It's immediately obvious what to do in each case, and as an added bonus, it's literally impossible to pull a door with a metal plate — so users have no choice but to open the door properly.[22]

In UI design

When you're designing a digital product rather than a physical one, the toolkit changes but the core ideas stay the same. With one look at your product, it should be immediately apparent what users can do and how they do it.

Concretely, this means that your *call-to-action* (*CTA*) buttons have to be easy to find, well-labeled, and given the proper contextual styling. A signup button should be big, bold, and centered; a button that does something "dangerous" like deleting a file should be red; disabled buttons should be grayed out; less important buttons should get less visual prominence; and so on.[23]

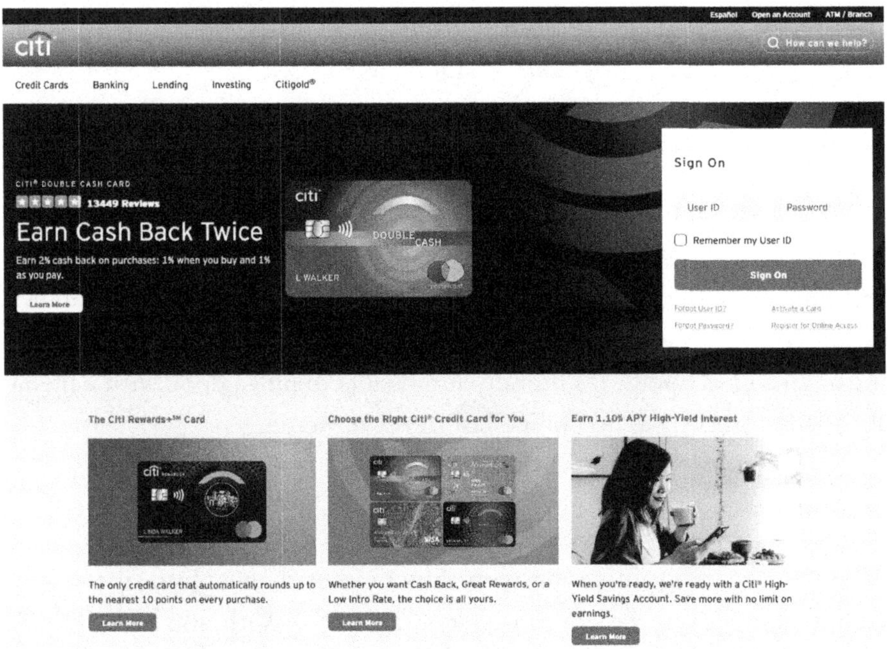

Citibank's promotion-stuffed homepage has poor discoverability. It's hard to figure out how to do something as simple as opening an account — turns out that the button is buried in the corner, inexplicably between the button to change language and the button to find a branch. Source: Citi[24]

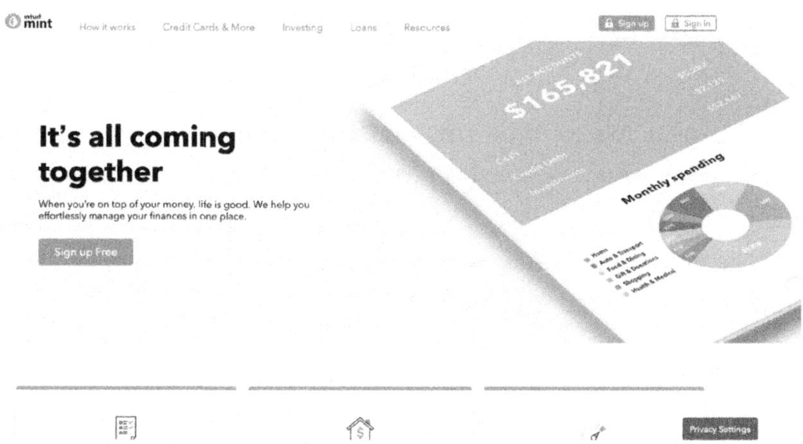

Mint's homepage is great at discoverability. The big orange "sign up" buttons guide users directly to the most important action they might need to take. Source: Mint[25]

Similarly, the various features of your product should be easy to find. Don't hide important things deep inside menus, especially unrelated menus.[26] Bank websites, for instance, are infamous at putting features deep within multiple layers of menus. Windows 8 was also criticized on this front because it was nearly-impossible to find the "shut down" button: you had to go to the settings menu, of all places, to find it.[27]

Principle 2: Feedback

Another principle from Norman is that of *feedback*: the object should tell you whether or not your action worked. The increase in resistance when you tighten a ketchup bottle's cap, the tearing sound of a tape dispenser, and the rumbling sound of a black pepper grinder are all instances of objects giving you useful feedback.[28]

To take a tech example, you've probably noticed the small bumps on your laptop's 'F' and 'J' keys. These are a crucial method of delivering feedback: they let you know if your hands are in the right place for typing without making you look down.[29] More generally, *all* physical keys on a keyboard give you some feedback, helping you find and push buttons just by touch. Computer screens, meanwhile, are just single slabs of glass, so they don't help you find buttons by touch alone. This is why so many users howled when Apple removed the physical Escape key in favor of a digital button on the Touch Bar in 2016 MacBooks.[30]

Without feedback, you don't really know if you've actually made the change you wanted to make. If your car doesn't beep when you try to lock it, you might get confused and walk back to the car to try again. If you press a button to submit a form and nothing happens, you might try pressing it again — which could actually be dangerous, since you might be making a purchase twice.

Multisensory feedback

It's easier for people to notice things when multiple senses get involved:[31] if the toast in your toaster catches fire, you'll know by sight, smell (of smoke), and taste (again of smoke).

Tech products often have trouble engaging multiple senses, since the main way users interact with them is through a flat piece of glass. Visual feedback, like the sight of a button getting pushed, is good but not enough. This is why *haptic feedback* — giving off a slight vibration when something happens, thus engaging the sense of touch and creating a bit of sound to boot[32] — is so popular on mobile devices.

If done well, sensory feedback can overcome other shortcomings in a product's UX. We mentioned earlier that laptop touchpads have poor discoverability. Fortunately, most good touchpads give you multisensory feedback when you click: the sight of the pad getting pushed down, a small clicking sound, and a bit of resistance against your finger. Apple's popular Force Touch touchpads take this a step further by adding two "levels" of clicking: a shallow one that greets you with a bit of vibration and a deep one that triggers a much richer vibration.[33a] This rich feedback is a big reason why touchpads have remained popular, despite their discoverability flaws.

Bad feedback

Objects that don't give feedback are problematic, but giving wrong or misleading feedback can be just as bad. One type of bad feedback is delayed feedback. If you double-click to open a file and nothing happens for a few seconds, you might click it again several times in a row — only to be greeted with fifteen different windows a little later.[35]

---

[a] What's even cooler about the Force Touch trackpad is that you don't actually click: the touchpad never gets depressed. But Apple calibrated the haptic feedback so perfectly that you think you pressed the pad down.[34]

Another problematic, but more subtle, feedback pattern is if the object gives you feedback that you made the action, but no feedback that it actually worked (known as "result feedback"). The classic example of this is a garage door opener: when you press it to open or close your garage, the light flickers, but that light only tells you that the opener itself is working. It doesn't tell you whether or not the garage door actually opened or closed; the only way to do that is to look at the door or listen for its rumbling sound.[36]

You can probably work around your garage door opener's lack of result feedback, but the engineers at Three Mile Island weren't so lucky. Recall that their control panel had a light that showed when the valve was told to close, but this light never told them if the valve had actually closed. So when the valve got stuck open, they were none the wiser — which led to the disastrous meltdown.

Finally, there are objects that might give you feedback but make it hard to find or notice. Most liquid measuring cups have this problem: you pour the liquid while standing up, but you can only see the measurements when the cup is at eye level. This means you have to go through the annoying process of pouring a little, bending down to see how much you've poured, standing back up to pour a little more in, and so on. These cups technically give you feedback, but it's so frustrating to measure that many people would rather just eyeball it.

Fortunately, the kitchen utensil brand OXO found a way around this. They created a measuring cup whose labels were at an angle, so you can see them as you pour. This way you can get the exact right amount of liquid without having to bend down.[37]

OXO's famous angled cup, which lets you see exactly how much liquid you're pouring without having to bend down. Source: Sur la Table[38]

In UI design

Giving feedback in digital products follows similar patterns. The user should always know their location in the product, the current status of their action, what's going to happen next, and what the ultimate outcome of their action was.[39] *Breadcrumbs*, UI components that show where the user is in your product and helps them "drill up" to a higher level,[40] are very helpful for the first item. Progress bars to show completion status, *snackbars* (also known as *toasts*) to show error or completion messages,[41] and pop-up *modal dialogs* to show important information are all useful for the latter items.

Snackbars, seen here on Google Keep, let you give users feedback without interrupting them. They're good for showing success or error messages.

Ecommerce sites often make good use of breadcrumbs to help users navigate the many layers and categories of products. Source: Best Buy[42]

Another useful rule of thumb is borrowed from Newton's laws of physics: every action should have an equal and opposite reaction.[43] Buttons should look "pushed in" when clicked, checkboxes should light up when selected, phones should vibrate or show a push notification when an alert comes in, and so on. Most UI design libraries and frameworks take care of this for you, but keep an eye out for it as you're building your product.

Principle 3: Forgiving

In baseball, if you fall behind by 12 runs to 2, you don't stand much of a chance of coming back — making such games demoralizing to play in and not much fun to watch either.

Most sports' scoring systems work like this: both sides rack up points from beginning to end, and the person with more[b] points at the end wins. And so most of them aren't much fun if they're a blowout.

Tennis, meanwhile, has developed a uniquely compartmentalized scoring system. You win points each time you beat your opponent, getting scores like 40–15; get enough points and you win a game. Win enough games and you win the set; win enough sets and you win the match.[44]

Crucially, though, the points won in one game don't carry over to the next game, and the games won in one set don't carry over to the next set. This means that, even if you get destroyed 7–0 in one set, you're back on equal footing at 0–0 in the next set. The mistakes you made in one part of the game don't haunt you for the rest of the game. This means that players always stand a fighting chance, no matter how badly they did before, and thus there's always something exciting at stake for the fans.[45]

[b]Or less, in golf.

The point is that tennis's scoring system is *forgiving*: if you make mistakes, as we all do, you aren't sunk. A similar principle applies to well-designed products, which help users avoid and recover from their mistakes. Specifically, a forgiving user experience minimizes the chance of mistakes, reduces the damage caused by mistakes, and makes mistakes easy to undo.[46] Let's step through each in turn.

Avoiding mistakes

The best way to make a product forgiving is to help the user not make mistakes in the first place.

The first way to do this is to hide "dangerous" or irreversible actions so users won't accidentally click on them.[c] For several years, the iPhone's mail app put the "delete" button right next to the "reply" button, leading many users to accidentally delete emails.[48] Meanwhile, Gmail on iOS hides the "delete" button by default and replaces it with the less-dangerous "archive" button; the user can switch out the buttons in the settings if they like.[49]

On the topic of avoiding misclicks, you want to be sure that your *touch targets* — buttons, checkboxes, and other widgets — aren't too small. Research shows that touch targets should be at least 9 millimeters (0.35 inches) to minimize the risk of misclicks.[50] Similarly, it's helpful to add "safety latches" so users don't take actions accidentally: "swipe to unlock" phone lock screens[d] have prevented many an embarrassing "butt dial."

You can also make users think twice before taking dangerous actions. GitHub makes users who want to delete a repository type in the repository's name before making the action.[51] This unusual UX pattern grabs users' attention, alerts them about the dangers of what they're do-

---

[c]In the popular show Family Guy, the acupuncturist Dr. Ling keeps his box of normal needles next to his box of poison-tipped needles.[47] Don't be like Dr. Ling!

[d]We've been itching for a chance to use that phrase.

ing, and ensures they don't accidentally make a destructive action while on "autopilot."

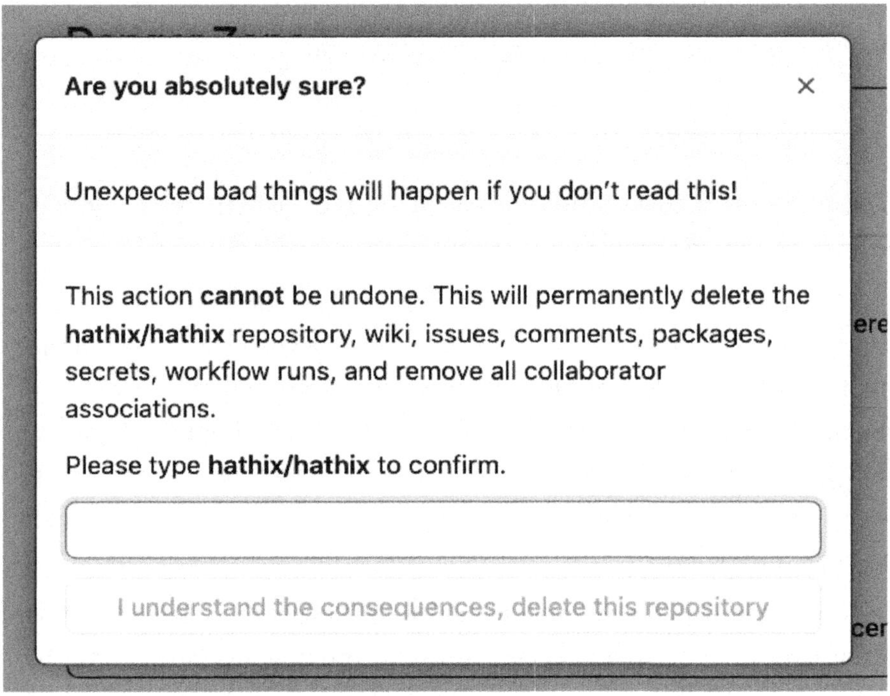

GitHub purposely adds friction to the repository deletion flow so users don't make careless mistakes. Source: GitHub[52]

Finally, you'll want to ensure that your product isn't leading users to make mistakes. Avoid jargon and confusing language that might lead users astray; make sure that users know exactly how dangerous an action is before they commit to it. GitHub is again a good example here: it helpfully marks all high-impact actions with red buttons and puts them in a clearly-labeled "danger zone."

Making mistakes less dangerous

With the above steps, you should be able to make mistakes less likely, but you'll want to have another line of defense: ensuring that mistakes aren't too costly.

One way is to automatically fix small errors. Google Search's autocorrect is a great example; it ensures that a single typo doesn't make your query useless.[53] Really, any type of autocorrecting, from phone keyboards turning "grllo" into "hello" to Excel adding missing parentheses to your formulas,[54] falls into this category.

User testing will usually reveal some of the more common small mistakes. These are trivially easy for you to fix but can really make users happy. For instance, if you're booking a flight on Google Flights and enter a return date that's before your departure date, the app will automatically reverse those dates for you.[55] These simple instances of the app "knowing what you mean" are satisfying yet easy to build.

When users make mistakes that you can't automatically fix, make sure it doesn't set them back too far. We've all been there: you're filling out a long form to apply for a bank account or whatnot and hit submit, only to realize that you made a single mistake and now have to fill the *entire* form in again.[56] It would be best if all the correct form fields stayed filled — or, even better, if the incorrect form field glowed red before you even hit "submit."

You can also help users catch their mistakes before they become dangerous. For instance, the default Android clock app has a lifesaving feature that tells you how far in the future an alarm will go off once you set it. If it's 1am and you're trying to get up at 5am to catch your flight, setting your alarm right is critical. If you accidentally set your alarm to 5pm, the app will alert you that the alarm will go off in 16 hours — which will instantly show you that you put the wrong time and help you avoid missing your flight.

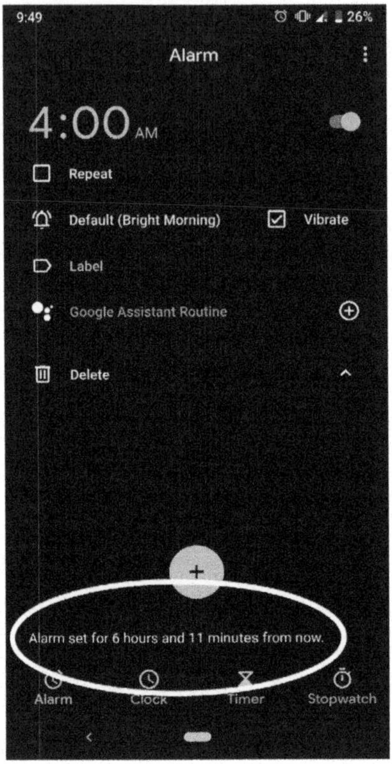

The Android clock app tells you how long it'll be until your alarm goes off, helping you catch mistakes.

Reversibility

One of the simplest and most popular ways to make a product's UX forgiving is to offer some kind of "undo" button for every action. Dropbox lets you undo accidental file deletions,[57] Gmail lets you "unsend" an email in some situations,[58] and so on. This lets you quickly recover from a mistaken action.

But you don't need to limit yourself to literal "undo" buttons. Every command that isn't explicitly irreversible (e.g. deleting something from a database or sending money) should have an opposite command. Thus, "add" buttons should be paired with "remove" buttons, "OK" buttons should be paired with "cancel" buttons, "install" buttons should be paired with "uninstall" buttons, and so on.[59] This ensures users never get into a state they can't get out of, and it also helps users simplify their mental models.

You can also offer users intermediate states where they can mull over their decisions before committing to them. Ecommerce websites' shopping carts and operating systems' recycle bins serve this purpose: they let you back out before making an irreversible action like sending money or permanently deleting files.

Many PMs build in reversibility without thinking about the other ways of making products forgiving. The best user experience is if users can't make the mistake in the first place — so it's helpful to think of undo buttons and the like as last resorts rather than primary solutions.[60]

Error messages

Despite all your (and your users') best intentions, errors are going to happen. It's inevitable. This is why good error messages are important. Instead of giving some obscure error number or vague message like "Incorrect information," you should explain exactly what went wrong and what the user can do about it. Make sure it's in conversational language and uses the active voice so it's clearer.[61] Thus, a mediocre error message might look like:

> *Bad password, try again.*

Meanwhile, a good error message might look like:

> *The password you entered includes your birthday, which isn't allowed. Remove that from your password and try again.*

This tells the user what they did wrong and how they can fix it. An excellent error message might include a button that offers to generate a random password for the user so they can fix their error with one tap.

Principle 4: Intuitive

Finally, a good user experience is intuitive: it fits with our mental models and is thus predictable and easy to learn. Unintuitive products are jarring to use; recall how confused Neel's friends were when they tried using his erasable pen. Chances are that you've experienced these fleeting moments of confusion before when using tech products.

Hidden features

One way this problem shows up is when an important affordance is hidden. How many times have you opened a small tub of ice cream and run around looking for a spoon, only to notice later that a small wooden or plastic spoon was hidden inside the cap the whole time?[62]

Popular tech products aren't immune from this either. For many years, Dropbox's mobile apps let you download a file offline by pressing the "Mark as favorite" button. But that connection makes no sense — why do favorite files have to go offline, and why can't you save files you don't like offline? Users were confused, searching high and low for a "save offline" button, not realizing that the button to achieve that goal was in front of their noses the whole time. People got so confused, in fact, that Dropbox had to put up help center articles to explain how the button worked.[63]

Mental models

In the last chapter, we mentioned how important it is that a product conform to people's existing mental models. When a product doesn't, it becomes unintuitive. For instance, the average user's mental model for how to operate a podcast player probably includes an expectation that you'll be able to listen to any episode at any time. But one popular podcast app doesn't let you listen to episodes of a podcast unless you subscribe to that podcast — a jarring and confusing experience.[64]

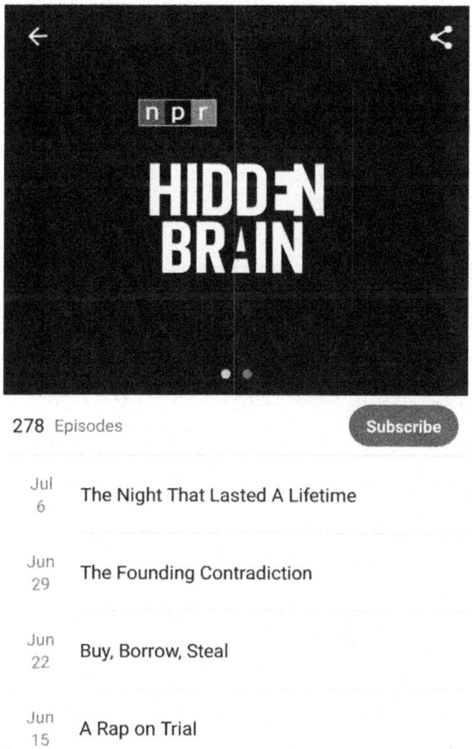

One popular podcast player doesn't let you listen to episodes of a podcast unless you subscribe to that podcast. Source: CastBox[65]

Note that you don't have to follow every single convention of related apps — if you did, your app would hardly be unique! You can break some of the standard assumptions, but make sure it's clear to users so their mental models don't get confused. The dating app Coffee Meets Bagel intentionally gives users a limited number of matches per day, a departure from most dating apps, which tend to offer an unlimited number. This isn't confusing to users, though, since Coffee Meets Bagel gives a good reason for it: it forces you to be more selective[66] and lines up with the app's branding as an app for finding long-term relationships.[67]

This confusion also happens when users form unspoken assumptions about how your product will work, only to find that they aren't true. For instance, there are three ways to engage with a tweet on Twitter: like it, comment on it, or retweet it. Most Twitter users have a mental model that, if someone retweets or comments on a tweet, all their followers will see it.[68]

But, on the flip side, they expect that likes are more private and aren't broadcast to your followers — if the like button behaves just like the retweet button, what's the point?[69] The trouble is that Twitter sometimes shows the tweets that someone likes to their followers, thus treating likes as semi-retweets. What's more, this behavior is inconsistent; there's no apparent rhyme or reason for why a particular liked tweet shows up in someone's timeline. This has caused users a lot of confusion[70] and spawned countless articles that try to find ways to turn off this mystifying feature.[71]

You might notice a theme here: if you feel the need to write a help center article to explain how a feature works, or if you notice third parties writing articles about how to make it work, that's a good sign that it's unintuitive and has to be fixed. Instead of making a whole article on how to save files offline with the "favorite" button, Dropbox should have just changed the button to say "save offline." (To their credit, Dropbox did that eventually.[72])

Mappings

An important subset of intuitiveness is *predictability*: the user should be able to, well, predict what the outcome of any interaction will be.[73] If the mapping of controls to outcomes isn't clear, users will get confused and inevitably make mistakes.

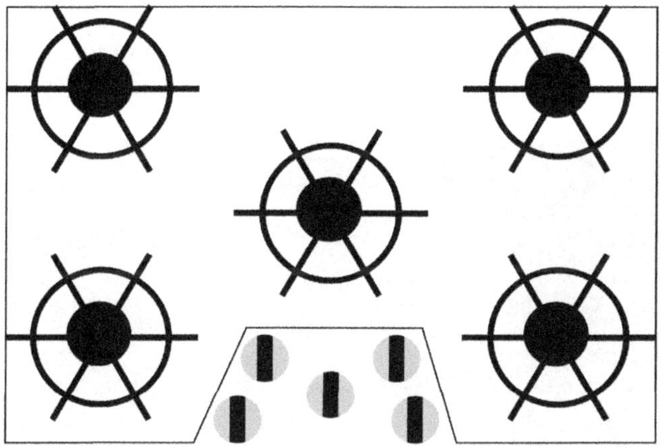

A stove with an intuitive spatial mapping of knobs to burners. You can easily predict which knob goes with each burner.

The classic example of this comes from stoves. They usually have four or more burners, each of which has an associated knob to control the heat. A well-designed stove will place the knobs in an arrangement that looks similar to the arrangement of the burners. This way, the *spatial mapping* of knobs to burners is clear. The top left knob controls the top left burner, and so on. A badly-designed stove, on the other hand, might place the knobs in a row while the burners are in a different configuration — making it hard to know which knob goes with which burner.

A stove with knobs in a bad arrangement could work if the knobs were labeled, but — as we've said before — the best interfaces don't need labels at all. Intuitive interfaces, by definition, can be picked up without the need for labels or manuals.

Another great example comes from Mercedes-Benz cars, whose driver's seat controls are shaped like a seat. This way, drivers can easily figure out what each button does and can quickly adjust the headrest, seat back, seat bottom, and other parts of the seat.[74] It's much more intuitive than having buttons laid out in, say, a grid, in which case drivers would have to memorize which button goes with which part of the seat. That might even require a dreaded label.

This Mercedes-Benz's seat control buttons look like a seat, making it very easy to predict which button controls which part of your seat. Source: Pikist[75]

When you're building software products, creating a good spatial mapping is relatively straightforward, since you can put a click target on pretty much anything. A good rule of thumb is to put the controls for an object on the object itself instead of somewhere else on the screen. For instance, if your app has a list of contacts, the user should be able to tap on each contact to bring up the deletion option instead of having to, say, check a box on the contact and then press a delete button in the corner of the screen.

Another kind of mapping is *cultural mapping*; the culture a user comes from dictates the kinds of mappings they expect.[76] In languages written with a left-to-right script (like English and Hindi), we expect the back button to be on the left and the forward button to be on the right. But in languages written with a right-to-left script (like Arabic and Hebrew), users expect the exact opposite.[77]

The Hebrew-language website for Haaretz, the Israeli newspaper, flips the spatial mappings we're used to in a left-to-right world. The menu button is in the top right instead of the top left, the sidebar with additional stories is on the left instead of the right, and captions are to the left of images instead of to the right. Source: Haaretz[78]

It's not limited to human cultures; the broader context in which someone experiences an object determines how they expect the object to behave. For instance, Macs use so-called "natural scrolling," where moving your finger up on the touchpad moves the contents of the page down, and moving your finger left moves the contents right.[79] (This is "natural" because devices with touchscreens usually operate this way.) Meanwhile, Windows PCs usually use traditional scrolling, where moving your finger up moves the contents up.[80] So if you're building an app for Macs, users will expect it to scroll "naturally," but if you're building the same app for Windows, users will expect the traditional scrolling regime.

✿ Try this

Now that you know what makes a good user interface, try this tongue-in-cheek game that challenges you to work around some of the absolute worst — and most hilarious — UI design patterns ever created.

userinyerface.com/game.html

Chapter 18

Usability

When PMs think about what makes a great product, we often think about powerful features, clever growth hacks, or good-looking user interfaces. But one thing we often overlook is simple user-friendliness.

Ease of use has made many famous products extraordinarily successful. The graphical user interface (GUI), popularized by Xerox and Apple in the 1970s, was revolutionary. Instead of having to memorize long lists of computer commands, users could just point and click.[1] The Apple II's GUI put Apple on the map and sold over two million units in a time when few people had even heard of personal computers.[2]

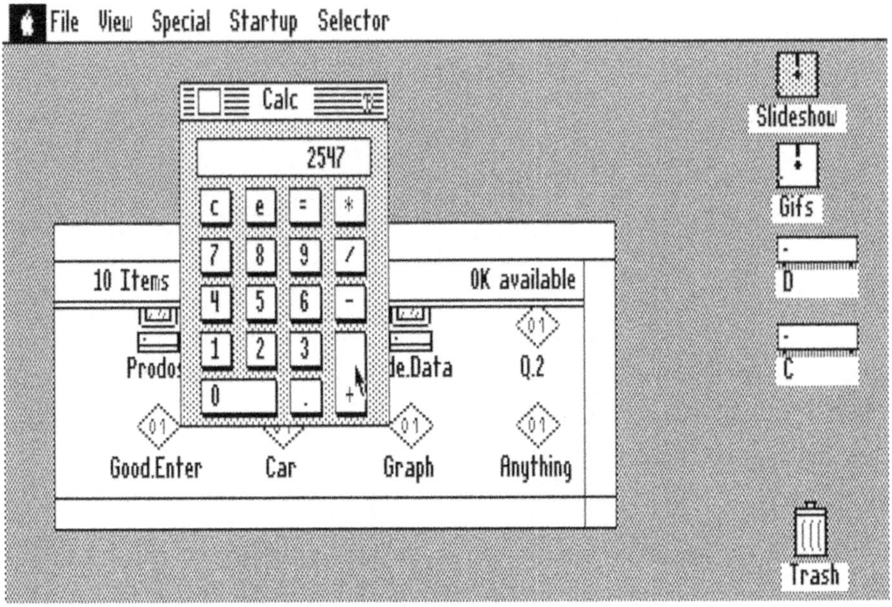

The Apple II's GUI. Source: ToastyTech[3]

Apple struck again with the iPod's famous click wheel, which, with just five buttons and a dial, was incredibly easy to use. People who had never used handheld electronics before were perfectly comfortable with it,[4] and the iPod sold hundreds of millions of units.[5]

Then Google came out with ChromeOS, the web-based operating system. It was a revelation: you no longer had to deal with antivirus programs, worry about managing drivers and system libraries, or constantly check for operating system updates.[6] Even the interface was simple: the desktop started with a single button (the browser shortcut), making the OS remarkably straightforward. ChromeOS "just worked" and was much harder to mess up than a Windows PC,[7] and it quickly became a hit among grandparents[8][9] and kids alike.[10]

There are plenty more examples like this, but the thread between them is clear: creating simple, easy-to-use products that account for humans' shortcomings is a great way to make products that people will love. It may not be that sexy, but focusing on usability pays dividends.

Memory limits

You may have seen those viral images of people "grandparent-proofing" their TV remotes: they cover the vast majority of buttons with tape, sparing only essentials like the power, channel, and volume buttons.[11] This reduces the remote's feature set, but in doing so it makes the remote more user-friendly — and thus *more* useful despite being able to do less.[12]

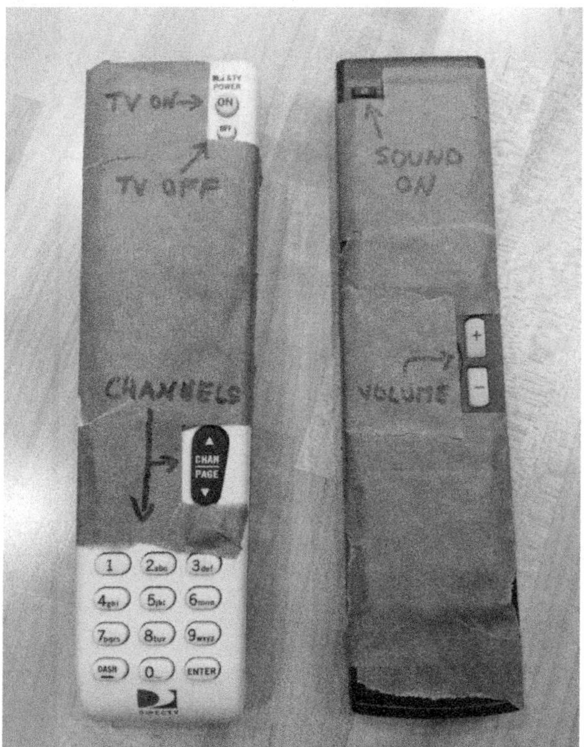

A "grandparent-proofed" pair of remotes with only the power, channel, and volume buttons available. Source: thecre8ivewon via Reddit[13]

Humans aren't perfectly-intelligent automatons; we get confused and stressed, especially when we're overwhelmed with choices and information. The rise of "grandparent-friendly" remotes shows how prevalent the problem is. It also rears its head when we're shopping. In one study, experimenters set up two display tables at a food market; one offered 24 varieties of jam, the other just 6. You might expect more shoppers to buy from the table that had more flavors, but you'd be wrong: more people visited the 24-jam table, but people who visited the 6-jam table were ten times more likely to buy a bottle.[14]

Apple TV's slick remote, which cuts out all but the essential buttons. Source: Wikimedia[15]

This problem goes by many names, from *analysis paralysis*[16] to the *choice paradox*[17] to *Hick's Law*,[18] but the idea is the same: the more choices someone is confronted with, the longer it'll take them, and the more stressed they'll be. The timeless advice of "Keep it Simple, Stupid" is always useful here.[19]

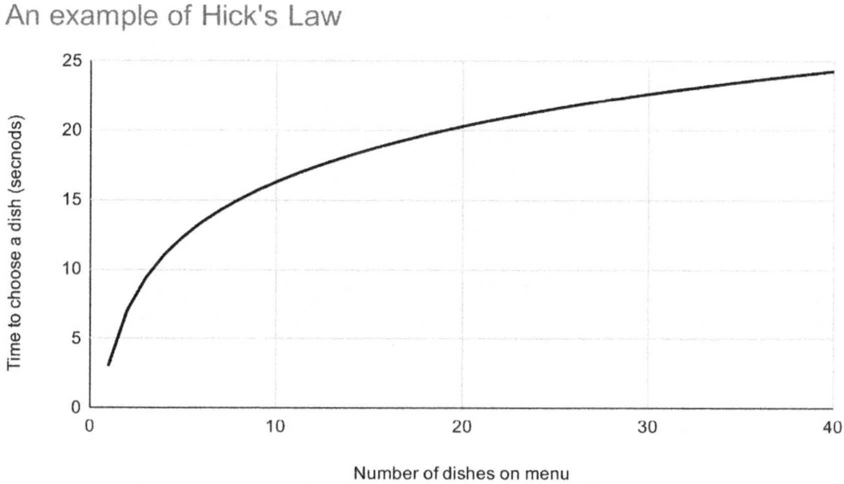

An illustration of Hick's Law using example data about a restaurant menu. The law says that that the time it takes people to make a decision grows as they're offered more choices. The formula is $r = a + b \times \log_2(n)$*, where r is the time taken to make the decision, n is the number of choices, and a and b are arbitrary constants. Source: Interaction Design*[20]

Removing irrelevant options

Everyone suffers when they're bombarded with information and choices, so a great product will design around it. The meditation app Headspace is great at this.[21] Instead of asking for paragraphs of text or requiring new users to set up a complicated meditation routine, Headspace's onboarding asks a single question: why you're looking to meditate. It only offers a few simple answers, and it stresses that there's no wrong answer. It's a fittingly zen onboarding flow.

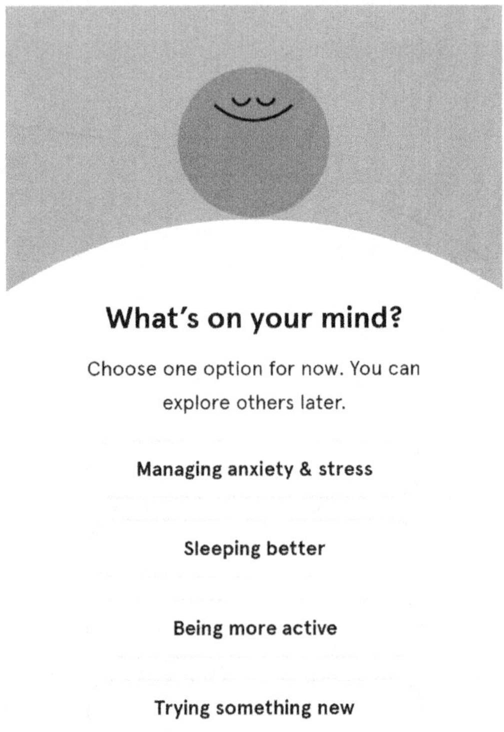

Headspace's onboarding flow is a single, easy question with no wrong answers. Source: Headspace

TurboTax, for all its flaws,[22] does a great job at simplifying the monstrously complex and confusing process of filing your taxes. Instead of throwing people into a gigantic form with hundreds of fields, it steps users through a series of simple questions with just a few answer choices at each step, often just "yes" and "no." Simplifying the tax code into simple questions, along with keeping the user focused on just one task at a time, is a great way to reduce the cognitive load of doing taxes.[23]

Seven, plus or minus two

The general theme here is that human brains can only handle so much incoming information at once, whether it's a bunch of buttons on a remote, jams at a table, or questions on a tax form. A successful product will reduce the flow of information to avoid overwhelming users.

An interesting special case of this problem affects our *working memory*, which is the hyper-short-term memory we use when we're trying to remember the phone number that someone told us to type in.[24] We're only able to hold seven, plus or minus two, items in our working memory; if we try to cram more in, we'll inevitably drop something. This relationship, known as *Miller's Law*,[25] explains why it's so hard to remember a ten-digit phone number that someone reads out to you.

The practical implication is that, when designing a user interface, you should break content into groups of five to nine items each.[26] This is why it's useful to put only a few items in each section of a toolbar, limit yourself to seven bullet points on a slide,[27] offer no more than nine products for sale on a single screen, and so on.

Conservation of complexity

Every product has a certain amount of *irreducible complexity*: a certain amount of information or tasks that have to be done.[28] For instance, when you're sending an email, you don't have to include body content, a signature, attachments, or even a subject line. But even the most stripped-down email has to have two fields: To and From.[29] These two bits of information are the irreducible complexity of sending an email.

The user interface designer Larry Tesler argued that every product has irreducible complexity, and that someone has to deal with it: either the developer or the users. This is known as *Tesler's Law* or *the law of conservation of complexity*.[30] Developers of user-friendly products will take on as much of the irreducible complexity as they can, thus minimizing the amount of work the user has to do. In the email example, email apps will auto-populate the From field, so all the user has to do is fill in the To field. The complexity doesn't disappear; it's just shouldered by software.[31]

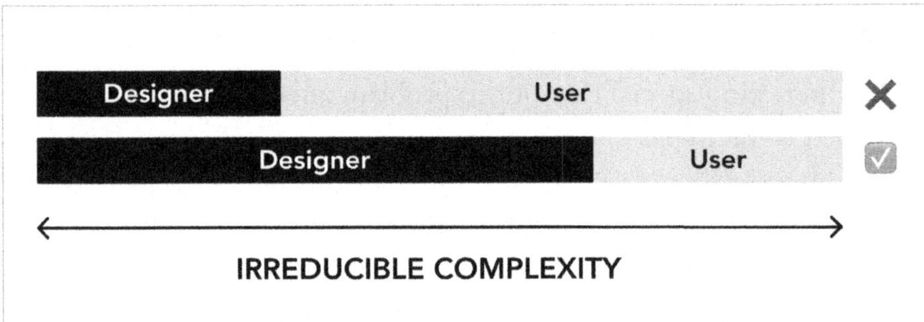

Every product has a certain amount of irreducible complexity. Well-designed products shift the burden of that complexity off the users and onto the developer. Source: Harish Jose[32]

Another way to think about it: imagine a million users spend one minute doing something they don't need to, like entering the From field in an email. If the developer spends a few hours doing it automatically, hundreds of thousands of users' hours will be saved.[33]

There are many small friction points where developers can save users a little bit of time. For instance, when users are inputting their credit card details into a website, the site has to know information like the credit card number, expiration date, network (like Visa or MasterCard), and a few other fields. Most well-designed websites will automatically figure out the network based on the credit card number, so the user doesn't have to enter it themselves.[34] A few hours, at most, of developer time will save millions of people a few precious seconds each.

Face authentication is another great example: the system has to verify the identity of the person signing in. Requiring users to sign in with a username and password is easy on developers but painful for users; face auth is harder to implement but saves users a lot of time.[35]

Reducing the burden on users helps your product in other ways, too. One theory is that users have a fixed amount of energy that they dedicate to using your product, so if you reduce the amount of energy they have to spend on simple tasks, they'll have more energy left to do more complex tasks[36] — and thus they'll become "power users," engage more with the product, and probably become more likely to pay.

Accessibility

It's estimated that 15% of the world population lives with a disability,[37] so products must accommodate the challenges their users might face if they want to be truly usable.

We'll discuss the tactics for how to build accessible products in a later chapter, but for now, suffice it to say that thinking about disabilities is actually a powerful lens as you try to improve your product's user-friendliness. Identifying places where people with disabilities might struggle with your app can help you find opportunities to improve your product for everyone.

The classic example of this comes from the world of kitchen equipment. In the 1990s, a businessman named Sam Farber was vacationing with his wife in southern France. One day he walked into the kitchen and found her crying because her arthritis made it impossible for her to use a metal peeler to peel an apple for an apple tart. Farber's wife, Betsey, grabbed a lump of clay and started designing an arthritis-friendly handle for the peeler.[38]

It dawned on Sam Farber that people with arthritis needed more comfortable and usable kitchen equipment, so he turned Betsey's workaround into OXO, a line of ergonomically-designed kitchen equipment[39] ranging from peelers to spatulas to whisks to colanders.[40]

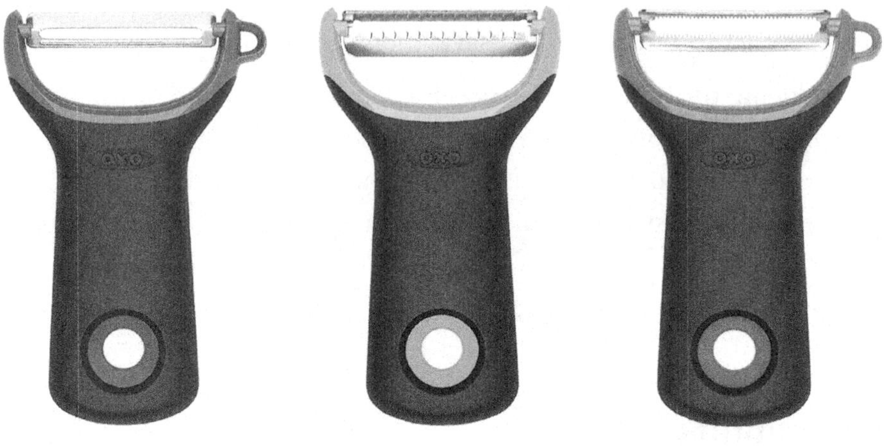

Ergonomic fruit and vegetable peelers from OXO. Source: The Pepper Mill[41]

It turned out that everyone, not just people with arthritis, loved OXO's comfortable rubbery handles and easy-to-hold design. OXO equipment now graces kitchens around the world[42] — including, perhaps, your own. It goes to show how everyone benefits from products designed for accessibility.

To take a tech example, an *inclusive design* team at Microsoft was investigating ways to make the company's products more usable for the blind. The team came up with a tool that would automatically create captions for PowerPoint presentations, which morphed into real-time captions for Skype.[43] Anyone who's been on a conference call with people with different first languages knows how a feature like this would be useful for anyone, not just people with disabilities. That same team improved text wrapping and formatting to help people with dyslexia read text more easily, which ended up helping even people without dyslexia read faster.[44]

Simulation

When you're trying to improve your product's UX, then, it's helpful to work with users with specific disabilities, or even simulate those disabilities yourself, to sniff out usability problems that you might never notice. One common tactic is to artificially blur your product's UI to simulate how a visually-impaired (or just shortsighted) person might experience it. You'll quickly notice if your call-to-action buttons are hard to spot, if important alerts are easy to miss, and so on.[45]

Or you could force yourself to only use your non-dominant hand to interact with your phone to simulate how someone with motor disabilities might experience your app; you'll quickly find out where you wish your app accepted voice input or where you wish fewer taps were needed. (Of course, nothing beats working with users who experience these disabilities themselves.)

Some UX designers even get drunk and try using their products to see what becomes confusing or where it becomes easy to make mistakes (say, if the delete button is right next to the edit button).[46] Most people aren't going to be using your product drunk,[a] but you can quickly pick out problems that people in a hurry or with less technical experience might encounter. (Remember, most users are probably not like your hyper-tech-savvy team!)

Constraints

It's helpful to think of accessibility not as an annoying set of hoops you have to jump through at the end of development, but rather as constraints that can help you be more creative as you craft your UX. Constraints drive creativity.[47]

To illustrate this, try thinking of an idea for a new board game. Put the book down and think for a minute.

---

[a] Well, maybe you run a dating app.

You might have had trouble with that. Now let's add a constraint: think of an idea for a board game, except with the rule that your game has to involve eating food as a core mechanic.[48] See what you come up with.

If you're like us, you probably came up with much more interesting ideas once the food constraint was added. Maybe you thought of a game like "High Tea Assassin," where everyone eats a cupcake and uses the fruit embedded inside the cupcake as clues to figure out who the killer was. Or maybe you thought of an edible Pictionary, where players close their eyes, taste food combinations like raspberries and Nutella, and then try to guess what they just ate.[49]

This worked because the added constraint gave your brain something to latch onto. Instead of stabbing around in the dark for an idea, you had a beacon of light to start your exploration with.

One great way to find constraints is to think about accessibility. The Farbers, for instance, found a very specific problem with kitchen equipment — the painful metal handles — and focused themselves on improving that. This focus, in turn, helped spur their now-famous innovations.

So when you're looking for creative ways to improve your products, look to accessibility not as a hurdle but as a source for constraints. With this, you'll be able to come up with ideas that won't even approach the average PM's radar.

Screen layout

One thing that often gets overlooked when designers and PMs are creating user interfaces is the constraints of the user's device. That is, when you're creating prototypes on Post-It notes or in Figma, it's easy to forget that people are going to consume your app through some kind of device, and the physical nature of the device introduces some constraints.

Phones

For instance, people tend to cradle phones in their hands with their thumbs over the screens, and so buttons in the natural range of their thumb are easier to press. It may look great if your button is in the far corner of the screen, but it'll be really awkward for the user to reach it. (Try holding your phone in your right hand and reaching your thumb for the top-left corner of the screen. It can be physically painful!)

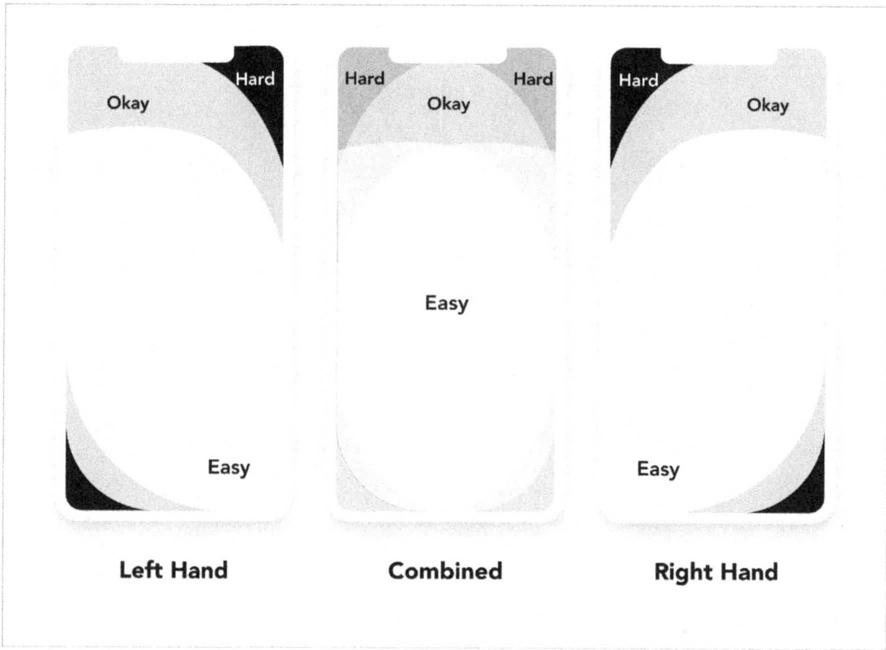

The "thumb zones" for an average phone screen. Depending on how the user holds the phone, the thumb zones will differ; place your buttons so that they're easy to reach no matter how the phone is held. Source: Smashing Magazine[50]

Generally speaking, the buttons that people will want to press the most should go in the "thumb zone," located near the arc of the user's thumb(s). Since people can hold their phones in either hand (or in both hands), your most important buttons should go toward the lower center of the screen, since that's where the "thumb zones" for all grips intersect.[51]

In fact, this is exactly what Google's Material UI does: the most important button in the UI floats in the bottom of the screen, offset toward one side but still in the thumb zone. You'll notice these so-called *floating action buttons*, or *fabs*, in many Google apps, and indeed all across Android.[52]

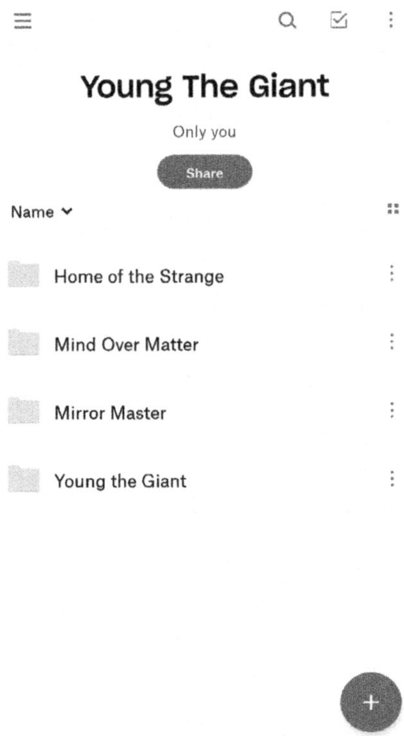

Dropbox's Android app features a prominent floating action button, located squarely in the thumb zone.

The exact size and shape of the optimal zone for buttons depends on the device's *form factor*. The thumb zone for larger phones, where your hand can't wrap around the entire device (if you don't know how this feels, try holding your phone sideways in one hand to simulate it), is smaller and more linear because your thumb is more locked in place.[53] The thumb zones for tablets, which users usually hold in two hands, might look more like two distinct zones in the bottom corners. You'll have to experiment with the form factors of your target devices to figure out the best zones for buttons.

The thumb zone on a large phone or tablet looks different than that of a smaller phone. The user's hand is more locked in place, so less of the screen can be reached easily. Source: Practical Ecommerce[54]

Laptops

Users interacting with your UI with a mouse and keyboard will experience different constraints than those using touch. The mouse is quite different from the finger, after all.

For these users, a useful rule to keep in mind is *Fitts's Law*, which states that the time taken for someone to move a mouse to a button depends on the button's size and the distance they have to move the mouse. The farther-away and smaller a button, the longer it takes to get there. This explains the intuitive advice to group similar buttons together and ensure your buttons are large enough.[55]

Fitts's Law also explains why drop-down and right-click menus are so helpful: they let the user take a variety of actions without having to move their mouse too far.[56]

One less obvious insight from Fitts's Law is that the corners are very powerful. On computer screens, the cursor can't go off the edge of the screen, so it's actually quite easy to find a button that's nestled at the edge of the screen: you don't have to worry about overshooting it. It's even easier to hit a button in the corner of the screen; you could close your eyes and move your mouse as far up and to the left as possible, and you'd be virtually guaranteed to end up in the top-left corner of the screen. This means that the effective size of buttons on the corners is infinite, so that Fitts's Law says that they're very easy to find and click.[57]

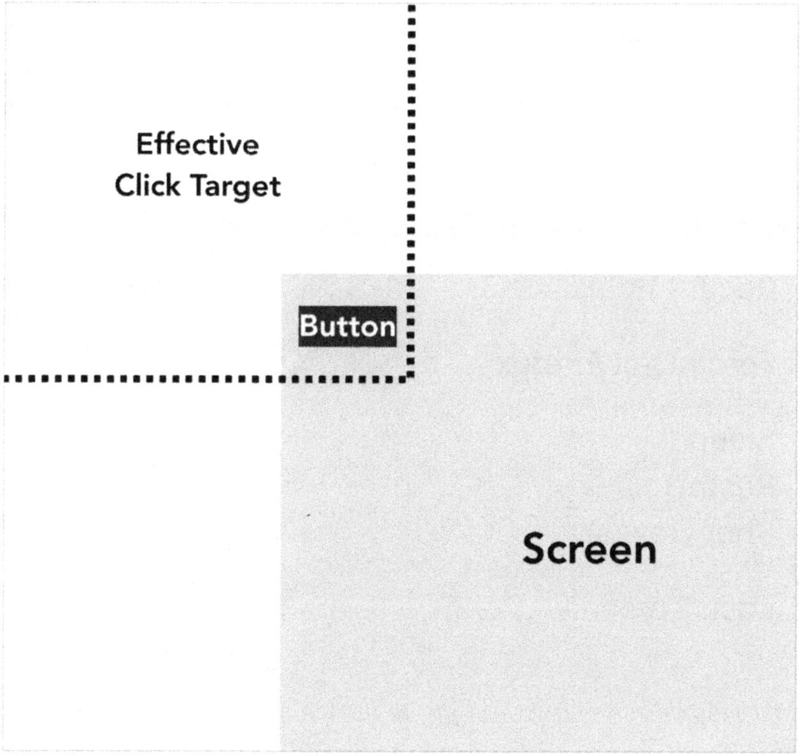

Putting a button in the corner of the screen gives it an effectively infinite click target. This makes such a button very easy to click, per Fitts's Law. Source: Wikimedia[58]

This is why operating systems tend to put important buttons in the corners of the screen. Windows 10 puts the Start menu in the bottom-left corner;[59] Macs put the Apple menu in the top-left corner and the notification center button on the top right.[60]

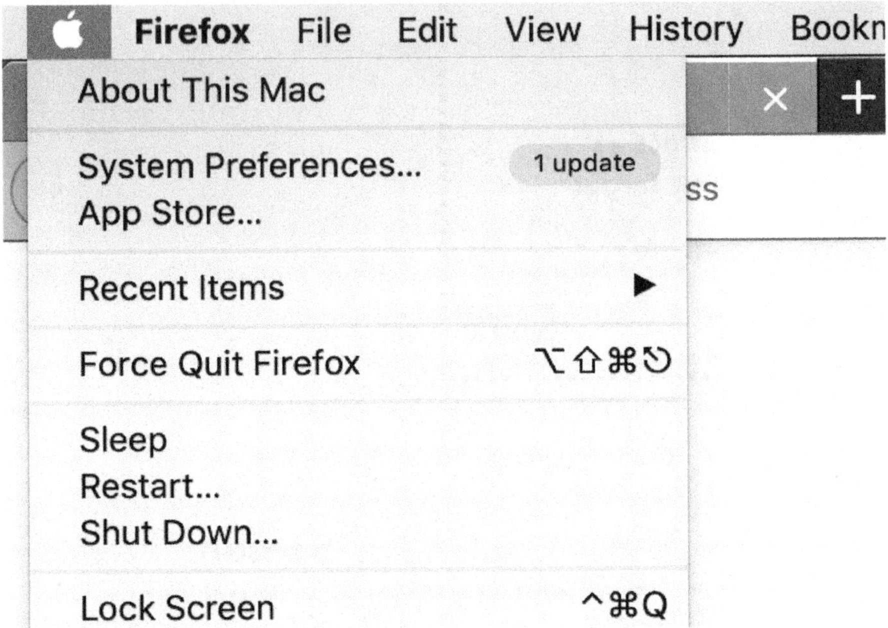

A Mac's Apple button is located just to the left of the top-left corner of the screen. But the button activates even if you click to its left, in the absolute corner. This subtle twist makes it very easy to hit to the button: no need to aim, just sling your mouse to the top left corner of the screen.

Note that entirely different patterns emerge when users are reading. Many studies have generated heatmaps of where users tend to look on webpage and found several unique patterns. The most common is the *F-pattern*, where users start at the top-left corner and read a few lines, then only look at the left side of the page as they go down. Another is the *Z-pattern*, which emerges on less-dense websites as users skim text, moving their eyes left-to-right and then jumping down a line.[61]

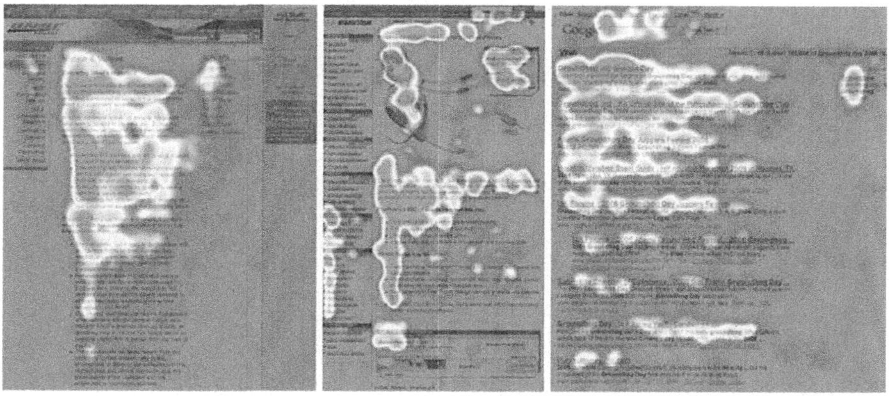

These eye-tracking heatmaps show how users' eyes move across various webpages. A rough F-pattern emerges. Source: Norman Nielsen Group[62]

Some users also follow a *layer-cake pattern*, where they read headings and skip everything else; others create spotty patterns by jumping around the page while looking for a specific item, like a phone number or a link.[63] So the appropriate UI layout for reading-heavy products (Medium, newspapers, etc.) differs from the appropriate layout for more action-oriented apps.

🎁 Bonus video

We've seen how you can optimize the layouts of screens. But let's talk about the next big thing: no screens! Watch this bonus video to learn how voice input is the next frontier of usability.

productalliance.com/videos/voice

Chapter 19

Customer vs. Business

EVER NOTICE HOW milk always seems to be found way in the back of the supermarket? That's no accident: supermarkets purposely put staples like milk at the back of the store so shoppers have to wander through the entire store, getting bombarded with offers and impulses to buy other stuff as they go.[1] Supermarkets are also known to put profitable junk foods near eye level on shelves so people will feel tempted to buy them;[2] the same logic explains why there's so much candy at the checkout lines.[3]

Supermarkets know very well that there's often a tension between user goals (getting through a store quickly and avoiding junk food) and business goals (getting shoppers to buy as much stuff as possible), and they design their stores to promote the business's needs.

Tech products realize this too: who hasn't felt a pang of rage at Uber charging you 3x surge pricing after a night at the bar, when public transit is closed and you have no alternative? Or when you book a Lyft, see the driver going in circles for five minutes, and cancel, only to get slapped with a cancellation fee?[4] These ridesharing products, like supermarkets, prioritize making money over providing a good customer experience.

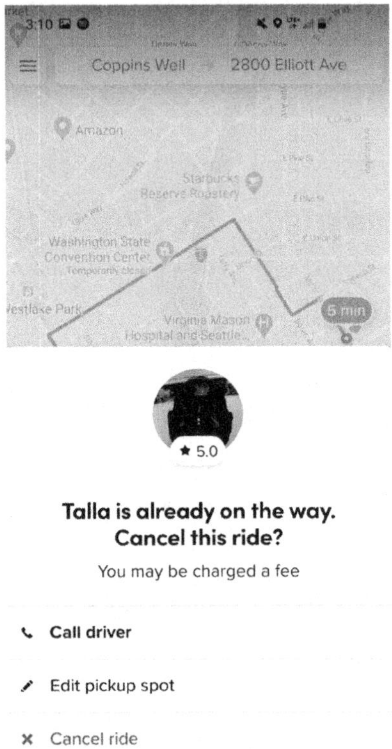

Lyft charges you a fee for canceling a ride after you've hailed it. The app's wording makes you feel a tad guilty, too.

It doesn't have to be like this, though. Explicitly putting the user experience last is a surefire way to get unhappy customers, and they'll eventually get fed up with you. A good user experience aligns the business and user goals so everyone wins, and that's the foundation of many a successful product and business.

Dishonest patterns

Before we look at companies that have successfully aligned business and user goals, let's investigate some anti-patterns: dirty tricks that companies use to advance their business goals while ruining the user experience. These are often called *dark patterns*,[5] though we prefer to call them *dishonest patterns*.

Note that there's nothing wrong with a company making money: that's what companies have to do, after all! The problem comes when companies are *actively hostile* to the user to make a buck. We've seen examples of these dishonest patterns from supermarkets and ride-hailing companies, but they're much more widespread. Let's look at just a few examples of these dishonest pattern as they've shown up across the tech industry.

Roach motels

Perhaps the most famous type of dishonest pattern is the colorfully-named *roach motel*, which refers to services that are easy to sign up for but very difficult to get out of.[6] It takes its name from the Roach Motel, a popular roach bait device with the catchphrase, "Roaches check in… but they don't check out!"[7]

You've probably experienced this with credit cards before. You can sign up for a credit card with a quick online form, but canceling a card requires jumping through a lot of hoops. You have to call a support agent, endure excruciating elevator music as you sit on hold, and dance through nagging and "retention offers" before you can cancel.[8] One gym even makes members print and fill out a form, then send it via snail mail, before they can cancel their subscriptions.[9]

Many online services make it difficult to cancel your account, too. It's very hard to delete your Amazon account, for instance. There's no button in the "Your Account" menu, where you might expect it to show up. Instead, you have to find the tiny "Help" button at the bottom of the screen, click "Need More Help?", hit a button to contact Amazon, and dig through menus until you find a button to cancel your account.[10] (It's easier to turn off Prime, fortunately.)

Hidden fees

Another tricky but widespread dishonest pattern is the hidden fee. The event ticketing firm Ticketmaster is infamous for inflating the cost of tickets with these fees. By one estimate, Ticketmaster inflates the price of a ticket by 30% with fees that only become apparent once you go to check out.[11] A ticket advertised for $100, then, would actually set you back $130, something you'd only realize once you'd mentally committed to making the purchase. More infuriatingly, some of these fees are clearly cash grabs, like the vague "convenience," "facility," "processing," and "delivery" fees.[12]

It's easy to beat up on Ticketmaster, but plenty of other products bundle in hidden fees. The fees on home-rental services like Airbnb and Vrbo are usually between 25%[13] and 50%[14] of the list price. But in one particularly egregious example, a one-night stay at a property listed for $275 a night came with $289 in fees, bloating the real price to $564.[15]

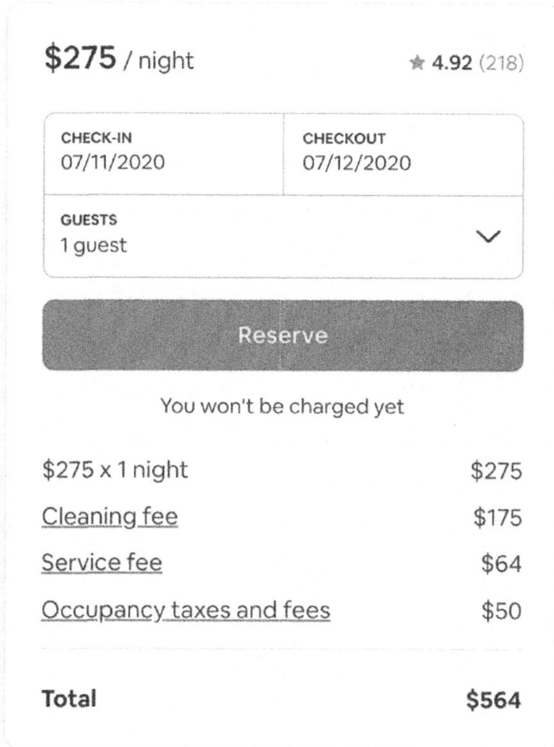

One Airbnb listing was advertised as $275 a night but actually cost $564, a blatant instance of hidden fees. Source: MissChang via Reddit[16]

Other products sneak in fees with no discernible user benefit. In 2014, for instance, Uber added a $1 "Safe Rides Fee" to all rides, claiming that the fee would be used to fund "background checks," "driver safety education," and "insurance." But an investigation found that the money raised from this fee never went to safety projects and instead just padded Uber's margins.[17]

Bait-and-switch

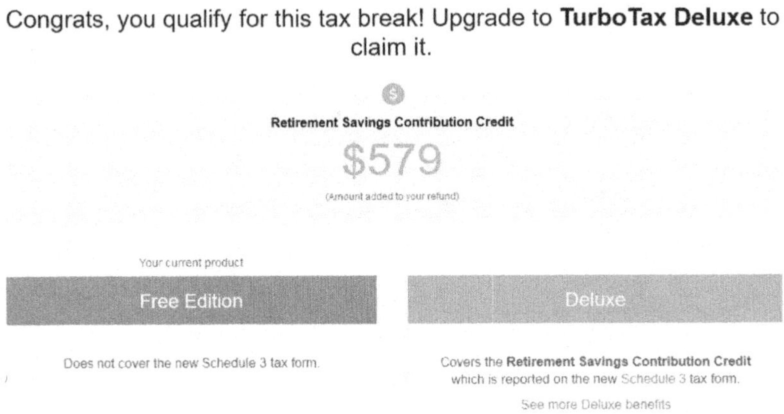

TurboTax's free edition will sometimes hit you with a paywall once you've gotten deep enough into the app. Unless you pay to upgrade, you'll lose all your progress. Source: CurtainClothes on Reddit[18]

There are plenty more examples of dishonest patterns, which you can read about on entertaining subreddits[19] and Twitter accounts,[20] but we'll only cover one more here: the bait-and-switch.[21] Here, the product "hooks" you by promising you one thing, only to deliver something else.

The best-known example of this comes from comedian Hasan Minhaj, who called out tax preparation products like TurboTax and H&R Block. These companies promised users 100% free tax preparation — only to slap them with a paywall once they were halfway through, refusing to let them continue their work unless they upgraded.[22]

Another infamous example came from Microsoft, which wanted reluctant Windows 7 users to upgrade to Windows 10. A popup appeared on Windows 7 users' screens, saying that their device would be upgraded to Windows 10. The popup's "X" button didn't cancel the upgrade, as people thought — it actually made the device upgrade![23] Windows drew sharp criticism for working against established UX patterns and upgrading users' computers without their consent.[24]

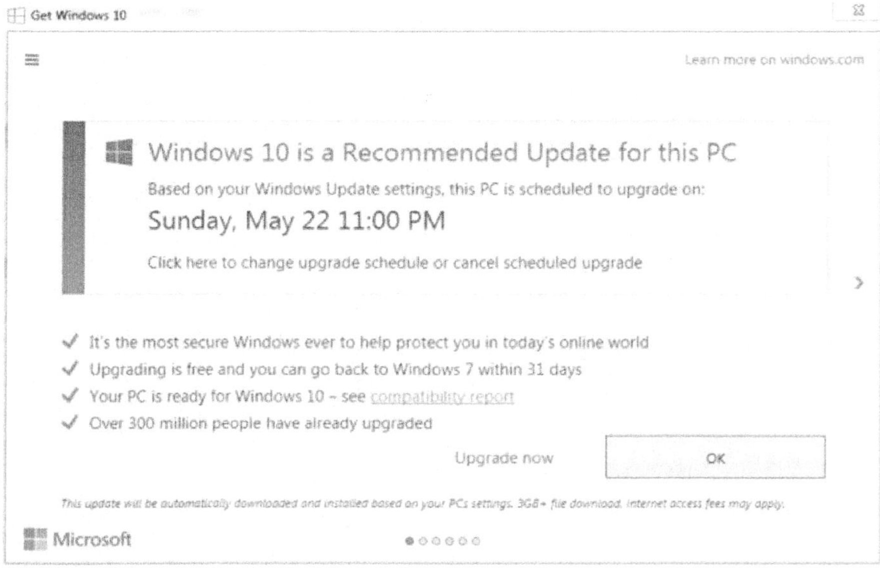

The confusing — and deceptive — popup that Microsoft showed to Windows 7 users. It was intended to get users to upgrade to Windows 10. Source: Dark Patterns[25]

Plenty of smaller products are even more brazen in their use of this tactic (a recurring trend). The grammar-checking site Grammarly is infamous for "finding" grammar errors and plagiarism in free users' uploaded writing samples, prompting these users to upgrade to the paid tier to find and fix these issues. But when you upgrade, these issues mysteriously disappear.[26]

The sleaziest of all came from the image-hosting site Photobucket, which once emailed free-tier users implying that the site had their NSFW pictures and would only let them take the pictures down if they signed up for the paid tier.[27] Needless to say, Photobucket probably didn't have pictures like that.

Win-win experiences

The whole idea of dishonest patterns rests on the mistaken assumption that the tension between business and user goals is zero-sum — that the only way for the business to win is for the user to lose. Great PMs know that that's not true, though.[a] For one, angering your users doesn't pay off in the long run. And more importantly, it's very possible to craft user experiences that make both users and your bottom line happy.

The IKEA hero's journey

To see this, look no further than IKEA. Few people would consider furniture shopping a fun family outing, but IKEA shoppers would beg to differ.

In most big-box furniture stores, there's no sense of progress as you move through the store. Items are scattered — bedding here, desks there, chairs over there — so you're endlessly trudging back and forth, never feeling like you're getting closer to finishing. Every minute feels the same.

Meanwhile, IKEA stores are laid out to make the very experience of shopping an adventure — a *hero's journey*, to borrow a term from literature.[28][b]

[a]The corollary: dishonest patterns are a sign that the PM doesn't have this important experience.

[b]The hero's journey, also known as the *monomyth*, refers to a common narrative arc[29] that's found in stories as diverse as Harry Potter, Star Wars, the Bible,[30] and the Indian epic the Ramayana. The hero is called to action, leaves their homeland to fight some great evil, and returns with blessings for their fellow people.[31]

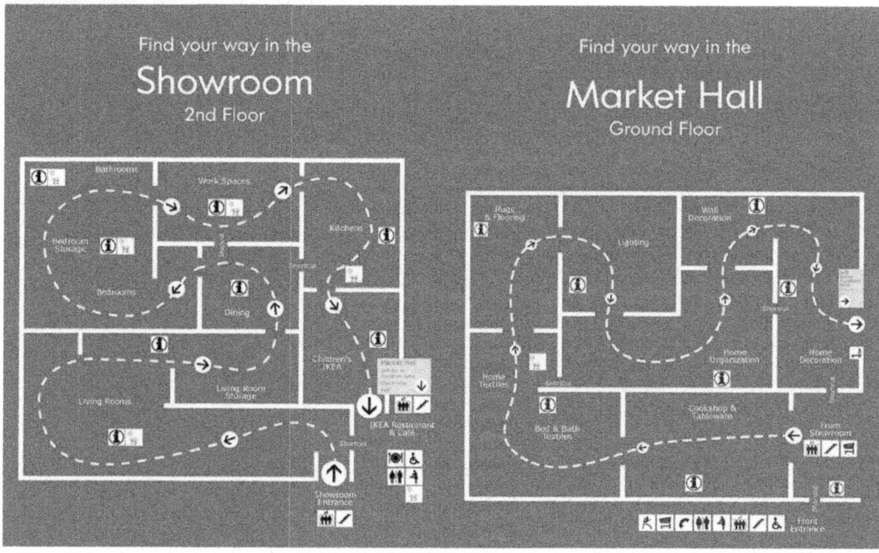

A map of an IKEA store, showing that the stores aren't confusing mazes but rather linear "adventures." Source: Shouts from the Abyss[32]

You might not have noticed this, but IKEA stores are anything but a maze: while the hallways are full of twists and turns, the experience is highly linear.[c] Part one of your adventure is finding furniture; you walk through living rooms, dining rooms, bedrooms and kitchens. You take a break and grab a cinnamon roll at the restaurant, then enter the "Marketplace" to pick up goodies like cooking wares, rugs, and wall decor.[34]

Then, at the conclusion of your epic journey, you enter the majestic warehouse to pick up the spoils of your adventure, the massive cardboard boxes that contain the goods you worked so hard to identify with your miniature pencils and paper pads. Just listen to how one IKEA shopper

[c] IKEA is thus a labyrinth rather than a maze. A maze is a puzzle with branches and dead ends, while a labyrinth is a single twisting path. A labyrinth isn't about the challenge but rather the experience of going through an epic journey. Incidentally, this is why labyrinths are common in churches.[33]

described her family's experience entering the warehouse:[35]

> *The stacks of boxes reach far into the sky like leaves in a Redwood forest. The smell of cedar, pine, chestnut, and wicker flood the senses and massages away the stress of the day. Children have been emancipated from their colorful holding cells and they screech happily throughout this room like parrots during a mating ritual.*

The point of this parable is not to teach you about retail store design but rather to show that IKEA's design is both profitable and a lot of fun. IKEA becomes a fun family outing, packed with adventure, playrooms for kids[36], sweet treats[d], and the thrill of a bargain. It's less a chore than a day trip.

And yet IKEA gets shoppers to pick out furniture, drag it to the checkout, and assemble it for free, which helps keep costs down.[37] The linearity of the store reduces the need for associates on the floor, which further cuts costs;[38] linearity also ensures that customers have to look at everything on display, which helps drive additional sales. The wafting smell of cinnamon rolls and meatballs throughout the store also helps IKEA make money off food sales.[39] Combined, these have helped a previously obscure Swedish store become a fixture in over three dozen countries around the world.[40]

IKEA shows us, in short, that profit and user experience don't have to be at odds. In fact, they can reinforce each other and let you get the best of both worlds.

Glossier

There are many glowing things we could say about the user experience of Glossier, the popular direct-to-consumer beauty company.[41]

[d]Make sure you get Daim chocolates at your next IKEA trip.

Glossier's iconic pink bubble-wrap pouch, which all Glossier products come packaged in. Source: Catalyxta[42]

For one, the physical products are delightful: Glossier products, which range from skincare to makeup to fragrances, all come swaddled in an iconic pink bubble wrap pouch with a white-and-red zipper.[43] These pouches are so beloved, and so useful, that many customers repurpose them as makeup bags, clutches,[44] passport holders, and even pencil cases.[45e] This establishes a sense of deep customer loyalty,[47] which in turn helps the bottom line by letting Glossier charge higher prices.

[e] You can even buy the pouches by themselves on Glossier's website![46]

Glossier encourages its customers to become "micro-influencers" by taking photos of themselves wearing Glossier makeup and tagging them with #YesGlossier on social media. Source: Instagram[48]

Then there's the app, which lets users see how a given product looks on women of many different skin tones. This solves a major pain point — it's hard to know how most makeup products look on your exact skin tone — and also makes users of all skin tones feel included.[49] Welcoming customers who feel left out by the usual beauty companies is great for those customers, but also for Glossier's business.

But Glossier's most creative way of aligning business and user needs comes from its social media strategy. Glossier encourages its customers to take pictures of themselves wearing Glossier products and post pictures tagged with #YesGlossier on Instagram; Glossier amplifies chosen customers on its website.[50] In fact, Glossier even uses these customer pictures on its product pages in place of professional models' pictures![51]

Glossier uses customer-submitted pictures on its product pages. Here, a woman showcases a tube of blush. Source: Glossier[52]

This is great for both Glossier and customers. Aspiring influencers can get exposure across the internet, while Glossier gets free word-of-mouth marketing and gets people to take beautiful pictures of its products for free.[53]

Glossier shows that it's possible — and, indeed, encouraged — to achieve both user and business goals. "Honest patterns," if you will, are very much in reach.

Conclusion

GROCERY STORES AREN'T always the most pleasant places to go. Standing in a checkout line feels like a waste of time, while self-checkout stations require you to obey the irritating requests of a machine and work for the store for free. Plus, the robotic sound of "Unexpected Item In The Bagging Area, Please Wait For An Attendant" is beyond grating.[1]

So Amazon's cashierless Go stores were an instant hit when they debuted in Seattle in 2016.[2] The Go stores didn't try to make the self-checkout process friendlier or shorten the lines for the human cashiers — it eliminated the "interface" of paying for products entirely. Amazon uses cameras to track your movement throughout the store and automatically charges your Amazon account once you walk through the gates with your items.[3]

Inside an Amazon Go store in Seattle. Source: Wikimedia[4]

No cashiers, no lines, no waiting — the store was tremendously convenient. And it was enormously popular. By 2020, Amazon had expanded to over two dozen Go stores across the United States.[5]

If conventional grocery stores' irritating checkout "interfaces" are like those confusing Norman doors, then Amazon Go stores are like automatic sliding doors: the interface completely disappears. With no interface, there's no friction, no source of accessibility problems, and no mental overhead. Once you get over the initial shock of being able to walk out of a store without pulling out your wallet,[6] the Amazon Go store becomes so simple that even someone who's never been to a store before could use it. In short, many times the best interface is no interface at all.[7]

Granted, you can't always eliminate the interface: you can't do a CT scan without a CT machine. And sometimes people enjoy using ornate interfaces like those of record players or expensive watches. But most of the time, people aren't using your product for the interface. Nobody goes to a store because they enjoy the checkout process; nobody watches Netflix to see the video-picking screens. If it's possible to make the interface fade into the background, it's usually a good idea — just look at Amazon Go.

This humility is important for product managers. People are seeking certain utility, experiences, and delight out of your products. The more that you can get out of the way and deliver that to them, the happier they'll be. ❦

88 All QR codes from Part IV

In case you skipped over any QR codes from the last few chapters, here's a roundup. Scan them with your phone to watch bonus videos and try interactive demos.

A game that challenges you to work around some of the absolute worst UI design patterns ever created:

userinyerface.com/game.html

Voice assistants and the future of user interfaces:

productalliance.com/videos/voice

V

Data Science

Data! Data! Data! I cannot make bricks without clay.

— Sherlock Holmes

Introduction

On January 13, 2000, Bill Gates stepped down from his post as Microsoft CEO, and his longtime ally Steve Ballmer took the reins.[1] Ballmer was a businessman at heart: he joined Microsoft after dropping out of Stanford's MBA program[2] and rose to become the company's VP of Sales.[3] And as a businessman, he knew his goal had to be to boost Microsoft's revenue and profits.[4]

Ballmer spent his 14-year tenure at the helm milking Microsoft's cash cows, pumping resources behind Windows and Office and seeking to make them more dominant than ever.[5] He fended off competing operating systems like Linux and office suites like Google Docs,[6] built the $8.9 billion Xbox division to protect Windows from Sony's PlayStation video gaming line,[7] and shored up Office by buying Skype for $8.5 billion.[8] He even set up a $20 billion new enterprise business, creating business tools like SharePoint, Exchange, and Dynamics CRM.[9]

Ballmer had set out to improve the bottom line, and he delivered. Microsoft's annual revenue tripled from $23 billion in 2000 to $78 billion in 2013, Ballmer's last full year as CEO. Ballmer also nearly tripled the company's annual profit to $22 billion by 2013.[10] By this data, Ballmer was a phenomenal CEO.

It's said around Silicon Valley (and Redmond, for that matter) that data wins arguments.[11] Data is how your team and company measure their success, it's a key part of how you decide your strategy, and it informs your product decisions. Ballmer focused hard on the financial numbers, and many of Microsoft's actions during the 2000s were a direct result of that.

Knowing how to measure data is important, and knowing how to move the numbers you care about is important as well. We'll cover that in this part of the book. But even more important is knowing how to choose the right data to care about in the first place — and that's one of the PM's most important jobs. We'll cover that, more than anything, in this part.

And we'll find that your choice of data matters. In Ballmer's case, a slightly different look at the data shows why he may not have been all that great after all.

Chapter 20

Distributions of Data

ONE OF THE CORE PARTS of your job as a product manager is to look at data: user data, sales data, logs data, economic data, and so on. Data tends to form shapes and patterns — and you have to be able to read it to find insights. Let's start by looking at the shapes that data can take.

The normal distribution

Perhaps the most famous "shape" that data can take is the *normal distribution*, also called the *bell curve* or the *Gaussian distribution.*[1] It shows the spread of data that clusters around an average and falls off above and below that average; real-life examples of normally-distributed values include people's heights,[2] blood pressures,[3] test scores, prices of goods,[4] and so on.

In tech, ratings (of ecommerce products, Airbnb houses, etc.) are often normally distributed. For a good real-world example, take Uber driver ratings, which were leaked in 2015:[5]

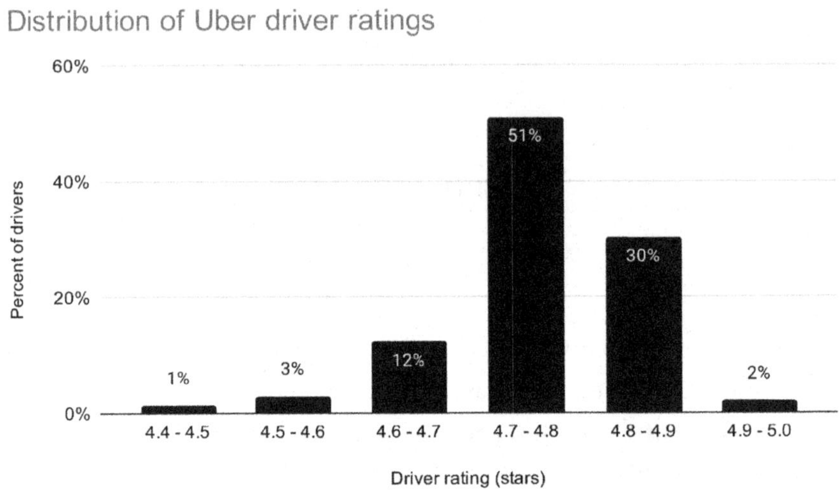

The distribution in the ratings of Uber drivers (from one to five stars). Source: Business Insider[6]

From a glance at the graph, you see that the distribution looks pretty bell-shaped, or normal, though it's a little fatter on the right side (4.8 to 4.9 stars) than on the left side (below 4.6 stars). The reason for that, incidentally, is that Uber deactivates drivers whose ratings stay below 4.6 stars.[7]

Describing the distribution

We can describe the shape of a normal distribution using two variables, or *parameters*: the mean, represented with the Greek letter μ (mu), and the *standard deviation*, represented with the Greek letter σ (sigma). The standard deviation, roughly speaking, measures how spread out the distribution is. Higher standard deviations lead to taller peaks around the mean and thinner tails.

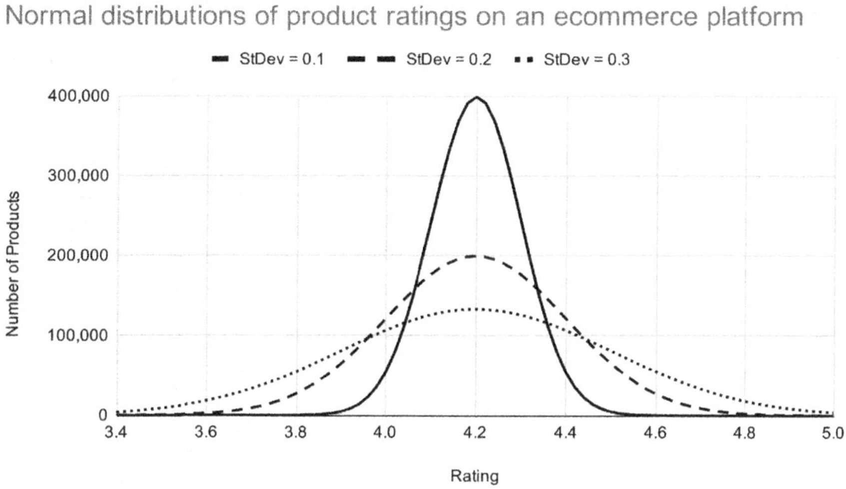

Three normal distributions, each with the same mean (μ) but different standard deviations (σ).

We can summarize the distribution using the notation $N(\mu, \sigma)$.[8] Looking at the Uber rating graph, it looks like the average rating is somewhere between 4.7 and 4.8 stars; let's call it 4.75. So $\mu = 4.75$.

The standard deviation is a bit harder to read off the graph. For this, we can use the rule of thumb that about 68% of data points fall within one standard deviation of the mean, 95% fall within two standard deviations, and 99.7% fall within three standard deviations.[9] This is known, quite conveniently, as the *68–95–99.7 rule.*

Looking at the Uber graph, we can see that 93% of drivers (12% + 51% + 30%) had a rating between 4.6 and 4.9. That's roughly 95%, so we can say that 4.6 is two standard deviations below the mean and 4.9 is two standard deviations above. Since each end of the range is 0.15 stars away from the mean, that means $2\sigma = 0.15$, or $\sigma = 0.075$. So, if you were a PM at Uber and wanted to concisely describe the distribution of driver ratings to an executive or data scientist, you could say that it's roughly $N(4.75, 0.15)$.

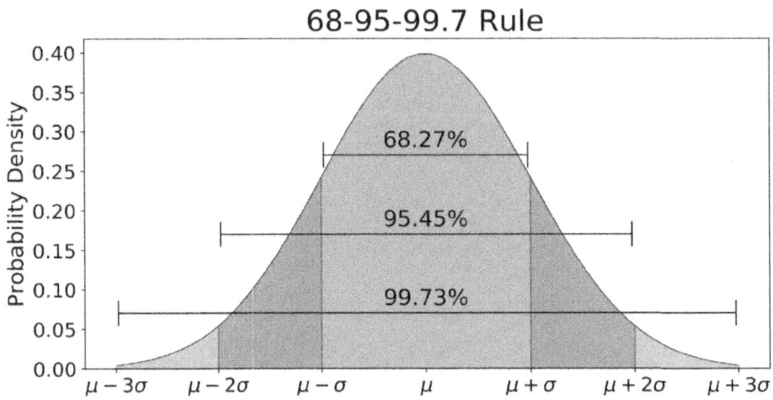

About 68% of items in a normal distribution fall within one standard deviation of the mean. Mathematically speaking, that's $\mu - \sigma$ to $\mu + \sigma$. About 95% fall within two standard deviations, and about 99.7% fall within three standard deviations. Source: Michael Galarnyk[10]

Skewed distributions

Not all distributions are normal, or even close to it. Many of them are fatter on one side or otherwise lopsided; you'll see this a lot with usage data or financial data like customer spending.

For instance, take the distribution of household income in the United States:[11]

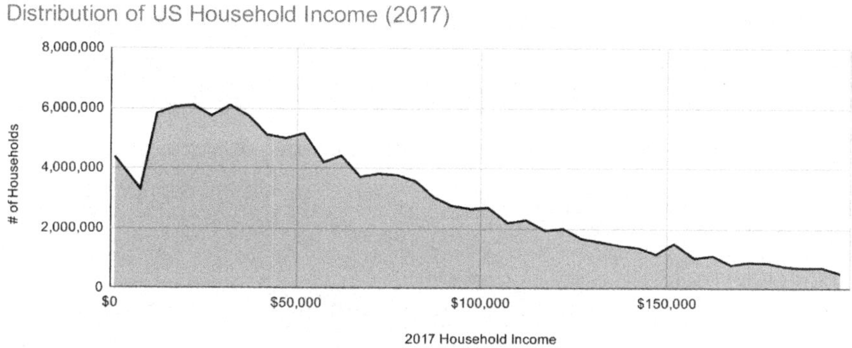

The distribution of income in the US has a long right tail. It's so long, in fact, that including people who make a billion dollars a year would require this graph to be over a thousand times wider. Source: US Census Bureau[12]

You can see that it looks somewhat like a normal distribution that got stretched out to the right. As you might expect, there are a lot more people clustered at the lower end of the distribution, with a long tail going out to higher incomes. (This graph doesn't even include people with incomes over $200,000 a year — meaning that this tail could go on for a long while.)

Because this distribution is asymmetrical, the mean isn't always the most useful metric here. Because the mean sums up everyone's incomes, it's very sensitive to outliers. In this case, those outliers would be named Bill Gates, Jeff Bezos, et al. The *median* is more useful here because it represents where the "middle" American is and doesn't get as wildly skewed by outliers.[13] If Jeff Bezos made a few extra billion dollars a year, the mean would get inflated while the median would stay the same — making the median more representative of the typical American's financial situation.

When there's a long right tail — as in this case — the mean tends to be dragged higher than the median; the opposite is true when there's a long left tail. In this example, the median US household income is \$61,423[14] while the mean household income is \$87,643.[15] (If you're curious, the mean income of every American would grow by \$8 if Bezos made an additional billion dollars, while the median would stay the same.)

Case study: social media

Another well-known example of a long-right-tail distribution is the distribution of the number of followers of social media users. Most people have a few dozen or hundred followers, while a handful of mega-influencers get multiple millions.

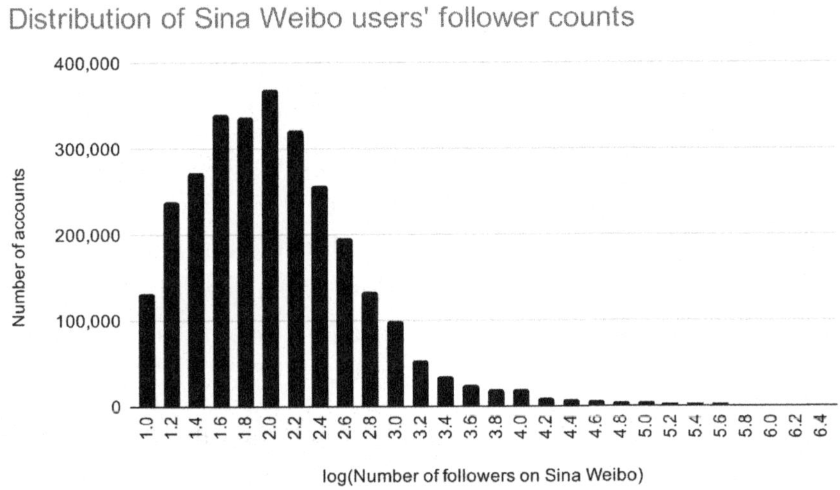

The distribution of followers of Sina Weibo users; Sina Weibo is a Chinese version of Twitter. It's strongly right-tailed; note that the X-axis uses a logarithmic scale. Source: Zhenkun Zhou[16]

Long-right-tail distributions, also known as *right-skewed distributions*, are common whenever a few people can command massive amounts of a scarce resource, whether it's money or social media followers. The distribution is somewhat normal for people on the lower end, but people at the higher end (the right tail) can really run up the score.[17]

The author Nassim Nicholas Taleb calls this situation *extremistan*: those with a small edge meet with outsized success because many human institutions provide non-linear rewards.[18] An especially lucky or talented mechanic might make 50% more than her peers, but an especially lucky or talented movie producer could create a hit movie that earns 20 times as much as the average movie.[a]

Power-law distributions

The distributions we saw earlier, while skewed, still look somewhat like a bell curve. But, as a PM, you'll probably see even more distributions that are so skewed that they don't look anything like a bell curve. These distributions peak right around zero, with a very long tail to the right.

Power distributions are very common when you're ranking things: there's a steep drop-off from the top things and the lower-down things. You'll notice this when you are, for example, ranking websites by the number of monthly visitors they get. The likes of Google, Wikipedia, Twitter, and Facebook get hundreds of millions of views, but beyond the top or so sites, there's a steep decline.

These right-skewed distributions are also common when you're ranking things: the #1 thing will obviously have a higher "bar" than the #2 thing, but the drop-off is usually quite steep. Consider a graph of the top 100 websites in the US.[19]

---

[a]Extremistan applies to PMs and entrepreneurs, too: many people will create moderately-successful products, while a few will make the next unicorn. We hope we can help you be among the latter group!

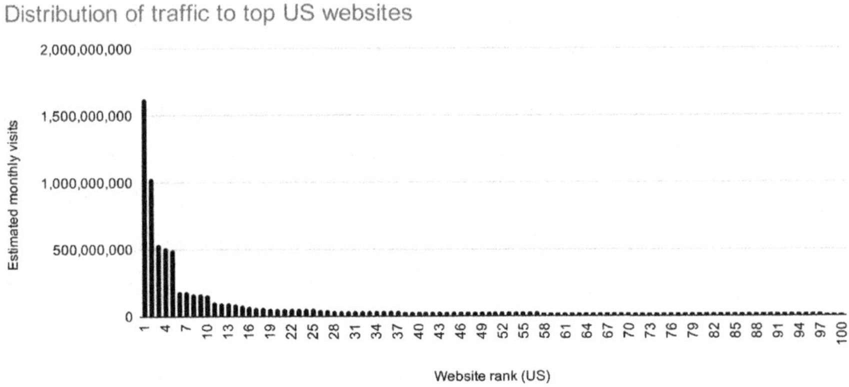

The distribution of visitors to the most-visited websites follows a power law. Source: Ahrefs[20]

Or consider the distribution of app downloads for the top US publishers on iOS and Android. The most successful publishers are many times more successful than the rest, leading to a quick drop-off with a long tail (though the tail here is fatter than the top websites example).

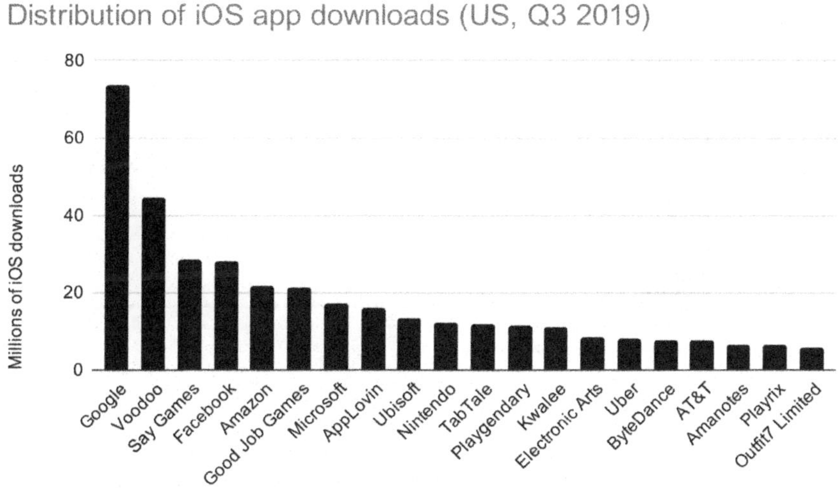

The ranking of the most-downloaded iOS app publishers shows a power-law distribution. Source: SensorTower[21]

The underlying math

Mathematically speaking, these long-right-tail distributions are often called *power-law distributions* because the underlying equation is something like $y = ax^{-b}$; note that the input variable x is raised to a "power."[22] For instance, the distribution of website hits can be approximated pretty well by a power law curve:[b]

[b] In this case, it's roughly $y = 1,600,000,000x^{-1}$.

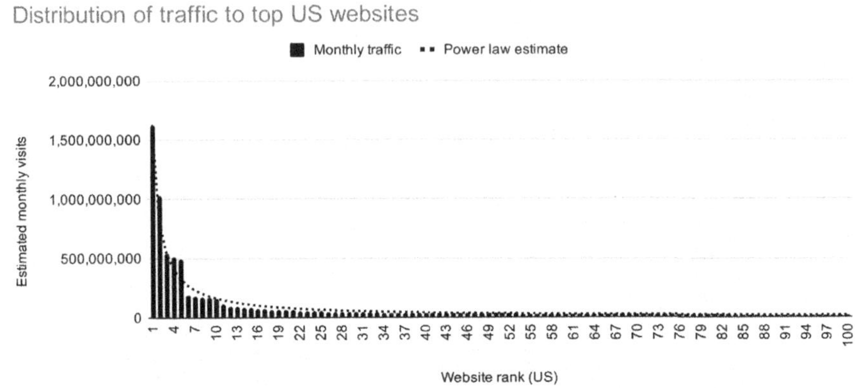

The website visitor distribution from before, except matched with a power-law curve to show how strongly it fits. Source: Ahrefs[23]

While a good PM knows that many distributions are right-skewed, a great PM can earn data scientists' respect by knowing how to identify and name a power law distribution.

Whales

There are several analytical tools that you can use once you've noticed that a distribution follows a power law. The most famous one is the *80/20 rule*, or the *Pareto principle*, which describes the usual shape of power-law distributions.[24] The rule is that about 80% of the action comes from 20% of the actors, or, more generally, the top 20% of a distribution contributes about 80% of the output. 20% of bugs cause 80% of crashes (as Microsoft famously found), 20% of customers produce 80% of revenue, 20% of features account for 80% of sales support calls, and so on.[25] (Some distributions are more or less skewed — for instance, the top 10% of US households owns 85% of stocks[26] — but the 80-20 rule is a good average.)

In our top websites example, the top 20 websites together account for 72.5% of the traffic of all the top 100 websites. In our example distribution of customers' monthly spending, the top 20% of users bring in 79.7% of revenue.

That bit about revenue is especially important, since it's key to many products' business models. In free-to-play games, for instance, developers put a lot of focus on a handful of extremely profitable customers that they call *whales*.[27] One gaming studio, for instance, found that 40% of their revenue for a phone game came from the 2% of players who spent $1,000 or more on the game; 90% of revenue came from those spending over $100. One whale even spent $6700![28] These studios' strategies revolve around finding and cultivating whales, who effectively pay for the massive pod of free-tier players.

The term "whale" isn't used as much outside the video game industry, but the 80/20 rule shows up in a lot of industries. In social media and other user-generated content products, there's a similar rule of thumb called the *90–9–1 rule*: 90% of your users are "lurkers" who post very little, 9% are "contributors" who comment on or share posts but don't make many posts of their own, and 1% are "creators" who actively create content.[29]

You could expect this rule to hold for Twitter, Facebook, Yelp, Rotten Tomatoes, and other such sites. In Twitter's case, one study found that 85% of tweets came from the top 15% of users[30] — something roughly between the classical 80/20 rule and the 90–9–1 rule.

Interview tip

Whenever a company earns variable amounts of money from a customer (whether you're selling in-app purchases or earning money from ads), think about how you can get more whales, since whales will be the source of most of the company's profit. If you can mention whales off the bat in an interview with such a company, you'll stand out immediately. For instance, you can bet that Slack, which charges companies for every employee, makes a lot of money from Fortune 500 companies, and that Instagram gets a lot of ad revenue from people who spend multiple hours on the app every day.

Note that the concept of whales isn't relevant if everyone's paying you the exact same amount, which is the case with consumer subscription services like Netflix.

The 80/20 rule can even apply to your job as a PM. One common rule of thumb is that 80% of your results will come from 20% of your tasks — so you should focus your energy on those 20% and cut out the activities that yield lower returns.[31] For instance, your team could get 80% of the impact by working on the top 20% of bugs — yielding a higher *ROI*, or return on investment, for your team's time.

Chapter 21

Experiments

ONE OF THE KEY TOOLS in a PM's toolbox is the experiment: it's the simplest, fastest way to see if a product change gets you closer to achieving your goals. While you may not be coding up the experiments yourself, you'll probably be tasked with designing the experiments, reviewing the data, and figuring out what to do next.

A/B testing

The most common type of experiment you'll run is an *A/B test*, where you compare how two *variants* of your product — "A" and "B" — perform on certain metrics you care about. You randomly assign one group of users to "A" and the other group to "B" and see how the metrics shake out; the theory is that, if the only thing that separates "A" and "B" is the version of the product they used, any metrics changes between "A" and "B" can be chalked up to your product. (You can compare more than two versions with a similar technique called *multivariate testing*,[1][a] but we'll focus on A/B testing here since it's simpler.)

A/B testing is a cheap way to see if your potential feature and product launches will help you meet your goals,[3] catch potential bad ideas before you ship them,[4] and test if your prototype ideas are worth pursuing. There's a reason that it's a key weapon in any PM's arsenal.

[a]Sometimes given the colorful name of *multi-armed bandit experiments*.[2]

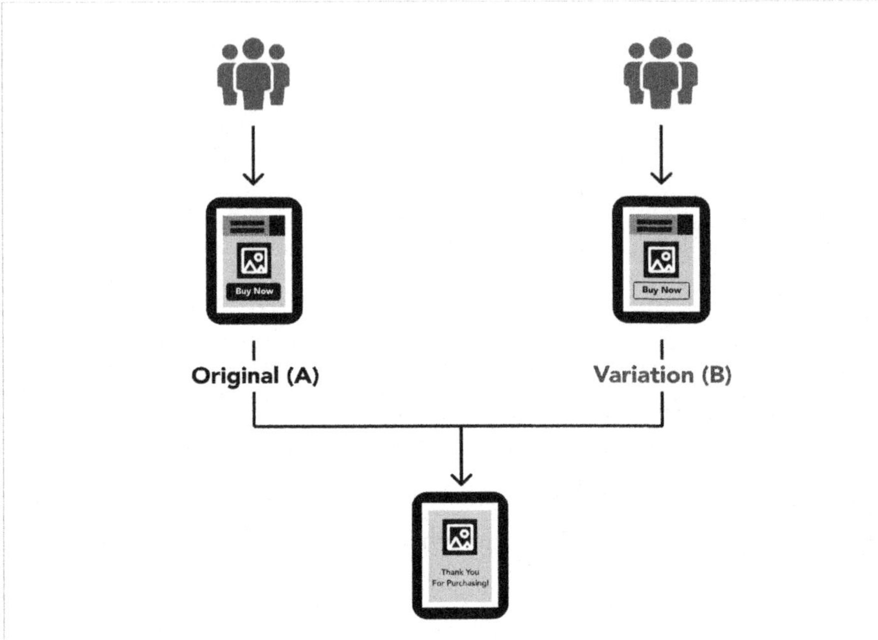

A/B tests show one variant of a feature to one group of users and a second variant to another group. Source: Optimizely[5]

The classic example of A/B testing is tweaking buttons on a website: does changing the text, color, size, or other features of the button increase how much people click on it?[6] But A/B testing is done in many, many places: Spotify A/B tests new user interface features,[7] Airbnb tests changes to its house-booking flow,[8] and Uber tests redesigned versions of its apps.[9] The most famous example of A/B testing, though, is when Google tried out 40 different shades of blue for its advertising links[10] and found that the winning color increased ad revenue by $200 million.[11]

It's hard to overstate just how common A/B testing is. All the way back in 2009, Google ran 12,000 A/B tests, and while just 10% of those led to noticeable improvements, those small wins add up.[12] Chances are that, every time you open a popular app, you're enrolled in one or more

A/B tests without even knowing about it.

Significance testing

Let's step through an example to show how you'd make sense of an A/B test.

Suppose you work at Facebook and wanted to launch a new feature designed to get users to spend more time on the Facebook website. You run an A/B test with two versions of the product: version "A" is the *control*, which doesn't include your feature, while version "B" is the experimental version, which does. You don't want to subject too many users to an experiment, so you give the control to 150 users but the experimental version to just 50. You plot your data on a graph.

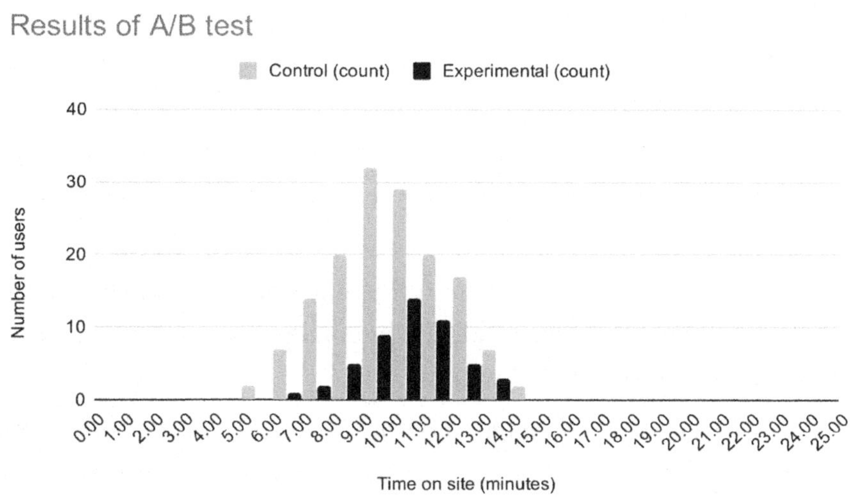

Example results from an A/B test that tests whether a new feature increases the time that Facebook users spend on the site.

The results look normally distributed, but more importantly, it *looks* like your experimental group of users spent a bit more time on the site! You run the numbers and find that the mean time on site (or *ToS*[13]) is 10 minutes for the control and 10.5 for the experimental.[b] It worked! You run to your boss's office to tell her the good news.

But hold on — you can't be so sure. You only tested on a small *sample* of your entire user base, so you can't be sure if the difference you saw was real. Perhaps your feature doesn't have any impact, and you just happened to choose a sample of users that spent more time on the site.[15]

Confidence intervals

To know for sure if the A/B test result was real, you have to run a *statistical significance test*. The idea is that you have some *null hypothesis* that you're trying to reject.[16] The null hypothesis is the most pessimistic view: that your new feature didn't actually change anything, and that the result you saw was just noise.

To figure out if we can reject the null hypothesis, we have to figure out whether or not the pattern we saw in our testing sample applies to the whole population. When we tested 200 people, we saw a ToS increase of 0.5 minutes; what would happen if we released the feature to our entire user base?

To estimate the impact on the full population, we construct a *confidence interval*, or *CI*. The confidence interval gives us a range that the actual value will probably fall within.[17]

Think of our experiment like shooting an arrow at an archery target. We aim our arrow at the bullseye, but we know that when we actually shoot (i.e. release to the entire population), the arrow might land somewhere else. The confidence interval tells us which "ring" our arrow is likely to fall in.

---

[b] Facebook's actual time on site is closer to 60 minutes per day,[14] but bear with us for this example.

An archery target, with rings radiating outward from the bullseye. Source: NeedPix[18]

The confidence interval is made with a specific *confidence level*, which represents how cautious we want to be. To use the archery example, we might say that we're 90% confident that we'll hit somewhere within the five innermost rings, or that we're 99% confident that we'll hit somewhere within the eight innermost rings. The higher confidence level we need, the wider our confidence interval needs to be. Practically speaking, 95% is the most commonly-used confidence level, though cautious statisticians and PMs might use 99%.[19]

To construct a confidence interval, we use a tool called *Student's two-*

tailed t-test.[c] You'll never have to compute this yourself — many companies have statistical software to compute it, and even humble Excel can calculate it for you.[20] Suffice to say that it'll give you a confidence interval for the difference of means.

In our Facebook example, the 95% confidence interval for the difference in means comes out to -0.080 to 1.065 minutes, written in shorthand as (–0.080, 1.065). This means that we're 95% certain that, if we launched this feature to the entire world, the ToS would change by somewhere between -0.080 and 1.065 minutes. Our 99% confidence interval, by the way, would be wider: (–0.261, 1.246). But let's stick with our 95% interval for now.

Notice that our 95% confidence interval includes both positive and negative numbers. This means that, if you released your feature to all Facebook users, there's a substantial chance that you'd actually *hurt* the time on site metric! (The exact chance that the real difference in means is zero or less, also known as the *p-value,*[21] is 0.092 in our experiment — that is, 9.2%. So there's a 9.2% chance that we actually hurt ToS!)

When our confidence interval includes zero, we fail to reject the null hypothesis.[d] We want to be 95% confident that anything we launch will improve our metrics, and the only way we can be this confident is if the entire 95% confidence interval is above zero. Thus, our A/B test isn't good enough to justify launching the feature to all of Facebook.

Had our confidence interval been, say, (0.1, 0.9), then we would have been able to say with 95% confidence that the feature would have increased ToS for all Facebook users. Or, simply, if our interval was all above zero, our result would have been statistically significant, and we would have been able to launch. (The p-value here would have been

[c]This only applies if you're measuring a *continuous variable* like time on site, which can be measured with a sliding scale. For *discrete variables* with a fixed number of values, like whether someone did or did not click on a button, you'd use *Pearson's chi-squared test.* Either way, you'll get a confidence interval at the end.

[d]You can never "accept" the null hypothesis; you can just fail to reject it.

less than 0.05, which is another way to show statistical significance and justify launching the feature.)

On the flip side, if our confidence interval was all below zero, like $(-0.6, -0.2)$, we would have been confident that our feature definitely would have reduced ToS for all Facebook users, and thus we probably would have canceled the feature.

Note that getting a confidence interval that includes zero isn't the end of the line for your feature. If your mean was above zero, you could try to shrink the confidence interval so that the entire interval is above zero. The best way to shrink the confidence interval is to run a bigger trial;[22] if you worked at Facebook and really got a result like our example, your next step might be to test on 1000 users instead of 200.[e]

Sampling

Now that you know how to interpret an A/B test, it's worth looking at how you choose who gets placed in the "A" and "B" buckets.

On one hand, you want there to be enough people in your experimental group to get good results. As we mentioned before, the larger your sample group, the tighter your confidence interval and thus the easier it is for you to get a statistically significant result.[24] Usually, quadrupling your sample size will cut the width of your confidence interval in half (it's a $1/\sqrt{n}$ relationship).[25]

On the other hand, it's risky to roll out a feature with an unknown metrics impact to a wide range of users, and people may get confused or annoyed if they see many of their friends getting a feature while they don't get anything (remember, your average user has no idea what an A/B test is and assumes products are the same for everyone).

---

[e] This is why political polls try to have the biggest possible n, or number of participants: it minimizes their *margin of error*, which is similar to the confidence interval.[23]

Big tech companies have developed a rule of thumb to balance these competing desires: the *1% experiment*, pioneered by Google.[26] Here, 1% of your user base should get the experimental feature, while 99% should be in the control group. If your user base is big enough, even 1% of users should be a large enough sample size to give you a good chance of getting conclusive results. If you're working on a much smaller product — say, a startup product with a few hundred users — you will likely need to roll out the change to a larger percentage of your user base to get statistically significant results.

Staged rollouts

A/B testing is such a common tool for product managers that many companies build it into their regular product deployment processes. At companies like Google and Facebook, for example, most features are automatically deployed to 1% of the user base once they're coded up. After a few days of data collection, the PM reviews the A/B test results to ensure the metrics changes look good. Only then can the feature be released more broadly.

But features rarely go straight from 1% to 100% of users; there are many intermediate steps. At each step, the feature gets more and more exposure and the PM can get more and more data about the metrics impact. Each step is thus an A/B test with a progressively larger experimental group.

Right after the 1% experiment, a feature might go to beta testers outside the company. New Windows features, for instance, go to "Windows Insider Preview" customers before they reach the average Windows user.[27]

After that, the feature might slowly ramp up to the general public: first 5%, then 10%, 20%, and so on. Eventually it'll be ready for prime time, but even at that point, it won't go all the way to 100%. At big tech companies, features are usually launched to just 95% or 99% of users, with the rest in a *holdback* group that doesn't get the feature.[28][29]

This gives you one last chance to make sure that the launch will have the desired metrics impact, since once you go to 100% there's no more control group and thus no ability to run A/B tests. Only once you're dead-set on the feature should you go to 100%. (In fact, some features never actually hit 100% and are permanently set at 95% or 99%, since that lets you do A/B testing forever.)

Established companies usually have a workflow that automates all these steps, but smaller companies may not — which is where you, the PM, come in.

The New Zealand strategy

The sampling strategy we've explained so far is pretty simple: give the feature to a randomly-chosen subset of users. It works fairly well because your experimental and control groups will be very similar; the only major difference between them is that the experimental group gets the feature while the control group doesn't.

This strategy is fine for features that only impact the individual user, like "Buy Now" buttons and redesigned user interfaces. But many features rely on users interacting with each other and thus don't work very well with random sampling.[30] Imagine if you launched a feature that let users pay each other: it's only useful to a user if they can use it with all their friends, but if you did a 1% experiment, users with the feature would have a very hard time finding friends to use the feature with. When Twitter rolled out its Group DM feature, the company couldn't roll it out to every 100th user — the feature would be useless to the people who got it, since they couldn't write to most of their friends.[31]

Social networks often have this problem, since few features are used by people in isolation. Most of their features are, obviously, social. To get around this, Facebook has developed a "New Zealand strategy": when

A/B testing a new feature, give it to everyone in a small, isolated country like New Zealand.[32] If you assume that New Zealanders mostly talk to fellow Kiwis, everyone in New Zealand will be able to test the feature effectively, since everyone they know will also have the feature. And yet only a fraction of the global population will get the feature, similar to a 1% experiment. (Why New Zealand? It's a Western country with a culture similar to the United States', so it'll give a good approximation of how the feature would work in the US.)

For example, in 2017 Facebook launched a feature called Discover People in New Zealand before taking it to the rest of the world. This feature lets users easily find people who have things in common with them, perhaps people who work for the same company or who've gone to the same events.[33] This feature only really works if everyone involved has access to it, since it would be weird to get a friend request from someone through the Discover People feature if you didn't have access to it yourself. Thus, the New Zealand strategy was a perfect fit.

Interestingly, many companies besides Facebook have discovered the power of testing in New Zealand. Microsoft first launched the website creation tool Sway here, Dominos tested out drone-powered pizza delivery on the islands, and Kiwis were among the first people to get Pokémon GO.[34]

💼 Interview tip

If you're interviewing at a big company, the New Zealand strategy is a great one to mention when you're talking about A/B tests. You can go a step further by slowly rolling out to progressively larger English-speaking countries before you hit the United States. From New Zealand (population 5 million), you could hit Ireland (5 million), Australia (25 million), Canada (40 million), and the UK (65 million) before hitting the US (330 million).[35]

More generally, you can A/B test social features with any small community whose members mostly talk to each other. For instance, a social network could roll out a polling feature to just members of one of those "X Memes for Y Teens" meme groups.[36]

The dangers of non-randomness

The pitfall with strategies like this is that you're breaking the assumption of randomness, so you aren't guaranteed that your experimental group will be exactly like the control group. (If New Zealanders are especially tech-savvy, for instance, they may use a feature differently than the general population.) You have to be able to prove that your experimental group is *representative* of the general population.

Also remember that features may resonate differently with users in different cultures. The classic example is colors: red is associated with danger in the West, but good luck and spirituality in South and East Asia, for instance; while white is associated with purity and peace in the West, but death and mourning in China. Users in different countries might react differently if you, say, change your buttons' colors, so it's often not enough to test in just one country.[37] (Incidentally, blue is considered the "safest" color since it has generally positive associations everywhere[38] — which is a big reason why so many tech products use blue in their user interfaces and logos.[39])

Pitfalls

While A/B testing is a powerful tool, it comes with a lot of caveats and pitfalls. You should never blindly run A/B tests and automatically do whatever they say.

Metrics aren't always law

The main reason for this is that metrics don't always tell the complete story. The classic example of this is Google's 40-shades-of-blue experiment to find the best shade for ad links.[40] This experiment angered Google's designers, who felt it was yet another example of Google blindly obeying A/B tests and building a Frankenstein's monster of a product that had no consistent design language.[41] That is, a well-designed product has a consistent user interface, color scheme, and behavior, but running a bunch of A/B tests to micro-optimize each part of the user interface leads you to create a mishmash of styles that gives the product no coherent design. It's great that A/B testing is objective, but it doesn't account for subjective things like design; blindly obeying A/B tests will anger your designers at best and give you a bad-looking product at worst.

A disgruntled ex-Google designer explained his complaints about this case well:[42]

> *When a company is filled with engineers, it turns to engineering to solve problems. Reduce each decision to a simple logic problem. Remove all subjectivity and just look at the data. Data in your favor? OK, launch it. Data shows negative effects? Back to the drawing board. And that data eventually becomes a crutch for every decision, paralyzing the company and preventing it from making any daring design decisions.*

What's more, improving your metrics in the short term may not actually help your business in the long term. For instance, Bing once ran an experiment that raised queries per user by 10% and revenue per user by 30%. It looked like a slam dunk.

But, on closer inspection, it turned out that the experiment contained a bug that made the search results terrible, which forced users to run more searches and click on more results to get answers to their questions, thus increasing the number of searches and ad clicks. But it frustrated users and would have led them to abandon Bing down the line.[43] Making the search results worse would temporarily boost metrics but hurt them in the long run. This means two things: the PM should have chosen a better metric to optimize for (like the number of times a user returned to Bing, which would have captured potential frustrations[44]) and not placed so much stock in metrics in the first place.

Opt-in features

One mistake we see a lot is PMs running A/B tests on opt-in features.[45] Risk-averse executives might suggest that PMs make a controversial or risky feature opt-in before running an A/B test, since they wouldn't want to risk giving the feature to average users who didn't ask for anything so risky. (This has happened to us before!)

An example was Twitter's ambitious "2.0" redesign in 2015;[46] PMs at the company decided to make early versions of the redesign opt-in so that users who liked the old design wouldn't be forced off it. But then Twitter PMs decided to run an A/B test, where they'd compare metrics for the users who opted into the new design against metrics for users who stayed with the old one.[47]

The problem was that the control and experimental groups were very different — the people willing to try the redesign were probably bigger Twitter fans than the rest — so the A/B test results couldn't be trusted. If the test results showed that people using the redesigned app sent more tweets, was that because the redesign helped people tweet more, or because the people using the redesign tweeted more to begin with? There was no good way to tell.

In our minds, the best way to A/B test risky features is to give the feature to a randomly-chosen subset of beta testers. Users who are comfortable with risk opt in to the beta version of the product, so they've given their "consent" to get risky features. And, while beta testers are quite different from the general population, the beta testers you randomly chose to get the feature won't be significantly different from the beta testers you didn't give the feature to. This strategy lets you run an effective A/B test while minimizing risk, though you have to be sure that you have enough beta testers to get large enough sample sizes and that your beta-testing group is representative of the broader population.

The big splash theory

You may not always want to stealthily roll out a feature via A/B testing. In some cases, there's more benefit to making a big splash.[48]

For instance, major tech companies like announcing new products at conferences like Google's I/O[49], Microsoft's Ignite[50] and Inspire,[51] or Facebook's F8.[52] Making big splashes like this is a great way to draw positive press, excite users, and show investors that your company is taking big steps.

The downside, of course, is that you can't back out of launching the product once you've publicly committed to it. If the numbers look bad after launch, you won't be able to cancel the product very easily. Still, you can launch the product to just a few users at the start, run A/B tests to fine-tune it, and only then release it to the wider world. This is, in fact, exactly what Facebook Dating did: Facebook announced the product at the F8 conference in 2018[53] and rolled it out to 20 countries in 2019[54] before it tried to launch to the wider world.[55]

That said, you can always announce a big feature at a conference and roll it out slowly with A/B tests. But, since you've already committed to the feature, you can't roll it back if your metrics look bad. Still, A/B testing can let you tweak certain parameters of the product before you give it to everyone.

Also note that you can't A/B test hardware, since it's far harder to tweak hardware, and you certainly can't do it on the fly. Hardware products rely far more on internal testing, or *dogfooding*, or prototype pieces of hardware.[56] That's the closest you can get to an A/B test for hardware products.

Cherry-picking

One unscientific tactic that shows up around the world is cherry-picking: looking through a sea of data that doesn't support your viewpoint and picking out the few pieces that happen to support you, thus making it look like the data overall is in your favor.[57]

This happens at tech companies, too. Twitter's A/B tests report hundreds of metrics, and chances are that even an "unsuccessful" A/B test would randomly make statistically-significant-looking changes to a few of those metrics.[58] An otherwise ineffectual A/B test might, say, lead to a statistically significant increase in retweets from iPhone users in Argentina (but nowhere else). It would be unscientific (and a sign of an unskilled PM) to claim that this result was a sign that the experiment was a success — there's no good reason that iPhone users in Argentina would behave differently than everyone else.

In fact, these freak "results" are always going to happen. PMs usually use 95% confidence intervals in A/B tests; that means that, if our confidence interval excludes zero (i.e. it looks statistically significant), we think there's a less than 5% chance that the true value is zero or less.[f] This means that, if you run enough tests, it becomes likely that at least one of them mistakenly shows statistical significance.[59]

The same logic applies in sports. If you only make 5% of your shots in a basketball game, you're not a very good player — but, even if you're that bad, you'll probably make at least one basket if you shoot enough times. (Indeed, the math says that you'll make an average of one basket over 20 shots.)

The webcomic *xkcd* satirically explained this by having scientists test if jelly beans cause acne using 20 different colors of bean; there's no real

[f]If you run a two-tailed t-test, as we suggest in this chapter, and get a confidence interval that's all positive, there's actually a less than 2.5% chance. This is because the 5% of the "area" outside the confidence interval is split across two tails: one below the lower bound (which includes zero) and one above the upper bound (which is even higher).

connection, but since scientists are comfortable with a 5% error rate, it was expected that one color of bean would show a phantom connection to acne. The scientists found that green jelly beans had a connection to acne (while none of the other 19 flavors did), leading an unintelligent newspaper to make a sensational headline that green jelly beans cause acne — when, really, anyone could have found a phantom result like that just by testing enough colors.[60]

A satirical piece by the webcomic xkcd, *poking fun at the media for cherry-picking scientists' outlier findings. Source: xkcd*[61]

Because A/B testing will often lead to some phantom "statistically significant" metrics changes, you shouldn't look at all the metrics after you run your experiment and cherry-pick the ones that happen to look good (or bad). This tactic is known as *HARKing*, or Hypothesizing After the Results are Known, and is considered scientific malpractice.[62] PMs should do what Twitter suggests and decide which metrics they want to consider before they run the experiment — and only look at those once the experiment is done.[63]

Neel once ran into this problem when he was working on Google Search. He was working on a feature that would add Google Doodles animations to the Pixel phones' home screens[64] and knew users would be excited. The problem was that people on other teams worried that adding a dancing cartoon to the home screen could hurt Android or Search metrics.

A Google Doodle appearing on a Pixel phone's home screen search bar. Source: XDA Developers[65]

So Neel ran a 1% experiment and found that most relevant metrics weren't significantly affected, which was good news for his team. But at an executive review, someone found that one of the dozens of metrics was significantly down (the whole confidence interval was below zero) and used that to argue against his feature.

Neel showed that metrics related to this one weren't negative, and because of the 5% error rate that statisticians are comfortable with, it's very likely that one of the dozens of metrics would randomly happen to turn out negative, even though nothing was really happening. This explanation satisfied the critics, who let the feature launch to 95% of users.

And when the results from that broader experiment came in, the team found that the original offending metric hadn't changed significantly, supporting Neel's argument that the drop during the 1% experiment was just an illusion.

▶ Watch this

There are all kinds of statistical pitfalls you have to watch out for when analyzing data. Watch this mock interview with a Microsoft PM where she walks through a seeming statistical paradox: the average Uber driver rating in Washington state is higher than the average Lyft rating, and the same is true for Oregon, but when you combine the two states' data the average Lyft rating becomes higher. (This is called *Simpson's Paradox*.)

productalliance.com/videos/explainer

Countermetrics

It's also not enough to look at success metrics, the metrics you hope will go up if your experiment is successful. You also need to look at so-called *countermetrics*, which are metrics that might be hurt if your success metrics are helped.[66]

For instance, a Netflix experiment that increases the quality of videos sent out to users (like, say, giving everyone 4K movies) might increase customer satisfaction — but it might also increase Netflix's server and bandwidth costs. Similarly, bringing a lot of casual new users to your website's landing page might give your new-user numbers a boost but might also increase the rate at which users leave your product (known as the *churn rate*).[67]

You can also think of countermetrics as pairs of metrics that would be incomplete without each other. For example, the customer acquisition cost (CAC) and the customer lifetime value (LTV) are countermetrics because you need to know both to know if your customer acquisition strategy is good: recall that you succeed when your CAC is sufficiently lower than your LTV. Just knowing one of the two doesn't give you a complete picture: your CAC going up is no big deal if your LTV is also going up, but if your CAC goes up while your LTV flatlines, then you have a problem.[68]

Countermetrics are closely related to the notion of *cannibalization*,[69] which happens when one of your products eats up the market share of another product. It looks good for the one product, but your company overall is no better off. Suppose your company offers an $11-per-month subscription service and you test out a new $9-per-month student tier. Your success metric would be the uptake of your student tier, but your countermetric would be the usage of the original tier. If millions of people fled the $11 tier for your $9 tier, your success metric would look good — but your countermetric would help you catch that you weren't really helping the company at all.

Novelty and learning

Finally, we'll note that the effects you initially see in your A/B tests may not last. Because of the *novelty effect* and the *learning effect*, your initial metrics might be higher or lower than their long-term values, respectively.[70]

The *novelty effect* describes changing a feature might draw users' attention to it and make them temporarily click or engage more — a change that evaporates over time. For instance, a link on the MSN.com homepage normally opens Hotmail in the same tab, but Microsoft once ran an A/B test that made Hotmail open in a new tab instead. Microsoft saw a large jump in the number of people who opened the Hotmail link — but it wasn't because the user experience was better. Instead, users were just surprised by the link's new behavior and clicked the link more to see what was happening. The effect eventually died out.[71]

Had Microsoft declared victory after just a few days of testing, they might have implemented a change that didn't have a durable impact on user behavior. To avoid wasting effort, it was important that Microsoft waited.

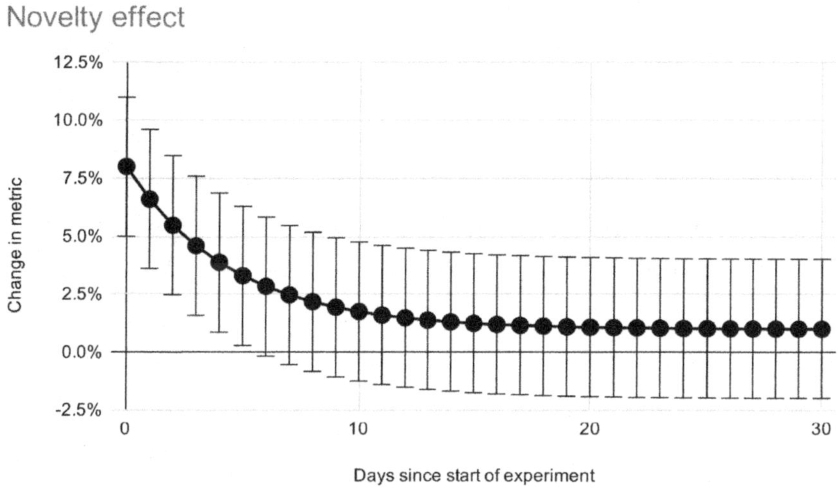

The results of an example experiment over time, showcasing the novelty effect. The error bars show the uncertainty around the metric's value: if the error bars cross zero, that means that the metrics wasn't significantly changed. In this case, the change looks significant at the start of the experiment but becomes insignificant in about a week once the novelty wears off.

PMs should take a critical eye to A/B tests that claim to show a large jump in metrics from a small user interface change. When Google earned millions of dollars just by changing the color of ad links, was that because users actually preferred that color, or because changing the color surprised users, leading them to temporarily click more but revert to their old habits within a few weeks?[72][g]

---

[g]There's a meta-strategy here. If making small user interface tweaks temporarily boosts metrics due to novelty, what if you always cycled between small changes so you could constantly get this metrics boost? Users may get tired of your constant changes, though, so the strategy might not be that effective, but it's an interesting one to think about nevertheless.

On the other hand, your metrics might start out *lower* than their long-term values due to the *learning effect*. Users may not know how to use your experimental version at the start of the A/B test but learn over time — meaning that your metrics could start badly but improve over the course of the experiment. This happens often with user interface redesigns: users may not initially know how to take their desired actions, leading to a metrics hit, but as they learn the metrics will pick up.[73]

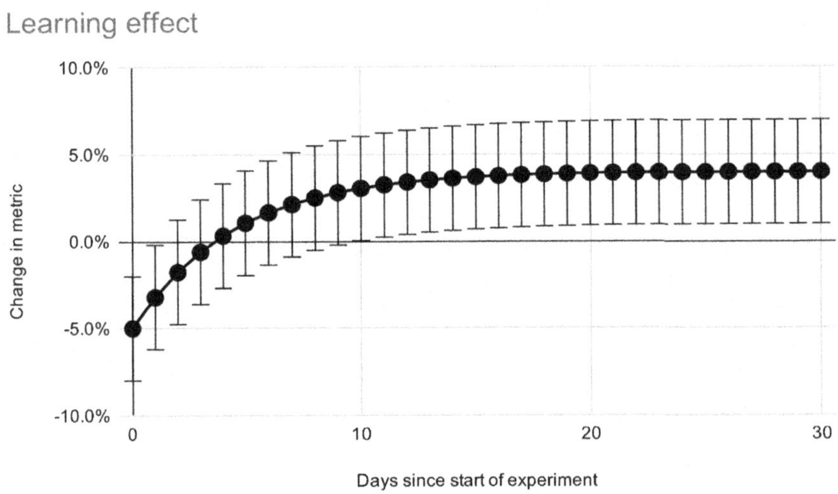

Data from an example A/B test that shows the learning effect in action. The data initially shows a negative effect on metrics, but over time we see that the long-term effect is positive.

In both cases, the lesson is the same: don't declare victory (or defeat) after just a few days of the experiment. If you think the novelty or learning effects could apply, be patient and see what the metrics' long-term value is.

Interview tip

Many beginner PMs will say in interviews that they'd run an A/B test for a week or so to get results quickly. But, as we can see, that's usually not enough time to know whether any change in metrics is sustainable or just caused by the novelty or learning effects. Thus, it's good practice to run your A/B tests for longer: perhaps three or four weeks.

Peeking

In traditional scientific research, you only look at the data after your experiment is done. But in product management, you're usually working on a live product, so you can start seeing live data as soon as you launch your A/B experiment. It can be addictive to constantly watch the stats in your A/B experiment, eagerly hoping that your confidence interval and p-value end up significant.

But *peeking* in this way can lead you to make false judgments.[74] Because you're testing in real time, your confidence interval and p-value will constantly be shifting around, and there's a lot of temptation to cut off the experiment as soon as the lower end of your confidence interval inches over zero (or, equivalently, as soon as your p-value goes below .05, which is considered the boundary for statistical significance[75]).[76]

As we've seen, you might see an artificially large rise or fall in your metric in the first few days due to the novelty and learning effects. But sometimes a metric can temporarily wander into or out of the significance zone by random chance before settling out to its final value.

It might be tempting to cut off an experiment as soon as you get a result that looks significant, but that's intellectually dishonest. It's no better than cherry-picking data, since you're trying to find a positive trend where there might not be any. Plus, if you launch the feature and find out later that it has no long-term benefit, you'll look foolish for recommending the launch.

Your best move is to avoid peeking altogether:[77] before you start the experiment, commit to ending the experiment at a certain date or once a certain sample size is reached. Only look at the data once these conditions have been met, and you'll ensure you aren't making the mistake of peeking.

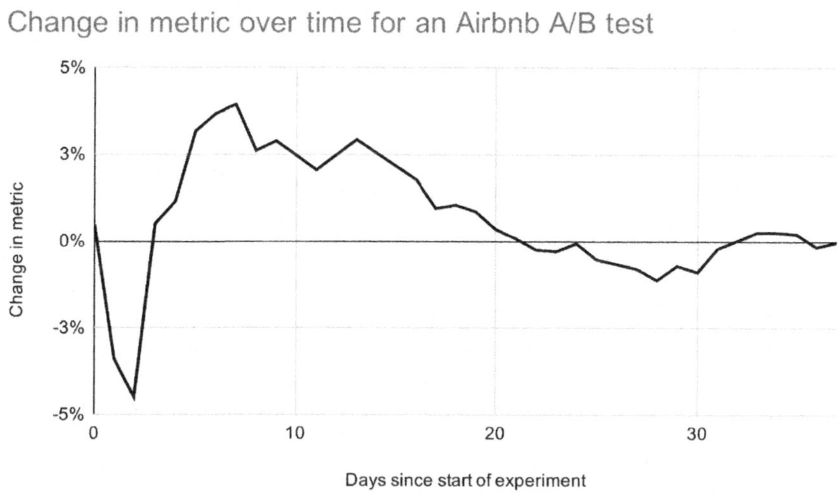

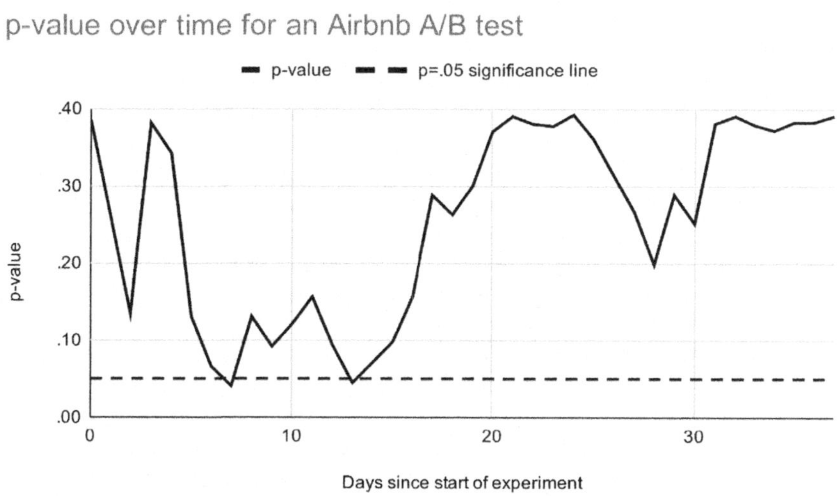

The change in a metric and the associated p-value fluctuated over the course of an A/B test run by Airbnb. Notice that effect seemed significant toward the start but quickly became insignificant — a sign of the novelty effect. Source: Airbnb[78]

Chapter 22

Metrics

METRICS ARE a PM's lifeblood: it's the way you can tell if your product is doing well, a key part of your toolkit for deciding what to do next, and (of course) a big part of getting promoted.

It's easy to say that you like metrics, but it's hard to know exactly which metrics are the right tool for the job. And while it's easy to root for your graphs to go "up and to the right,"[1] the proper use of metrics is a bit more nuanced, and there's a lot more power than meets the eye.

Startup metrics for pirates

The best place to start when thinking about metrics is the categories of metrics you should care about. The most famous categorization of metrics is Dave McClure's *Startup Metrics for Pirates*. This colorfully-named framework explains that metrics fall into five major categories, each one corresponding to a different stage of the user lifecycle:[2]

1. Acquisition: getting people to know about your product and visit your homepage, or *landing page*.[3]
2. Activation: getting people to sign up for your product and thus become users.[4]
3. Retention: getting users to keep coming back.[5] It's closely related to the concept of *engagement*.
4. Referral: getting users to bring their friends on board.[6] In other words, going viral.[7]

5. Revenue: earning money from your users. Also known as *monetization*.[8]

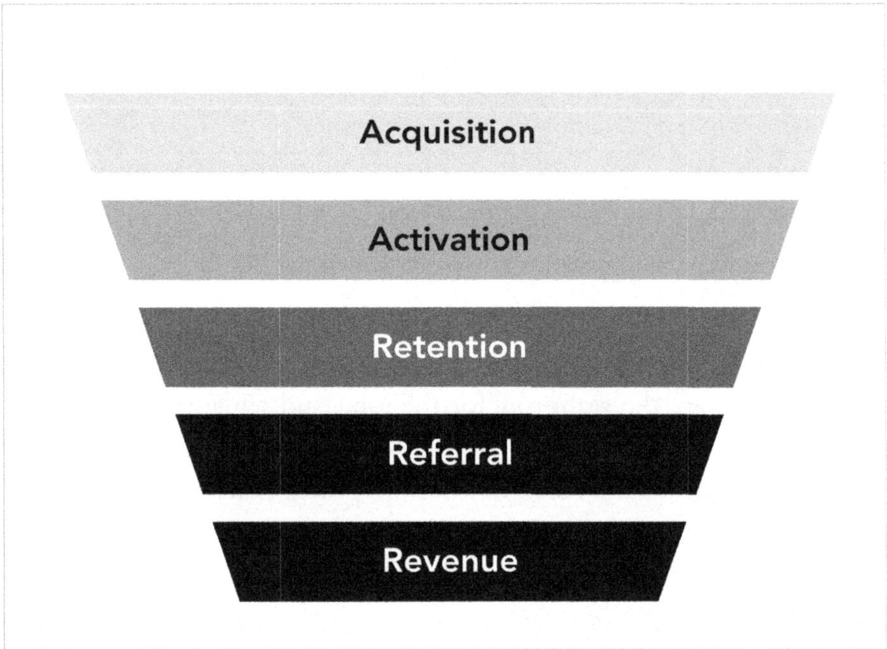

The "AARRR" metrics shown as a funnel. Users travel from top to bottom; some "leak" out of the funnel at each step. Source: SalesMate[9]

(That's AARRR — get the pirate joke?[a])

The metrics you care about will usually fall into one of these five buckets. It's not enough to know what those buckets are; your job as a PM is to figure out which metrics you'll use for those buckets. Let's look at some examples.

[a] The "revenue" bucket is sometimes called "monetization," thus giving this framework an alternate name of AARRM or, if referral is excluded, AARM. The pirate name is much catchier, though.

🗂 Interview tip

When asked to choose metrics for a feature, many PM interview candidates just say a single word: "retention," "acquisition," "engagement," etc. But that's not specific enough: interviewers will want to see you give a specific mathematical formula. If you say you'll measure engagement, for instance, you need to give a numerator and denominator.

We'll help you think through the math throughout this part of the book, but make sure you use it during your interviews!

Acquisition

Acquisition is just about getting eyeballs. Most acquisition metrics track just how many eyeballs you're attracting: the number of views on your company blog[10] or landing page,[11] your rank on Google for your most important search keywords (also known as *search-engine optimization* or *SEO*),[12] the percent of people who click on links in your newsletter (known as *click-through rate* or CTR)[13] and so on. These metrics are pretty simple, so you won't have to dwell too long on choosing a perfect acquisition metric.

Slightly more advanced are acquisition metrics that look at your *return on investment*, or *ROI*. How much are you spending on marketing per click to your website? Or, how much are your ads on Google, Facebook, and other platforms costing you?[14]

Activation

Activation metrics are also quite simple. The focus here is on *conversions*, or the percent of eyeballs that you turn into users.[15] Once you've acquired potential users to your website, activation is about *converting* them into users with accounts.

The most obvious metric here is the number of signups for your product: how many people (or what percent of people who landed on your website) filled out the new account form and gave you their email address?

But not all new users are created equal; users who fill out their account profiles and start using the product a bit are more likely to become fans and eventually pay you. Thus, another metric could be the percent of users who finished the *onboarding process.*[16][17] Twitter, for instance, might measure the percent of people who visited twitter.com and registered for an account, but they might also measure the percent of new signups who added a profile picture and chose some starter people to follow.

The exact line between acquisition and activation is blurry. We'd argue that getting users to sign up for a free trial of a *software-as-a-service*, or *SaaS*, product like Notion or a subscription service like Netflix is part of the activation step. Others have said that getting users to sign up for free trials is part of acquisition, since this gets their eyeballs on your *real* product, the paid version.[18] You can go either way — just be consistent.

Retention

Retention metrics, also known as *engagement metrics*, are the most famous, and the most hotly debated, metrics. Keeping users around is much cheaper than constantly bringing in new ones, and given that about 65% of small business sales in the US are to repeat customers,[19] it's essential to keep users around once you've *activated* them.

The first bucket of retention metrics simply measures how many active users you have. These include the famous *MAU* (monthly active user) and *DAU* (daily active user)[b] metrics, which measure the number of users who have used your product at least once in the last month or day.[20][c]

[b]Around Silicon Valley, these are usually pronounced to rhyme with "cow."

[c]There's also *WAU* — weekly active users — but it's not used much in practice.

MAUs, in particular, are the most common retention metric — indeed, perhaps the most common metric of all — used to measure the success of consumer products. Consider how proud Google is of its half-dozen-plus products with over one billion MAUs,[21] and how Facebook likes trumpeting its billion-active-user social products.[22]

While MAUs and DAUs measure your user base at a snapshot in time, a second bucket of metrics helps you measure how well you're hanging on to your users over time. There are two related metrics to consider here: *retention rate* and *churn*. Retention rate measures the percent of your users at a given time who are still users a certain amount of time later. Churn is the inverse (i.e. 100% minus retention rate), measuring the percent of users who quit.[23]

Retention rate and churn can work for a variety of time periods: you can measure retention after one day, one week, one month, one year, etc. Retention rate, in particular, is commonly reported using a trio of metrics: *D1*, *D7*, and *D30 retention*, which measure the percent of users who are still active 1, 7, or 30 days, respectively, after first joining.[24] (The day a user joined is known as *D0*. Thus, *D0 retention* is usually considered to be 100% by definition, since nobody has had time to stop using the product yet.[25] Some PMs, though, use D0 retention to measure the percent of users who logged in twice in the first 24 hours.[26])

Churn is usually measured using *cohorts*: you pick a set of users who were all active at a given time and track their activity over the following days and months.[27] If 8% of people in your cohort quit within a month, your last-30-day churn rate is 8%.

Churn and retention rate are often shown on a *user retention curve*, which tracks the number of users from a cohort who are still active on a given day or month.[28]

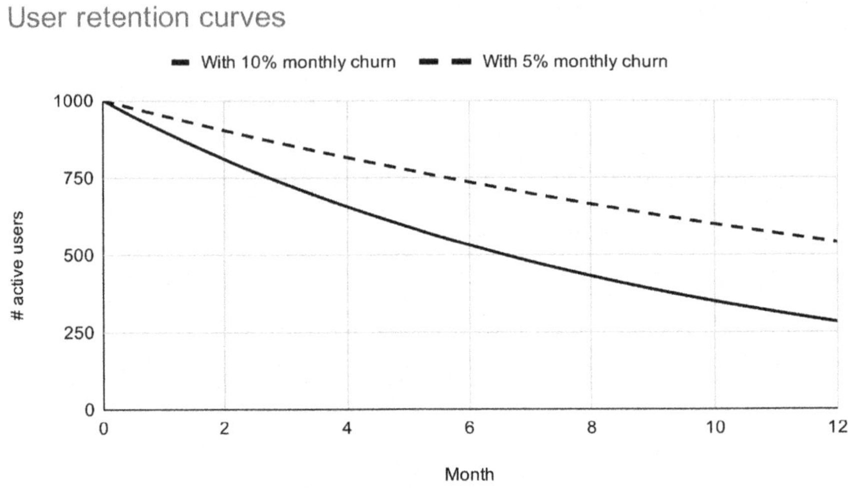

Churn matters: reducing the churn rate by 5%, in this case, almost doubles the number of users in a cohort you keep after a year!

🗂 Interview tip

The average churn rate varies between industries. For SaaS companies, it's 5% per year, but for consumer goods companies, it can be as high as 10% per year.[29]

Note that "average" doesn't necessarily equal "good." Entrepreneur David Skok insists that healthy SaaS companies have to keep their churn rates below 2%.[30]

Also note that retention rate, churn rate, and DAUs/MAUs are connected. Everyone who's a MAU will either be retained or churned over the next month. If you have 1000 MAUs in January and 200 quit in February, then your D30 retention is 80% while your D30 churn is 20%.

The final bucket of retention metrics measures just how excited your active users are. Not all active users are created equal, after all: someone who uses your product twenty times in a month is more valuable than someone who uses it just once. There are a bunch of metrics you can use to measure excitement: time between visits,[31] the percent of users who visit more than X times a month,[32] and so on.

Our favorite engagement metric, though, is *stickiness*: the ratio of DAUs to MAUs (DAU/MAU). Stickiness measures the average number of days your monthly-active users use your product.[33] If DAU/MAU = 20%, that means the average monthly active user visits your product 30 × 0.2 = 6 days a month. (It helps to think about the extreme cases: if DAU = MAU, everyone who uses your app is visiting every day; if DAU = MAU/30, everyone who uses your app is just visiting once a month.) The higher the stickiness, the more "addictive" or "engaging" your product.

Note that the expected stickiness ratio differs between product types.[34] Social media and messaging apps might expect users to log on every day, whereas a financial tool like Mint might be happy if someone logs on once a week or so and Airbnb might be thrilled with one visit a month.

Interview tip

Though stickiness varies across industries, we can create some rough rules of thumb. A stickiness of 10% is usually considered average; 20% is considered good; and 25% is considered excellent.[35]

Referral

The poor referral bucket is often overlooked — some versions of the pirate framework leave it out entirely[36] — but we think it's just as important as the rest. *Word-of-mouth* (*WOM*) marketing is considered the best way to bring users to your product, since people trust their friends and family far more than a random internet ad or blog post.[37] If you can get people to refer their friends, you have a free source of new users.

There are two key parts to getting referrals: getting users to like your product in the first place, then getting them to invite their friends.

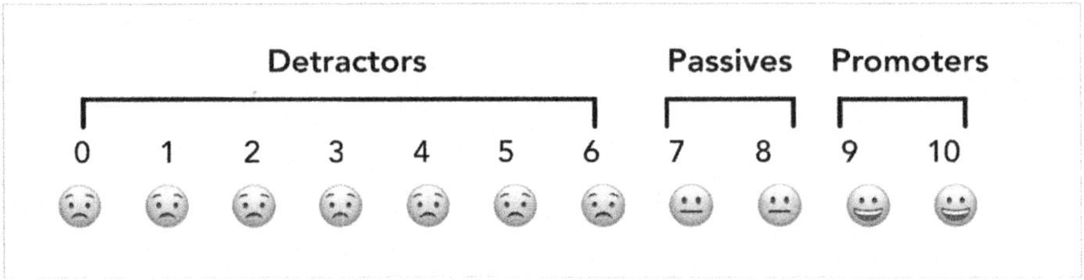

In the Net Promoter Score calculation, each user tells you how much they like your product on this scale from 0 to 10. Source: GetThematic[38]

For the first part, the gold standard metric is the *Net Promoter Score*, or *NPS*. To measure NPS, you ask all your users (or at least a random sample of them) a simple question: "On a scale of 0 to 10, how likely are you to recommend this product to a friend or a colleague?"[39] People giving a score of 0 to 6 are called *detractors*, who will actively criticize your product; people giving 7 or 8 are called *passives*, who are satisfied but won't say much; and people giving 9 or 10 are called *promoters*, who will actively recommend your product to friends.[40]

Calculating the NPS is simple: it's the percent of promoters minus the percent of detractors.[41] A score of 100 means every single user loves your product; a score of -100 means everyone hates it.[d] (Let's hope you aren't at that extreme.) It's more likely that your NPS will fall somewhere in the middle: if 60% of users are promoters, 20% are passives, and 20% are detractors, your NPS will be 40.

What's a "good" NPS, you ask? Obviously, you have to compare to your competitors and the average for your industry and country,[42] but

[d]The percent sign is usually dropped when reporting NPSes.

generally, a negative NPS is considered bad; 0–30 is considered average; 30–50 is good; 50–70 is great, and 70+ is world-class.[43]

Tech companies tend to have high NPSes — usually above 60[44] — so the bar is high. Certain segments of tech, of course, have worse NPSes. File-sharing services have pretty mediocre NPSes, with Dropbox at just 8 and Microsoft OneDrive at -10. The top-rated one (Google Drive) only scratches out a 35.[45]

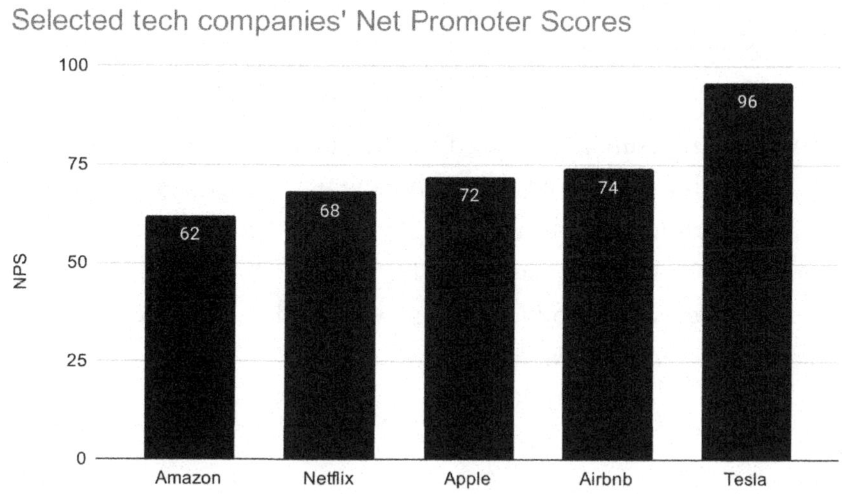

The Net Promoter Scores (NPSes) for selected tech companies. Source: Retently[46][47]

Obviously, you want to increase your NPS and grow the number of promoters, since they'll be the ones referring friends and creating viral growth loops, bringing more and more people onto your product. But you also have to listen to your detractors and address their concerns, since nothing throws cold water on a glowing recommendation from one friend than a harsh criticism from another friend.[48]

Once you've gotten users to like you, you have to get them to invite users. Metrics for this are simpler, including the number of users who invite friends, the number of invitations sent, and the percent of invitations accepted.[49]

A more advanced metric is the *viral coefficient*, also known as *K*,[50] which measures the number of new users an average user generates. This equals the average number of invitations sent multiplied by the invitation acceptance rate.[51] The higher this value, the more "virally" your product will grow.[52] This is, incidentally, very similar to the unfortunate R_0 metric popularized in the COVID-19 pandemic, which measured the number of other people that an infected person would infect.[53] (So you may not want to speak glowingly about "viral growth" anymore.)

Another unfortunately-named virality metric is the *viral cycle time*, or *VCT*, which measures how quickly new users invite friends.[54] If you sign up for a product on Monday and invite your friend, who signs up on Friday, the VCT was four days. The higher your K and the higher your VCT, the faster your product will go viral and experience the much-desired *hockey-stick growth*.[55]

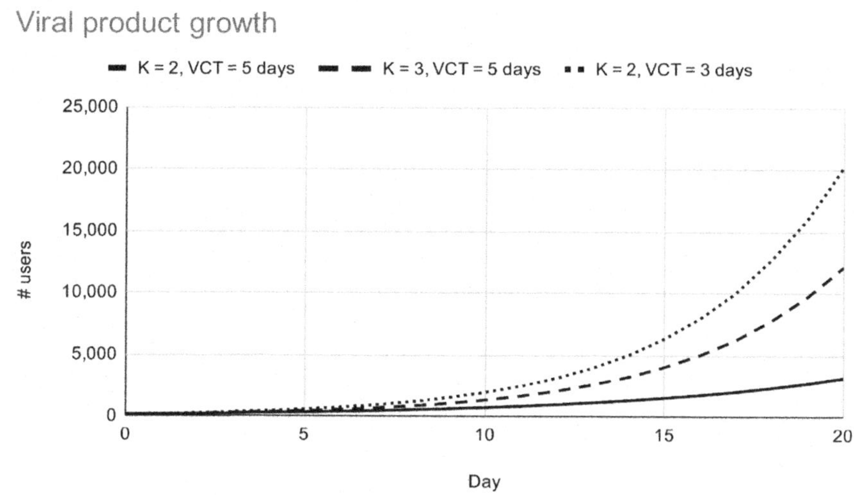

A model showing how the viral coefficient (K) and the viral cycle time (VCT) affect a product's growth.

Different products' VCTs can vary quite significantly. Memes have a very short VCT, since they can be screenshotted and forwarded along to friends in just a few seconds. Meanwhile, something like tax preparation software will have a very long VCT. If you get TurboTax this year and really like it, you might not tell your friends about it until just before next Tax Day — almost a year in the future!

That's not to say that you can't reduce the VCT. Without the retweet button, Twitter's VCT would be maybe ten seconds: you'd have to copy a tweet's text, paste it into the tweet composer, add a line crediting the original author, and then hit send. But with the retweet button, circulating a tweet to your followers takes just one or two seconds.

Revenue

The final bucket of metrics, and the one that matters the most for your bottom line, is revenue. The appropriate revenue metric depends on your business model. If you're selling ads, for instance, you might care about the percent of users who click on ads and your average earnings per ad (usually measured as the earnings per 1000 ad *impressions*, or views, and known as *cost-per-mille* or *CPM*[56]). If you're in ecommerce, alternatively, you might care about the average price per purchase, known as *average order value* (*AOV*)[57] or *cart size*.[58] And if you're selling phones, you might care about the *average sale price* (ASP)[59] of your phones.[60]

Besides the raw number of dollars you're hauling in, it's useful to think about how much money you need. It's great if all your users are making you a few dollars, but ideally your users would be earning you more money than it cost you in advertising and server costs to bring them on. So you might want to measure the percent of users who are turning you a *profit* instead of just bringing in revenue.[61]

Putting it all together

One useful exercise is to think of one metric in each of the five pirate buckets for your product (or, if you're looking for a job, a particular company's product). Let's run through an example with the digital pinboard company Pinterest.

Our user acquisition would probably come from ads or posts on other social networks, so our acquisition metrics might include average cost per ad (recall CPM) and number of visits to the site from Facebook (known, somewhat confusingly, as *referral traffic*, since Facebook is referring users to us[62]).

For activation, we can simply look at the percent of visitors who sign up for a new account. It's useful to slice-and-dice it, though, to see our strongest "funnels" for bringing new users in. We might want to compare the sign-up percent on the homepage to that of an influencer's profile page[63] or a post page.[64] We could further compare the sign-up percentages of different kinds of post pages: recipes, fashion, home decor, and so on.

We'd look at a pretty standard set of retention metrics: MAUs, DAUs, churn, D1/D7/D30 retention, and stickiness. Note that social networks love talking about "engagement," which is a flashy but vague term. If we wanted to measure engagement, we might look at average usage numbers: the average number of new posts per user per week, the average amount of time spent on the site per day, and so on.

For referral, we'd naturally look at the average number of invitations sent. But even something as simple as sharing a link is a form of referral, so we could look at the number of people who first visited Pinterest by clicking on a link sent by a friend. We might also look at the NPS of different kinds of users — are avid cooks more satisfied with Pinterest than travelers? Which ones are the most likely to spread the word about Pinterest?

And for revenue, we'd follow a standard playbook for ad-driven companies: ad CPM, ad *click-through-rate* (*CTR*), and so on.

Leading indicators

One of the most powerful uses of metrics is to correlate some easily-observed metric with a harder-to-measure, but very valuable, outcome. One of the hardest but most important things to predict is what makes a new user likely to become an active, and thus profitable, user. If you can figure out the actions that future active users take and future churned users don't, you can push new users to adopt those actions and thus improve your activation and retention (and thus, eventually, revenue).[65]

Take a practical example: Slack found that teams who sent at least 2000 messages were far more likely to stay active on Slack and upgrade to a paid plan.[66] You can imagine that Slack got this number by comparing the number of messages a team sent to their average upgrade and retention rates and found a sharp jump around 2000 messages. Perhaps the curve looked roughly S-shaped, with the steepest slope at 2000.

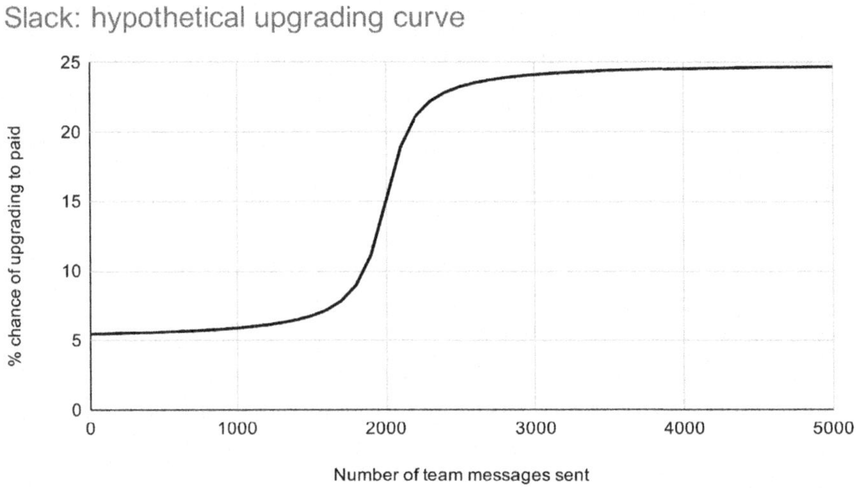

A graph containing hypothetical data that Slack might have collected. It shows that customers are far more likely to upgrade once they pass 2000 messages sent.

The number of team messages sent is known as a *leading indicator*:[67] it's a simple, easy-to-measure metric, and when it crosses a certain critical threshold, some highly-valued outcome becomes much more likely.

Growth PMs love finding leading indicators, since they provide a satisfying "aha" moment and help rally the whole company behind achieving a concrete goal.[68] Telling PMs to "get more teams to upgrade" isn't very actionable, and it's not clear exactly how to achieve that goal. But telling PMs to do whatever it takes to get teams to send 2000 messages is a much better rallying cry — you can probably think of a dozen strategies to achieve this off the top of your head.

Many notable growth PMs have found the leading indicators for their companies. Former Facebook growth lead Chamath Palihapitiya found that users who made seven friends within ten days of signing up were likely to become active.[69] Twitter PM Josh Elman found that casual users become active once they follow 30 accounts and ten of them follow back.[70] A Dropbox PM found that users who create a folder and upload a file to Dropbox are likely to become active. And a former Zynga product manager found that users who played a game two days in a row were likely to become paying users.[71]

Insights about leading indicators are especially powerful for designing new user *onboarding* experiences since they usually deal with how to turn a new user into an active one. It should be no surprise, then, that Twitter revamped its onboarding flow in the mid-2010s to include a long list of suggested accounts to follow.[72]

How can you find a leading indicator for your product? You need to find a metric that correlates with some success criterion: usually a user becoming active or profitable. If you notice that people who do X become paying customers while people who *don't* do X don't become paying customers, then X could be a good leading indicator.

User interviews or looking through logs of what new users do can be a good place to start, but remember to turn a critical eye toward patterns you see. (If users who sign up on Tuesdays are more likely to become paying customers, there could be a good reason for it — or it could just be noise.)

Vanity and real metrics

There are a lot of numbers you can dig up about your product, but not all of them are good ones. You can always find numbers that'll let you make an attractive graph that's going "up and to the right," but those numbers might not be at all relevant to the bottom line — and presenting them as good news might actually mask deeper problems.[73]

For instance, suppose we had a startup that racked up signups over time; after a year we had over 20,000 total accounts. The curve was definitely going up and to the right; in fact, it was curving slightly upward!

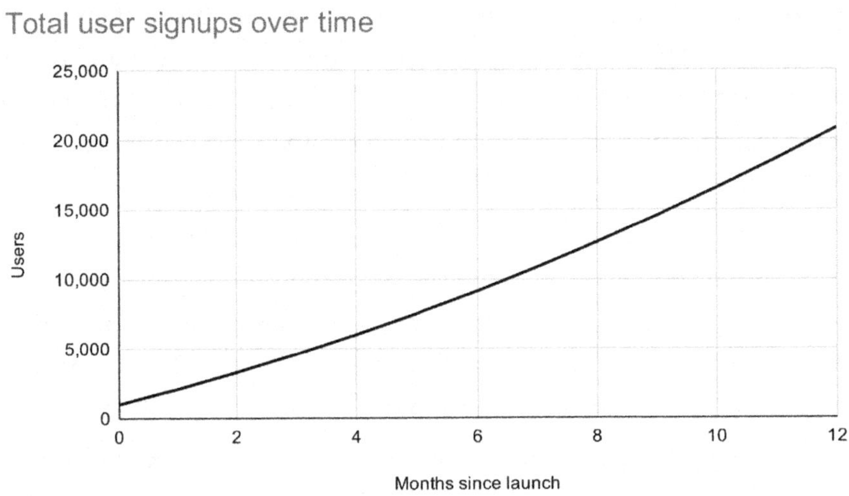

Example data from a startup that shows total user signups increasing nicely over time.

But the cumulative number of accounts *always* goes up and to the right, and what's more, it doesn't actually have any bearing on how much money you're making (which is the ultimate metric). Only *active* users will make you money.

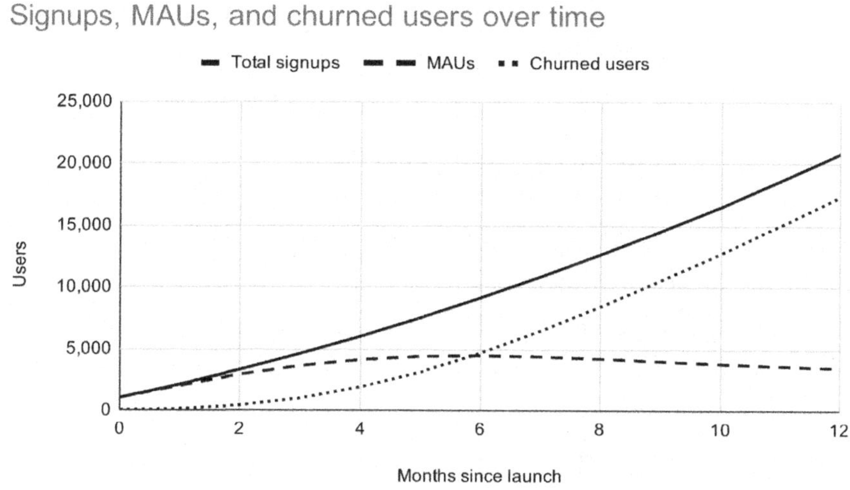

A closer look at our startup's data shows that most users are churning; we're actually losing active users over time.

What if we discovered that our original rosy picture was misleading? Perhaps we found that, while we kept adding new users, most of them churned, or quit the app, within a few months. We were actually slowly losing MAUs, which probably boded poorly for our startup!

So don't pay attention to the metrics that look good but have little bearing on how well you're *actually* doing. Most "total" numbers — like total signups, number of visitors to your webpage, or downloads in app stores — fall into this category of vanity metrics since they only tell you how well your product did in the *past*, not how well it's doing right now.

Case study: Xbox's MAUs

One interesting twist is that metrics that start out useful might become vanity metrics over time. In the video game industry, success has traditionally been measured by the number of consoles sold over time.[74] More sales equals a better console. (Total sales was indeed a vanity metric, but time-based metrics like quarterly sales were pretty good.)

Sales metrics were fine when console companies made money just by selling the hardware. They were thus the most important metrics for Xbox for many years. But in 2016, Xbox announced that it would stop measuring or announcing Xbox sales numbers — instead focusing on monthly active users of the Xbox Live service,[75] which lets gamers chat with friends, rack up achievements, and livestream.[76] Crucially, Xbox Live also offers a paid Gold tier that enables online multiplayer gaming and periodic free games.[77]

Why the switch? Xbox likely realized that console sales actually accounted for just a fraction of their revenue, especially once a few years had passed since a given console was released. Much of Xbox's money came from active Xbox Live users who were likely to buy more games and upgrade to Live Gold, both of which would give Microsoft more money than the consoles themselves. And focusing on MAUs was more forward-looking than focusing on total sales: someone who bought an Xbox but left it gathering dust in the corner will be worth a lot less to Microsoft than someone who plays every day.[78]

Gray areas

It's easy to beat up on vanity metrics, but there are a lot more subtle errors you can make in choosing metrics.

One subtle error is to find metrics that look good but are only useful for companies with different business models. For instance, MAU is a great metric for social networks and SaaS companies, but not all that useful for two-sided marketplaces. If an Airbnb PM bragged that they raised MAUs by 20%, that's a vanity metric — you'd want to ask them if they had increased nightly bookings, which correlates far more with revenue and is thus more useful.

While it's good to have one "north star" metric your whole team can rally behind, don't overemphasize it, since it might make you ignore other important ones. MAU is a fine north star metric to have, but if your users start visiting just once a month instead of once a week (i.e. your stickiness decreases), you're in trouble — but your MAU number wouldn't catch that at all. You need to track multiple metrics to get the full picture.

Chapter 23

Metric Models

WHICH SET OF METRICS is right for your product or business? It depends on your business model! Modern software companies usually fall into one of five categories, each with its own business model and appropriate set of metrics:[a] software-as-a-service with subscriptions, freemium apps, user-generated content with ads, two-sided marketplaces, and ecommerce.[1,2]

There are two interrelated sets of metrics PMs need to care about: revenue metrics and user metrics. We'll investigate in turn the metrics that determine revenue for each business model. Since the overarching goal for each business model is to turn non-users into paying users, we'll also show how users might move from start to finish and which metrics will tell you how well you're doing at this "funnel."

Software-as-a-service

Pretty much all software for businesses — known as *enterprise software* or *B2B* (*business-to-business*) *software* — is sold on a subscription model these days.[3] Gone are the days when companies bought CDs with prepackaged software on them. Instead, companies pay a monthly or yearly fee to access cloud-based software.[4]

This *software-as-a-service*, or *SaaS*, model comes with several advan-

[a]Here, we're adapting business model categorization frameworks introduced by the book *Lean Analytics* and the blog *Stratechery*.

tages. It helps companies get constant updates and smooth out their payments (so they pay a consistent recurring fee instead of making a few giant purchases that wreck the budget). And it helps the software makers get consistent revenue instead of "feasting" when they release a major new version and enduring "famine" at all other times.

Almost any enterprise software you can think of — Trello, Asana, GitHub, Zendesk, Slack, and so on — follows this business model. As such, their revenue and user metrics are surprisingly similar.

Funnels

The revenue and user metrics for SaaS businesses are closely linked, since the number of paying users you have correlates very tightly with the amount of money you make. We'll start with the user metrics. You generally want to guide users along a path that makes them ever more profitable: from a non-user to a free-tier user to a paying user. You'll want to measure the drop-off rate between each step of this path, or *funnel*.

Key metrics

The most important metric, though, is the one that bridges the user and revenue halves: the percent of users who upgrade from the free tier to the paid tier. This determines how many paying users you have. And the number of paying users you have, along with your fee structure (including your *average revenue per paying user*, or *ARPPU*), determines your revenue.

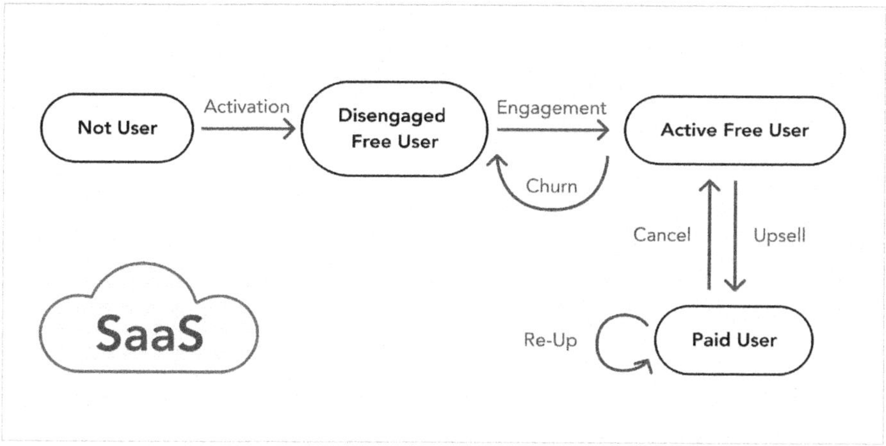

The stages that a SaaS product user flows through.

One formula you'll see throughout this section is the monthly active users formula. The number of MAUs you have this month includes all the MAUs from last month, plus the new ones (which is where the viral growth formulas come in), minus the ones who quit, or churned.

Freemium apps

The remaining four business models, including this one, are for consumer software: products that make money off everyday people like you and us. This category includes any product that's free to use but offers paid upgrades in the form of *in-app purchases* or subscriptions (like the SaaS businesses above, but for consumers).

Most mobile games, plus a handful of other apps, offer in-app purchases.[5] Candy Crush lets you buy extra lives with real money if you die,[6] Fortnite lets you buy outfits with "V-Bucks" (which you buy with real money),[7] and *gacha games*[8][b] like Nintendo's *Fire Emblem Heroes* let

[b]The term comes from the Japanese word *gachapon*, which refers to "capsule toys"

you buy *loot boxes* that contain random virtual goodies.[9] In-app purchases are a bit rarer outside gaming, but dating apps like Tinder often let you buy extra "swipes," "boosts," and "super likes" to improve your chances.[10]

Meanwhile, all kinds of consumer apps offer subscriptions: Spotify Premium,[11] Netflix,[12] Dropbox Plus,[13] the meditation app Calm,[14] and so on. Paywalled media publications like the *New York Times*[15] and *The Atlantic*[16] also fall in this category. (Note that most of these apps offer entertainment content like videos, music, or news, while straight-up software tools don't make an appearance — the saying around Silicon Valley is that people are willing to pay for content but not for software.)

Key metrics

The revenue and user metrics for subscription-based freemium products like Netflix are quite similar to those of SaaS products. In other words, Spotify Premium and Slack's paid tier have surprisingly similar metrics.

you can buy in vending machines across Asia. You put money into the machine and get a random toy out — an old-fashioned version of digital loot boxes. (We spent a lot of money on *gacha* toys in Tokyo... it's addictive!)

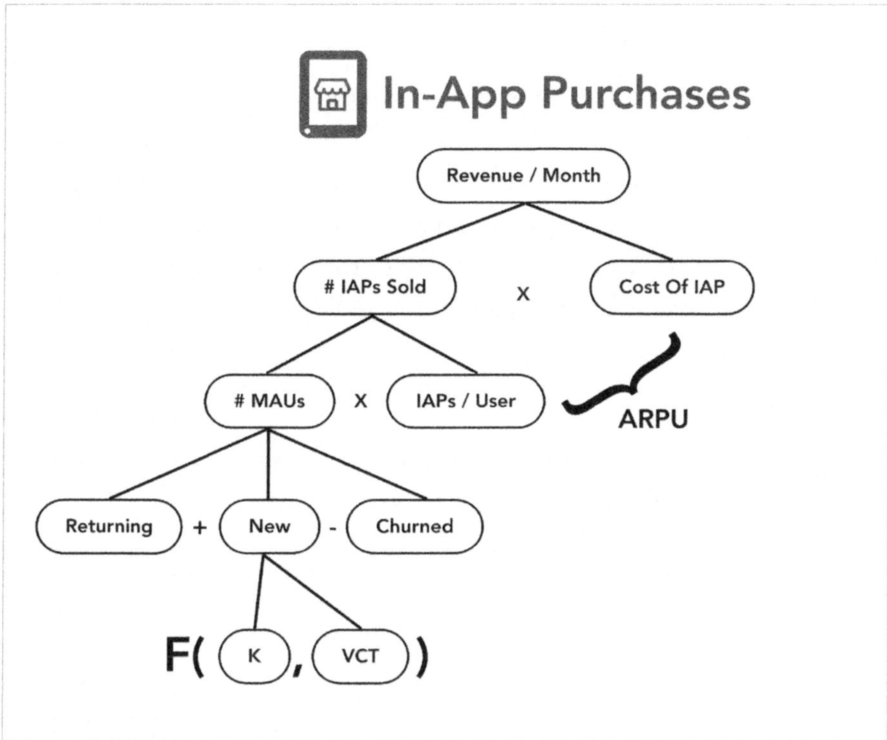

A "tree" that shows how various sub-metrics roll into the top-level metric (revenue) for a product that monetizes with in-app purchases.

In-app purchase metrics are slightly different. At a surface level, the core metric is not the number of subscribers but rather the number of in-app purchases sold. It's the same way a buffet restaurant cares about the number of customers served while an *a la carte* restaurant cares about the number of dishes served.

And while all users of subscription services are created equal (you pay Netflix the same fee whether you watch one movie or one hundred), the same doesn't hold for products powered by in-app purchases. More dedicated players pay more than less dedicated users — in many cases, a lot more. These are the "whales" we discussed earlier in this part of the book.

Thus, in-app-purchase powered products care less about the raw number of players and more about the number of whales they can snag. Growing the number of whales by 25% is probably more impressive than growing the number of free players by 50%. (Attracting more free players helps grow your app's popularity, thus drawing in even more players, but ultimately it comes down to the whales.)

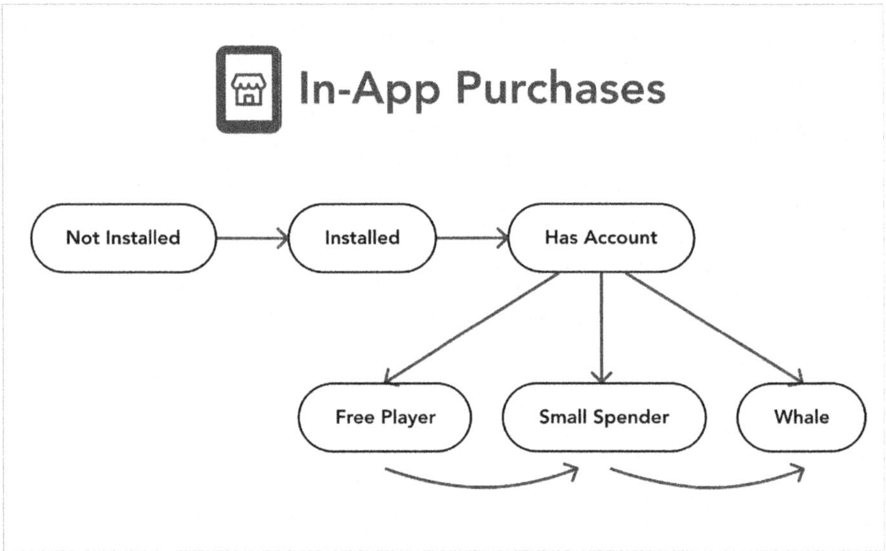

Users of apps with in-app purchases flow through these stages. Ideally, you'll be able to turn them into "whales."

For game developers in particular, stickiness (DAU/MAU) is very important, since whales are hard to come by and they're always at risk of being lured away by the latest hot game. And, while *average revenue per user (ARPU)* is always important, ARPPU is even more important for games, since it measures how well you're monetizing your whales.[17] For instance, the best-performing mobile games (84th percentile) had seven times the ARPPU of the worst-performing games (16th percentile).[18]

Interview tip

By one estimate, about 2% of the users of a typical freemium app will pay you money, whether through subscriptions or in-app purchases.[19]

User-generated content with ads

This bucket's name is a mouthful, but it's pretty simple at its core. *User-generated content* (*UGC*) products center around users making posts,[20] so this category includes all social networks, review sites like Yelp, microblogging sites like Twitter or Medium, video- and photo-upload sites like YouTube and Flickr, and so on. Unlike with the Netflixes of the world, users aren't willing to pay to interact with their friends or digital communities, so the only way to monetize is to show ads between posts.

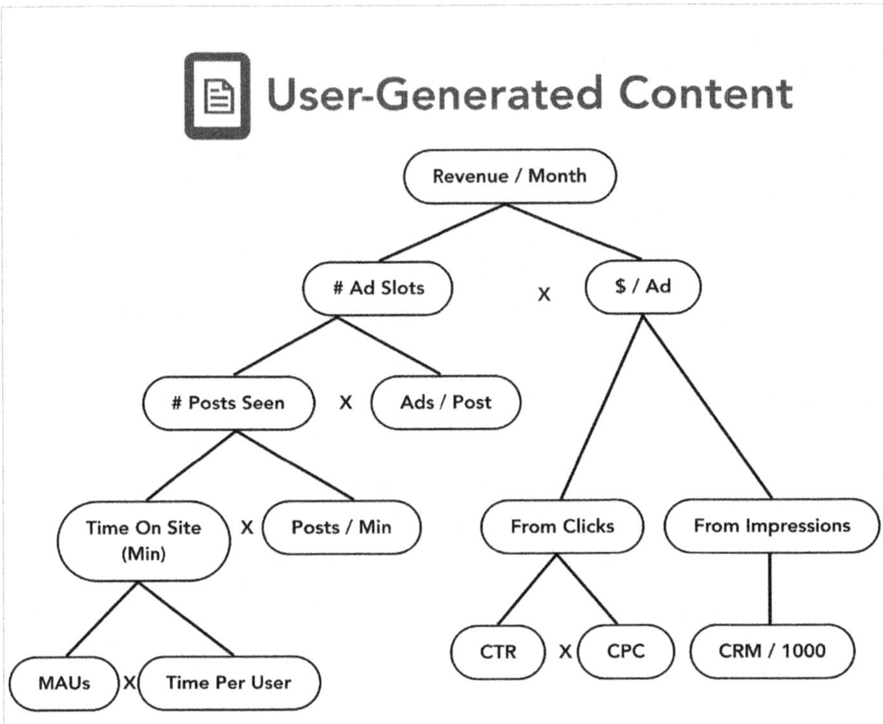

The tree of metrics for a User-Generated Content product. Revenue ultimately comes down to your ads.

For these products, the goal is simple: get people to spend a lot of time on your site, show them a lot of ads, and profit. The "tree" of metrics is quite intricate, though, giving PMs many levers to pull. For instance, you can increase the number of ads someone sees per post, like when Facebook[21] and YouTube[22] started showing *pre-roll* and *mid-roll* ads before and in the middle of videos, respectively. Or you can show more ads per post, such as by showing ads every nine posts instead of every ten (though this can degrade the user experience).

Time on site

The most important sub-metric for these platforms, though is the total time spent on the site, since more time equals more ads and thus more money. Time on site, often abbreviated as *ToS*, is so crucial that many UGC companies, like YouTube[23] and Facebook,[24] mention ToS in the same breath as revenue numbers. That is, time on site is so strongly correlated with revenue that the two are mentioned side by side.

The average time on site varies between platforms, but the most successful platforms can get users to spend nearly an hour a day. Check out the numbers from one study of popular social media apps:[25]

Platform	Avg. time on site
Facebook	58 min.
Snapchat	50 min.
Instagram	53 min.
YouTube	40 min.
WhatsApp	28 min.
Pinterest	14 min.
Twitter	1 min.
LinkedIn	1 min.

(The tiny usage numbers of Twitter and LinkedIn don't necessarily mean that people are opening these apps for one minute a day. It's more likely that people use the apps for longer periods but do so less frequently; using LinkedIn for fifteen minutes twice a month averages out to one minute per day.)

To maximize your time on site, you can either get more users through the usual viral means or get your current users to spend more of their time on your platform.

The most straightforward way to get people to spend more time on your platform is by simply adding more content. The more posts there are, the more time users can spend on your platform "consuming" those posts. This is why product teams at UGC companies spend so much time developing new *formats* for posts; for instance, in 2016 Facebook started letting you ask friends for tips on the best dentists, babysitters, nail salons, and other local services with the new "Ask for Recommendations" post type.[26]

Stories have become popular formats around the internet ever since Snapchat pioneered them; because stories are so easy to create, they're great for people who don't have the time or energy to make a "full" post. Rolling out stories, as YouTube did in 2019[27] and LinkedIn did in 2020,[28] thus lets UGC companies access previously-untapped reservoirs of creativity and create a lot of new content. And, of course, more content equals more time on site.

▶ Watch this

Features for ad-supported consumer products should seek to increase time on site (ToS), since that leads to increased revenue. It's hard to directly measure a feature's impact on ToS, so PMs need to find other usage metrics that correlate with ToS, known as *proxy metrics*. As an example, check out this mock interview we did with a Facebook PM to see how he'd define proxy metrics that correlate to ToS for Facebook Dating.

productalliance.com/videos/metrics

You can also get people to spend more time on your platform by making your existing content catalog stickier. PMs seeking to do this have created the (often-criticized) techniques of autoplaying videos and infinite scroll.[29]

User metrics

As for user metrics, MAU is the gold standard, but remember from before that UGC sites tend to follow a 90-9-1 rule: 90% of users are lurkers and don't post anything, 9% are contributors who post occasionally, and 1% are creators who make most of the posts.[30] A great UGC PM can know the lurker-contributor-creator breakdown for their product and find metrics to measure how people can move between those buckets.

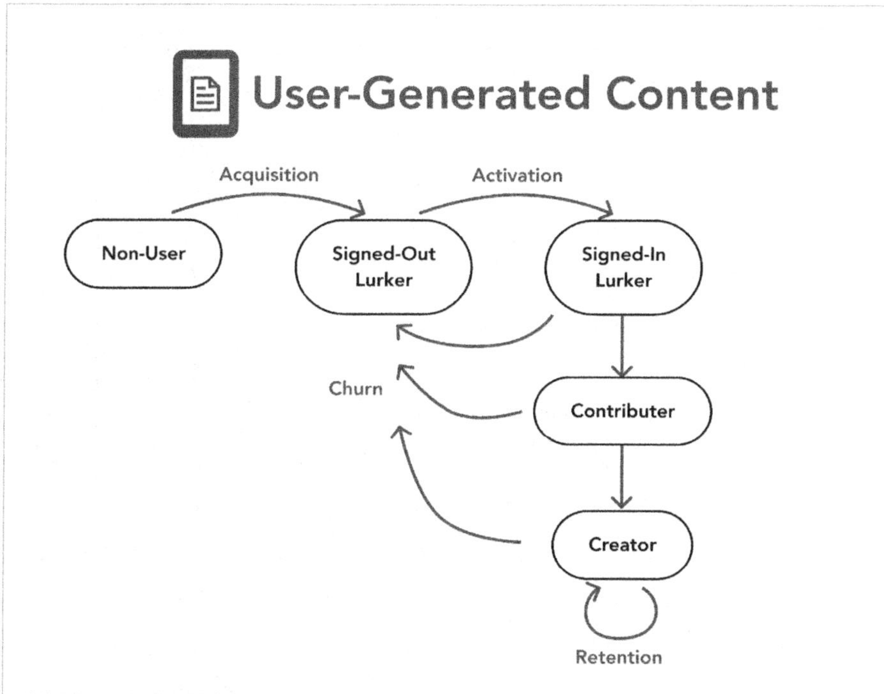

Users of User-Generated Content products flow between these stages. You want to get everyone to be a creator.

Two-sided marketplaces

This bucket includes products that match "buyers" and "sellers," taking a commission off every transaction. Notable two-sided markets include Uber, Lyft, Airbnb, DoorDash, Etsy, eBay, and the hundreds of "Uber for X" startups.[31] Amazon is partially a two-sided market, since it lets "third party" small businesses sell on the platform alongside products offered directly by Amazon.[32]

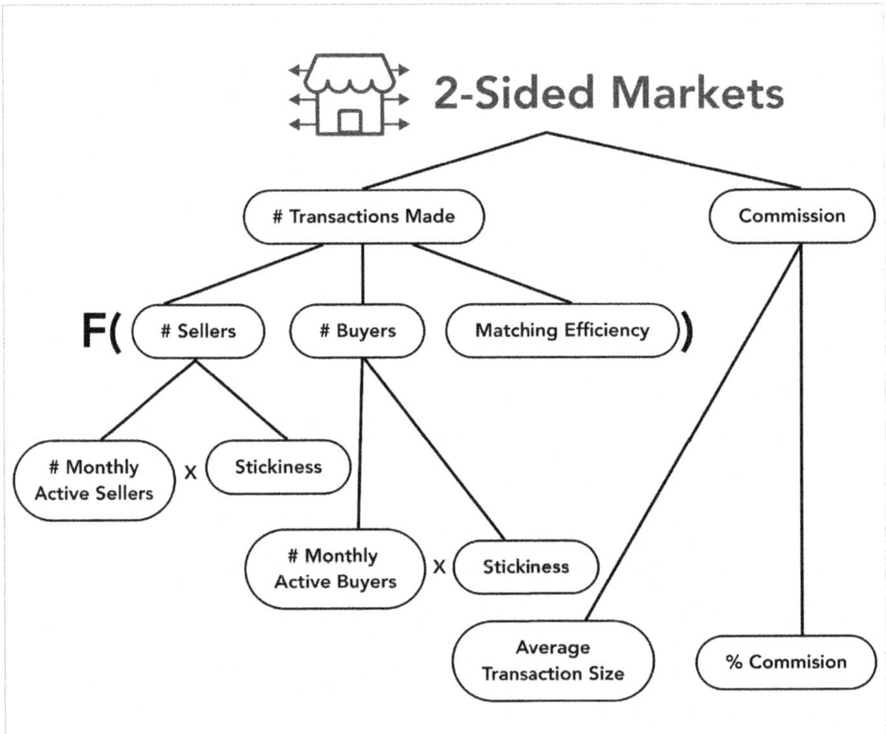

The metrics tree for 2-sided market products. The number of transactions made is a function, F, of the number of buyers and sellers on the platform, as well as the matching efficiency.

The revenue strategy of a two-sided market company is relatively simple: match buyers and sellers so transactions can happen, then take a cut of each transaction. The more buyers and sellers you bring on, and the more efficiently you can match them, the more money you'll make.

Improving matching efficiency is straightforward: you have to make sure that people who want to buy can always get matched with people who want to sell. Improving the eBay search algorithm or changing the Uber driver-rider matching algorithm, such that drivers spend less time waiting around for a rider, can boost this.

Supply and demand

The hardest part about two-sided markets is that they suffer from the infamous *chicken-and-egg* problem, where the product is no good for buyers until there are enough sellers on board, and it's no good for sellers until there are enough buyers on board. Nobody's going to drive for Lyft in a town where nobody has the Lyft app installed, and nobody's going to open Lyft in a town where there are no drivers.[33] In other words, there's no demand without supply and no supply without demand.

The way out of the chicken-and-egg problem is to artificially create buyers or sellers so that the other side will join. When entering Seattle, Uber created "sellers" (the supply side) by buying cars and hiring drivers, paying them by the hour to shuttle riders around. Only after there was a critical mass of riders did Uber start paying drivers with commission. Meanwhile, Amazon started out selling books and assembled a legion of customers (the demand side), which made sellers of other products flock to the platform.[34]

Pundits disagree over whether you should focus on the supply[35] or demand[36] side first, but history shows that focusing on supply first is the best move. The reason is that demand comes automatically once you've built the supply; word-of-mouth marketing among consumers is very powerful. Convincing suppliers to join the market is a harder task, since suppliers usually don't invite other suppliers (their competitors!) through word-of-mouth. Put another way, demand grows organically through positive feedback loops, while no such loop exists for suppliers in most cases. Thus, you're better served by manually building out the supply first.[37]

One analyst tested this theory by looking at seventeen popular two-sided marketplaces. As expected, fourteen of these startups focused on supply first, while just three focused on demand first! Check out the full list:[38]

Built supply first	Built demand first
Airbnb	Rover
AngelList	TaskRabbit
Breather	Zillow
Caviar	
DoorDash	
Etsy	
Eventbrite	
GrubHub	
Instacart	
Lyft	
OpenTable	
Patreon	
Thumbtack	
Uber	

Balancing growth

No matter how you start, you have to balance the growth of buyers with the growth in sellers. Adding more buyers will drive more transactions, but only to a point — if sellers run out of goods to sell, having all the buyers in the world won't help. The same applies to adding more sellers.

Let's take Airbnb as an example to see how this math plays out. Suppose that guests will book more nights when there are more hosts available, but they'll book no more than five nights a month (people have to go home at some point!) Thus, adding more hosts per guest would have diminishing returns in terms of the number of nights booked.[c]

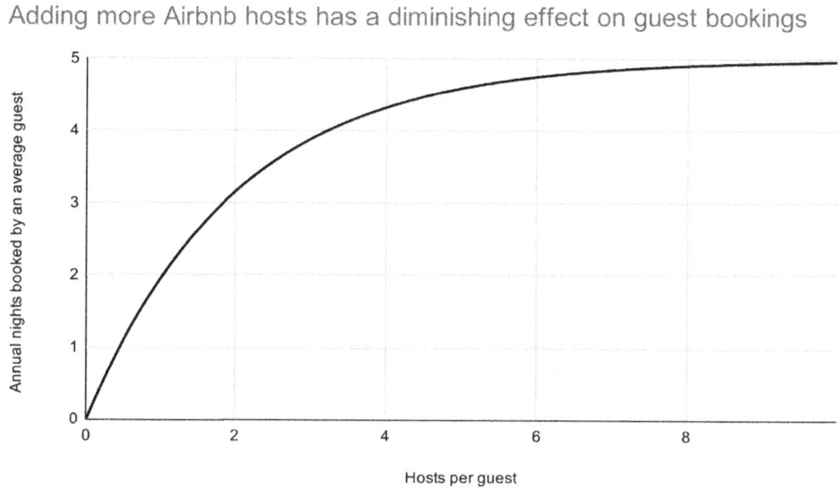

Adding Airbnb hosts gives users more choice and thus increases the number of nights they'll book every year, but there's an upper limit. Using our example data, the average user won't book more than five nights per year no matter how many hosts are available to them.

Now, imagine Airbnb has a lot of guests but not many hosts. The number of nights booked, based on the number of guests and hosts on the platform, is shown on the below graph.[d39] Adding more guests won't help much: if Airbnb had 20 hosts and doubled the number of guests from 20 to 40, they'd only grow total nights booked from 39 to 44. It would be a waste, then, to invest in features or marketing campaigns

[c]The formula we're for the number of nights booked per guest is $N(x) = -5e^{-0.5x} + 5$, where x is the ratio of hosts to guests (if there are h hosts and g guests, $x = h/g$).

[d]The formula for total number of nights booked is $B(g, h) = N(h/g) * g$, where there are g guests and h hosts, and N is the hosts-per-guest function we showed earlier.

designed to add guests. The PM's money would be better spent attracting more hosts: if there are 20 guests and 20 hosts, adding just 10 more hosts would increase nights booked from 39 to 53.

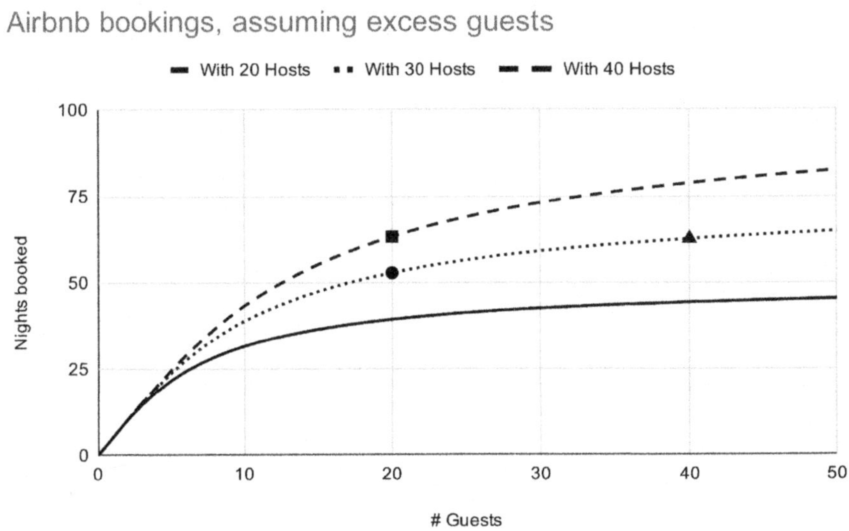

A model of how many Airbnb nights would be booked given a lot of guests and not many hosts. Adding guests (going from the circle to the triangle) doesn't increase bookings much, while adding hosts (going from the circle to the square) has much better returns. Moral of the story: don't add even more of a resource that you already have in excess.

On the flip side, if Airbnb has excess hosts, adding even more hosts won't help. With 30 guests and 150 hosts, Airbnb would get 138 nights booked. Adding 100 more hosts would only add 10 more nights booked, while adding just 10 guests would add 31 more nights booked.

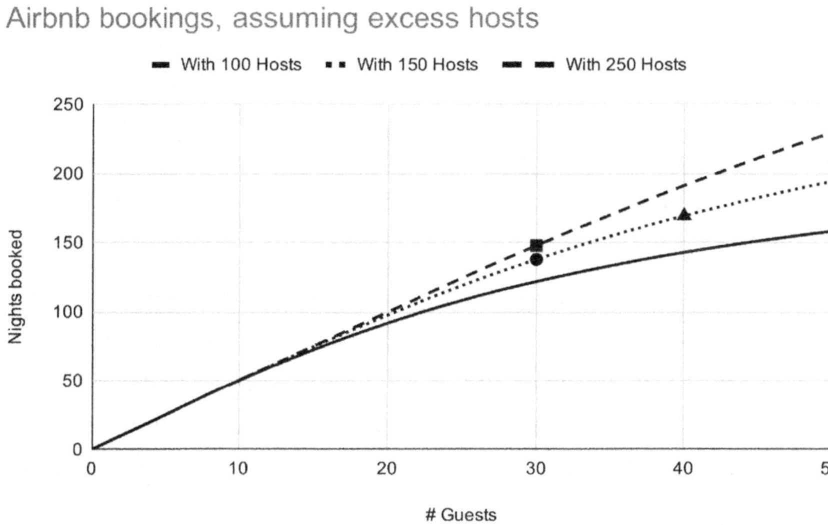

A model of how many Airbnb nights would be booked given a lot of hosts and not many guests. Adding even more hosts (going from the circle to the square) doesn't grow bookings much, while adding guests (going from the circle to the triangle) has a big impact.

The moral of the story: stay focused on your top-line, or *north star*, metric, which for two-sided markets is usually the number of transactions made. It's good to increase the sub-metrics like number of buyers or number of sellers, but they may not always improve your top-line metric. A great PM for a two-sided marketplace will know the balance of buyers and sellers, and thus the best metric to move to increase the number of transactions.

Ecommerce

Ecommerce is slightly different from the four other business models we discussed in that it engages far more with the "physical world": you have to move physical goods around, not just bits of digital data. It's just a digital version of a typical store: people buy goods on your website, and you ship the goods to them.

The main tech company in this space is Amazon, but it also includes the ever-popular *dropshipping* businesses (which ship straight from the manufacturer to the buyer)[40] and *direct-to-consumer*, or *D2C*, companies like Casper, Warby Parker, Glossier, and Dollar Shave Club.[41] (D2C companies aren't *really* tech companies,[42] but since they hire PMs like tech companies[43] we'll discuss them here.)

As we mentioned earlier, the fundamental revenue model of an ecommerce business is the cart size, or *Average Order Value* (*AOV*).[44] Increasing the number of users is good, but the cart size affects profitability more directly. Ecommerce businesses usually need larger cart sizes to offset the fixed costs of acquiring users, shipping products, and running the store.[45]

Another important metric is the *conversion rate*, which simply measures the percent of visitors who buy something. It's a bit of an oversimplification, since it splits visitors into only "buyers" and "non-buyers" without accounting for the fact that some buyers spend a lot more money on your site than others. But still, it's such a common ecommerce metric that it's good to track. By one estimate, the average ecommerce conversion rate hovers between 2% and 3%.[46]

A third metric that ecommerce PMs need to worry about is the cart conversion rate — or, more specifically, its inverse, the *abandonment rate*. By one estimate, over 60% of carts on ecommerce websites are abandoned; shoppers fill them up but never check out.[47] If you can help nudge users toward buying the items in their forgotten carts, you'll be able to rake in a lot of money that would otherwise be left on the table.

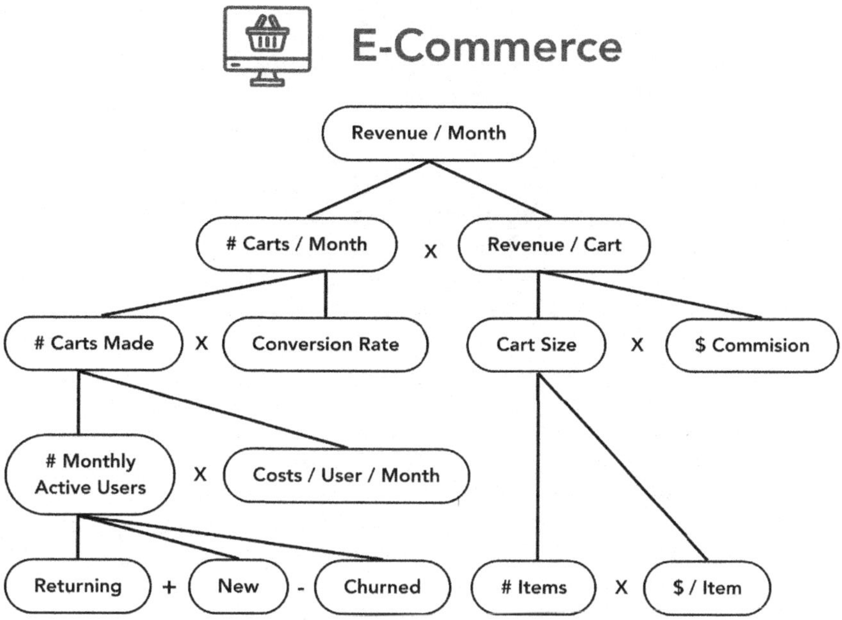

The metrics tree for ecommerce products. Revenue comes down to the number of carts sold and the revenue per cart.

User metrics

On the user metrics side, ecommerce companies focus much more on getting users to buy — or *convert* — than other software companies, which focus on keeping users entertained and engaged. Someone who visits Facebook every day is probably worth a lot to Facebook, but someone who visits Amazon every day without buying anything is of no economic value to Amazon. Thus, ecommerce companies really focus on pushing users through the "funnel" of visit–see–click–buy.[48]

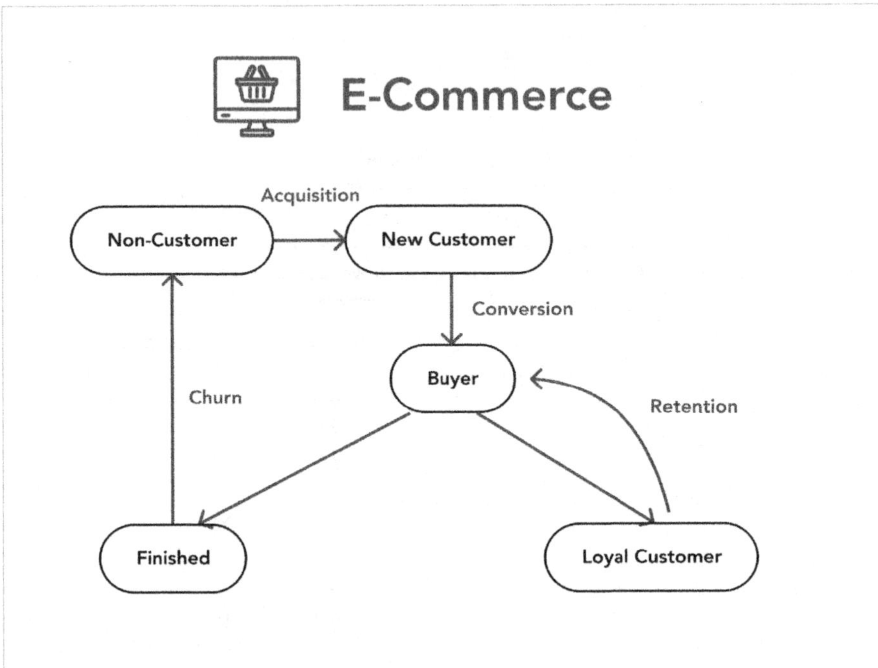

The stages that ecommerce users flow through. Notice how important the AARRR metrics are here.

It's worth noting that the AARRR metrics are at their most powerful for ecommerce websites, since the flow from A to A to R to R to R is so important. Ecommerce PMs should use the AARRR framework liberally.

Loyalty

An interesting twist is that ecommerce PMs have to decide whether to focus on one-time or loyal customers, whereas most other software PMs just try to get all users into the "loyal" bucket.

Many ecommerce sites, such as those selling wedding materials, will probably mostly have one-time customers — and that's OK! One rule of thumb is to look at your *annual repurchase rate*, or the percent of last year's customers who bought again this year, to figure out where to put your energy. If your annual repurchase rate is less than 40%, you should focus on bringing in new customers since you aren't likely to get loyal customers; if your rate is over 70%, you should focus on customer loyalty.[49]

Chapter 24

Storytelling with Data

As we've learned, data is a key part of telling convincing stories, winning people over, and rallying people to act. "Data wins arguments" is a popular saying around Silicon Valley.[1]

But there's more to storytelling than raw data. You can't win over VPs, users, and potential investors by plopping a spreadsheet on their desk or throwing numbers at them. Making a bunch of graphs and charts helps, but data doesn't speak for itself. You can use data to support your arguments, but you have to have a compelling story and vision first. Let's explore some of the more valuable lessons we've learned about the best ways for PMs to marshal data to support their claims.

A T-shirt being given away by a data-analysis startup at a conference in 2016. Source: Interana[2]

Engage people's imaginative side

When the three of us — your authors — worked at Microsoft, we wanted to convince company leaders to create an "internal startup incubator," where Microsoft employees could take a few months off their day jobs to work on a startup and get funding from Microsoft — all while staying employed at Microsoft.[3] A key part of our argument was that Microsoft was losing valuable employees and missing out on a lot of potential revenue and innovation, and our proposal would stop the bleeding.

We knew we had to get data to support this argument. We found that several hot companies were formed by ex-Microsofties: Zillow,[4]

Glassdoor,[5] the video game company Valve (the makers of Steam),[6] and the car data company INRIX.[7][a] They had a combined valuation of about $12 billion at the time.

We considered emphasizing the $12 billion in lost capital but instead decided to emphasize the companies that Microsoft missed out on. Why? We knew that, if we emphasized a dollar figure, people would go into "spreadsheet mode" and get bogged down thinking about financials. We knew they'd find ways to contradict the argument. *"Microsoft is worth hundreds of billions of dollars — who cares about a measly $12 billion? We could easily make that much money with Office. Those companies would have been worth less had they stayed with Microsoft."*

By emphasizing the companies Microsoft missed out on, we made people think wistfully about what could have been. *"Man, wouldn't it have been cool if our Xbox division owned Steam? Imagine how much better LinkedIn would be if we could connect it with Glassdoor."* And so on. We engaged the creative and imaginative part of people's brains instead of their mundane, number-focused sides.

To strengthen our argument further, we decided to draw on the power of *FOMO*, the *fear of missing out.* We argued that competitors had been offering this perk for years: Google's Area 120 has been a huge draw for talented techies who want the opportunity to pursue their dreams without giving up their jobs.[8] Just imagine how many talented employees turned down an offer from Microsoft because it didn't have such a valuable perk!

Again, numbers would have only weakened our argument. It was more effective to just make it seem like the company was at a permanent disadvantage, missing out on some potentially incredible opportunity, and then to let people's imaginations run wild.

---

[a]Expedia is the most famous ex-Microsoft company, but it was actively spun off from Microsoft in the 1990s. We focused on companies made by people who had left Microsoft just before founding the company.

We took our number-light, emotion-heavy argument to company leadership, and it worked: Microsoft implemented a moonlighting program like the one we described.

The lesson is that you can't rely on data to carry your argument; it won't give it any emotional heft. You should build your argument around examples, stories, and "what-if" scenarios that engage people's imaginative side, and only use data to back up your claims. Data isn't enough to win people over.

Tell people what to think

Suppose you work at Lyft and want to convince leaders to try your bold new product idea. You compile data on your and Uber's stock prices and throw them on a slide deck:

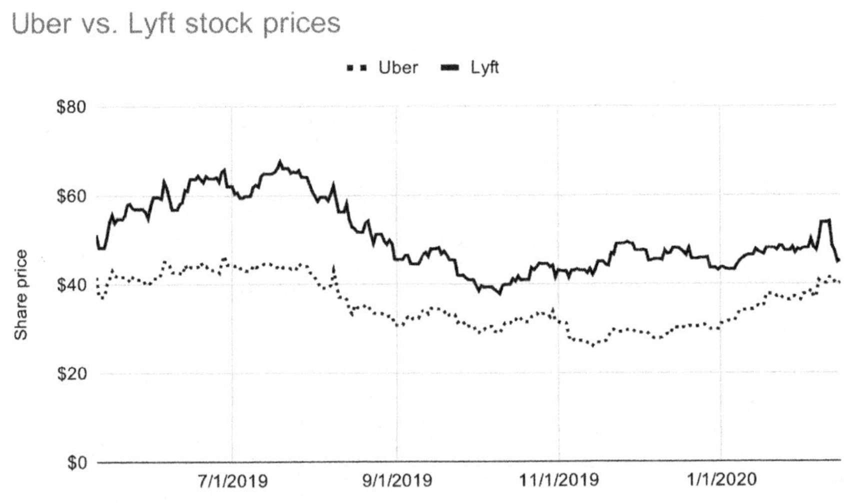

A straightforward graph that shows Uber and Lyft's stock prices over time. Source: Google Finance

The graph you make doesn't say much by itself. It tells you that Uber and Lyft stock prices have moved pretty much in lockstep over the selected interval, but it doesn't explain your argument at all. When a VP looks at this graph, they'll probably get caught up looking at the lines and fail to see your point. But the remarkable stability of the two companies' stock prices can be spun to make an argument.

You could take the exact same graph and just change the title to read, "Lyft has failed to outcompete Uber," emphasizing that Lyft's stock price hasn't zoomed ahead of Uber's at a time when it really needs to.

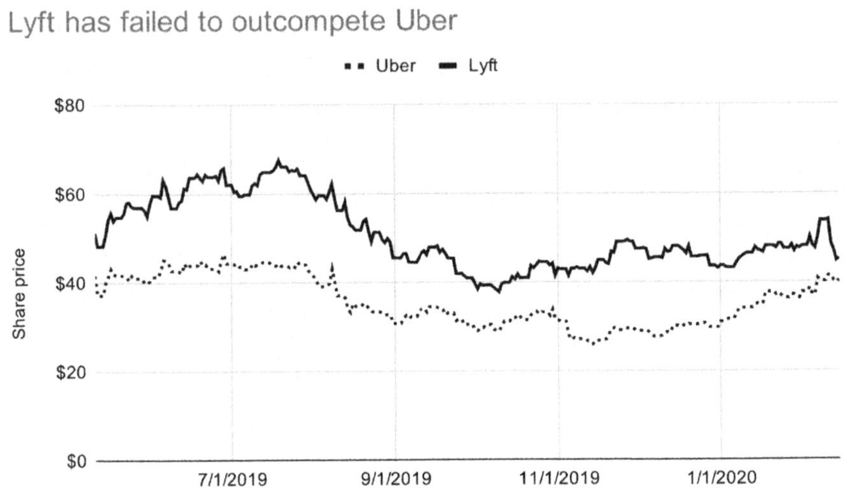

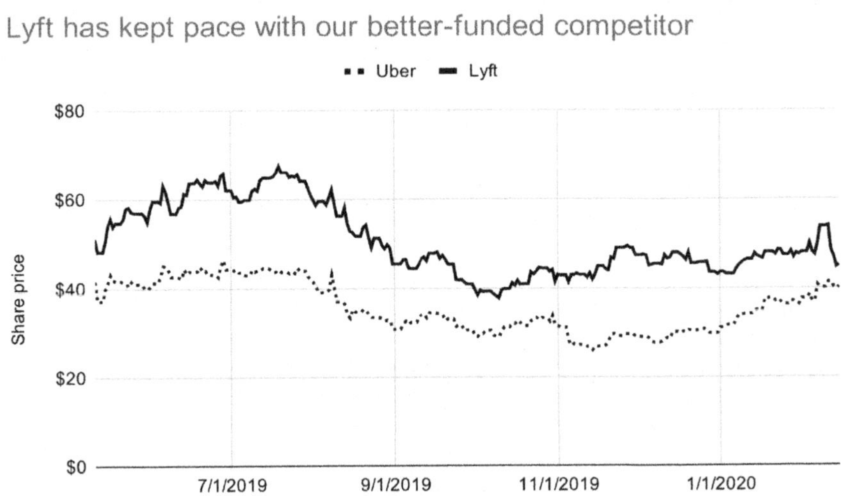

The exact same graph of Uber and Lyft's stock prices can take two very different meanings depending on the title attached to the graph. Source: Google Finance

All of a sudden, this graph reads as a damning indictment of Lyft's business practices. It gets the VPs thinking, *this PM is right — why haven't we done anything bolder*? Just by making the graph title tell people what to think, you can get data that otherwise looks ambiguous to make a convincing case for you.

This tactic is so powerful that it could take the exact same data and tell a completely different story. Suppose, instead, that you wanted to make Lyft executives more cautious. Then you could take your exact same graph and change the title again, this time to, "Lyft has kept pace with our better-funded competitor."

Now the stable stock prices look good for Lyft, and the graph's meaning changes yet again. The graph is reassuring, leading executives to pat themselves on the back and start thinking that they may not want to take any additional risk — they should just keep doing what they're doing.

Even if you have a dataset that you think speaks for itself, you should make sure the title explains your key takeaway. You've spent much more time looking at the graph and underlying data, so you'll be able to see all the nuances. Someone seeing it for the first time may not grasp exactly what it means — so you need to guide them along. And in doing so, you can steer the audience toward your desired point of view.

Avoid misleading scales

One of the most common shady data visualization tactics is to distort data scales to make your product or work look better than it really is. Consider this infamous Microsoft ad designed to show how much better Edge was than competing browsers:

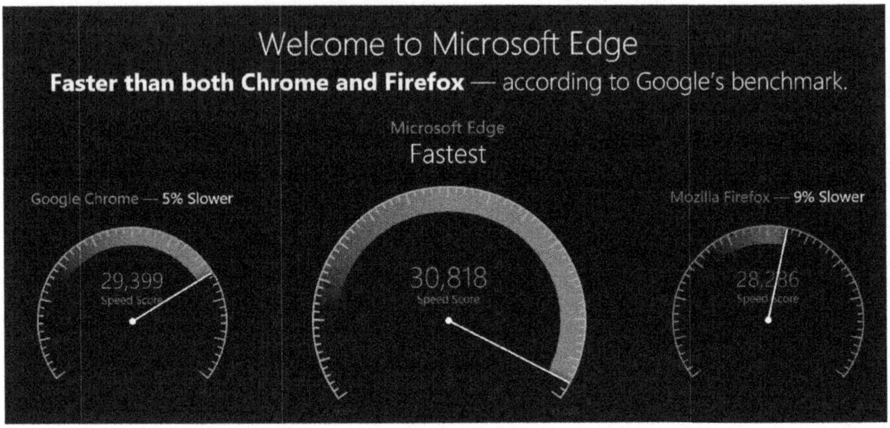

A misleading graphic that Microsoft made to make Edge look far superior to other web browser. Source: Mr. Banewolf on Reddit[9]

Edge has a 5% and 9% edge on Chrome and Firefox respectively, but the graphic makes it look like Edge leaves the rest in the dust. This is because the ad starts the "speedometer" at 25,000 and ends it at 31,000.[b] Graphing the numbers accurately would show that the three browsers were nearly tied, especially when you consider that there was some margin of error:

[b]This visualization would have been perfectly fine if the test only gave out scores from 25,000 to 31,000, like how all SAT subject scores are between 200 and 800. (Though it would be hard to assign a percent difference in that case.)

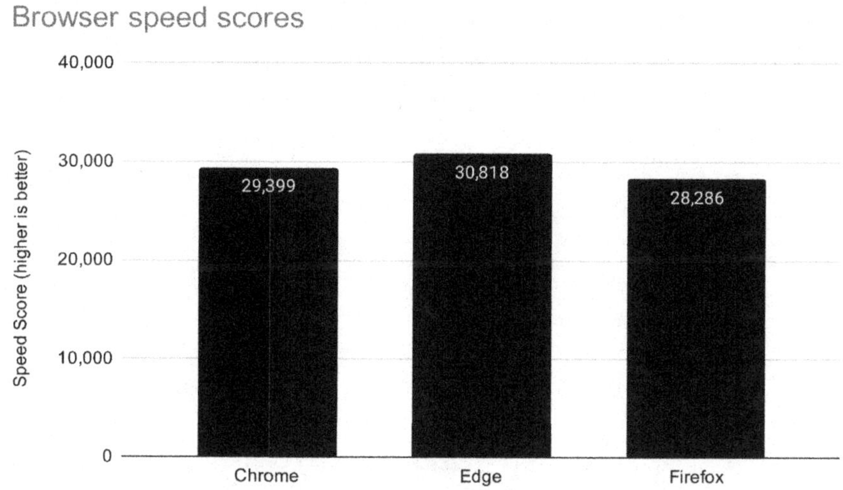

With a normal axis, we see that Edge isn't much better than its competitors. Source: Mr. Banewolf on Reddit[10]

Misleading scales might fool people who look for just a second, but they'll see right through it given enough time — and this tactic would probably make you look bad.

Control the narrative

Back in 2009, Verizon circulated a map bragging about how much better its 3G coverage was than that of its archrival AT&T. AT&T only covered patchy areas around the coasts and big cities; Verizon, meanwhile, bathed the entire continental US in a glorious sea of ruby red.[11] Verizon correctly argued that it had *five times* more coverage than AT&T, a powerful boast.

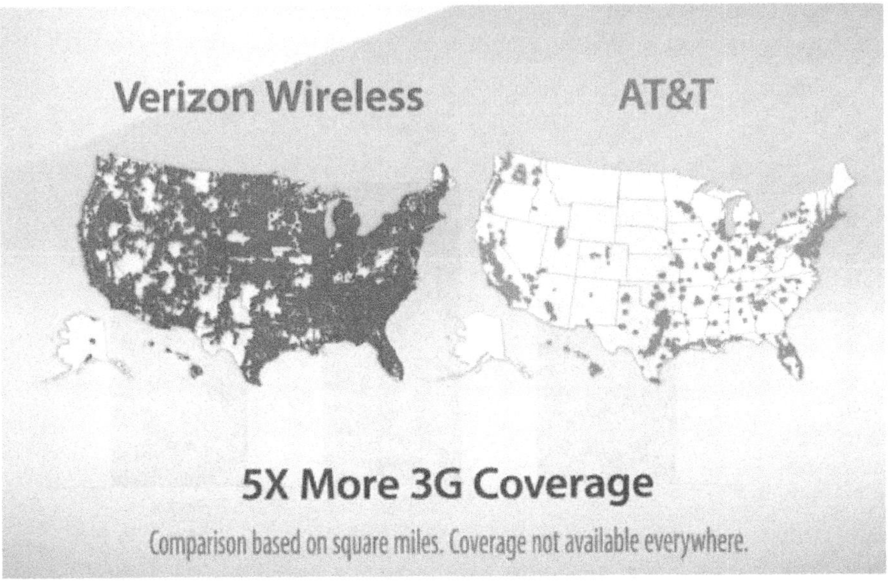

An ad that Verizon put out to showcase how much more land its 3G network covered than rival AT&T. Source: Fast Company[12]

AT&T struck back, saying that Verizon's boast was meaningless. Sure, Verizon covered a lot more land in the middle of Wyoming, but who lived there? Cows don't need 3G coverage. AT&T argued that, while their network only covered one-fifth of America, it covered 97% of *Americans* — and that's what mattered. [13] AT&T even sued Verizon for making the misleading graph.[14]

This story shows how the exact same data can be interpreted in two very different ways, each serving a very different narrative. Verizon savvily interpreted the data in a way that made them look good, while AT&T found another interpretation that made them look reasonable and Verizon look sleazy. Your competitors will often spin the data to make you look bad — so you have to wrest control back by putting out a more favorable interpretation.

Conclusion

LET'S GO FULL CIRCLE by revisiting Ballmer's story. By the metrics of revenue and profitability, he excelled. But those aren't the metrics that matter the most.

Microsoft's stock price stagnated during Steve Ballmer's tenure as CEO. Source: Google Finance

Just look at the stock price, one of the key signals of a CEO's success.[1] Microsoft started the 2000s as the most valuable public corporation on Earth, but the stock price stagnated for the entirety of Ballmer's tenure. By the time Ballmer left, Microsoft's stock price was lower than it had been when he'd joined, and Apple's stock price had left Microsoft's in the dust.[2]

In optimizing so relentlessly for short-term revenue and profit, Ballmer caused the company a lot of long-term harm. The shortsighted drive for money led to higher-ups stifling any ideas that threatened the Windows cash cow; this led to massive bureaucracy and the death of many ideas that the company should have invested in for the sake of its long-term health.[3] Microsoft missed the boat on smartphones, tablets, music players, and ebooks — teams in the company had prototypes of these products, but these products were killed in the infighting[4] because they didn't prop up Windows.[5]

Ballmer also allowed a destructive culture to take root — something that didn't affect the short-term revenue numbers but hollowed out the company that was once the "hippest company on earth." The most infamous example was Microsoft's practice of "stack ranking," where employees were graded on a "curve;" only a fixed percent could get positive reviews, and a fixed fraction of the lowest scoring employees were fired every year. This led to terrible incentives: people tried to sabotage their colleagues' ideas so they could go higher on the bell curve, engineers spent more time playing politics than building great products, good employees were graded badly because their boss had sold them out for political gain, and teams would avoid collaborating with other teams to preserve their ratings.[6]

Ballmer maximized the metrics, but he missed all the other parts of being a leader. By the end of his tenure, Ballmer was rated one of the worst CEOs in the world.[7]

When Ballmer's successor, Satya Nadella, took over, his first order of business was to fix the culture, pivoting away from a Windows-centric model and encouraging cross-company collaboration again.[8] Stack ranking was out; the idea of a "growth mindset," which encourages employees to make mistakes and learn instead of always trying to be perfect, was in.[9] The company would no longer try to crush rivals;

instead, it would work with them.[10] Even the company's mission statement changed from dominating the PC market to "empower[ing] every person and every organization on the planet to achieve more."[11]

None of these things immediately moved the bottom line, but they drove Microsoft's revival. The improved culture helped Microsoft reclaim its spot in the list of best companies to work for.[12] Without the short-termist obsession with Windows, Microsoft was able to discover cloud computing with Azure, which eventually became a multi-billion-dollar business.[13] In 2018, Nadella was named the best CEO of a large US company.[14]

Nadella didn't do much for Microsoft's revenue: during his first few years at the helm, the company's revenue grew at about 10% a year, virtually unchanged from Ballmer's tenure.[15] But pretty much everyone would agree that Nadella was the more effective CEO.

So while we've talked at length about the importance of quantitative metrics, you can't put on your blinders and ignore everything else. The qualitative side matters, especially for the long term. As Nadella shows, understanding the intangibles is just as important for a leader as maximizing the tangibles.

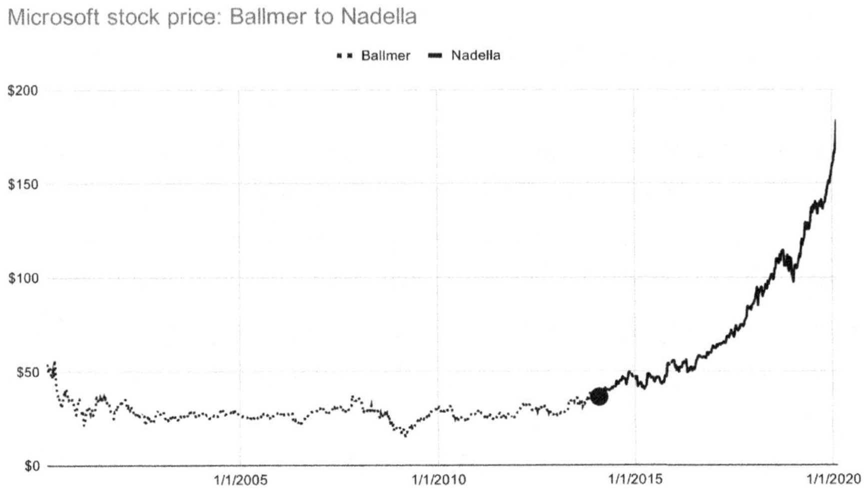

Microsoft's stock price started skyrocketing as soon as Satya Nadella took over as CEO. Source: Google Finance

(Fittingly enough, Nadella has *also* been better for Microsoft's stock price than Ballmer: the price nearly quintupled over Nadella's first six years, handily outpacing the S&P 500 and even beating Apple.[16] It turns out that focusing on qualitative metrics ends up helping you with quantitative metrics in the long run!) ❦

All QR codes from Part V

In case you skipped over any QR codes from the last few chapters, here's a roundup. Scan them with your phone to watch bonus videos and try interactive demos.

A mock interview that discusses Simpson's Paradox, a common pitfall to avoid when analyzing data:

productalliance.com/videos/explainer

A mock interview where a Facebook PM defines proxy metrics for time on site (ToS):

productalliance.com/videos/metrics

VI

Law & Policy

Laws without morals are in vain.

— University of Pennsylvania motto

Introduction

Uber got away with a lot in its early years. In its birthplace of San Francisco, the SF transit agency slapped the company with a cease-and-desist order in 2010, yet the company kept sending drivers out on the roads.[1] Uber famously engaged in tactics like "greyballing"— showing regulators fake cars on the Uber app but never actually letting them get a ride, thus stifling sting operations.[2] The company even hired contractors to call and cancel Lyfts to frustrate Lyft drivers.[3] These same contractors would then ultimately get in Lyfts and aggressively try to persuade the drivers to switch to Uber.[4]

Uber's luck started running out in 2017. That year, it was hit with a $20 million fine for allegedly lying to drivers about how much money they could reasonably earn.[5] It was the same year that Google's self-driving car subsidiary, Waymo, sued Uber for stealing its secrets,[6] leading Uber to pay Waymo $245 million in a settlement the next year.[7] These scandals were among the factors that led Uber's founder, Travis Kalanick, to resign from his post as CEO by the end of the year.[8]

The moral of the story is that you can only get away with breaking the law for so long: it'll catch up with you eventually. We've seen that our peer PMs often consider the legal department a nuisance standing in the way of rapid product growth. But it's foolish to believe that. Knowing the law and knowing how to comply with it can help your company avoid some expensive fines — and it can even give your business a decided advantage.

Chapter 25

Antitrust

OUR FAVORITE THING about Lyft is that it keeps Uber in check. Without Lyft, you'd have to pay Uber whatever it asked if you needed a ride home at 3am.

A market with just two competitors isn't ideal, but it is a lot better for the consumer than a market dominated by a single player. By clearing the market of competitors, a monopoly can drive up costs, shut down innovation, and put customers at its mercy.[1]

In the tech industry's infancy, tech companies were seen as ambitious young upstarts, bravely disrupting powerful companies like Walmart and CNN. But as the industry has grown, the big tech companies have become tremendously powerful[2] and eager to acquire competitors and consolidate the market.[3]

To stop monopolies, governments have instituted *antitrust* laws, the most famous of which is the United States' Sherman Antitrust Act of 1890.[4] The Sherman act, which makes it illegal to unfairly restrict competition, helped counter John D. Rockefeller's domination of the American oil industry[5] and Andrew Carnegie's ownership of most of the US steel industry.[6]

Antitrust laws like the Sherman Act may be over a hundred years old, but they're still potent, and in recent years politicians like Senator Elizabeth Warren[7] have called for big tech companies like Facebook, Google, and Amazon to be broken up. This has, predictably, caused fear around Silicon Valley.[8]

It's not as simple as "this company is big, so break it up." That's a mistaken assumption that many PMs who only casually follow the news take away. Let's dig into the depths of monopolies and antitrust to understand what's really going on.

Amazon and the shifting definition of "monopoly"

What is a monopoly, anyway? The US Federal Trade Commission (FTC) is tasked with regulating monopolies in the US, and over the years it's developed an opinion on that question. The FTC notes that some companies become monopolies by just being better than the rest: they have a better product, a better business strategy, a stronger brand, and so on. The FTC is fine with these.

Rather, the FTC takes issue with companies that exhibit *anticompetitive behavior*: those firms that abuse their market power to unfairly gain more market share or wipe out competitors, leaving an unequal playing field.[9] The Department of Justice's rule of thumb is that companies with over 50% market share in an industry may be monopolies and should be scrutinized; anyone with less market share can't be a monopoly.[10]

But there's a fine line between hard-nosed business strategies and outright anticompetitive moves, so when judging if a company is a monopoly, lawmakers try to apply tests to figure out where a company falls.

The European Union (EU) uses the *"as efficient competitor,"* or *AEC*, test to determine if a company is using anticompetitive tactics. It's quite straightforward: would a competitor that's just as competent (or "as efficient") stand a fighting chance? If the answer is no, the playing field isn't level, and competition and innovation that could help consumers is being suppressed.[11] The AEC test is in line with the FTC's framing from earlier: it's fine if a company gains power by being better than the competition, but it's not fine if a mediocre company abuses its power to stop companies that would otherwise be good enough to compete.[12]

While the FTC has its theoretical framing, it applies a quite different test when actually judging if a company is being anticompetitive. Since the 1970s, the US has applied the *"consumer welfare standard"*: anything goes, so long as it keeps prices for consumers down.[13] This framing lets companies that keep prices low but shut down innovation off the hook, so it misses out on a big part of the problem with monopolies.

The case of Amazon

The EU's innovation-focused test and the US's price-focused test often give the same answer: when conventional companies like airlines merge, it's bad for innovation *and* drives up prices, so both governments would say it's anticompetitive. But in tech, products remain cheap or even free no matter how much anticompetitive behavior is going on, so tech companies largely get a pass from antitrust regulators in the US, even as the EU seeks to crack down on them.

The most infamous case of this split is Amazon. The company that pulls in over $250 billion in revenue a year[14] is infamous for its aggressive practices to drive out competing ecommerce websites. In 2009, Amazon approached an up-and-coming ecommerce startup called Quidsi, which sold diapers on its website, Diapers.com. Amazon offered to buy the company.[15] When Quidsi refused, Jeff Bezos went scorched-earth, slashing prices for baby products on Amazon by 30%,[16] thus undercutting Quidsi and forcing Diapers.com to sell diapers at a loss. Quidsi lost $30 million a month, lost most of their customer base, and nearly collapsed. Amazon then bought the hollowed-out shell of Quidsi on the cheap.[17]

This is a common tactic for Amazon. Its Amazon Web Services (AWS) division produces vast amounts of profit — in 2017, all of Amazon's profit came from AWS[18] — which lets Amazon's ecommerce divisions offer incredibly low prices, thus undercutting and driving out competitors.[19]

But, obviously, this keeps prices low, which means that Amazon gets a free pass under the American "consumer welfare" regime. Customers know that they're getting incredible deals from Amazon: it's repeatedly named among the top five most loved brands in America.[20]

As the Quidsi story shows, though, Amazon fails the EU's AEC test for ecommerce. Even mighty Walmart can't keep up, posting barely half the annual growth rates of Amazon.[21] Amazon Prime is a powerful loyalty engine, which makes it hard for ecommerce competitors to get even a second look from Amazon shoppers.[22]

Amazon's sheer stock of capital has let it handily outpace its ecommerce rivals in shipping. It offered two-day shipping before Walmart and Target caught up[23] and is now leading the way on one-day shipping.[24] Walmart, in its mad dash to catch up with Amazon, estimated it lost over $1 billion in 2019 on its ecommerce platform.[25] (You know it's bad when even the world's largest employer[26] is struggling to keep pace.) You can imagine that smaller ecommerce firms stand no chance of keeping up with Amazon; Amazon's dominance thus restricts innovation and startup formation.

Besides low pricing, Amazon's other trick for dodging antitrust regulation is how it redefines the market. By 2020, Amazon controlled over half the US ecommerce market;[27] remember that 50% is the threshold at which the DOJ starts suspecting that companies are monopolies. But if you redefine Amazon's market as the broader retail market, Amazon has just 10% market share as of the time of writing.[28]

But Amazon's favorite tactic is to redefine itself not as a scrappy company competing in the retail space but rather as the *enabler* of other small businesses. In response to antitrust claims, Amazon points at the thousands of small businesses that operate on its platform, selling and distributing products with Amazon's website and logistics services.[29] That is, Amazon leans into its bigness, saying, "we may be huge and we may be swallowing the retail market, but many small businesses need our platform to survive."

If Amazon's position seems contradictory, that's because it is. Amazon wants to seem like just another small business when it helps them escape scrutiny, but it also wants to look like large and essential infrastructure when it helps make the case for retaining its power. It's a strange dance, but it's effective.

Microsoft's browser wars

Microsoft is known today as a gentle giant, and Bill Gates known as one of the world's most famous philanthropists, but that wasn't always the case. The company had two famous brushes with antitrust law in the past. The first was in the 1990s browser wars.

Riding high after antitrust actions weakened IBM — its chief rival — in the 1980s, Microsoft went to war with its remaining competitors in the personal computing space. In 1995, Gates noted that the internet was the future, calling it "the tidal wave."[30]

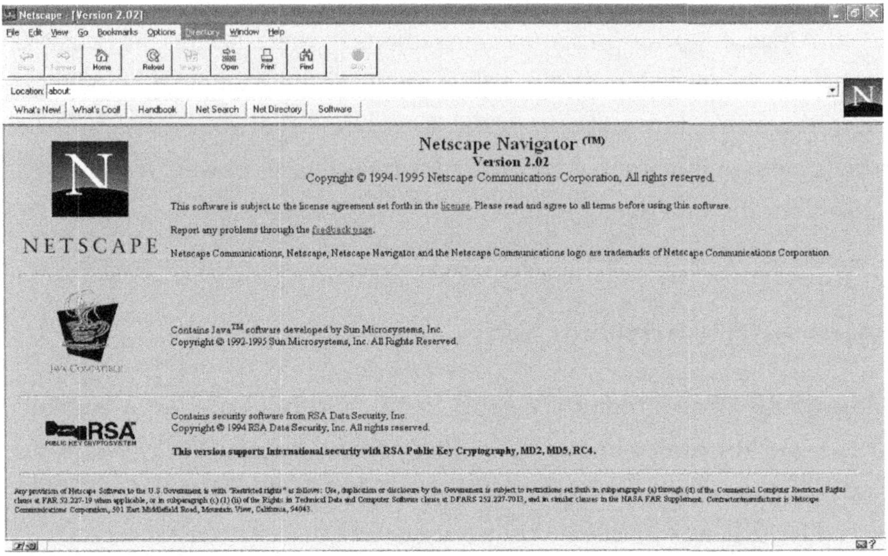

The Netscape Navigator browser in 1995. Source: Wikimedia[31]

Netscape Navigator

Windows' main competitor in the internet space, at the time, was a company called Netscape, which ran a popular web browser called Netscape Navigator.[a] Gates attempted to "smother" Navigator by bundling Internet Explorer for free with Windows and pressuring prominent companies to stick with IE instead of switching to Netscape.[32] By monopolizing the browser market, Microsoft figured it could control the web, and thus the future of personal computing.[33]

Microsoft's strategy worked: Navigator's market share crashed from well over 80% in 1996, to 48% in 1998, to just 6% in 2001.[34] Netscape saw heavy financial losses in this time, culminating in a round of almost 400 layoffs in 1998,[35] and the company slid into a long decline, with AOL acquiring the company in 2002[36] and disbanding the company

[a] The browser is often just called Netscape.

in 2003.[37] Microsoft's Internet Explorer became the new king of the hill, with over 94% browser market share in 2004.[38] (The browser that began to knock down IE in 2004? Mozilla Firefox, the open-source web browser that was created from the original source code of Netscape Navigator. The irony![39])

Embrace, extend, extinguish

Microsoft's even more famous anticompetitive tactic was called "embrace, extend, extinguish." The idea was that, if the rest of the market had agreed on a particular technical standard, Microsoft would *embrace* these standards, *extend* them with incompatible additions, and thus *extinguish* the competition.[40]

The term was coined in Microsoft in the 1990s as a tactic to bring down Netscape. Web pages have always been written in a programming language called *HTML*; it's an open standard, meaning that anyone can see the proper way to interpret HTML and draw a webpage.[41] This makes it easy for new web browsers to enter the market: anyone can read the standards and create a *rendering engine* to interpret the HTML of webpages. But Microsoft's plan was to create a proprietary extension to HTML that nobody else could implement, thus locking in Internet Explorer's advantage.[42]

It went like this: Internet Explorer was compatible with HTML, as were Netscape and other browsers, so IE could render any webpage that anyone else could. (Embrace.) But, in 1996, Microsoft introduced ActiveX,[43] a proprietary technology that let webpages embed special code that would only run in Internet Explorer.[44] (Extend.) This meant only IE, and not Netscape, could render every site on the web. Even Netscape fans had to install IE as a backup, and over time, people tired of having to switch between two browsers and settled with IE.[45] (Extinguish.) The browser market was no longer easy to enter, or even stay in.

Microsoft innovated hard on Internet Explorer until 2001, but Microsoft's various strategies, including "embrace, extend, extinguish," cleared the field, Microsoft stopped trying. Internet Explorer 6, released in 2001, achieved the aforementioned market share, and Microsoft didn't make serious changes to the browser[46] for a decade.[47] In the meantime, IE became a buggy mess and the bane of web developers' existence, given that it had a hard time rendering websites properly.[48] This was the danger of monopoly.

Microsoft gets the corner office

The web wasn't the only place where Microsoft used the "embrace, extend, extinguish" strategy. In 1998, Gates said he didn't want Microsoft Office documents to render well in other office suites, because that would be "suicide for our platform."[49] Most competing office suites used open document formats that anyone could implement, or at least they used formats that were compatible with other editors. Microsoft Word's biggest rival, WordPerfect, stored documents in the .wpd format, which Word could easily open.[50]

Word had thus embraced the standard formats of the time. Microsoft Word, though, stored documents in a proprietary .doc format, extending the open formats in an incompatible way. The effect was to extinguish the competition: the switching costs of leaving Word for WordPerfect or other competitors were too high, so Word became the *de facto* standard.[51] (Microsoft Office's dominance was, no doubt, helped by the fact that Gates crippled WordPerfect by not giving them access to key Windows *APIs*, or programming toolkits that let you interface with the operating system, in 1994, in a bid to help Microsoft Office.[52])

Lawsuits strike

These strategies led Microsoft to be hit with a wave of antitrust lawsuits, including one by WordPerfect in 1995.[53] The most consequential lawsuit was United States vs. Microsoft, an antitrust case begun in 1998 and closed in 2001.[54] (Yes, the United States of America took Microsoft to court, spurred by twenty state attorneys general starting similar suits.[55])

The suit aimed to break up Microsoft[56] so its hyper-popular Windows division couldn't unfairly help Internet Explorer and Office.

In 2000, Microsoft was found guilty of using anticompetitive practices. In a scathing verdict, a federal judge said that Microsoft put an "oppressive thumb on the scale of competitive fortune" and argued that:[57]

> *Microsoft mounted a deliberate assault upon entrepreneurial efforts that, left to rise or fall on their own merits, could well have enabled the introduction of competition into the market for Intel-compatible PC operating systems.*

While Microsoft narrowly avoided getting broken up, Bill Gates was pressured into stepping down as Microsoft CEO.[58] It was the end of an era for Microsoft, both in terms of its leadership and its use of aggressive, anticompetitive tactics.[59]

This case was credited with weakening Microsoft's dominance of personal computing, ensuring that it would never own the web the way it owned PCs and office suites. This, in turn, helped the rise of two hot internet startups in the early 2000s: Google and Facebook.[60] Microsoft has become far less brutal in its competition, now forming partnerships with rivals like Dropbox, Salesforce, and Amazon.[61]

What's more, Microsoft has since become a proponent, not an opponent, of open standards. Its new Edge browser, which succeeded Internet Explorer, embraces HTML without making incompatible extensions.[62] And, since 2007, Office has used open-source file formats, such as .docx, .pptx, and .xlsx, that are explicitly designed to be compatible with other editors.[63]

One thing to note from this saga is that a lot of Microsoft's individual decisions were perfectly defensible. Office suites are within their rights to create proprietary file formats. It's fine to introduce special technologies into your web browsers. And creating synergies[b] between two of

[b] We apologize for the buzzword, but it really is the right word for the job here.

your products, such that they work better when paired together, is usually OK when done judiciously. But Microsoft's actions, when looked at over the span of several years, painted a clear picture: Microsoft was abusing its power, especially with Windows, to give its products an unfair advantage. That is, no one tactic by itself made a drastic shift in the playing field, but combined, they made it stacked against competitors. PMs would do well to think about how their individual product decisions might feed into a broader story of anticompetitive behavior.

BrowserChoice.EU

The 1998 antitrust case was the most significant of Microsoft's history, but the company had a small second skirmish with antitrust lawyers a decade later, this time in the European Union.

In 2009, the EU was accused of not giving users a fair choice in browsers, given that Internet Explorer was still bundled with Windows and still heavily encouraged to be the default. The EU said that this move suffocated the browser ecosystem, thus reducing customer choice.[64] Recall that the EU takes threats to innovation more seriously than the US does — in this light, it should come as no surprise that the EU sued Microsoft for being anticompetitive with this tactic.[65]

Microsoft and the EU reached a deal: Microsoft could keep bundling IE with Windows, but it would have to offer European users a choice of several browsers when they first launched Windows.[66] This site was called BrowserChoice.EU,[67] and it included well-known browsers like Firefox, Google Chrome, Opera, and Apple's Safari (which, at the time, still had a Windows version),[68] as well as lesser-known browsers like Rockmelt, Flock, K-Meleon, and SRWare Iron.[69]

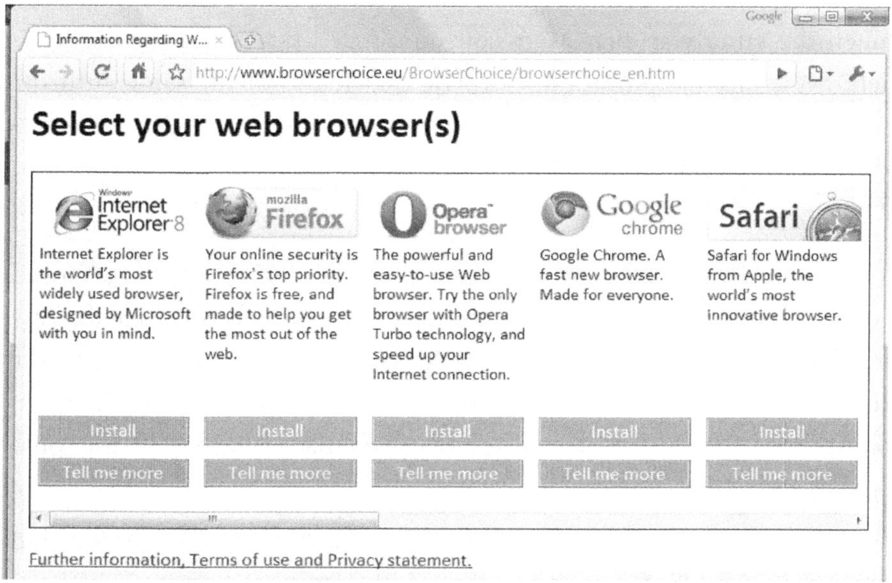

BrowserChoice.EU in 2010. Source: Pietro Zanarini[70]

Microsoft agreed to keep the website up until 2014.[71] That wasn't the end of the story, though: a 2013 update to Windows 7 stopped showing the BrowserChoice page, breaking the agreement.[72] When the EU found out, it slapped Microsoft with a $730 million fine.[73]

(Let this be a lesson to PMs: listen to your legal department! Small product decisions like removing a screen you thought was outdated can, quite literally, cost your company a fortune.)

Google's echoes of Microsoft

There's a strong case to be made that today's Google is similar to the 1990s' Microsoft. Google Chrome is now the world's most popular web browser,[74] and Google dominates the consumer technology space — browsers, phones, email, cloud storage, documents, maps, etc. — in much the same way that Microsoft dominated that space decades earlier. So it should come as no surprise that many of the same antitrust complaints have hit Google.

Tying

The most obvious example of this is when, in 2016, the EU charged Google with unfairly using Android — which controlled 75% of the European phone market at the time — to promote Google products over competitors.[75] By preinstalling products like Google Maps and Chrome on Android phones, the charge goes, Google made it far harder for competing services to get a foothold.[76]

(This is yet more proof that the EU values protecting innovation more than the US. "Google has abused its dominant position... [their] behavior has harmed consumers by restricting innovation in the wider mobile space," said the EU's antitrust chief.[77])

The EU refined this argument in 2018 when it fined Google $5 billion for breaking antitrust laws. The EU's executive arm, the European Commission, said that Google abused its market dominance with Android by forcing phone manufacturers to install various Google apps, like the search app and Chrome, to get access to the Google Play Store, which is by far the best way to find and install apps on Android. That suit also alleges that Google banned phone manufacturers from getting the Play Store if they used a spin-off, or *fork*, of Android.[78]

In other words, Google was using Microsoft's playbook of using one extremely powerful platform — Android, like the Windows of old — to give other products an unfair edge. In the world of law, this practice is known as *illegal tying*, where customers are forced to get a product they don't want to get a product they do want. The argument is that this arrangement gives those otherwise-unpopular products an unfair advantage.[79] (One classic example: if a novelist has written five bad books and one good one, it would be unfair if the publisher forced bookstores to buy all six books as a package instead of selling the good one by itself.)

Feeling the heat, Google quickly changed its approach. In 2018, Google changed its licensing agreements with European phone manufacturers, allowing them to preinstall non-Google browsers and search apps.[80] And in 2019, Android started showing Android users in Europe a page to let them choose a browser and search engine when they first opened their phone.[81] (In other words: BrowserChoice 2.0.)

Remember: there's a fine line between bundling products and illegal tying. Using products to support each other is a smart business move, but illegal tying is grounds for legal action. This is one of the topics PMs should bring up consistently with their legal teams, who can advise the right course of action.

This website only works on Chrome

Google may not have had the same "embrace, extend, extinguish" policy as Microsoft, but in the 2010s, we saw a similar, albeit smaller, outcome for the web. As Chrome became the most popular browser in the world — by far — it became the default for web developers as well. Web developers only built their sites to work for Chrome; they only tested for Chrome; and they only expected users to be using Chrome. In 2017, for instance, Airbnb and Groupon customer support staff explicitly said that their sites were only designed to work in Chrome and advised that users encountering problems should just switch to Chrome.[82]

Now, Google embraced open web standards quite admirably — it makes sure that standard HTML features and more cutting-edge features in the *HTML5* suite of web technologies[83] — and it hasn't extended them like Microsoft did. But the web ecosystem has evolved such that many popular sites are only compatible with Chrome, making many people who don't use Chrome daily keep the app around as a backup. What's more, Google has accelerated this trend by making first-party web apps like Google Earth[84] and key features like Google Drive offline storage[85] only work in Chrome. This has a chilling effect on the adoption of any other web browser.

Like Microsoft's "embrace, extend, extinguish" policy, this has the effect of making it harder for competing browsers to gain footholds. Competing browsers have adapted by copying Chrome's guts and just slapping a new layer of paint (and some special features) on them. This is what Microsoft's 2020 edition of its new web browser, Edge, did,[86] and it's what upstart browsers like Brave[87] and Vivaldi[88] did as well. While this is a short-term fix for those browsers, they're still at Chrome's mercy, since Chrome ultimately decides the browsers' core feature set. The theme with Google and Microsoft is consistent: trying to privatize a public ecosystem is generally seen as an anticompetitive move.

Facebook's social monopoly

When Mark Zuckerberg was testifying to Congress in 2019, he was asked to name a competitor to Facebook. He couldn't think of one.[89]

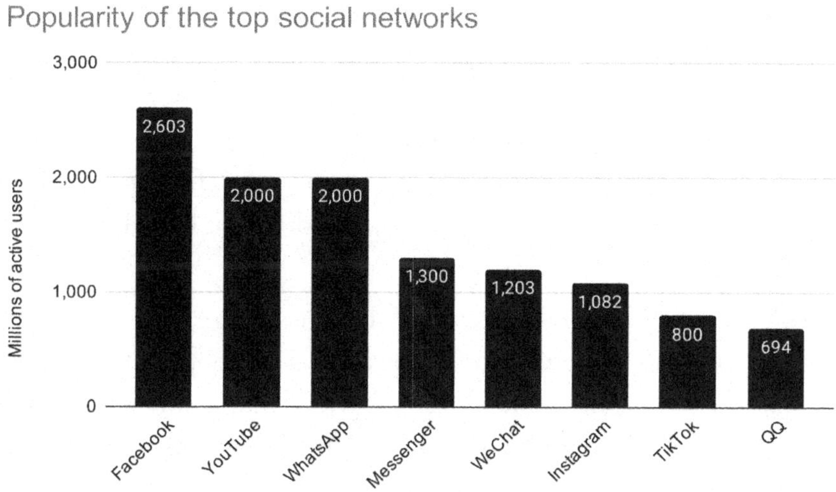

The top social networks by usage. Facebook controls 4 of the top 8. Source: Statista[90]

Like with Google and Microsoft, politicians and tech analysts alike have named Facebook as potentially monopolistic. In 2020, when claims about Facebook's anticompetitive practices, reached a fever pitch,[91] Facebook owned three of the top four social networks (WhatsApp, Messenger, and Facebook's flagship app). The other one is YouTube, but that's hardly a startup either.[92]

There were a handful of mostly-Chinese apps that could challenge Facebook farther down the list. WeChat came in at #5, TikTok at #7, and the instant messenger service QQ[93] at #8. But guess what was at #6? Facebook's Instagram.[94]

The dominance extends to revenue, too. Facebook cofounder Chris Hughes estimated in 2019 that the company controlled over 80% of the world's social media revenue.[95] This clearly fulfills the DOJ's criteria that any company with above 50% market share could be a monopoly.

Indeed, Facebook shows some telltale behaviors of a monopoly: it can set the prices for ads as it likes, since there aren't any major competitors who could offer similar ad slots for cheaper. Facebook reportedly artificially controls the number of available ad slots to drive up ad prices; in 2017, total ads shown on Facebook grew just 15% from the previous year, but ad prices surged 29%.[96] It's not that different from how OPEC controls oil prices.

(Isn't Google Facebook's archrival in advertising? Both sell digital ads, but they serve somewhat different markets. Google mostly serves *direct response ads*, which aim to get the viewer to immediately make a purchase, while Facebook has traditionally specialized *brand advertising*, which aims to build a positive brand impression with the user so they'll eventually buy more.[97][98] Think of it as "Buy Doritos online right now" versus "Reach for Doritos the next time you're in the supermarket." Google and Facebook serve a lot of overlap, but their core goals are different, so Google and Facebook aren't exactly head-to-head competitors.)

Buy or copy

Facebook achieved a lot of power through the *network effects* of its core apps, but one very important contributor to Facebook's rise has been its strategy of buying or copying competitors. The first social network that threatened Facebook was Instagram, which burst onto the scene in 2011;[99] the photo-first, mobile-first network was a much better fit for the era of smartphones than the text-first, desktop-first Facebook. Facebook bought it in 2012.[100]

The messaging app that most rivaled Facebook Messenger was WhatsApp, which by 2014 had nearly half a billion users[101] and was strong in the very places Facebook wasn't: India, Latin America,[102] and Africa,[103] among others. Facebook, as you can probably predict, bought WhatsApp in 2014.[104]

The next social network to challenge Facebook was Snapchat, which by 2016 had a rapidly-growing user base of 100 million people.[105] Snapchat was *the* app for people tired with Facebook and stood out by enabling spontaneous, silly communication and disappearing "stories." But that year, Facebook copied Snapchat's iconic stories feature, adding it to Instagram — and chopping off Snapchat's growth.[106] (Stories found their way into Facebook's core app[107] and WhatsApp[108] in 2017.) This move drew criticism in a way that Facebook's earlier acquisitions didn't; people around the tech world argued that Facebook was winning not by innovating but by free-riding off smaller competitors' innovations.[109]

Now, it's perfectly legal to copy features, and companies late to the market often do better than the first entrant: Google wasn't the first major search engine (there were AltaVista and Yahoo before[110]) and Facebook wasn't the first major social network (that was MySpace[111]). Even Airbnb wasn't the first house-rental platform; VRBO launched in 1995, a full decade before Airbnb.[112]

A chilling effect

But, like before, you have to look at the big picture; the combination of a bunch of otherwise innocuous moves can often be anticompetitive. And note that moves that don't seem anticompetitive at the time often become seen as such later. Chris Hughes said that, in retrospect, the FTC should never have let Facebook buy Instagram, calling it one of the FTC's all-time biggest mistakes.[113] US Senator Elizabeth Warren made a high-profile call to roll back the Instagram and WhatsApp purchases, calling them consolidation moves that people didn't take seriously enough at the time.[114]

The end result of Facebook's actions is that the Western tech ecosystem has become far less welcoming to social networking startups. If you're an American social networking startup, it seems like your only options are to get bought out by Facebook or to get copied — and beaten. Yes, there is the growth machine that is TikTok,[115] but it's telling that the app emerged out of the one major market that doesn't have Facebook: China.[116]

Data portability

To Mark Zuckerberg's credit, he's proactively called for Congress to create rules around *data portability*, which is the ability to move your posts, friend list, and other data automatically between social networks.[117] This is admirable because the *lack* of data portability makes it hard to switch social networks: having to start totally afresh is frustrating, especially since the #1 thing that makes social networks useful is the number of your friends who are on it.

In other words, *network effects* (when your platform gets exponentially more useful as more people join) and user investment (when users have already sunk a lot of time and energy into a platform) are powerful ways to preserve the status quo. Those aren't bad in and of themselves; they usually improve the user experience and give users more tools at their disposal. But, at the same time, they make it hard for new companies to enter the market. And when the status quo companies get too powerful, it becomes nigh impossible for a new entrant to take hold.

These data portability rules would let new social networks import the powerful network effects of older companies, thus making it easier for new companies to enter the market, thus increasing innovation. Data portability, in other words, can be a weapon against tech monopolization.

There have been promising moves in this space already: in 2019, the Data Transfer Project, a collaborative effort between Apple, Google, Microsoft, Twitter, Facebook, and other big tech companies, announced a tool to let you export your Facebook photos to the Google Photos app.[118] Rules like this will make it easy for new entrants to the photos space to experiment with new features and business models.

How big tech gets away with it

Antitrust enforcement in the United States has unquestionably gotten weaker in the last few decades. From 1970 to 1999, the US brought about fifteen antitrust cases per year. From 2000 to 2014, that number dropped to just three a year.[119] The FTC has been noticeably laxer in watching mergers. The airline and telecom industries, which were already controlled by a few big players, saw further consolidation in the 2010s and through 2020 as the FTC greenlit mergers like American Airlines–US Airways (creating what was then the world's biggest airline[120]) and Sprint–T-Mobile (reducing the number of major carriers in the US to just three).[121][c]

The path less scrutinized

While those airline and telecom mergers went through, they got a lot more scrutiny than tech mergers did. Why? One reason is that, as we mentioned earlier, the US is more focused on prices than innovation. It's pretty clear that reducing the number of airlines will drive up the average ticket price, but when most tech products are cheap or even free to begin with,[d] that concern doesn't get raised.

The more interesting reason, in our minds, is that the FTC focuses a lot on big head-to-head mergers;[122] they pay a lot of attention to major, direct rivals like T-Mobile and Sprint merging, but they don't scrutinize companies in adjacent spaces merging or companies buying upstarts. Big tech companies like to use those last two strategies: consider how Google bought YouTube (instead of another search engine like, say, Bing); Microsoft bought LinkedIn (instead of another cloud company like, say, Salesforce); or Amazon bought Twitch (instead of, say, eBay). And big

[c] As a consolation prize to consumers, Sprint agreed to sell some of its telecom business to Dish Network to create a new fourth telecom business. But just because there's a new business doesn't mean that it'll be large enough to succeed.

[d] Though you could argue that you pay for the "free" apps with your personal data.

tech, of course, likes the strategy of buying small companies that nobody pays much attention to: Instagram wasn't on regulators' radar before Facebook bought it, and most people probably still don't know the story of Amazon's purchase of Diapers.com.

Moving the goalposts

Another common strategy, and a quite shrewd one, is just redefine the market so you don't come close to dominating it.[123] It's hard to know if tech companies do this, but you can see how they would, in theory.

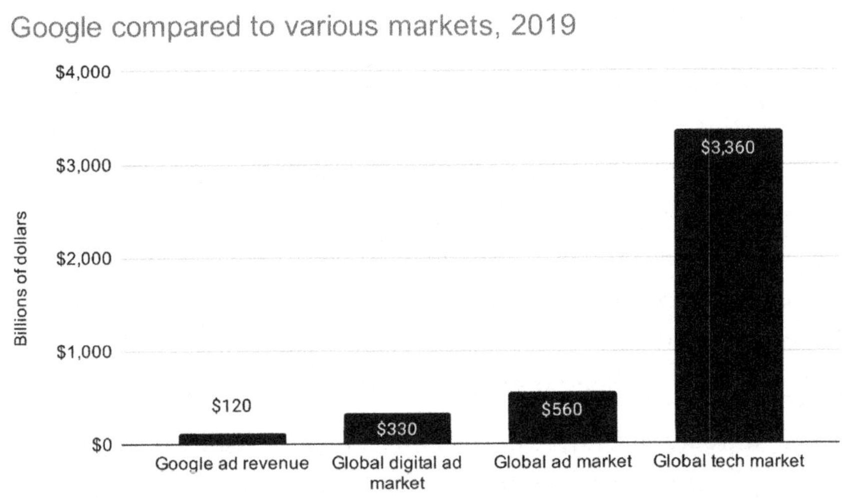

Google's 2019 revenue compared to the sizes of various global markets. Sources: Forbes,[124] eMarketer,[125] Statista[126][127]

Take Google. If Google called itself a search engine company, it would be dominant, with upwards of 90% market share.[128] That's alarmingly deep into monopoly territory.

But if Google called itself a digital ads company, it would only have 36% market share; Google's 2019 ad revenues were about $120 billion[129] out of an approximately $330 billion global digital ad market.[130] 36% is smaller, but still hints at Google's dominant position.

Google could go a step farther and call itself an ads company (dropping the "digital"). Google would then own just 21% of the $560 billion global ad market.[131] But if Google really wanted to slip under the radar, it could just call itself a consumer tech company. Google's $170 billion in total revenues[132] would comprise just 5% of the $3.36 trillion global tech market.[133]

In short, the smaller you look, the less attention regulators will pay to you. So it should be no surprise that tech titans regularly redefine who they are as they attempt to avoid scrutiny.

Chapter 26

Intellectual Property

MOST COMPANIES' most valuable assets are their warehouses, equipment, machines, trucks, and other physical goods. This is not the case for most tech companies, which care much more about their *intellectual property* than any physical item. Accordingly, anyone working at tech companies — but especially PMs — need to know the law around IP.

Types of IP

The United States, like most countries, recognized four kinds of intellectual property, or IP: copyrights (which protect original artistic and technological creations), trademarks (which protect a brand's use of particular names, logos, colors, or other symbols), patents (which protect the right to use an invention), and trade secrets (which protect a company's proprietary knowledge).[1] The two most relevant to PMs are copyrights and patents, but let's break down all four.

Copyrights and trademarks

The first important distinction is between copyrights and trademarks. Copyrights protect creations, like software, books, blog posts, and music. You're automatically granted a copyright whenever you create something new, and it lets you strike back against people who try to steal your ideas or claim them as their own.[2] While anyone can slap a "©" on their creation, you can register a copyright with the US government to make sure you can enforce your copyright claims in court.[3]

While copyrights apply to products, trademarks (and their cousins, service marks) apply to brands. When you consistently use a particular word, logo, color, sound, or other symbol to represent your brand, it becomes associated with your brand in the public eye — and then you can claim that symbol as a trademark. These trademarks are thus automatically granted with use, though you can register a trademark with the US Patent and Trade Office (USPTO)[4] and upgrade your "TM" symbol to a "®."[5a]

As an example, iPhones' default wallpapers and emoji sets are Apple creations and thus are copyrighted,[6] while Apple's logo, its brand names like "Mac" and "iPod," and its slogans are trademarked.[7] If a phone manufacturer tried to use Apple's emojis on its phone without permission, they'd be infringing Apple's copyrights; if a video game company tried to call their console the "iGame," they'd be violating Apple's copyrights.

Patents and trade secrets

The difference between patents and trade secrets is more interesting since it explicitly requires a tradeoff. When a company makes an invention, it can publish the details of that invention and get a patent, thus giving it the exclusive right to use that invention for a certain number of years[8] and letting it license the patent to other companies, earning a royalty each time other companies use that invention.[9] Or it can choose to keep that invention secret and not register it with the government, which gives the company a limited amount of protection against the theft of that secret.[10]

The benefit of keeping your knowledge as a trade secret (as opposed to patenting it) is that nobody else can reverse-engineer it or, worse, start using it for free once the patent's temporary monopoly is over.[11]

---

[a] The "R" stands for "registered copyright."

A famous example of a trade secret is KFC's "11 herbs and spices" mix, used to create the signature breading on its fried chicken.[12] If you're curious, the recipe is rumored to be:[13b]

Nº	Ingredient	Amount
1	Salt	1/3 tbsp.
2	Thyme	1/2 tbsp.
3	Oregano	1/3 tbsp.
4	Black pepper	1 tbsp.
5	Celery salt	1 tbsp.
6	Dried mustard	1 tbsp.
7	White pepper[c]	3 tbsp.
8	Garlic salt	2 tbsp.
9	Paprika	4 tbsp.
10	Ground ginger	1 tbsp.
11	Basil	1/2 tbsp.

The secret recipe is allegedly kept in a safe in KFC's Louisville headquarters, available to only a few trusted executives. If KFC patented the recipe, they would be able to charge other restaurants a royalty each time they used the recipe, but everyone else would be able to see the ingredients and thus reverse-engineer or tweak the recipe. And, once the patent's monopoly expired, anyone would be able to use the recipe for free.[14] That would probably be disastrous for KFC's business. Meanwhile, keeping the recipe a trade secret means its secrecy will never expire (as long as nobody in the company leaks it).

Tech has its fair share of trade secrets, such as Google's search algorithm,[15] self driving cars' blueprints and routing algorithms,[16] Facebook's algorithm that decides what goes on your news feed,[17] and so on. (Notice how algorithms are the stars of this list — they're tech's ver-

[b]Colonel Sanders' nephew leaked this, but KFC denies that it's legitimate.

[c]Colonel Sanders said this was "the secret ingredient."

sion of KFC's spice recipe and Coca Cola's secret formula.[18]) Basically, anything that is used only behind the scenes and confers an "economic advantage" to the holder by being secret should be classified as a trade secret.[19]

Tech companies are especially happy to patent, though. IBM is a famously prolific patent filer, with over 140,000 patents to its name; at the time of writing, it had filed more patents than any other American company for 27 years straight.[20] Google, Intel, Samsung, and Apple also top the list.[21] Tech companies encourage their employees to file as many patents as possible, with some offering cash and prizes for each patent; Microsoft famously gives employees a "Patent Cube" when they successfully file for a patent.[22]

A patent cube, awarded to Microsoft employees when they file a patent. Source: Roy Patrick Tan[23]

Comparisons

There's a lot of overlap between the four main types of IP, but it's crucial to keep the differences straight. We can easily compare and contrast the four with a table:

Type of IP	Applies To	Length	How to Get
Copyright	Creative works[24]	70+ yr[25d]	Automatic[26]
Trademark	Brands[27]	Indefinite[28]	Apply to USPTO[29e]

Patent	Invention	<20 yr[30][f]	Apply to USPTO[31]
Trade Secret	Information	Indefinite[32]	Automatic

Working abroad

It's worth noting that each country's approach to IP law varies, and getting protection in one country doesn't necessarily mean that you get protection in other countries. Copyrights and trademarks apply automatically in the countries that recognize them, but you may have to refile for patents in other countries.

Fortunately, there are international agreements that let you easily apply for a patent in multiple countries at once or give you temporary protection abroad before you make a formal filing.[33] The best-known of these agreements is the Patent Cooperation Treaty (PCT), which lets you file for a patent in over 150 countries with a single application.[34]

Patents

As we mentioned before, patents are a key part of a tech company's toolkit — and thus knowing when to file patents and knowing how other companies might enforce patents is a key skill for PMs.

Offense and defense

First off, note that tech companies generally have two strategies around patenting: *offensive patenting* and *defensive patenting*.

Offensive patenting is what we usually think of: you file patents for your inventions to stop competitors from entering your space (or at least

[d] Technically, it's the life of the creator plus 70 years.

[e] Only if you want the registered "®" mark. The "™" comes automatically.

[f] It's 20 years from your earliest filing date.

making money off them if they try to.)[35] This strategy can be quite profitable; some tech companies even have entire business models fueled by patents. Qualcomm, which has filed thousands upon thousands of phone-related patents (mostly for wireless connectivity like 4G),[36] actually earns royalties for every single smartphone sold, since Qualcomm's wireless technology patents are used in the production of every phone.[37] Patent royalties account for over 75% of Qualcomm's annual profits![38]

Offensive patents can also be used to block competitors from implementing useful features that you happened to patent first. The most famous example of this is when Apple patented two key phone features: a "slide to unlock" login screen and a feature to turn phone numbers and addresses into links.[39] These are obvious features for a phone (or any computing device, really), and while it's unclear if Apple was the first to ever think of them, they were the first to patent them. This made it impossible for Android phones to use these features; Samsung tried and was slapped with a $120 million fine.[40] (This is why Android phones have always had to use alternative unlocking methods, such as "swipe to unlock,"[g] where you drag your finger in any direction instead of sliding it left-to-right.[41])

In defensive patenting, on the other hand, you aren't trying to get a patent yourself— you're just trying to stop someone else from patenting your invention later.[42] Since patents have to prove that they're a totally new invention, the existence of any "prior art" makes it impossible to file a patent.[43] So to block a competitor from patenting something, all you have to do is file a patent application for your invention. The application doesn't have to be any good; you just have to show that the idea was already thought of so that nobody can get a patent on it later.[44]

---

[g] We miss the days when screens like these were more popular. *Face Authenticate to Unlock* just isn't as catchy a book title.

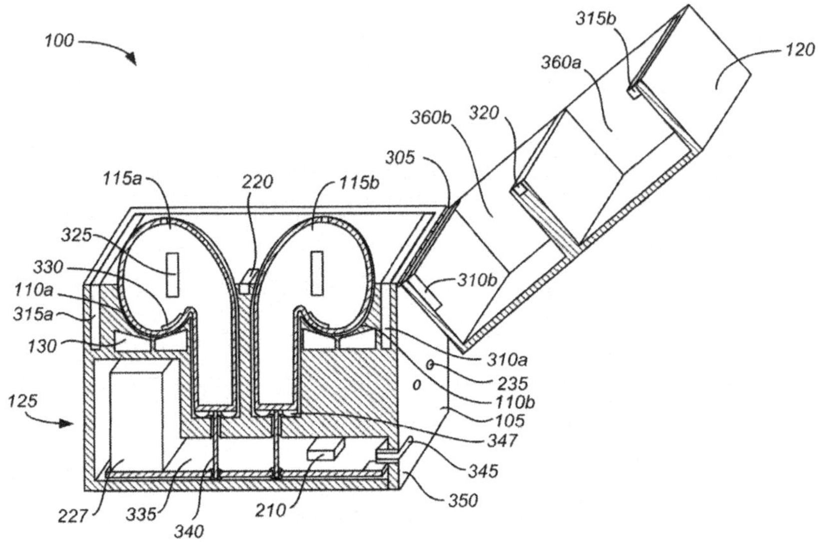

A graphic from Apple's patent application for AirPods — or, formally speaking, "Wireless Pairing of Earbuds and Case." Source: Google Patents[45]

In other words, it's easier to defensively patent than to offensively patent, since writing a patent application that's good enough to get accepted is much harder than just writing a basic application that'll serve as prior art. Defensive patenting is also useful when your invention is too minor or incremental to actually get patented;[46] it at least lets you get something of value (blocking your competitors) out of the deal.

Most big tech companies have armies of lawyers dedicated to filing patents; it's not uncommon for senior PMs to have dozens of patents to their names. In our experience, tech companies tend to prefer offensive patenting (their legal team is staffed well enough to be able to consistently get their patent applications approved), but defensive patenting is a good tactic to keep in your back pocket.

Patent trolls

We can't talk about patents without talking about patent trolls, those companies that don't do anything valuable of their own, making all their revenue from patenting things that already exist (but everyone else forgot to patent) and then suing everyone who uses them. These companies are usually aggressive and can bully the companies they sue — usually smaller firms — into settling out of court. The trolls might well lose in court, but they know that just lawyering up would cost the small firms too much money, leading those firms to settle.[47]

Patent trolling is a serious problem to the US: one study estimated that patent trolls shook down American companies for a combined $500 billion from 1991 to 2011,[48] and this constant fear of lawsuits has a chilling effect on startups, making them play it safe.[49]

Patent trolling can hit any industry, but it's especially bad in the tech industry, since software can be described vaguely, whereas something like a drug has to be described by its exact chemical formula. Because tech patents are so vague, they can be applied to nearly any product: Apple had to pay a patent troll $368 million in 2012 because FaceTime apparently violated some obscure, vague patents that referred to "VPNs and domain names."[50] (Needless to say, FaceTime doesn't really deal with either technology, and yet the troll managed to win!)

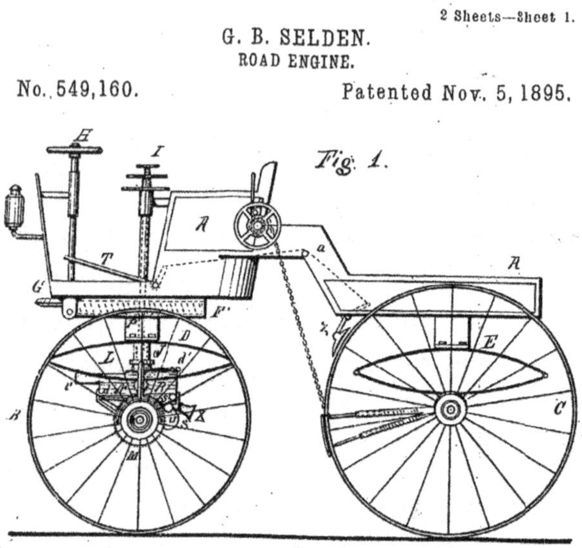

George Selden, born 1846, was the first patent troll. He never built a car but rather filed vaguely-worded patents for car technologies, which let him collect royalties from legitimate car companies.[51] *This is his infamous patent for a "road engine." Source: Google Patents*[52]

In many cases, trolls can get away with patenting things that are so obvious that they shouldn't be able to be patented, thus letting them sue a wide range of unsuspecting companies.[53] In 2011, a troll named Lodsys got a patent for in-app purchasing — an obvious behavior that shouldn't be patentable, the same way that rhetorical questions shouldn't be patentable — and used that to go after Apple and Google, hoping to bilk those companies of millions of dollars.[54]

There are signs that the US is trying to stop patent trolls, though, and it's succeeding. Before 2017, patent trolls could try their patent cases in any federal court district; most of them flocked to a handful of random districts that happened to be extremely friendly to patent trolls, including the northern[55] and eastern[56] districts of Texas. A Supreme Court ruling in 2017, though, announced that patent cases must be tried in the defendant's home district, not in a district chosen by the plaintiff (the troll), thus making it far harder for trolls to fight on favorable terrain.[57]

An even more notable Supreme Court ruling was 2014's *Alice Corp v. CLS Bank International*,[58] which severely limited the range of software patents that could be filed. In short, the Court's *Alice* ruling said that you could no longer patent basic things that were done on a computer, such as using a bank to reduce the risk in a financial transaction.[59] This made patent trolls' lives harder, since a huge portion of trolls' business was trying to patent these obvious things that happened to be done digitally.[60] (A follow-up 2016 ruling clarified that software patents must materially improve how the computer works, a philosophy known as the *technical effects doctrine*. Trivial changes, including most of the trolls' ideas, aren't patentable.[61])

While American courts have somewhat reduced the danger posed by trolls, PMs still need to be watchful — and aggressively file patents of their own for protection. Indeed, it's sometimes worth buying entire companies just to get ahold of their patents: Motorola Mobility's 17,000 patents gave Google 17,000 reasons to spend $12.5 billion on the struggling phone maker in 2011.[62]

The link tax

The EU is notoriously friendly to copyright holders like newspapers, movie producers, and sports leagues, and thus unfriendly to the tech companies that show or link to copyrighted content. One of the prime examples is the so-called *link tax*, which was Article 15 (earlier known as Article 11) of a 2019 law called the EU Copyright Directive.[63]

The idea of Article 15 is that news aggregators like Google (the prime target of this law), by linking to and showing snippets of websites, could be infringing on the copyrights of those websites.[64]

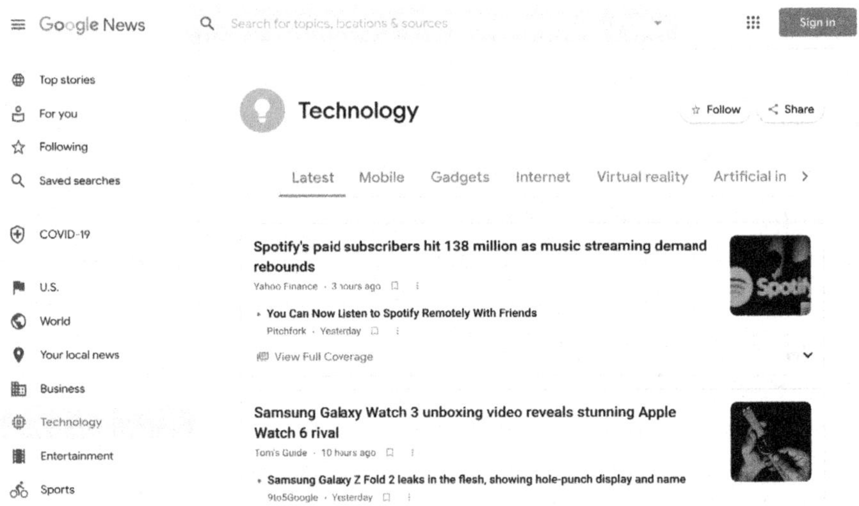

Google News, the popular news aggregation service. Source: Google[65]

As a result, the link tax forces news aggregators and search engines to buy licenses from media companies before linking to their content.[66] Google argued that this would make it impossible to run a news service like Google News, and it would make search results in Europe far less useful, since Google wouldn't be able to show any context about media webpages on the search result page.[67]

The real problem with this law was its vagueness. The law says that platforms don't have to pay if they're showing "mere hyperlinks which are accompanied by individual words"[68] — but how many words count as "individual words"? Is just putting the title of the article or video too much? Is showing a snippet of, say, ten words too much? What's a "mere" hyperlink, anyway?

The law also exempts "legitimate private and non-commercial use of press publications by individual users," which we assume means that people posting on social media don't need to pay the link tax. That's good, but it's still vague.

Consider Twitter. If McDonald's tweets a link, do they have to pay? Twitter is social media, but McDonald's isn't "non-commercial." Another twist: an Instagram influencer who sometimes makes sponsored posts is an "individual user," but would they count as "private and non-commercial"?[69]

Ultimately, it's hard to know what impact the link tax will have, or really how it works in the first place. Even Google, which the law clearly targeted, wasn't sure exactly what the law meant for it.[70]

There also wasn't any evidence that a link tax works. When a similar law was enacted in Spain in 2014, a Spanish media group wasn't a big fan of it, since it forced Google to shut down Google News and threatened to stop Google from linking to media websites at all. This meant that the link tax would have sharply reduced the amount of traffic coming to media websites, thus depriving them of clicks and eyeballs. The law, in other words, hurt the very media companies it was supposed to protect. What's more, media outlets couldn't opt out of the law so that Google could link to them for free — the law made Google pay media companies whether the companies wanted it or not.[71]

A similar law was tried in Germany, to a similar outcome. The link tax, designed to protect publishers, just dried up their traffic.[72]

The takeaway here is that places like the EU often pass IP laws that are well-meaning but too vague to properly understand, and they don't account for unintended consequences. So when you hear about new laws coming out of the EU, don't stop at the text of the bill — read more deeply to see what the second-order effects might be. This can help you and your team adapt to the new environment before your competitors realize what's really going on.

Chapter 27

Platform Liability

WHO IS RESPONSIBLE for the content that people upload to the internet on sites like YouTube, Reddit, and Twitter? This is one of the central questions of tech policy, and it leads to a fundamental question about liability. Are platforms to be held liable for what they let people do and post? Or are they just neutral middlemen?

You might hold a newspaper liable for the information they publish, but you wouldn't hold the postal service liable for lies or copyright-infringing materials sent through the mail. Which model do tech platforms fall under?

DMCA and safe harbors

The first big example of this debate is in copyright law. IP law usually assumes there's a rights holder, like a movie studio or company with patents, and a rights infringer, like a shady company. But on the internet, there's usually a third party: a tech platform like the aforementioned YouTube, Reddit, and Twitter. Should the platform be held liable for hosting IP-infringing content?

The Digital Millennium Copyright Act, an American law passed in 1998, answers that question in the case of copyrights.[1] The DMCA strikes a middle ground: it says that tech platforms (which it calls Online Service Providers, or OSPs,[2]) only need to take down copyright-infringing content when the copyright holder asks them to.[3] There's no specific timeline, but OSPs are supposed to "act expeditiously" to remove material as soon as they're notified.[4]

Breaking that down, it means that websites like YouTube can't be sued just for hosting a copyright-infringing video (like, say, someone posting a pirated version of a copyrighted movie). The DMCA gives web platforms a "safe harbor," protecting them from lawsuits.[5] But web platforms have to take down copyrighted content when the rights holder, like the movie studio in this example, asks them to.[6] Rights holders have to submit "takedown requests" to the platform's legal team; pirated software, images and songs reused without permission, and pirated movies are among the most common targets.[7]

Why the web loves it

Internet companies love DMCA[8] since it means that they don't have to actively police their platforms for copyrighted content; they can let people upload whatever they want and only take down content when a rights holder complains. On the flip side, rights holders like movie studios hate DMCA[9] since it places the burden of finding every single piece of pirated content and filing to get it taken down on them.[10]

It's hard to overemphasize how vital the DMCA is to the health of the web ecosystem. Without the DMCA, the US's usual policy of "indirect copyright liability" would apply to tech platforms; websites could be sued for every piece of copyrighted content uploaded on their sites. This would give tech companies that rely on user-generated content, or *UGC*, two bad options: carefully filter every piece of content that people upload (which would be very expensive and lead to "draconian self-censorship"[11]), or don't filter content and get hit with lawsuits day in and day out.[12] Without DMCA, startups that rely on UGC would have a hard time getting off the ground.

There's a reason that the Internet Association, a trade group that represents companies like Google, Facebook, and Twitter, calls the DMCA "instrumental and indispensable" in the rise of internet platforms.[13]

SOPA and PIPA

The biggest threat to DMCA came in the form of a pair of bills introduced in Congress in 2011:[14] the House's Stop Online Piracy Act (SOPA) and the Senate's Protect IP Act (PIPA).[15]

SOPA/PIPA's stated goal was to take down foreign sites that trafficked in pirated digital materials, like the notorious Pirate Bay.[16] The DMCA only covers companies that operate in the US, so it was toothless to stop these foreign offenders.[17]

The infamous piracy website The Pirate Bay, which traffics in illegal copies of software, books, movies, and games. Source: The Pirate Bay[18]

There was nothing wrong with those goals; the problem was how the bill tried to implement its goals.

DNS banning

Early drafts of the bills would have required internet service providers, or ISPs, like Comcast and Cox to alter their DNS systems to block access to alleged piracy sites. DNSes, or *domain name services*, are like address books that convert website names (like www.apple.com) to strings of numbers called *IP addresses*[a] (like 17.172.224.47).[19]

The first problem with DNS banning system is that it didn't work: you wouldn't be able to pull up the website just by typing its name in, sure, but you could still access it by typing in its IP address. It's like blacking out books' titles on their spines but leaving all the books in the library.[20] Wannabe pirates could easily get around this hurdle.

The bigger problem is that this system was ripe for abuse: one piece of the bill, nicknamed the "vigilante provision,"[21] let ISPs essentially DNS-ban any website they wanted to, which means they could ban the websites of, say, competing ISPs or websites that disagreed with their political views.[22]

The DNS-banning provision was removed[23] in later drafts, but Vint Cerf, one of the fathers of the internet, said that the bill's alternate blocking mechanism was still bad for cybersecurity.[24]

More criticism

Another problem — and this one will remind you of the link tax — is that the bill was too vague and broad in choosing its targets. What exactly counts as a piracy website? The Pirate Bay, obviously. But what about sites that host user-uploaded files, like Dropbox, Google Drive, SoundCloud, and GitHub? SOPA and PIPA said those could count as piracy sites and would have ordered those sites banned if anyone uploaded pirated material to them.[25] Remember: several of those websites are *American* companies that would have been taken down by a bill aiming to stop *foreign* piracy.

Harvard Law School professor Lawrence Tribe took the criticism farther: he said that SOPA and PIPA would let the government take down any user-generated content site that had even a *single* piece of

[a]This IP stands for *Internet Protocol*; it's different than the IP for *Intellectual Property*.

piracy on it. Twitter, for instance, could be attacked for hosting a single tweet that pointed to pirated content.[26]

But the worst part of SOPA/PIPA was their "anti-circumvention provision," which would have made it illegal to teach users how to get around the bans against "piracy" websites.[27] Any site that, say, hosted a link to one of the Pirate Bay's many alternate domain names or a link to a browser addon that would let you bypass the SOPA/PIPA bans[28] could get sued. There were no "safe harbor" provisions like in the DMCA; internet platforms would have had to proactively scan their websites to make sure not a single piece of "circumvention" material got uploaded. This would have placed a crippling enforcement burden on these platforms.[29] Even tools like *VPNs*, which increase privacy and security by tunnelling your internet connection through secure channels, would have been banned, since VPNs would have let you get around the bans.[30]

Epilogue

In short, SOPA/PIPA would have made it far too easy to sue an internet platform (or get them banned), which would have led them to censor aggressively just to be safe, thus shutting down free speech on the internet. Weakening the DMCA would have crushed the tech industry as well.[31] (No wonder Hollywood backed SOPA/PIPA so strongly![32])

Tech companies won a resounding victory when widespread protests convinced Congress to kill the bills.[33] It's a sign that the tech industry has more power in Washington than the movie industry does,[34] and that popular opinion in the US is often on tech companies' side.

The fact that DMCA is alive, and SOPA/PIPA aren't, is good news for PMs in tech. But the constant tug-of-war around these laws should show that you have to take content moderation seriously, since you never know what your platform might one day become liable for. (This bit of history is especially important for PMs working in media; our friends who work on movie, music, and TV platforms report that there's still bad blood between Hollywood and big tech, which makes it that much harder to work with them!)

The EU's Article 17

But while the US has been very tech-friendly on platform liability in recent decades, the EU has — as you might expect — been less so. Article 17 of the EU Copyright Directive[b] (formerly known as Draft Article 13),[35] passed in 2019,[36] is the European version of DMCA, but it's less generous to tech companies in its protection.

Like the DMCA, Article 17 aims to reduce the amount of copyrighted material online, but unlike the DMCA, it puts somewhat stricter (and, in classic EU fashion, vaguer) rules on tech platforms.

General monitoring obligations

Article 17 says that "content sharing services" — that is, platforms that host user-generated content, from YouTube to Twitter — can be held liable for copyrighted content posted on them. To avoid lawsuits, the services must be able to prove that:[37]

1. They make "best efforts" to get a license for copyrighted material hosted on the platform.
2. They make "best efforts" to not show copyrighted content.
3. They quickly take down copyrighted content when the rights holder files a takedown request.
4. They make "best efforts" to stop users from re-uploading previously removed content.

Article 17 claims that, like the DMCA, it doesn't force a "general monitoring obligation" on companies, meaning that tech platforms only

[b]This is the same law that includes the link tax (Article 11/15).

have to *reactively* take down content when notified, instead of having to *actively* police the platform.[38]

But critics point to the second item that platforms have to be able to prove: that they made "best efforts" to not show copyrighted content in the first place. It's a vague requirement, but it implies that tech companies should actively police their platforms. Critics say that tech companies will "inevitably" start proactively removing content just to be sure that they don't fall on the wrong side of the vaguely-worded law.[39] For that reason, Article 17 is popularly known as the "upload filter"[40] law, since, in the worst case, it would effectively force companies to proactively filter all uploaded content.[41]

Granted, the law exempts "non-commercial" platforms like Wikipedia and says that it will place a lighter regulatory load on startups.[42c] But critics say that the law still applies in some form to startups, and they probably lack the money or resources to build automated content-scanning tools to make sure no copyrighted material gets onto the platform.[43] (Remember, the margin of error is zero — even a single infringing video could get a video site sued — so companies have to invest a lot of money in making a foolproof system.) This is why Jimmy Wales, the founder of Wikipedia, feared that Article 17 would just entrench the "corporate giants" that already dominated the web.[44]

The meme ban?

In 2019, rumors started circulating that Article 17 would ban memes on websites like Reddit, since many memes — including the ones that slap funny text on a still from a movie — are built on copyrighted material.[45]

[c]The European Parliament's statements were vague about what defines a "startup." The exact revenue or user number cutoff is probably up to their discretion.

A meme made to mock the EU's supposed ban of memes due to Article 17. Source: Yamezj via Reddit[46]

Fortunately, that fear didn't come true, since Article 17 specifically exempted memes. Article 17 said that internet platforms can freely host "quotation, criticism, and review," as well as "caricature, parody, and pastiche," of copyrighted works.[47] Memes fall into the latter category and thus are protected.

There's a name for this carve-out from Article 17: the *fair use* doctrine.[48] Fair use says that it's OK to reuse copyrighted material if you're trying to educate the public,[49] such as by parodying a movie, copying a snippet from a book to leave a review, or summarizing and quoting from an article.

Because Article 17 exempted fair use and thus memes, Reddit didn't have to take down memes. But critics feared (and still fear) that companies would go overboard in taking down fair use content, including memes, just to be safe.[50]

The broad view on the EU

Like the link tax, Article 17 was well-intentioned: it's fine to try to uphold copyright laws. But, again like the link tax, the EU didn't think about the knock-on effects of their law. And it was a major loss for big tech companies around the world.[51]

More broadly, this shows that tech companies don't hold nearly as much sway in Brussels as they do in Washington.[52] This means that PMs for international products should always have special plans for how they're going to handle European regulations, since European tech laws have diverged from American tech laws, and that trend is accelerating. You'll have to think hard about whether your product should operate in Europe: are the potential legal risk and monitoring obligations worth the additional user base? If you decide to keep your product running in Europe, you'll have to work closely with European allies to make sure you build the necessary workarounds to comply with EU laws.

Section 230

We saw how DMCA protects platforms from being sued for copyrighted material hosted on their platforms: the "safe harbor" provision means that platforms don't have to actively police material on their sites. But what about all the other kinds of "bad" content, from violent threats to fake news to child porn? Should platforms be liable for that kind of content?

The Communication Decency Act, passed in 1996, answers that question.[53] The official wording of the law's key part, Section 230, is refreshingly clear, so it's worth reading some excerpts:[54]

> *No provider or user of an interactive computer service shall be treated as the publisher or speaker of any information provided by another information content provider.*

And:

> *No provider or user of an interactive computer service shall be held liable on account of... any action voluntarily taken in good faith to restrict access to or availability of material that the provider or user considers to be obscene, lewd, lascivious, filthy, excessively violent, harassing, or otherwise objectionable, whether or not such material is constitutionally protected.*

In short, internet platforms (called "interactive computer services"[d]) can't be sued in civil courts for the content they host, as long as they make "good faith" efforts to take down bad content. Specifically, platforms are immune from privacy, negligence, defamation, and tort (causing someone emotional or physical injuries[55]) lawsuits.[56] It doesn't consider criminal lawsuits (which platforms can still be held liable for) or IP, the latter of which is covered by the DMCA.

This is an incredible level of protection for internet companies, and it's the primary reason that user-generated content websites — Reddit, Twitter, Twitch, LinkedIn, you name it — can exist.[57] For this reason, it's been called "the internet's most important law."[58]

A history of liability

Before Section 230 was passed, the incentives for internet platforms were quite strange. If you *didn't* try to moderate content, you were seen as a "platform," a neutral conduit for information to pass through. Think of it like FedEx or an ISP: they let most anything pass through without censorship. If you were classified as a platform, you couldn't be sued for the content you hosted.[59]

[d]It's charming how quaint these 90s terms for internet companies are.

On the other hand, the moment you started trying to moderate content, you became seen as a "publisher," like a newspaper, and you'd be held liable for anything hosted on your site.[60]

This was the status quo before the Communications Decency Act: you were either a "platform" or a "publisher." You were either a "library" or a "newspaper."[61] This incentivized websites to not monitor their platforms at all, since even a good-faith effort to clean up some of the worst content would leave them open to a wave of lawsuits. This let bad content proliferate around the web.[62]

Section 230 defined an intermediate level of liability for companies, giving them some protection if they made a reasonable effort to remove the worst posts. This aligned incentives properly: both society and tech companies would be rewarded for tech companies doing their part to police their websites. This intermediate classification has been called a "distributor": you aren't exactly a dumb pipe like a "platform," but you're not making editorial decisions like a "publisher," though you are deciding what gets seen.[63]

That's not to say that everyone was on board with Section 230. Critics have called it *too* powerful because it gives websites a "Teflon shield" against lawsuits for anything they host.[64] As Georgetown Law legal scholar Rebecca Tushnet put it, internet companies get "power without responsibility."[65]

Regardless of its merits, Section 230 — like all the laws we've discussed here — plays a huge role in determining what tech companies can and can't do. You as a PM need to pay attention to these laws, especially if you work on platforms that accept user-generated content. A good PM can listen to legal and implement changes they ask for, but a great PM stays up-to-date with what's happening on Capitol Hill (and around the world) and prepares for the impacts of potential legislation without having to wait around until they're told.

Chapter 28

Privacy

IS YOUR PHONE listening to you? To many people, it certainly seems that way. Perhaps you've had a friend or family member who's talked about, say, rugs for their living room and then seen ads for rugs start appearing on their social media feed.[1]

Whatever its truthfulness, this rumor is heard around the world and shows just how much people distrust the big tech companies that produce their devices and the apps on them. As the question implies, this distrust comes largely from tech companies' suspected privacy abuses: they're always listening, always scooping up data on you, always using it in some shady back room to make a buck off you.[2]

If people don't trust you, you'll have a difficult time getting them to use your products.[3] That shows just how important it is for PMs to understand the privacy landscape and learn how to protect user privacy as much as possible. This understanding has to begin with looking at the most important privacy laws and regulations.

GDPR and friends

The world's most famous tech privacy law, and perhaps its most famous tech law in general, is the EU's General Data Protection Regulation, or GDPR. The EU boasts that the law, passed in 2018, is the "toughest privacy and security law in the world."[4]

The EU created this law because, in the mid- and late 2010s, there were mounting concerns that major tech companies like Google and

Facebook were collecting needlessly large amounts of data on internet users — including those who weren't actively visiting their websites — and profiting handsomely from it.[5]

The gist is that GDPR makes tech companies get consent from people before they collect their data, give people control over that data, and limit the amount of data they collect in the first place.[6] But, as with any law, there are a lot of moving pieces.

Rights and responsibilities

GDPR applies to any tech company that's based in Europe or serves European users[7] and lays out a set of requirements for these companies, as well a set of rights for their users. The requirements are:[8]

- Data minimization: companies must collect no more data than they need to do their job. The standard example is that an online retailer has no reason to collect data on your political orientation — and thus they shouldn't be able to.
- Security: companies must take proper measures to make sure their user data doesn't get stolen.
- Accountability: companies must explain how they handle user data, only let approved people see the data, and report data breaches to the government.

The data minimization provision is really the heart of GDPR. It doesn't say this explicitly, but it clearly targets companies — like Google and Facebook — that track users around the web, grabbing personal data that they can use to make targeted ads.[9] The provision threatens these targeted-ads companies, since their entire business models are based on knowing everything possible about you. (A social network doesn't need to know your favorite brand of chips, but that information sure helps sell ads!)

Along with the requirements for companies are a set of rights for consumers:[10]

- The right to access your data. You must be able to see the data that tech companies have about you and download a copy of it. This is what tools like Google Takeout, which let you download all your Google account data, are for.[11]
- The right to delete your personal data in some circumstances, like if it was unlawfully processed, if the company has no legitimate need for your data, or if you "withdraw consent" to let the company collect it. That last piece effectively means that you should be able to delete your data at any time, since GDPR says consumers can withdraw consent at any time.
- The right to data portability (though this has been only spottily enforced). As an example, Google, Facebook, Twitter, Microsoft and others teamed up to create a tool to let you export your Facebook photos to Google Photos.[12]

Broader than before

It's important to know what "user data" means here. Privacy laws have traditionally only covered a narrow set of *personally identifiable information*, or *PII*: your name, address, phone number, geolocation, and other information that can uniquely identify a person and thus should be kept private.[13]

But GDPR greatly expands the definition of PII to include almost *any* data about a person, including not only those personal details but also biometric data like fingerprints and sensitive data like race, sexual orientation, and political opinions.[14] The idea is that, even if you don't have someone's name, you can still uniquely identify them from a set of people if you have enough random data points about them. And certain pieces of data, like sexual orientation, would be too dangerous to reveal, so they should be kept private no matter what.[15]

So GDPR's definition of "user data" is broader than before; its definition of "user" is also broader. GDPR applies to all "data subjects" —

that is, anyone whose data you gather, whether or not they actually use your product.[16] Tech companies have a history of gathering the data of non-users; consider how Facebook came under fire in 2018 for creating "shadow profiles" of people who weren't on Facebook.[17] And advertising companies can install tracking cookies on any visitor's browser, letting them track the visitor around the web — even if they never log into the company's website.[18]

GDPR truly is comprehensive: it covers almost all data a tech company collects about almost anyone.

Fines

The EU, as you've seen by now, liberally fines tech companies that violate its laws. Companies that violate GDPR can be fined up to 4% of their global revenue[19] — that's not European revenue, that's *global* revenue!

And tech companies have gotten in hot water for the GDPR before. One well-known example comes from terms of service: since tech companies need to get your consent to gather your data, they write extremely long terms of service that give them a blank check to gather almost any kind of data from you. Europeans complained that tech products' terms of service had become a coercive, "take it or leave it" affair — either you sign away all your privacy, or you can't use the app.

But GDPR forbids companies from penalizing people who opt out of data collection, and privacy advocates claimed that the companies were doing exactly this. Privacy advocates slapped Google and Facebook with lawsuits totaling $9.3 billion in damages just hours after the GDPR went into effect.[20]

Another area for fines comes from consent. Remember that GDPR requires that tech companies have to get consent from people before collecting their data, and that consent has to be freely given; companies also have to explain what they're doing with the data. But in 2019 a French regulator ruled that Google didn't properly explain how it was using user data and failed to gather consent properly simply because the checkbox to let Google collect user data (usually labeled as "Personalize Ads") was ticked by default when people signed up for new Google accounts. Yes, simply turning data collection on by default was seen as coercive and not letting people give consent freely. The regulator fined Google 50 million euros.[21]

The "Personalized Ads" framing[22] is telling: tech companies need to find a way to convince you to hand over your personal data, so they have to show that it's in your best interest to do so. But companies can't withhold certain unrelated features from you if you don't opt in, since that would be coercive.

So companies have to explain why giving them your data *directly* helps you — in this case, the argument is that giving the company your data will let them show you ads that are more interesting and relevant to you. *If you're going to see ads anyway*, the thinking goes, *why not see ones that you might actually like?* If you're working on a product that'll be used in the EU, you may have to think about how to make a similar pitch to your product's users — and, of course, you'll have to think about how to stay on the right side of the law and avoid fines.

The California Consumer Privacy Act

The GDPR was a trailblazer in the realm of privacy law, but other countries and states have started catching on. The UK passed a very similar bill called the Data Protection Act of 2018.[23a]

At the time of writing, the US hasn't passed a comparable bill (the EU has really led the way in tech regulation). California, though, passed a bill very similar to GDPR in 2018. It's called the California Consumer Privacy Act (CCPA)[24] or AB375, and it became the toughest data privacy law in the US.[25]

[a] Yes, the UK passed this bill *before* Brexit officially happened.

Like GDPR, CCPA expands the personal data rights for consumers and expands the definition of PII. And, like GDPR, CCPA makes businesses explain why they're collecting and selling personal data, protect the data, and let users see the data that businesses have on them in the first place.[26]

CCPA explicitly mentions data rights for kids, as well. It requires that companies get parents' permission before selling the personal data of children under 13 or otherwise using it for profit.[27] (Note that Google, Facebook, and the like don't actually sell user data — they sell *access* to it in the form of targeted ads.) CCPA also says that kids from 13 to 16 must opt in themselves before companies can sell their data or use it for ad targeting.[28]

The biggest difference from GDPR is that CCPA, unlike GDPR, doesn't require companies to minimize the data they collect in the first place.[29] In our opinion, it's a matter of time until California — or perhaps the whole US — adds that provision, so PMs would do well to proactively start minimizing data collection in their products.

One thing to watch out for: as more and more polities enact their own data laws, it'll get harder and harder for multinational tech companies to comply with all of them. Fortunately, GDPR, CCPA, and the UK's Data Protection Act are similar, but they're not the same, and it's possible that the US or other countries might implement quite different laws. This is why you might see tech companies' legal teams pushing for unified data laws across countries.

💼 Interview tip

Some of the most exciting product ideas include using big data or machine learning. But when you pitch ideas like these, make sure you discuss the privacy tradeoffs that come with using so much user data. Sometimes, the risk to user trust and safety — not to mention the cost of complying with laws like GDPR and CCPA — outweighs the benefits of the feature.

Biometrics

One of the most sensitive pieces of data is *biometrics* — biological data like your DNA profile, scans of your face, or your fingerprints — since those things are locked to you and can never be changed, unlike, say, a password or even a name. That is, once someone has your biometric data, they can always use that data to uniquely identify you.

Facial recognition

Facial recognition is probably the hottest spot for biometric privacy battles. There are horror stories of authoritarian regimes using facial recognition to identify and punish protesters based on video feeds of public areas.[30] More generally, the idea of never being anonymous again can make people always feel followed, afraid, and on edge.[31] And as more and more tech starts using your face to log you in, people are worried about the possibility of abuse.

So far, most of the agitation against facial recognition has played out in the world of government, since facial recognition has emerged as a favorite tool of police, who use it to monitor protesters, find people committing identity fraud (like having multiple driver's licenses), and identify suspects in criminal cases.[32] Recognizing the potential for abuse, San Francisco, Oakland, Seattle, and Somerville, Mass. banned facial recognition by city agencies in 2019, and states like California and New Hampshire limited police's ability to use facial recognition around the same time.[33]

Note that the facial recognition used by governments is subtly different than the facial recognition used in consumer tech products like the iPhone: governments use facial *identification*, where they try to match a particular face against a database of known faces, while consumer tech products usually use facial *verification*, where they just check if a given face is the same as one known face.[34]

Facial identification is much more problematic than facial verification, since the former enables surveillance and discrimination by police and oppressive regimes. Since facial verification only works if you know what you're looking for, it'd be impractical to use it to, say, identify protesters in a crowd. Tech products, which almost exclusively use facial verification,[35] thus get a pass from the law.

But while the *law* has let consumer tech products off the hook, users are still wary of letting tech companies get scans of their faces,[36] in part out of privacy concerns and in part out of fear that the face data could get stolen or leaked, including to hostile police.[37] PMs working on biometric authentication should be watch out for these concerns and, like Apple,[38] explain how their face authentication data is stored safely and privately.

A good example of facial recognition that's technically legal but ethically problematic is the secretive startup Clearview.AI. Clearview has scraped images from public websites like YouTube and Instagram[39] to create a massive database of 3 billion faces, which it claims to offer for sale to law enforcement agencies around the world.[40] Clearview's software lets law enforcement identify anyone in the database and get all publicly-available information about a person within 10 seconds.[41] In a world with Clearview, there's no such thing as anonymity anymore, and protesters can be singled out and tracked down.

Because the US has no nationwide law banning the use of personal data in this way, Clearview can scrape photos and sell its database to anyone[42] — including, apparently, the governments of Saudi Arabia and the UAE[43] — with impunity. If anything illustrates the importance of laws like GDPR and CCPA, it's Clearview.

DNA

In recent years, at-home DNA test kits have become popular ways to learn about your ancestry[44] and any rare medical conditions you might have.[45] Ancestry.com and 23andMe run some of the more popular services.

As you might expect, though, there are rampant privacy concerns with home DNA testing. If you have a doctor run a proper DNA test, medical privacy laws like HIPAA[46] limits how your data can be shared. There's no such limitation on the companies that offer at-home test kits, meaning that they have free rein to sell your data. Indeed, most of these companies sell your data to third parties; some share your data with police, and many sell your data to insurance companies, and insurance companies can then use this medical data to change your insurance premiums or cut you out of insurance entirely.[47]

23AndMe's DNA testing kits on sale. Source: Mike Mozart[48]

To take an example, the FamilyTree DNA testing service gave the FBI access to its database of over one million users' DNA profiles for use in criminal investigations — without getting those users' consent. FamilyTree later said users could opt out, and competitors like Ancestry and 23andMe said they'll only give police that data if they get a search warrant or a subpoena.[49]

Meanwhile, Ancestry keeps your DNA samples on file and shares it with "research partners" (vague, huh?). To their credit, Ancestry lets you ask them to destroy your DNA samples.[50] Meanwhile, 23andMe says it destroys DNA samples after testing, but it gives its data to other companies owned by its parent company.[51] The common thread is that companies aren't at all clear about where your data goes, and once your data makes it out onto the data marketplace, it can get endlessly sold and resold by companies called *data brokers* until everyone on the internet has a copy of your DNA data.[52]

The lesson for PMs here is that customers *do* care about your data retention and sharing policies, as dry as they may seem on the surface. As we said before, there's a slippery slope in data sharing: the moment you start selling data to third parties, that data will make it to all corners of the internet. The only way to keep user data private is to never hand it over to anyone. This is why PMs working on products that handle sensitive user data need to be very careful before getting into even a single data-sharing agreement.

Financial data

Financial data — information about how and where you spend your money — is obviously attractive to companies who want to sell you things. It's one big reason that the "FinTech" industry drew over $25 billion in venture capital funding in 2019.[53]

But, as you might guess, there are privacy issues related to gathering and selling people's financial data. The biggest is that there's a sprawling web of companies who sell and resell people's financial data, and your data quickly gets spread throughout the whole web. One reporter for the *Washington Post* swiped his credit card to buy a 29¢ banana and found, after hours of digging, that data about his transaction ended up with banks, the credit card network (Visa or Mastercard), the store, the point-of-sale software system, mobile wallets like Google Pay, and financial apps like Mint.[54] And if any one of those companies wanted to sell data to a third party, the data would soon be all across the internet.

This reporter further checked companies' privacy policies and found how vague they were. Companies like Amazon, Visa, and Chase say they share data with "affiliates" or "co-branding partners" — but who exactly are those companies?[55]

Credit cards

The entire ecosystem of companies that use people's financial data for profit is staggeringly large, but we can take a few peeks inside it. Consider the credit card networks. Way back in 2013, an exposé found that Mastercard was working with Maxpoint, a digital advertising firm that combines public data with MasterCard data to build audience profiles for ad targeting. Maxpoint can build profiles for each ZIP code, showing how much people in that ZIP code spend on various categories of goods. For instance, if a Vietnamese restaurant finds that people in ZIP code 02138 spend 20% more on Asian food than people in neighboring ZIP code 02139, the restaurant would better know which kinds of users to target with Facebook and Instagram ads.[56]

Credit card companies also have lucrative consulting businesses on the side: in 2009, American Express opened a consulting arm that sold access to AmEx users' purchase data to marketers and advertisers.[57] As you can imagine, marketers would pay top dollar to learn about wealthy spenders' buying habits.

Finally, credit card companies feed customer data to "data management platforms," which are platforms that aggregate all kinds of financial data and sell it to digital advertisers.[58] When companies give customer data to platforms like these, customers lose all control over where it goes. As we said before, companies that handle user data have to be very careful before selling it to even one partner, since once the data is out there, it'll spread everywhere, and it's impossible to take back.

Home assistants

Another frontier of the privacy debate, and one that's especially relevant for PMs working in big tech, is the realm of digital assistants like Alexa and smart speakers. People are wary of installing a device that's always listening, always tracking what's being said in their homes. One tech writer issued this scathing critique:

> *But you shouldn't buy [an Echo]. You shouldn't buy one for your family. You definitely should not buy one for your friends. In fact, ignore any praise we've ever heaped onto smart speakers and voice-controlled assistants. They're bad!*[59]

If your company is going to sell smart home hardware or make digital assistants a core part of its business strategy — which is true for Amazon,[60] Google,[61] and Apple,[62] among others — you need to understand the reason why people don't trust assistants and what can be done about them.

An Amazon Echo. Source: Shinji[63]

Causes of distrust

Digital assistants (including the apps on phones and the specialized hardware like Echoes and Google Homes) are always passively listening for a *wake word* like "Alexa!" If the assistant hears the wake word, audio captured just before and after the wake word is sent to company servers for processing.[64] Usually, the servers figure out who's talking, turn the sounds you make into words, and turn the words into actions. This also means that the companies store snippets of your voice recordings on their servers.[65]

People are nervous to give tech companies their voice recordings. In one famous case, Alexa recordings were used to figure out what happened after a murder in a Florida home.[66] And lawsuits allege that assistants can create "voiceprints" — profiles of your voice that uniquely identify you, much like a fingerprint — without your consent, which lets them build up a "vast level of detail" about your life.[67] In other words, details about your voice are PII, but they don't seem to get any legal protection.

What causes the most outrage, though, are the revelations that big tech companies have let their employees and contractors listen to people's voice recordings. In 2019, news came out that Microsoft workers listened to Xbox users' Cortana recordings,[68] Google workers listened to Google Home recordings,[69] Amazon workers listened to Alexa recordings,[70] Apple workers listened to Siri recordings,[71] and Facebook workers listened to Messenger chats.[72] The stories about Apple were especially troubling because they revealed the wide range of sensitive topics that Siri listens to: Apple workers listened to drug deals, medical details, business dealings, and sexual activities from Siri users.[73]

To be fair, contractors listen in to recordings for quality control purposes,[74] and they usually make sure that recordings are anonymized. What's more, the recordings are usually of queries that the device failed to respond to correctly; this data helps product teams figure out how to improve the device in the future.[75] So these recordings do serve legitimate purposes.

But since we know that tech companies can make unique "voiceprints" of you, you can never be truly anonymous. So it's no surprise that each of those news stories led to significant backlash against big tech.[76]

Potential fixes

There are some quick product fixes that could reduce these privacy concerns, but they might be too little, too late. One obvious fix is for speakers to do voice processing on-device and only send the final, anonymized query to company servers; imagine if Alexa only sent words like "buy socks" to Amazon instead of your actual voice snippet. The problem is that this would force smart speakers to pack more powerful hardware, thus driving up the cost.[77] Doing processing locally also robs quality assurance teams of the ability to identify mishandled queries.

Given the tradeoffs, there's no easy answer to how much processing should be done locally. Some tech companies, for their part, think the privacy benefit is worth the tradeoffs and have moved closer to a model of on-device processing. In 2017, for instance, Apple announced that Siri wouldn't send any information to Apple's servers until you said "Hey Siri."[78] (At the time, Alexa would send some data to Amazon servers even when you weren't saying "Alexa," but Amazon has since adopted Apple's approach.[79])

The other quick fix is just to add a physical button to turn off the camera and microphone so that people can know the device is disabled when they aren't using it. Facebook's video-calling smart devices, known as Portals, included this feature to reduce some privacy concerns when they launched in 2018.[80] Besides the slight cost increase of adding a plastic switch, there aren't many downsides to physical shutters, so we think they're pretty easy to justify adding.

Remember, though, that no amount of tweaks can protect you from a bad brand perception. If people associate your company with spying on them or gobbling up their data for questionable uses, they won't buy products that they perceive to be privacy risks. This is why it's so important to think about how your entire company deals with privacy questions rather than slapping on an "off" switch and calling it a day.

Encryption backdoors

Law enforcement and governments want access to people's private conversations to track down criminals (and, sometimes, monitor citizens). Everyday people don't want others snooping on their conversations. Tech is often caught in the middle — and this tug-of-war has gone on for years.

End-to-end encryption

Encrypted messaging services keep your conversations private by *encrypting* them: the contents are scrambled, and only the sender and receiver have the keys to unscramble them.[81] (These messaging services are formally known as *end-to-end encrypted*, meaning that nobody besides the sender and receiver can read them; if anyone else gets the encrypted contents, it'll look like gibberish.[82])

An app called Signal was the trailblazer in the encrypted messaging space; it started offering encrypted calls and texts in 2015.[83] (Conventional SMS and phone calls aren't encrypted, which is why police can wiretap them.[84]) Many popular messaging apps followed suit: WhatsApp made all conversations encrypted by default in 2016,[85] Facebook Messenger offered optional encryption via its "Secret Messages" feature the same year,[86][b] and Telegram started offering encryption in 2017,[88] though the feature was off by default[89].

Apple is a confusing case: Apple says iMessages are end-to-end encrypted, but they're stored in iCloud, and Apple can decrypt your iCloud data. This means that Apple isn't really correct, since iMessages can be

[b] Mark Zuckerberg said in 2019 that all Facebook messaging products would become end-to-end encrypted, though he didn't offer a timeline.[87]

read by the sender, the receiver, *and Apple.*[90] (Apple's encryption algorithm for iMessage has also been cracked, according to one security expert, so hackers could easily decrypt iMessages.[91])

Encryption isn't just for messages, either: iPhones let you encrypt the entire contents of your phone, only decrypting them when you enter the password. This means that no hacker could read what's on your phone unless you log in. We'll see shortly how this feature became contentious.[92]

A history of backdoors

Law enforcement is fine with people using encryption, but they insist on messaging services building in a *backdoor*: a "bug" that lets law enforcement break the encryption and read people's messages.[93] Thus, messaging services with backdoors aren't actually end-to-end encrypted.

The rationale is that criminals plan all kinds of crimes on encrypted messaging services, and without a backdoor, police can't identify potential criminals or get messages to use as evidence against suspects. Telegram, for instance, is the go-to messaging app for American white supremacists, who flock to it precisely because law enforcement can't figure out what they're saying.[94]

The US government has been pushing for backdoors since the 1990s, when it tried installing "clipper chips" in phones and computers. These chips would store encrypted versions of all messages sent with those devices; the NSA had a special key to read the information on those chips. After massive backlash, the clipper chips quietly died off.[95]

The more famous example, though, was when the FBI sued Apple in 2015, trying to force Apple to install backdoors in iPhones. The FBI wanted to break into the iPhones of two suspects in the San Bernadino shootings, but those phones were encrypted, so the FBI demanded that Apple let the FBI build a "master key" to let them bypass the login screen and get access to decrypted data.[96] Apple CEO Tim Cook rejected the request, saying that any tool that Apple built for the FBI would let them unlock *any* iPhone, not just the suspects' phones.[97]

The legal battle was fierce: the FBI invoked a law that said law enforcement could force a phone company to "provide technical assistance" to give police customer data. Apple fought back, saying that being forced to write software would infringe on Apple's First Amendment rights.[98] The battle was never resolved, though, because the FBI found a third party that knew how to exploit a security hole in Phones to bypass the encryption, managed to crack the phones, and withdrew the case.[99]

Since then, law enforcement has continued to pressure tech companies to install backdoors, and tech companies have continued to refuse. In 2019, Facebook rejected a request from American, British, and Australian attorneys general who wanted the company to install a backdoor into WhatsApp. Facebook said such a backdoor would be a "gift to criminals, hackers, and repressive regimes" and would leave users open to "real-life harm."[100]

Public opinion has turned against law enforcement in this case, as well. Ever since former NSA contractor Edward Snowden revealed just how much the NSA surveilled American citizens in 2013,[101] the public has loudly rejected the idea of giving governments backdoors.[102]

The PM's view

Encryption has become so popular that it's practically mandatory for modern messaging apps to have it. There are obvious risks to enabling end-to-end encryption — it makes terrorists' lives a lot easier[103] — but it appears that the public is willing to put up with these risks to enable greater privacy for all.[104] On balance, encryption helps society.

Thus, it's relatively clear that PMs should add end-to-end encryption when possible. (Porting a large existing service over to end-to-end encryption can be tough, though; Facebook Messenger struggled to implement the feature for years.[105])

The more contentious question is whether you should build in backdoors. Besides the obvious user backlash that would ensue, this would also bake in a permanent security hole in the software. Security experts say that, if there's a security hole that governments can use, it's only a matter of time until hackers find out how to use it too.[106] That is, there's a slippery slope: build in a single security hole, and your product is as good as not encrypted. So the decision isn't "backdoor vs. no backdoor," it's "encrypted vs. not encrypted" — and we strongly advise you take the encrypted, non-backdoor route.

Chapter 29

Employment in the Gig Economy

THE *GIG ECONOMY* — nontraditional working arrangements where people earn money off apps like Uber, DoorDash, and TaskRabbit — has been called the "future of work,"[1] and, indeed, it's a big part of the *present* of work.

The gig economy is great for businesses, who find gig workers much cheaper and easier to hire than normal salaried employees.[2] Because gig workers like Uber drivers are classified as "independent contractors," companies don't have to pay them minimum wage or overtime, offer workers' compensation, or give them benefits like healthcare. This makes these contracts about 30% cheaper than hiring full-time employees.[3]

This is less great for the actual gig workers. According to a 2018 estimate, Uber and Lyft drivers make about $9 or $10 an hour — less than a third of the average private-sector employee.[4] And besides the benefits we mentioned above, gig economy workers don't get labor protections under the Fair Labor Standards Act, accommodations for disabilities from the Americans with Disabilities Act (ADA), and other protections.[5] Yes, gig work is more flexible than regular salaried work, but it gives only a sliver of the benefits.

California's AB5

In 2019, California wanted to change this unfortunate state of affairs and passed a bill called AB5,[6] which secures employee-level protections for gig workers. According to the bill, workers in California count as employees, not contractors, if their employer "exerts control over how they perform their tasks" or if "their work is part of a company's regular business." In other words, if someone works like a full-time employee, they should get paid like a full-time employee. People now classified as employees get unemployment insurance, minimum wage, overtime pay, and the other benefits we mentioned above.[7]

The bill's wording was tailor-made to target gig workers. Consider Uber: since its app literally tells drivers where to go and who to pick up, Uber does "[exert] control over how they perform their tasks." And while anyone could recreate the Uber app quite easily, Uber's key strength is its network of drivers, which isn't easy to recreate — thus, these drivers' "work is part of [Uber]'s regular business."

As a result, the bill affected one million Californian workers, including Uber and Lyft drivers, DoorDash and GrubHub deliverers, and other gig workers.[8]

Criticism

As you can expect, this new law quickly drew criticism from gig economy companies. Uber, Lyft, and DoorDash pledged to spend $90 million to support a ballot initiative that would exempt them from the law.[9] These companies' usual argument was that classifying gig workers as employees would "destroy" the flexibility that their workers enjoyed[10] and even destroy the gig companies entirely.[11] An oft-cited example: it's easy to be a contractor if you're retired or semi-retired but harder to have a full-time job, so AB5 would make it harder for retired or semi-retired people to work gig jobs.[12]

Another criticism was that the bill targeted much more than just the gig economy. It turns out that a lot of contractors are actually "part of a company's core business": construction workers, nail salon workers, fast-food workers, and so on.[13] Thus there is potential for unintended consequences; industries outside tech could become collateral damage. (As you've seen in this chapter, it's very common for tech laws to have unintended consequences because it's hard to precisely target who a law will apply to. Good PMs can understand how laws might unintentionally affect their business.)

The future of the future of work

While AB5 was ultimately struck down due to California's Prop 22 in 2020[14], the ideas behind the law remain popular, and it seems that laws like it will keep spreading around the world. AB5 wasn't even the first bill of its kind, in fact. The EU passed a similar gig worker protection bill earlier in 2019,[15] and the UK passed another similar bill in 2018.[16]

Notice another trend here? Tech law innovations start in Europe, then get a foothold in California, then (in some cases) make it to the US at a national level. PMs at American companies should watch European tech law carefully, because the hot legal topics there will eventually become hot in America.

Chapter 30

Accessibility

AN OFTEN-OVERLOOKED, but nevertheless important, part of tech law is accessibility: designing your products so they work for everyone, regardless of ability level.

Why accessibility matters

Since the Americans with Disabilities Act (ADA) was passed in 1990, physical spaces have had to be designed to accommodate people with disabilities. Building codes have been overhauled since then — wheelchair ramps are some of the more noticeable features of new buildings.[1]

Most techies know about the ADA, but few know that it applies to tech products as well! In 2019, a Supreme Court case called *Robles v. Domino's Pizza* set this precedent. Guillermo Robles, a blind man, sued Domino's because its website wasn't accessible: its website only showed graphics without text equivalents, so Robles couldn't see what he was ordering.[2] The Supreme Court ruled in Robles' favor, saying that the ADA should be interpreted to mean that websites must be accessible, just like physical spaces.[3]

The fines for disobeying the ACA can be quite hefty: Target was once fined $6 million because its ecommerce site wasn't accessible.[4]

Besides the legal responsibility, designing for accessibility is a savvy business move too. 60 million Americans have some form of disability,[5] accounting for $21 billion in combined discretionary income.[6] It's estimated that 15% of people worldwide have some kind of disability.[7] If you, like Domino's, don't design your products to serve people with accessibility needs, you're leaving 15-20% of your possible revenue on the table. (In a world where PMs fight tooth-and-nail to eke out 1% improvements in profitability, it's silly to ignore the massive market that designing for accessibility unlocks.)

Interview tip

One great way to stand out at an interview is to put accessibility on your long-term roadmap. While your minimum viable product (MVP) is probably going to focus more on validating hypotheses than building an accessible product, you can (and should) make accessibility one of the first things you add to a publicly-launched product. We'll talk about some key accessibility features later in this chapter.

Building accessible products can be a real differentiating feature, too. By one estimate, 85% of websites aren't accessible.[8] Consider the Xbox's Adaptive Controller, a large "gamepad" of sorts that's designed to work for people with physical, mental, visual, or other impairments. When Microsoft unveiled the controller in 2018,[9] it was quickly hailed as a "game changer."[10] In one fell swoop, the Xbox became the gaming platform of choice for people with disabilities, since Xbox's archrivals — Sony's PlayStation line, Nintendo, PC gaming, and the like — had absolutely nothing for this market.

The Xbox adaptive controller, which made playing Xbox games much easier for people with disabilities. Source: Wikimedia[11]

Finally, making a product accessible makes it better for everyone, even people without disabilities. Consider closed captioning on TVs: it's great for people with hearing impairments, but it's also great if you're in a noisy bar or airport and want to be able to understand the TV without being able to hear it. Those "push to open door" buttons are great if you're in a wheelchair or if you're carrying heavy grocery bags. And text-to-speech features are great if you have a motor disability or if you're just in a hurry: speech-to-text is about three times faster than typing.[12]

What's more, many — if not most — people are temporarily disabled at some point in their lives. When Neel sprained his wrist once, he realized how hard it was to do everyday tasks — from tying your shoe to typing on a laptop — with only one functional hand. Speech-to-text features on his phone and laptop were absolutely essential for him. When you're designing your product, it helps to think about all the times when you or your friends have been temporarily or permanently incapacitated. What features would have made all the difference for you in those times?

To zoom out, accessibility is often one of the last things on PMs' and engineering teams' minds; it's often treated as a low-priority, nice-to-have feature. But, for your own sake, you should treat it as a must.

Building for accessibility

So, how can you build your product to be accessible? For web apps, there's a clear answer: follow the Web Content Accessibility Guidelines (WCAG),[13] a set of guidelines for making websites accessible to people with a range of disabilities,[14] including mobile, visual, and cognitive disabilities.[15] These guidelines are even more comprehensive than what the ADA requires, so if you follow them, you'll definitely be on the right side of the ADA.[16]

Platforms like Android[17] and iOS[18] have their own accessibility guidelines, but the underlying principles are the same as the WCAG. So let's dig into what the WCAG suggests.

POUR

The Web Content Accessibility Guidelines are designed around four general themes, nicknamed *POUR*.[19]

P is for *perceivable*: users must be able to interpret your app with multiple senses, not just sight. This includes captions for images, high contrast between the foreground and background colors, a reasonable minimum text size, responsive design (so your app looks good on all screen sizes), and data visualizations that don't just rely on color (otherwise color-blind users will struggle to understand what you're showing[20]).

O is for *operable*: users must be able to control your user interface using whatever tools they have available: mouse, keyboard, finger, voice, etc. In other words, your app shouldn't behave in a way that could cause trouble for users. This means that your website must be operable entirely with a keyboard (you should be able to "tab" between elements), you should have large click targets, and you shouldn't flash images that could cause seizures.

U is for *understandable*: your website must be easy to understand. Text on your site should have a low-enough reading level, without jargon; your app should behave predictably and consistently; you should catch errors to make your users' lives easier; and you should make important actions like deleting documents or sending money reversible.

R is for *robust*: your site must be developed using commonly-adopted web standards that work across browsers now and in the future. This mainly means that you should follow the modern *HTML5* standards for writing your website's code.

Conclusion

THE YEAR WAS 2016, and the team chat app Slack was spreading like wildfire: its daily active user count had been growing exponentially since the app launched three years earlier and now stood at over four million.[1]

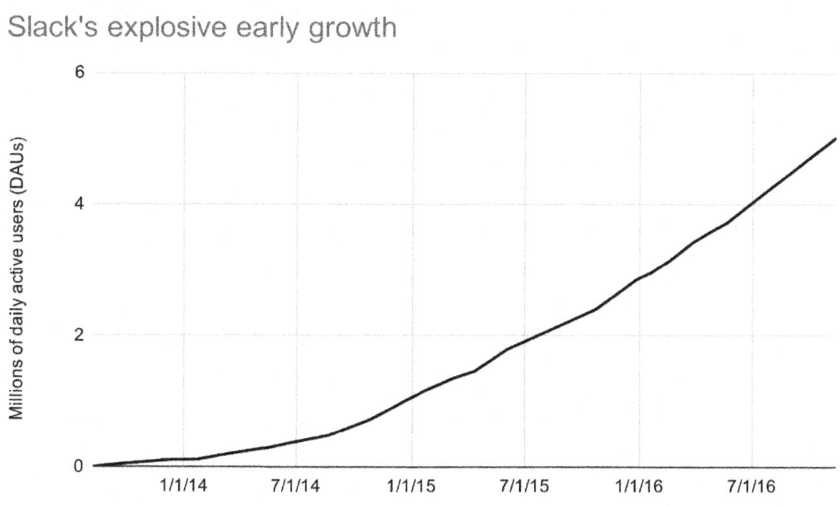

Slack's explosive growth from launch in 2013 through 2016. Source: The Verge[2]

Microsoft threw down the gauntlet in November of that year and announced Microsoft Teams, a chat app available for free to businesses that subscribed to Office 365.[3] How could Teams catch up?

Teams had many built-in advantages, including being free for many users, but one often-overlooked advantage was its advantage in legal compliance. There's an alphabet soup of data protection regulations that apply to multinational corporations, and thanks to its decades of experience building enterprise products that had to comply with these regulations, Microsoft was able to build support for them into Teams. The list, according to Microsoft, included "ISO 27001, ISO 27018, SSAE16 SOC 1 and SOC 2, HIPAA, and EU Model Clauses (EUMC)."[4] While Slack eventually added GDPR compliance, Teams complied with GDPR and even more laws out of the box.[5]

For enterprise products, this legal compliance was key, and it instantly made Teams a favorite among big businesses (who often have fat budgets and massive workforces), relegating Slack to the startup and small-business market.[6] This compliance edge, along with Teams' other advantages, helped Teams outgrow Slack, overtaking it in usage by 2019.[7]

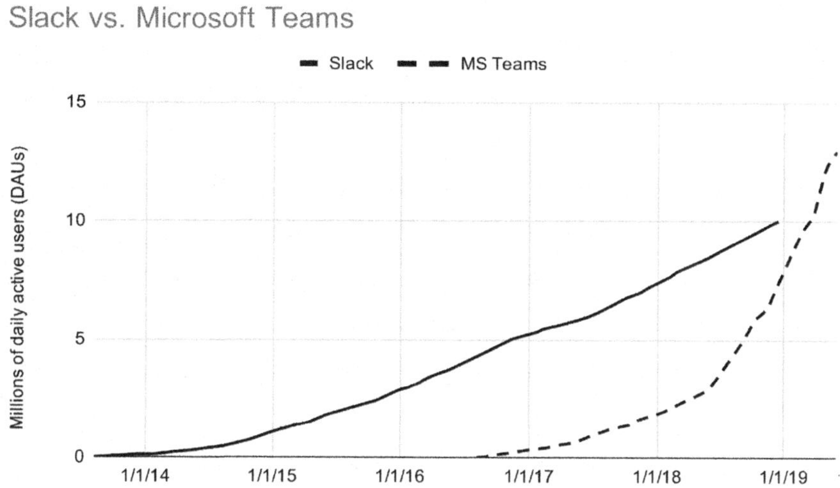

Microsoft Teams overtook Slack in usage within just a few years of launch. Source: The Verge[8]

In hyper-competitive markets, knowing the law, and knowing how to comply with it, can give your product the edge it needs. It's just another reason why knowing the law can pay dividends for product managers. ❦

VII

Marketing & Growth

Market growth alone doesn't give you enough tail-wind. You have to create your own. The way to do that is by designing products for consumers that wow them.

— Indra Nooyi, former CEO of PepsiCo

Introduction

Zappos, the shoe retailer owned by Amazon, is one of the most popular ecommerce companies on the internet. On the surface, it's just another ecommerce site; its shoes are good, but they're nothing out-of-this-world.

What makes Zappos special, rather, is its unparalleled commitment to customer service. Unlike most retailers, Zappos doesn't give its customer service employees scripts or time limits. Instead, employees are trained to be friendly and handle any request the customer throws at them — no matter how long it takes, and whether or not it's about shoes.[1] Overseers never tell employees to end calls early or upsell products.[2] It's about building relationships, not making sales.

Zappos's customer service has done some truly magical things. One employee stayed on the line with a customer for 10 hours and 43 minutes.[3] In another case, one woman called Zappos to ask about shoe returns. During the course of the conversation the woman explained that she had neurological problems in her hands and thus couldn't use a computer to do returns online. The Zappos employee answering her call revealed that his father had similar neurological problems and promised to pray for her. Two days later, a bouquet of roses appeared on the woman's doorstep. They were from the Zappos employee. The woman's family was so touched that they vowed to buy every pair of shoes from then on from Zappos.[4]

These instances of "wowing" the customer are commonplace at Zappos. It's not uncommon for an employee to give customers free expedited shipping so they can get shoes in time for special events, recommend ideal shoes for weddings, and let customers keep mis-delivered shoes for free so they don't have to bother returning them.[5] Zappos is so committed to "wow" that they famously offer new hires $2000 to quit on the spot if they don't think they can commit to delivering these magical experiences.[6]

In return, customers regularly rave about Zappos; Zappos's customer service has effectively become its most powerful marketing tool.[7] In a world filled with swarms of online shoe stores, Zappos has given people a very strong reason to choose their site — and it has very little to do with the shoes themselves.

This customer loyalty, in turn, has fueled Zappos's tremendous growth. Because customer retention is so high and customers advertise Zappos organically through word-of-mouth, Zappos can spend next to nothing on advertising. Instead, Zappos is able to plow their money back into growing Zappos's operations and making their customer service even more legendary, and the company can even keep a hefty chunk as profit. This was the engine that powered Zappos to grow its revenue from $1.6 million in 2000 to $800 million in 2007[8] and paved the way for Amazon's $1.2 billion acquisition of the company in 2009.[9]

You as a PM probably aren't selling shoes, but you're definitely trying to get people to use or buy your products. The average PM might think that making a great product — the ultimate pair of shoes — is all that matters.

But, as the Zappos story shows, products don't exist in a vacuum; selling a product isn't all about the product. A great PM knows that a strong brand, customer experience, and marketing strategy, like Zappos's, makes all the difference between mediocre sales and smashing success.

Chapter 31

Branding

We saw the importance of brands in the Zappos story. Intuitively, we know that strong brands are huge assets for the companies that have them: Zappos, Coca-Cola, Disney, Nike, Intel, and the like.[1]

However, it might be harder to lay your finger on what, exactly, constitutes a brand. A good first pass is that the brand is what people feel when they think about your company.[2] Apple evokes feelings of luxury, Coca-Cola makes you think about happiness and refreshment,[3] Volvo is associated with safety,[4] and, yes, Zappos makes you think about customer service long before you think about the shoes.

We can break down the concept of a brand more scientifically, though. Let's step through the pieces of the theory.

The origin of brands

It's easy to think of brands as some fluffy, buzzword-y creation of marketing teams, but the truth is that brands play a vital role in economic markets. Without brands, these markets would collapse.

A cow that's been branded to show the owner's identity. Source: Temple Daily Telegram[5]

The notion of "branding" goes thousands of years back. As early as 2000 BCE, farmers would use hot metal or wood "firebrands" to mark their livestock so people could tell whose cows were whose.[6] These literal brands were also a way for buyers to understand the livestock's quality: if all the cows branded with farmer Ezekiel's mark had been good in the past, a discerning buyer would have known to seek out those cows at the market.

Brands are also a form of accountability. Farmer Jedediah would have been incentivized to breed the best cattle he possibly could, because he knew that if a bad cow bore his brand, it'd hurt his business forever. Had there been no brands, farmer Jedediah wouldn't have cared much about quality — nobody would have been able to tell that a bad cow[a] came from him, so he'd have suffered no consequences.

[a] We were quite tempted to call this "a beefy lemon."

Ever since, brands have been a core part of the market economy, and getting rid of them has caused huge problems. For instance, the leaders of communist Russia thought that brands were filthy capitalist creations and outlawed them. Problems quickly started emerging at the steel factories that produced unbranded metallic rivets, which were used in the manufacturing of ships and heavy machinery. Factories were given ambitious quotas and expected to meet them.[7]

The problem was that every factory's unbranded rivets were pooled together, so if a given factory produced faulty rivets, nobody would know who had created them, and thus the factory would never be held accountable. This, combined with the incentive to churn out massive numbers of rivets, led to factories prioritizing quantity over quality. Communist Russia made a lot of rivets, but its ships also started falling apart. Only when Russia forced manufacturers to brand their rivets did quality improve.[8]

Hoverboards

To take a modern-day example, consider what happened with hoverboards, those wheeled mini-scooters that became popular in the mid-2010s but had the unfortunate side effect of bursting into flames.[9]

A person with their feet on a hoverboard. Source: IOChic via Pexels[10]

A big reason for hoverboards' poor quality was that no major brands sold them. There was no Samsung or Sony hoverboard. Instead, the gadgets were instead sold by an army of anonymous Chinese manufacturers.[11] Even the best hoverboards came from unheard-of companies: SISIGAD, Hyper GoGo, Epikgo, Swagtron.[12]

Because the hoverboard companies were so anonymous, they had no incentive to make their hoverboards *not* catch fire. They had nothing on the line, since their brands were almost worthless.[13]

Had Samsung built a defective hoverboard, they would have worked hard to fix it, since its multi-billion-dollar brand[14] would have been on the line. (Remember the Samsung Galaxy Note 7, which also burst into flames? The reason Samsung was so quick to recall millions of these tablets[15] was that their brand was at risk.)

In other words, companies with valuable brands (like Samsung) have a strong incentive to produce high-quality products, while companies with weak or nonexistent brands (like the hoverboard manufacturers) have no such incentive. This is another way that brands enforce accountability, and it's the reason that so many people prefer to buy brand-name products instead of generic equivalents.

Emergent brands

Brands are so essential, in fact, that people will go out of their way to find distinguishing features if the brand isn't marked. For instance, some companies sell knockoff Nintendo Switch docks, which are used to charge the gaming consoles and connect them to TVs. These knockoff docks look almost exactly the same as the genuine docks, down to the forged Nintendo logos, but they can fry your $300 consoles. Consumers were so desperate to find ways to distinguish fake docks from real ones that they literally tore open the docks to see if the silicon boards inside were different.[16]

The good news, for what it's worth, is that consumers discovered a tiny flaw in the fake docks. The fake docks copied all the consumer-safety logos from the real ones but failed to draw some tiny lines on a set of arrow icons.[17] This became the main way to spot fake docks — and consumers' meticulousness shows just how far people will go to find distinguishing brand marks if they aren't present. In other words, brands can emerge completely organically.

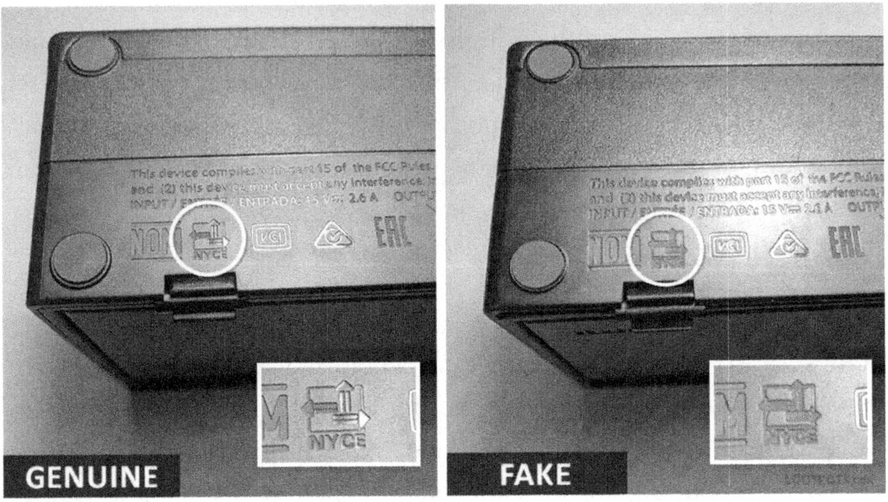

Fake Nintendo Switch docks look exactly like the real thing... except for some lines on a set of arrows. This flaw has become the "brand marking" of fake docks. Source: LootPots[18]

Brands, then, are a natural creation of market economies, because without them quality suffers. Branding your products is as much about marketing as about giving a signal of consistent quality.

Uber and the danger of a bad brand

Brands are like trust: they take a long time to create but can be destroyed in the blink of an eye. And if your company ruins its brand, the damage will take a long time to undo, hurting your bottom line the whole time.[19]

Take Uber, which was considered one of the coolest startups in the world when it first launched. There was something undeniably cool about being able to summon a black car at the tap of a button. You felt powerful, magical, even like a "baller."[20]

But in the mid-2010s, Uber's unsavory practices began coming to light. Uber was known to treat its drivers badly,[21] block inspectors from using the app to evade regulation,[22] and have an awfully sexist work culture.[23] Uber's reputation for coolness was replaced with a reputation for shadiness.

The last straw came in January 2017, when taxi workers near New York's JFK airport decided to strike, refusing to pick up passengers for an hour. Instead of honoring the strike and supporting taxi drivers, Uber turned off surge pricing near the airport, thus letting its drivers swoop in and break the strike. The public saw that Uber was trying to exploit a strike for profit — and they were furious.[24]

The #DeleteUber catchphrase caught fire[25] as people quit Uber in protest. The day after the strike, Lyft downloads surpassed Uber's for the first time ever.[26] Over the next year, Uber lost almost 10 percentage points of the US ridesharing market — boosting Lyft's market share from 29% to 41% in San Francisco, 17% to 27% in Philadelphia, 22% to 34% in Los Angeles, and similar amounts in cities across the country.[27]

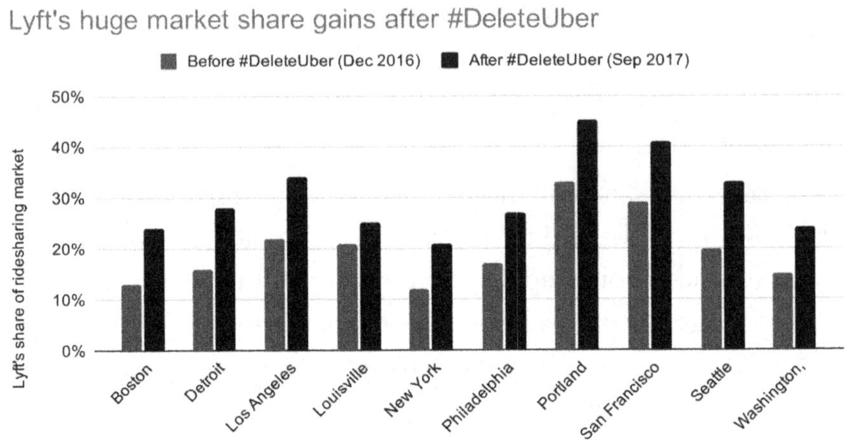

Lyft grew its market share at Uber's expense across the United States after the #DeleteUber movement took off. Source: Vox[28]

Uber's actions were a massive unforced error. By demolishing its brand, Uber gave its archrival a free 50-percent boost and permanently tarnished its standing with users. Brands matter.

Know your customer

Ron Johnson should have known that step one of building a brand — and, really, step one of marketing — is to understand your customers.

Johnson was an all-star in the world of retail; he'd previously served as Target's VP of Merchandising[29] and Apple's senior VP of retail.[30] He'd introduced Apple stores' iconic Genius Bars, open-floor demos, and free workshops on how to use Apple products.[31] So hopes were high when Johnson was tapped to be JCPenney's CEO in 2011.[32]

Johnson's first order of business was to reforge JCPenney as a high-quality retailer. He found JCPenney's constant sales, coupons, and clearances distasteful and threw them out.[33] Instead, he crafted a new strategy around consistently low prices[34] and added boutiques[35] and designer clothes[36] to cater to a higher-end market.

The results were disastrous. Johnson stepped down after just 17 months, during which time JCPenney stock cratered by 57%.[37]

Why? Among Johnson's many failures was his failure to understand who was shopping at JCPenney. It wasn't the same clientele as Apple's upscale stores. People shopped at JCPenney because they wanted inexpensive clothing and, more importantly, loved the thrill of finding great deals. These bargain hunters were probably mortified when Johnson's JCPenney started bragging that there would be "no coupon clipping, no door busting."[38] Johnson loved selling luxury goods, so he couldn't even imagine that people would find clipping coupons and hunting for discounts fun.[39] But they did, and Johnson drove them away.

As a PM, you have to know when your customers are different from you. Most of the people you're trying to win over are nothing like the stereotypical product manager — the jetsetting, 20- or 30-something who enjoys finding the best credit cards. A great PM does research and tries to get in their customer's shoes. Johnson would have done well to dress like a shopper and wander around a JCPenney for a few hours before making drastic strategy changes.

When users aren't customers

People in tech have a habit of equating users with customers, but they aren't always the same thing. Dogs eat dog food (they're the user), but humans buy the dog food (they're the customer). Mother's day gifts are bought not by moms but by their children, and so on.

When you're marketing a product, you need to market to the *customer*, not the user. Designing a great-tasting dog food won't help sales much, since dogs can't tell their humans how tasty their food was. Instead, you'd want to focus on things like how the food is organic or improves dogs' lifespans.

Dogs don't care how dog food looks, but owners sure do. And because owners are the ones buying the dog food, ads like these explicitly appeal to owners' desires and tastes. Source: NomNom on Instagram[40]

A great applied example of this concept is the toiletry brand Old Spice. Its marketers found that 70% of all men's toiletries are bought by women, yet most advertisements for men's body washes, shampoos, and deodorants like Axe are aimed at men, emphasizing how they'll feel more "manly." So Old Spice launched an ad campaign aimed at women, where a handsome, towel-clad actor said, "Hello, ladies" and explained how Old Spice could make their men look and smell more attractive. The campaign massively boosted Old Spice sales.[41]

Old Spice's body wash ad. It explicitly targeted women, despite the intended users being men. Source: YouTube[42]

▶ Watch this

Check out the Old Spice body wash commercial to see how the company advertised to women looking to buy products for the men in their lives.

youtube.com/watch?v=owGykVbfgUE

Case study: enterprise software

In tech, the classic example of customers not being users comes in enterprise, or *business-to-business* (*B2B*), software like the payroll software

Workday or SAP's expense-reporting software Concur. The people using this software are everyday employees, but the people who decide whether to buy it are in the finance and IT teams. These customers don't care very much about slick user interfaces and quick loading times; they want to maximize the number of features they get per dollar and make the software easy for the IT team to manage.

This is why PMs who make enterprise software emphasize the user experience much less than PMs who make *business-to-consumer* (*B2C*) software. And that, in turn, is why enterprise software gets a bad rap for being clunky, outdated, and crammed with rarely-used features.[43] The PMs who build that software would probably love to add a better user interface, but that wouldn't help the bottom line much, so it often gets deprioritized. (There are exceptions like Slack, which has a very user-friendly interface. These show that appealing to end-users can be helpful by making employees clamor for the software[44] — but, ultimately, the finance team makes the call, so a great UI can only take you so far.)

Indeed, the marketing strategies for a product might be totally different in consumer and enterprise channels. Google's Chromebooks, for instance, are sold to both everyday consumers and large businesses. The operating system is the same (and many times the same hardware is sold to both *channels*), but Google advertises it very differently. The marketing messages for enterprises emphasize how the devices are secure and easy to manage,[45] while the messaging for consumers emphasizes the battery life, speed, and synchronization with other devices.[46]

ChromeOS's advertising for consumers emphasizes the devices' excellent battery life. Source: Google[47]

Positioning

Once you've understood your user and their needs, the first step in building a branding strategy is to determine the *positioning*: the place in the user's mind that your product occupies.[48]

The simplest way to understand positioning is to think about the word or words that jump to the user's mind when they think of your product. For Apple, those words are likely "luxury" and "exclusive." For Google, they might be "useful" and "everywhere." Note that these aren't about product attributes but rather emotions and "personality." A useful question to draw out these personality-related words is, "if someone met my product at a cocktail party, how would they describe it?"[49]

You can summarize your product using a two-sentence *positioning statement* like so:[50]

> *[Product] is a [description] that helps [target market] [benefits]. People would describe it as [personality].*

For instance, the positioning statement for Waze, the popular mapping app that was later acquired by Google, might look like this:

> *Waze is a navigation app that helps commuters avoid hazards and slowdowns on the road. People would describe it as fun, clever, community-led, and friendly.*

You can (and should) have fun with it, too. Think hard about how it would act at a party:

> *Houseparty is a video-based party app that lets people hang out with their friends, play games, and meet friends of friends. People would describe it as rowdy, spontaneous, and chatty.*

Value propositions

One way to build on top of the formula is to show the *value proposition* for multiple types of users:[51]

> *YouTube is an online video community. It helps viewers find entertaining and inspiring videos, creators find and connect with fans, and advertisers get their message in front of one of the world's broadest audiences. People would describe it as witty and the life of the party, with clever trivia about every topic.*

When the value proposition is included, these positioning statement become especially useful tools because they effectively give you your *elevator pitch*. Once your team agrees on your positioning statement, you can update your website's homepage, your LinkedIn descriptions, your press materials, etc. The elevator pitch becomes a boilerplate bit of writing you can recycle anytime you're trying to introduce people to your product or company.[52]

Brand pyramid

Positioning is only part of your product's branding story. There are two more parts to add: the emotional benefits it brings and its broader social mission. How does it make users feel, and what kind of a change does it hope to make in the world?[53] The mission part often comes from your company's vision or mission statement.[54] For instance, Microsoft's mission is to "empower every person and organization on the planet to achieve more."[55] Most Microsoft products — from Office to Azure — inherit this mission as part of their brand.

You can then assemble a five-piece *branding pyramid.* The lowest levels are the most literal pieces of the product, and the higher levels are more abstract and visionary. In order, the levels are:[56]

1. Features and attributes: what your product does.
2. Functional benefits: what user problems your product solves.
3. Emotional benefits: how your product makes people feel.
4. Brand personality: your product's human characteristics, used to build an emotional connection with users.
5. Brand essence: your product or company's broader mission.

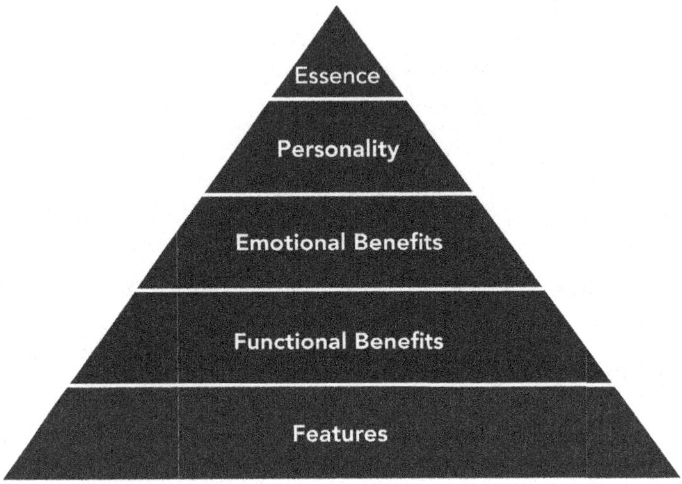

The brand pyramid. Each level builds on the levels below it.

The brand pyramid will be the foundation of all your future marketing work — all your advertising, growth strategies, sales tactics, and such will be based on it — so it's important to spend enough time on it.

Case study: Tesla

Tesla is nominally a car company that aims to protect the environment by swapping out gas-guzzling cars for electric vehicles, but a closer look shows that its brand isn't really that of an eco-warrior carmaker.

But a closer look shows that Tesla is more than just another electric car company. Teslas sell for as much as luxury cars[57] — a Model S will set you back over $70,000,[58] and Elon Musk himself admitted it's aimed at the "1%."[59] Musk bans the haggling, discounting,[60] and rows upon rows of cars found at most car dealerships.[61] Teslas have, indeed, become a status symbol for wealthy Bay Area residents[62] in a way that a Toyota

Prius never has. And then there's the fact that electric cars are only as clean as the electricity that powers them — and in many parts of the world, electricity equals coal and oil.[63]

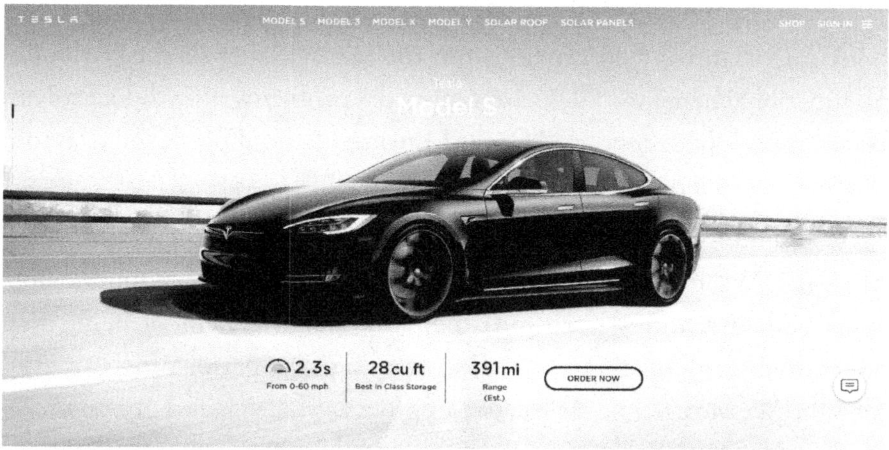

Tesla's website resembles Apple's far more than, say, Ford's. Source: Tesla[64]

If Tesla was really trying to spur an eco-revolution, they'd be building mass-market, hyper-efficient cars like the Toyota Prius or Chevy Volt,[65] and Musk would be turning his engineering prowess toward building, say, cars that run on incredibly clean hydrogen fuel cells.[66] Instead, Tesla refuses to sell cheap cars to dealerships,[67] and Musk calls hydrogen fuel cells "mind-bogglingly stupid."[68]

So we intuitively suspect that Tesla is more of a luxury brand — an "Apple on wheels"[69] — than a brand for eco-warriors. But Tesla is more complex than that. To rigorously analyze Tesla's brand, we want to build a brand pyramid.

At the base are features. Tesla's cars are all-electric, of course, but they pack a carload of high-tech and sports-car features. Tesla brags that its high-end Model S can go from 0 to 60 mph in just 2.3 seconds,[70] beating out Ferraris, Bugattis, Porsches, and McLarens.[71] Some Teslas even have the extravagantly cool falcon-wing doors.[72] On the tech side, Teslas can drive themselves on the highway through the Autopilot feature,[73] they drive themselves through the parking lot to their owners with Smart Summon,[74] and they automatically update their software *over-the-air*.[75] In short, these machines are high-tech sports cars: Apple meets BMW.

A car's features feed directly into the second layer of the pyramid: the functional benefits. These are simply the problems the product solves for the user. The legendary Harvard Business School professor Clayton Christensen called these the *jobs-to-be-done*.[76]

It's useful to compare the rival German car brands BMW and Mercedes. BMWs' ergonomically-designed interiors and light, nimble engines[77] (their features) feed into their functional benefit of being the "ultimate driving machine."[78] If you want a great-performing car, you get a BMW. Meanwhile, Mercedes' engines are heavier and guzzle more gas, but their exteriors are more stylish and their interiors feature lots of wood, chrome, and leather[79] — feeding into their functional benefits of luxury. If you want a good-looking and premium-feeling car, you get a Mercedes.

Teslas' functional benefits are quite like BMWs', and they come straight from their feature set. A Tesla's powerful electric motor makes it a fast, quiet, and smooth ride, with great acceleration and handling,[80] and Teslas' network of electric Superchargers give the cars a solid range.[81] Teslas' interiors are refined, clean, and high-tech, making them feel more like BMWs than Mercedes.[82]

A Tesla Model X with its "falcon doors" up. Source: Wikimedia[83]

But unlike BMWs, Teslas' regular software updates make Teslas always get better over time. In other words, you turn to a Tesla if you want a performant, innovative ride that's great for long roadtrips (the functional benefits). Compare this to the efficient, simple Priuses that are optimized for commuting.[84] It's also important to point out that Tesla isn't really going for luxury: the interiors are simple and the unusual features, like the "falcon doors" that open upward,[85] are more "cool" than luxurious.

These two base layers feed into the emotional benefits, which is where the brand pyramid starts getting more abstract. At this point it's clear that the cars' eco-friendliness is just a small part of their overall appeal. When you buy a Tesla, you're joining an exclusive club of forward-thinking technophiles, an enlightened group that has seen the future of cars — one without such dinosaurs as gasoline, sleazy car dealerships, and clunky digital interfaces.

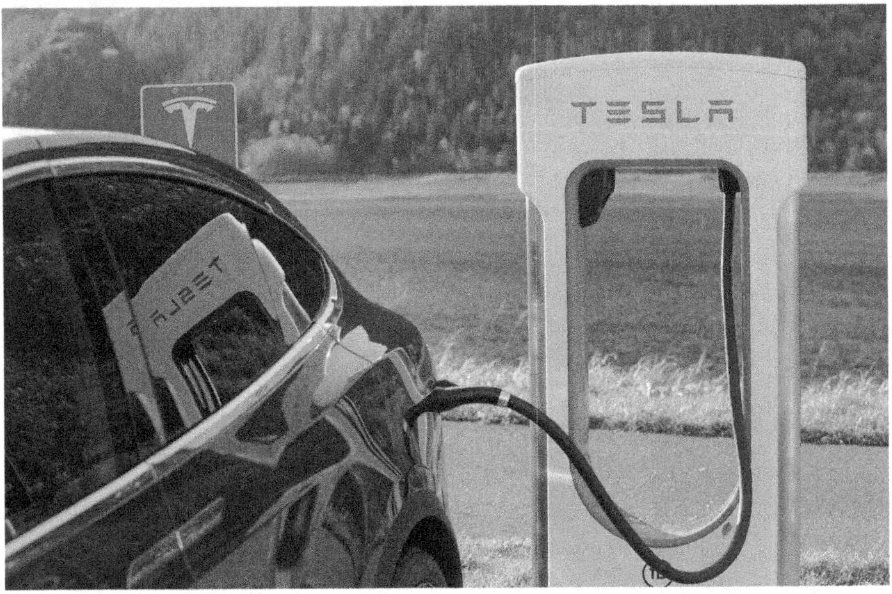

A Tesla Superchargers, where the electric cars can recharge. These are found along highways around the world. Source: Blomst via Pixabay[86]

Tesla's exclusivity starts with its network of electric Superchargers around the world,[87] which are only usable by Tesla owners.[88] Gas-car users can only look at these sleek, modern versions of the foul-smelling gas pump in envy, the thinking goes. Tesla owners even have exclusive forums and have created a sort of "us vs. them" mentality, contrasting the forward-thinking Tesla owners versus the masses stuck on the old technology.[89] This fosters an intense brand loyalty among Tesla customers.[90]

Owning a Tesla, in other words, makes you feel innovative, intelligent, bold, and part of a tight-knit group. This leads to the fundamental insight about Tesla cars: they aren't electric because it's eco-friendly (though that helps), they're electric because electricity is the future of cars, and Tesla drivers want to live in the future.

Tesla's desired emotional benefits explains part of its business strategy. Tesla intentionally started out at the high end of the market, with its debut Tesla Roadster selling for up to $110,000 when it launched in 2008. In part because of its high price, the Roadster quickly became popular with Hollywood celebrities including Brad Pitt and Jennifer Garner. Only later did Musk start creating cheaper cars.[91] This strategy aimed (successfully) to create a brand of exclusivity and innovation for Tesla. Starting at the low end of the market would have given people the first impression that the brand was ordinary — the opposite of what Musk intended.

The fourth layer is the brand personality, which is, effectively, Elon Musk. The eccentric billionaire is Tesla's face, brain, and soul. He's been portrayed in the media as a revolutionary, charismatic genius,[92] mentioned in the same breath as Steve Jobs and Albert Einstein.[93] Here is the man who, in addition to creating America's most exciting carmaker, has worked toward taking humans to Mars,[94] explored electric jets,[95] and designed a futuristic, high-speed underground railway called the Hyperloop.[96]

In short, Musk's fans call him a real-life Iron Man: Robert Downey Jr., who played Iron Man in the Marvel movies, even met Musk to understand the character of Tony Stark, the visionary tycoon who moonlights as Iron Man.[97] By buying a Tesla, the theory goes, you can be a little more like Musk, and you can have some of his more exciting qualities shine on you.[b]

The fifth level of the brand pyramid is the brand essence: Tesla's vision for changing the world. This one is pretty clear. Tesla's stated mission is to "accelerate the world's transition to sustainable energy."[98]

---

[b]The risk of using a person as your brand personality is that their quirks — like Musk naming his child "X Æ A-12" — rub off on your brand.

There's two parts here: the eco-friendliness and the revolutionary tone. When people buy Teslas, they feel like they're boldly fighting the moneyed, powerful old guard that makes their money off fossil fuels. Buying a Tesla thus becomes a rebellious act, using innovation to create a better world. It's one of the many reasons why Teslas are so attractive to people.

When you put it all together into the pyramid, Tesla's brand becomes clear: each level feeds into the levels above it. At the top is the brand essence: a revolution through sustainable technology.

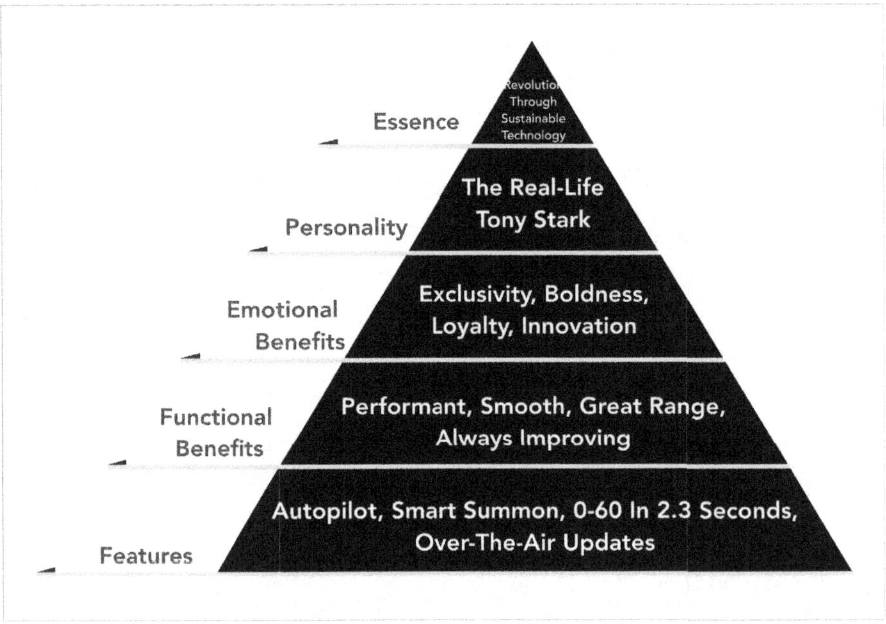

Tesla's brand pyramid.

After creating the brand, you have to deliver on it. Knowing the brand is thus essential to creating a feature roadmap. For instance, self-driving features don't initially seem relevant to electric cars. They're handy, sure, but they seem mostly independent of electric motors and environmental motives. But if you know that Tesla's brand is all about innovation, not just eco-friendliness, it all starts to make sense. Electric motors are innovative; self-driving cars are also innovative. A brand like Tesla thus has to have both.

Chapter 32

What Are You Hunting?

According to Ritesh Lal, a former PM at Yahoo, Yahoo in its heyday had a *nine-figure rule* for all its various businesses, from stocks to news to search. The rule was that a business had to have at least 100 million monthly active users or pull in at least $100 million in annual revenue for Yahoo to support it; anything less and it wasn't worth the giant company's time. This nine-figure rule has become common throughout Silicon Valley; many venture capitalists use it as a benchmark when evaluating startups.[1]

How do you go about earning $100 million a year? There are all kinds of tech businesses you could start, but they generally fall into one of five categories, according to what we call the *hunting model*, This model, which is popular among salespeople,[2] categorizes companies based on the average amount of money they hope to earn per customer per year,[3] or the *annual revenue per account* (*ARPA*).[a]

[a] This is just a more general term for the *annual revenue per user,* or *ARPU.* ARPA works in both consumer and enterprise settings, while ARPU is usually applied to just consumer products.

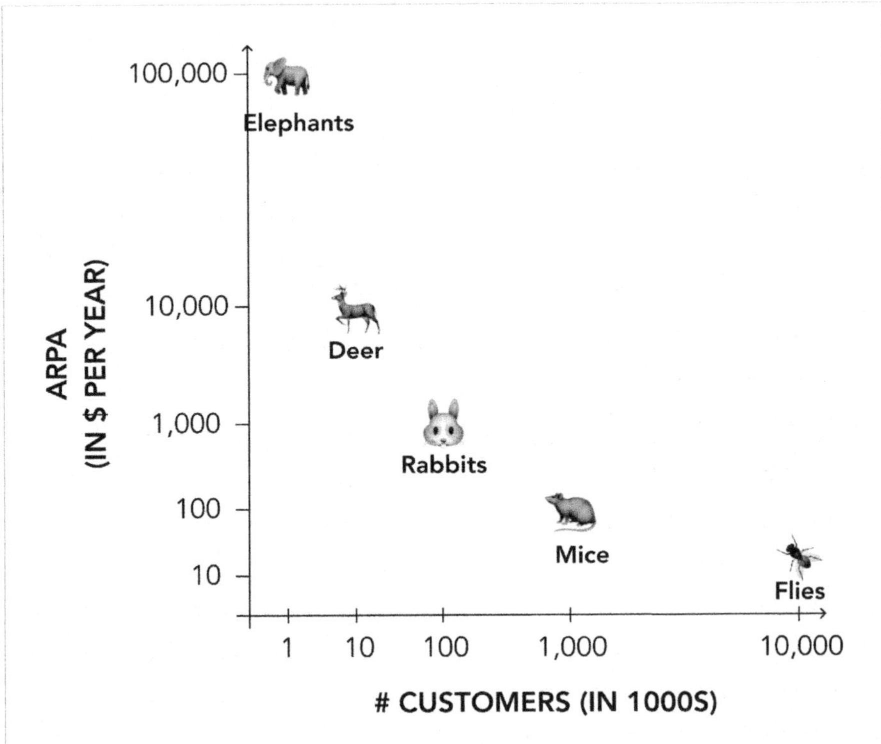

You can get to $100 million in annual revenue in five ways. Each way is represented as a different "animal" you can "hunt." At one extreme, you can earn a lot of money from a few users (elephants); at the other, you can earn a little money from a lot of users (flies). Source: Visual Capitalist[4]

This model treats different kinds of customers as different "animals" that you might be hunting. Based on what you're hunting, your marketing, sales, advertising, and growth strategies — in other words, all your methods for monetizing your products — will differ.

In this model, you have five options for earning $100 million in annual revenue: you can get $10 each from 10 million customers (flies), $100 each from one million customers (mice), $1000 each from 100,000 customers (rabbits), $10,000 each from 10,000 customers (deer), or $100,000 each from 1000 customers (elephants).[5] This model sometimes includes a sixth category, whales ($1 million each from 100 customers), but your marketing and sales strategies are pretty much the same as if you were hunting elephants,[6] so whales and elephants are usually lumped together.

Let's step through the ideal marketing, sales, advertising, and growth strategies for each type of animal.

Flies: $10 each

The first way to build a $100 million tech business is to earn $10 a year each from 10 million users. The central rule of the hunting model is that you shouldn't spend more to acquire a user (the *customer acquisition cost*, or *CAC*) than the user will spend (the *customer lifetime value*, or *LTV*). In fact, your CAC should ideally be less than one-third your LTV.[7]

Flies' LTVs are low — $10 per year they remain a customer — which means you shouldn't be spending much money marketing or advertising to them.[8] Super Bowl commercials, which cost over $5 million per 30-second slot, are probably out of the question.[9]

In fact, the LTVs here are so low that the only profitable way to hunt flies is to not advertise in the traditional sense at all. Instead, you want to bring in customers for free, and there are two main ways to do that: through *viral growth marketing* or through massive amounts of *user-generated content.*[10]

Viral growth marketing, or just *viral marketing*, relies on users bringing others onto the platform at no cost to you. This can take the form of social products where users can invite friends or family; think of Instagram, WhatsApp, or Snapchat. It can also, more abstractly, refer to social products with strong *network effects*, where users join the platform voluntarily once others join. Once enough attractive people on a college campus download a dating app like Tinder or Bumble, you can bet that others on campus will flock to it — no advertising needed.[11]

The other way to pick up a lot of users for free is to have Google funnel users to your website. Doing this requires creating a lot of pages so that large numbers of queries will lead to your site. Creating lots of pages, in turn, is only feasible if your users are making them — thus, these products live and die off their *user-generated content*, or *UGC*. After creating the content, these sites need to get Google to rank them highly, using techniques called *search engine optimization* or *SEO*. There are dozens of popular startups that use the combination of UGC and SEO to hunt lots of flies: Quora, Reddit, Yelp, StackOverflow, Pinterest, Medium, and so on.

Whether you're finding flies through social virality or UGC, the primary way to monetize them is through ads, since the average person won't want to pay money to use products like Reddit or Instagram. There are some exceptions, though; dating apps manage to make a few dollars from dedicated users through in-app purchases and subscriptions that boost users' chances of finding a match.[12]

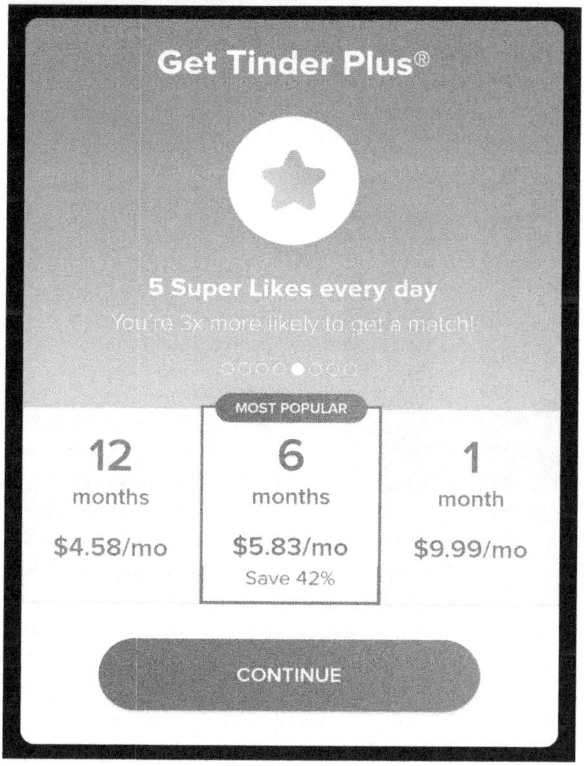

Tinder monetizes by selling Gold and Plus subscriptions, which offer goodies like unlimited swipes, "super likes", and no ads. Source: Tinder

Note that the actual amount of money you'll earn per user per year (your *average revenue per user*, or *ARPU*) isn't always $10, or even anything close. Facebook's ARPU is over $40 for users in the US and Canada but just $4 in Asia.[13] Most fly-seeking companies' ARPUs actually fall short of the $10 benchmark,[14][15] but $10 is close enough for the ballpark estimates that the hunting model needs.

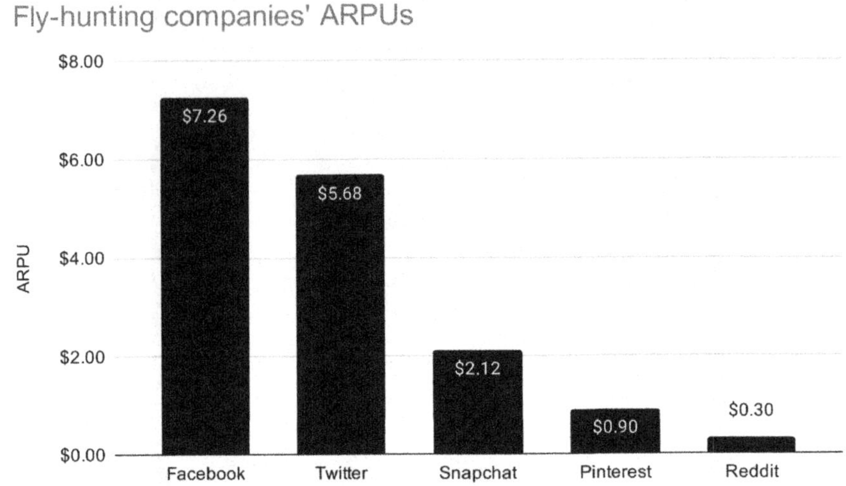

The Annual Revenue Per User, or ARPU, of several popular fly-hunting companies. Source: CNBC[16][17]

Mice: $100 each

Next up are mice, which are typically consumers and very small businesses (think LLCs and three-person consultancies) who spend about $100 a year on your product.[18] These include small-business tools like MailChimp and the website creation tools Wix and Squarespace; entertainment services like Spotify, Netflix, and Hulu; and various consumer services like Amazon Prime, the meditation app Calm, and Dropbox Plus.

The vast majority of these services monetize with monthly or annual subscriptions; while few charge exactly $100 a year, their *annual revenue per paying user* (or *ARPPU*) is in the same ballpark.

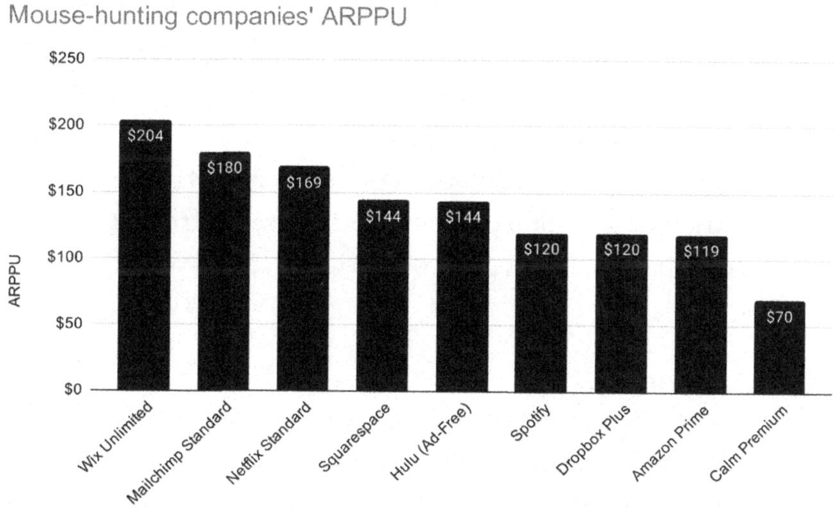

The Average Revenue Per Paying User, or ARPPU, of several mouse-hunting products. Sources: Wix,[19] MailChimp,[20] Netflix,[21] Squarespace,[22] Hulu,[23] Spotify,[24] Dropbox,[25] Amazon,[26] Calm[27]

(There's a subtle difference between ARPU and ARPPU: ARPU averages revenue across *all* users, while ARPPU only considers paying users. We use ARPU to analyze fly hunters because users don't "pay" for the services; the money mostly comes from ads, except for in-app purchase businesses. ARPPU is more precise when users pay for your service, which is the case for mice-hunting products.)

Because your customer lifetime values, or LTVs, are in the hundreds of dollars, you can start affording to spend good amounts of money on traditional advertising and marketing techniques: TV and Facebook ads, social media blitzes, newsletters, influencer posts, and so on.

But just because you *can* spend a lot of money on marketing and advertising doesn't mean you have to. It's estimated that, to get to one million paying customers, you'll need to get 10 to 20 million people to try your product. Running ads to recruit all those users will get expensive, so your best bet is to have a limited viral loop to bring in new users on the cheap.[28] Users may not join a paid subscription service for free, like they would for fly-hunting products. Instead, you'll want to use tactics like referral bonuses: for instance, Dropbox gives you 500 MB of free storage for inviting friends,[29] Airbnb gives users $20 for each friend they invite (but only once that friend has gone on a trip),[30] and so on.

Rabbits: $1000 each

After mice, you're no longer selling to everyday consumers. Your average Joe isn't going to shell out $1000 a year — the benchmark for a rabbit — for a tech product. Once you start hunting rabbits, you're entering the world of business, or *B2B*, products.

At this point, you no longer care about ARPU or ARPPU. You don't directly care about how many individual end-users you have. Instead, you care about the total amount of money each customer is paying you — the *average revenue per account,* or *ARPA*.[b] You don't care if the pizza shop has five employees or 50 as long as they're paying you $1000 a year.

Many familiar small-team productivity tools can count as rabbit-hunters, including Trello, Slack, Asana, GitHub, and Google Workspace. Slack's small-business tier costs $6.67 per user per month;[31] a 150-person business would thus spend exactly $1000 a year on Slack. But because these tools tend to be priced per employee, they could also be mice-, deer-, or even elephant-hunters depending on the size of the target customer. A tiny business of 15 people would spend just $100 a year on Slack; a larger 800-person company using Slack's $12.50 Plus tier would spend $10,000 a year.

[b] ARPA is effectively the same thing as ARPPU, but ARPA is the proper term for enterprise sales.

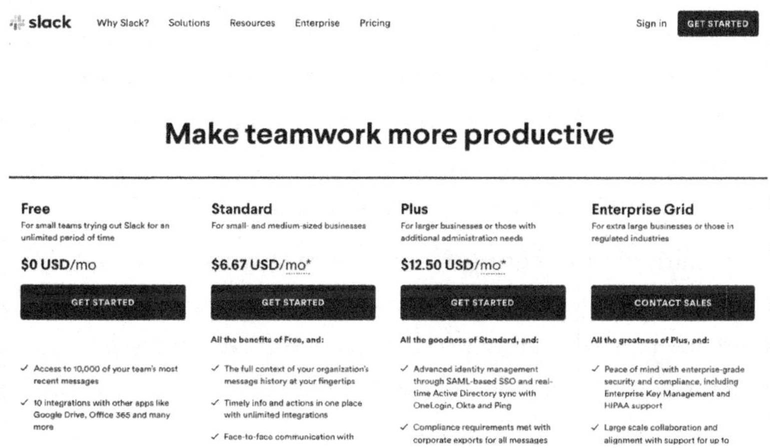

By charging companies per employee per month, Slack can cater to mice, rabbit, deer, and even elephants. Source: Slack[32]

But remember that, while your product might be hunting multiple types of animals at once, you'll need to use different marketing, advertising, and sales tactics for each animal.

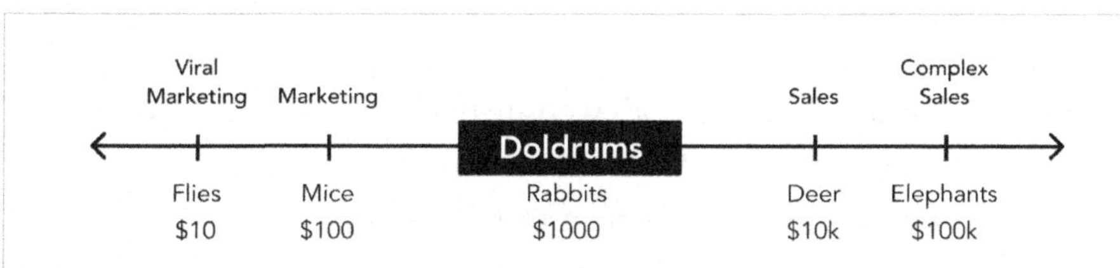

When hunting rabbits, you fall into a realm where neither traditional marketing nor traditional sales is particularly effective. This is often called the "Distribution Doldrums." Source: Zero to One[33]

Rabbits, in particular, are a hard customer to target. They're too large for traditional advertising and marketing to work; a small business isn't going to throw $1000 at Shopify[34] just based on some Instagram ad the founder saw. And yet they're too small for you to use classic sales teams; customers spending just $1000 a year aren't worth the salary of a salesperson, and besides, you won't have enough salespeople to cover 100,000 customers. The famous entrepreneur Peter Thiel calls this zone the "Distribution Doldrums" for this reason.[35]

The traditional marketing tactics we've discussed so far — ads, influencer posts, even cold emails — are what's known as *outbound marketing*, where you take your product to potential buyers and ask them if they're interested. The old-school door-to-door salespeople and trade conferences were the classic example of outbound marketing.[36] As we mentioned, these strategies aren't as useful for rabbits and larger animals.

Instead, your best bet is to embrace *inbound marketing*, where you get potential buyers to visit your site voluntarily. The theory is that getting people to make a purchase — in other words, *convert* — is much easier once you've gotten them on your home turf.[37] To get people to visit your site, you create content like blog posts, viral videos, free courses and ebooks, and such. People will visit your website to get this content, start to like your company, and thus become far more likely to buy.[38]

The digital marketing company HubSpot has been credited with inventing inbound marketing, and, fittingly, HubSpot itself is a skilled user of inbound marketing. HubSpot's website has hundreds of useful ebooks, blog posts, free courses, and free website tools for inbound marketers.[39] HubSpot knows that marketers turn to HubSpot to learn the art of inbound marketing — so when their companies want to buy marketing software, they'll naturally go to HubSpot.

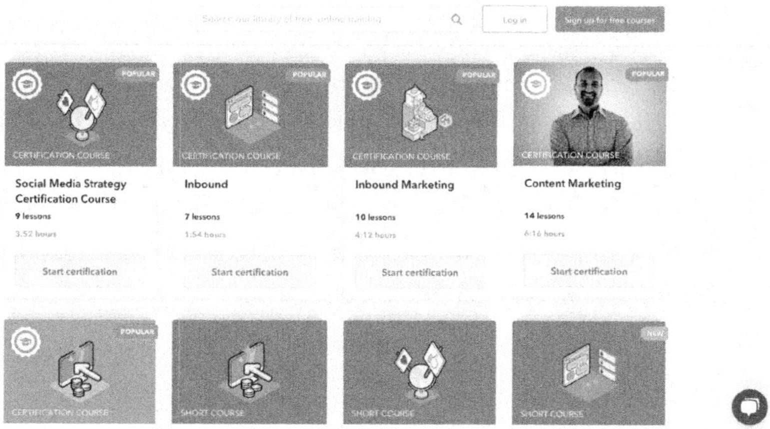

HubSpot offers dozens of free marketing courses designed to build goodwill with marketers — who will then trust HubSpot with their business. Source: HubSpot[40]

Inbound marketing works for rabbit hunting because it helps you attract the exact kinds of potential customers you want and build the kind of trust you need to make sales — all without requiring a human salesperson.

Deer: $10,000 each

At this point, you're starting to sell to medium-sized businesses (think 200-person startups) or smaller teams within huge businesses (like a particular division of a Fortune 500 firm). Companies like HubSpot, Atlassian, and Asana notably sell to such customers.[41]

Your customers are getting big enough that they'll probably want some human contact, meaning that the rabbits' inbound marketing strategies won't be enough.[42] Thus, you'll have to transition from marketing to sales. But customers aren't yet big enough to merit sending a huge sales force to companies' headquarters.[43]

Instead, you'll want to use an intermediate tactic called *inside sales* or *remote sales* — where customers do get sales representatives, but they only talk to those representatives over the phone or internet.[44] This keeps the cost of supporting each customer down. Also, each sales rep usually handles more than one customer, since a $10,000-a-year account usually isn't big enough to merit a full-time rep.[45]

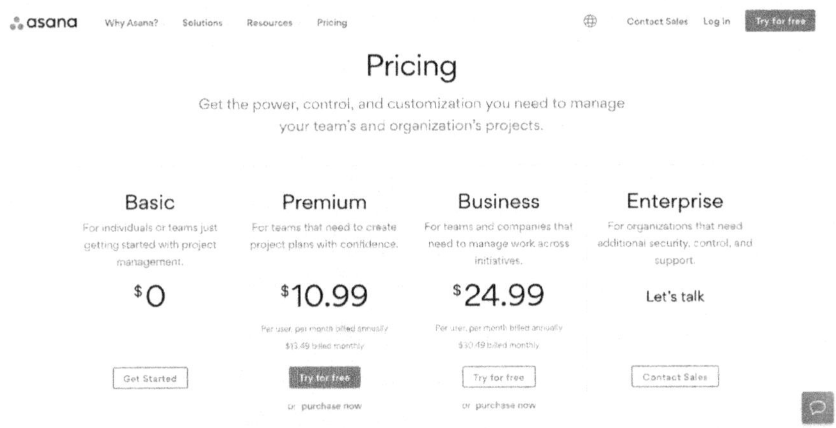

Asana offers a standard pricing system of $25 per employee per month; this is mostly targeted at deer. Elephants can't go this "self-service" route; they have to talk to the sales team. This is typical of most enterprise software that sells to both deer and elephants. Source: Asana[46]

Enterprise products can sell to rabbits, deer, or elephants, but some venture capitalists suggest that small or new teams focus on deer. Elephants require a lot of hand-holding, since you often have to promise them a large support staff, 24/7 help desk access, training sessions, and other services that a small team can't handle. Meanwhile, catching enough rabbits to "feed" your company is hard because these customers — like real rabbits — are hard to catch and pin down. Chasing after huge crowds of rabbits will only tire you out and leave you with too little "meat," the argument goes. But deer occupy a sweet spot in the middle: big enough that you don't need too many of them, but small enough that catching one isn't overwhelming.[47]

Elephants: $100,000 each

Elephants (and their larger cousins, the million-dollar-each whales) are the largest customers you can hunt. These are typically Fortune 500 companies or national governments. Think about the software that a typical Fortune 500 company might use: Microsoft Office, Amazon Web Services, Salesforce for *customer relationship management* (*CRM*), Workday for HR and payroll, and so on. These products are hunting elephants.[48]

Since elephants are so huge, you only need 1000 of them to hit the $100 million mark. But each one takes a lot of work to win. This is the realm of steak dinners, wining and dining CEOs, suited-up trips to corporate headquarters, and blowout customer conferences in Las Vegas. You can spend massive amounts of money to acquire customers, and in many cases you need to, since someone who's handing you $100,000 a year is going to expect a lot from you.[49]

As we mentioned earlier, hunting elephants isn't for the faint of heart. The sheer amount of support these customers need (and expect) will take time, energy, and resources away from your core product development teams, meaning that you'll be doing a lot more customer support and a lot less product building than you might have thought.[50] What's more, going for elephants out of the gate can paint you into a corner, since the products and teams that work well for elephant hunting aren't well-suited for rabbit or deer hunting. In other words, be careful before entering an elephant-hunting market.[51]

Chapter 33

Advertising

ADVERTISING IS, of course, a key part of most marketing strategies, and in the tech industry you often get to sit on both sides of the table. You'll have to use ads to grow your own product, and the products you work on (from Google Search to Quora to LinkedIn) will often use ads as a monetization strategy. So knowing this sub-industry is important no matter where in tech you want to work.

Brand and direct response

The first thing to know about advertising is that it's made of two very different parts: *direct response advertising*, which seeks to get viewers to take an action (such as buying a product) immediately, and *brand advertising*, which seeks to make viewers think more positively about a particular product or company.[1]

It's easiest to observe this split in the "real" world. Billboards are the classic example of brand advertising. When BMW puts up a billboard, they don't want you to head down to the dealership and buy a car that same day. No, they just want you to think more about the car so that, when it's time for you to buy your next car, you're more likely to pick a BMW. Meanwhile, those pieces of paper with tear-off tabs that you often see on notice boards — advertising babysitters, tutors, landscapers, and the like — are a great example of direct response advertising. They're not trying to boost their brand; they want you to tear off a tab with their phone number and book an appointment straight away.

A useful exercise is to start looking at ads you see in your daily life and classifying them as brand or direct response. A good rule of thumb is that any ad with a phone number, website, or *call-to-action* button like "buy now" or "install," is a direct-response ad. Anything else is a brand ad. Consider TV ads: most ads have no call to action, instead seeking to make products like cars and toothpaste look appealing, and are thus brand ads. (Super Bowl ads are pretty much all brand ads.) Meanwhile, those "call the number on your screen right now and get this specialty potato peeler for just $19.95" ads are the rare direct response TV ads.

State Farm published this brand advertisement on Snapchat. The insurance company isn't trying to make you sign up for a policy straight away — it just wants you to think more positively of the company. Source: Snapchat

This split applies in the digital world too. Marketers making digital ads for a product will likely use a mixture of brand and direct response advertising, and chances are they'll use different platforms for each. Frito-Lay, the company that makes Cheetos, might put a direct-response ad on Amazon so that Cheetos will pop up when you search for "party snacks." The goal of that ad is to make you click "add to cart."

Frito-Lay might also put a brand ad on Instagram, perhaps showing good-looking people at a party munching on Cheetos. The goal isn't to make you run out and buy Cheetos straight away — it's to make you associate Cheetos with parties and thus reach for Cheetos the next time you're shopping for party snacks.

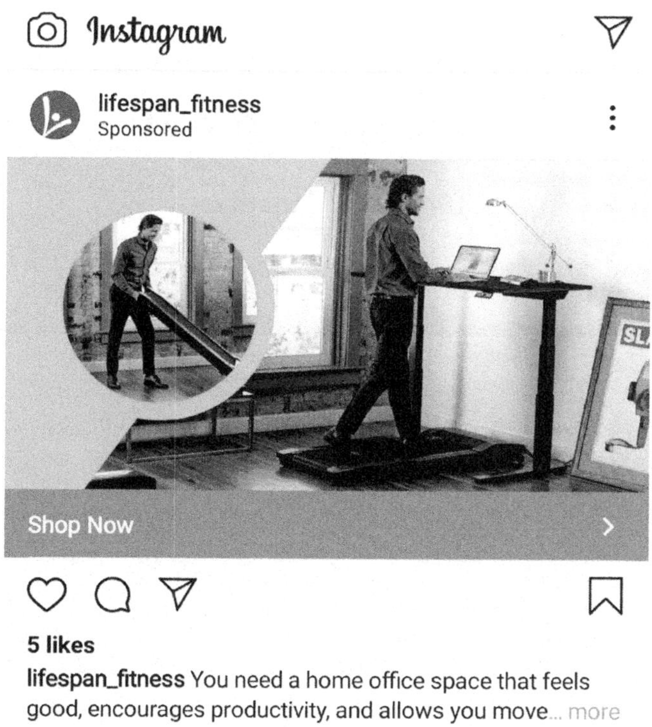

A direct-response ad for a walking desk on Instagram. The ad wants viewers to "Shop Now." Source: Instagram

Generally speaking, brand advertising works best when people are just browsing or seeking entertainment; these are *low-intent* activities where people aren't going to go out of their way to take action. People go to YouTube to sit back and be entertained — which makes it a bad place to seek a direct response but a great place to try to win people over. Twitter is another classic example of a brand advertising platform:[2] companies go there to showcase their brand personalities and charm users,[3] not to win sales directly.

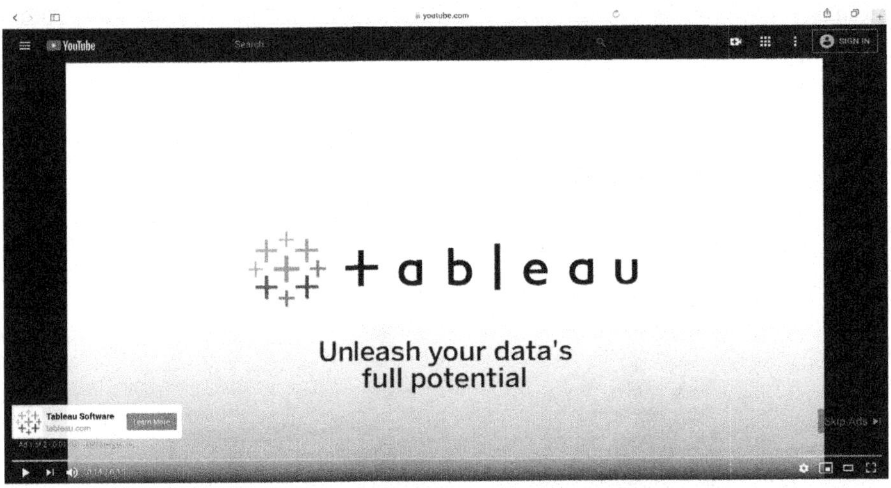

Some ads are hybrids between brand and direct-response. This YouTube ad for Tableau mostly exists to boost Tableau's brand awareness, but a small link in the bottom left corner lets you visit Tableau's website — thus mixing in an element of direct-response ads. Source: YouTube

Meanwhile, direct response advertising is best for high-intent activities, where someone is clearly seeking something out.[4] They're looking for something, not mindlessly scrolling. This is the case for Google[5] and Amazon — when someone searches for wireless earbuds, you know they probably want to buy them, so they'll welcome ads that lead them right to a purchase page. It would be a waste to just show them brand ads —

in fact, they might actually dislike brand ads, which would just distract them from their goal.

Other products are hybrids. Facebook and Instagram got their start in brand advertising,[6] but now they offer a fair number of direct response ads as well. If you've ever gotten an Instagram ad telling you to download an app or buy lip gloss, you've gotten a direct response ad.[7]

Purchase funnel

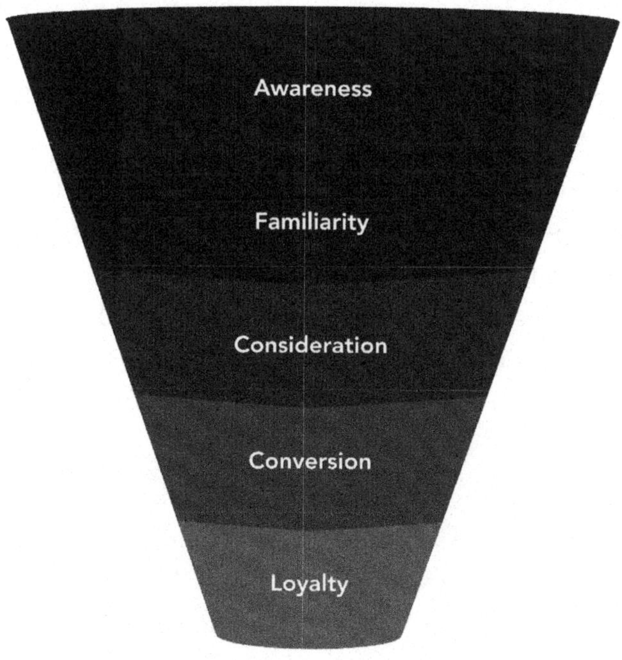

The five-step purchase funnel. Source: McKinsey[8]

Another way to think about brand vs. direct response advertising is with the five-step *purchase funnel*, also known as the customer decision funnel[9] or the customer buying funnel.[10] The idea is that people move through stages from "potential customer" to "loyal customer." Some people leave at each stage, but the remaining ones get more and more valuable. The stages are *awareness, familiarity, consideration, purchase,* and *loyalty*.[11]

The first step toward buying a product is knowing it exists (awareness). Then you have to form an opinion of it (familiarity). Then you have to think about buying it (consideration). Then you have to actually buy it (purchase), and then you become a loyal customer who buys again and tells your friends about the product.[12]

(You might also hear about the *AIDA funnel*, which is very similar. It cuts out the "loyalty" stage and renames the first four stages, *awareness, interest, desire,* and *action*.[13] It's more general-purpose than the five-step purchase funnel, so keep it in your toolkit.)

Brand advertising is usually toward the top of the funnel (awareness and familiarity) — getting people to know about and like your product. Direct response advertising is usually toward the bottom of the funnel (consideration)— getting people who already know what your product is like to take your desired action.[14] In this way, brand and direct response advertising aren't two totally different beasts: they're just two ends of a spectrum.

When you're seeking to advertise your product, it's useful to know which stage of the funnel you'd like to improve. Do you need more people to know your product exists (*top-of-funnel*)? If so, run some brand ads. But if you need to win over people hunting for things in your category, run direct response ads.

Meanwhile, if your product is going to monetize with ads, think about where in the funnel your users will be. People on app stores and ecommerce sites are probably going to be toward the bottom, while people browsing on social media or internet forums are probably toward the top. This knowledge, in turn, will help you figure out which kinds of ads you should run.

CPM, CPC, CTR

Whether you're advertising your product or selling ad slots, you'll want to pay attention to a trio of key metrics: *cost-per-mille* (*CPM*), *cost-per-click* (*CPC*), and *click-through rate* (*CTR*). These measure the price and effectiveness of an ad platform, so they're key tools for comparison.[15]

CPM and CPC refer to two dominant models of paying for ads. In the CPM regime, you pay a small amount of money each time someone views your ad (known as an *impression*). Since the price for each view is so low, ad platforms usually quote the price for one thousand views — thus cost per *mille*. In the CPC regime, you pay each time someone clicks your ad.[16]

As you might guess, the CPC/CPM distinction is strongly correlated with the direct-response/brand advertising distinction. Advertisers running direct response ads don't really care how many people see the ad — they just care how many people click through to, say, a purchase page. Thus, direct response ads usually follow the CPC regime. On the flip side, advertisers running brand ads just want to maximize the number of eyeballs that see the ad — clicks aren't all that valuable. Thus, brand ads usually follow the CPM regime.[17]

Platforms' favored models

Most platforms favor either direct-response or brand advertising, and as such, they favor either CPC or CPM. Google Search, for example, is all about direct-response advertising, so most ads are sold through CPC.[18] The ads on app stores like Google Play all ask the user to install apps, which is a form of direct-response advertising. Thus, these ads are monetized through a variant of CPC called *cost per install*, or *CPI*.

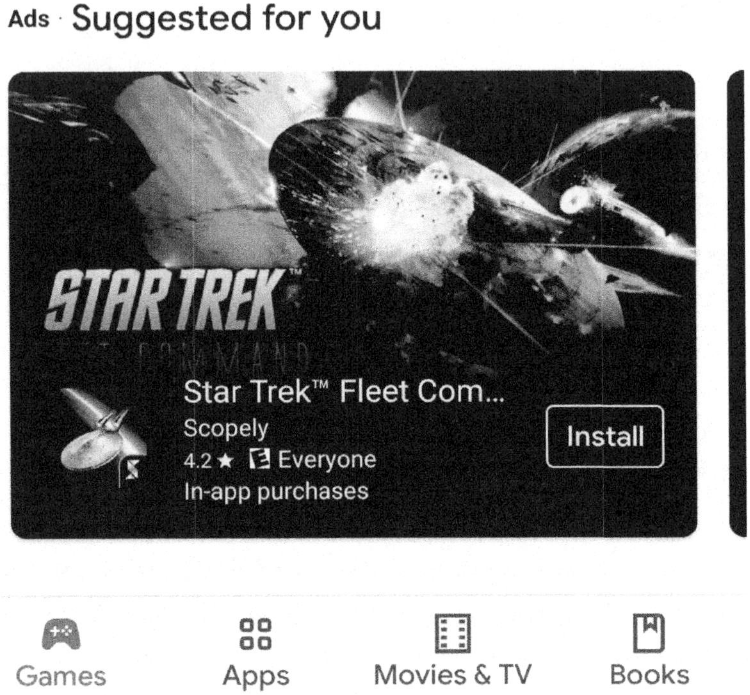

A direct-response ad on Google's Play Store. Source: Play Store

Meanwhile, YouTube is all about brand advertising, so ads are sold through CPM — or, more precisely, through *cost per view*, or *CPV*.[19]

That's not to say that ad platforms only allow one type of advertising. Most platforms let advertisers choose between CPM and CPC, along with some more rarer payment models that we'll discuss later. Most ad platforms even run CPM and CPC ads side-by-side.[20]

Comparisons

The CPM/CPC distinction gets interesting when we start to compare various platforms' CPMs and CPCs:

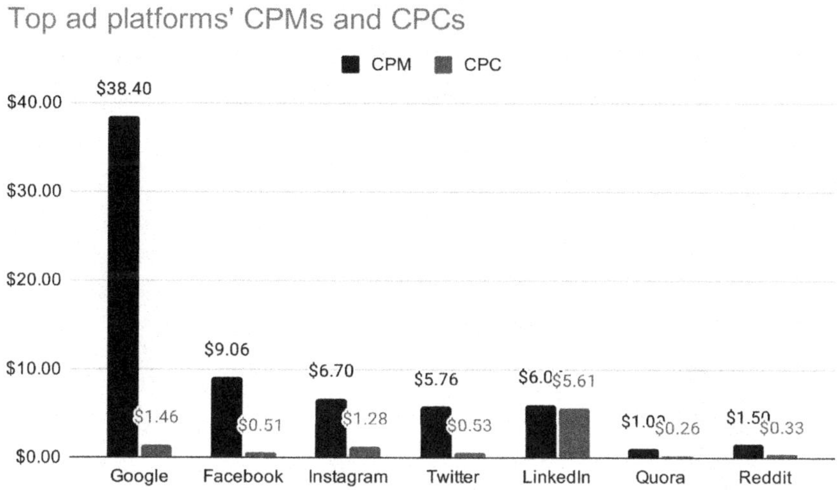

The CPMs and CPCs of several top ad platforms. Sources: Falcon,[21] *Lightning AI,*[22] *Ladder.io,*[23] *AdStage,*[24252627] *WordStream,*[28] *BannerSnack*[29]

Google's towering CPM was probably the first thing to draw your attention. What's up with that? And doesn't Google prefer CPC?

The trick here is that direct-response advertisers can actually choose the CPM regime, since people viewing ads can always click them, even if the advertiser isn't paying for clicks directly. The key factor is the ads' *click-through-rate.* With this number, you can "convert" CPM to CPC. If you pay $5 for 1000 ad views and 10 of those ad views lead to clicks, you've effectively paid $5 for 10 ad views — a CPC of $2.

And the thing about Google Search is that its users have high intent — they have literally told Google what they want to buy or look for — and, as such, ads on Google have a high *click-through rate*, or *CTR*.[30] Thus, advertisers are comfortable paying a high CPM for Google ads, since the high CTR means they'll get a reasonable "converted" CPC.

What's more, Google Search users are quite valuable in general, since they often search for high-value products like "lawyers near me" or "auto insurance." People selling those products would pay a pretty penny for ads on Google, since they know that anyone searching for lawyers or insurance is likely to buy — and spend a lot.

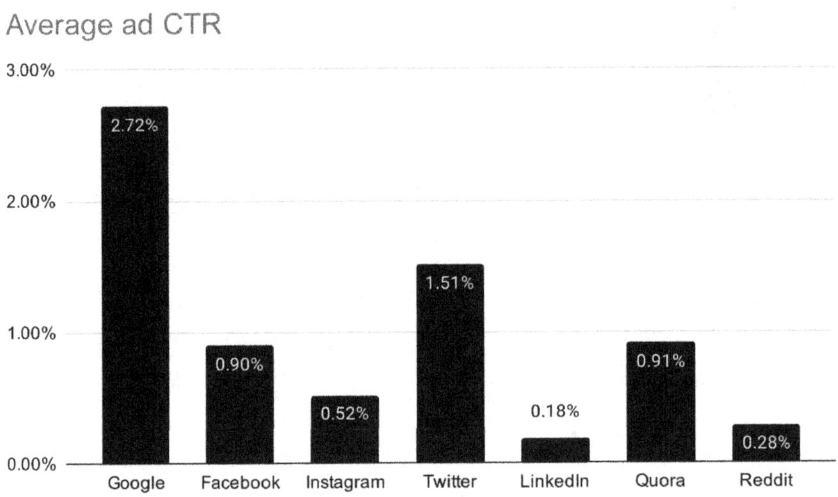

The average CTRs of several top ad platforms. Sources: Falcon,[31] Lightning AI,[32] Ladder.io,[33] AdStage,[34][35][36][37] WordStream,[38] BannerSnack[39]

🪪 Interview tip

It's useful to know ballpark CTR numbers when you're doing estimation interview questions, evaluating ad campaigns, or looking at financials. The simplest rule of thumb is that the average ad, across all flavors and platforms, has a CTR around 1%.

To be more granular, search ads, which show on search-result pages like Google's,[40], can hang around the 2-4% range.[41] Display ads, which are those banner ads you see on newspaper websites and the like, have CTRs around 0.4%.[42]

Meanwhile, if you're doing email marketing, you can expect about 20% of recipients to open your email and 2.5% of recipients to click a link in the email.[43]

Look back to the CPM and CPC graph. Besides Google, you'll notice that Facebook and Instagram have pretty high CPMs. This is because Facebook and Instagram have huge amounts of personal data — people literally tell Facebook which bands, snacks, and cars they "like," which makes it very easy to choose a good target audience for your ad. Even Google doesn't have that kind of personal information. You can also hit two birds with one stone by advertising with Facebook (the company), since the company lets you place the same ad on both Facebook (the app) and Instagram.[44] This convenience, of course, comes at a price.

You'll also notice that LinkedIn's CPC is quite high. This is in part because LinkedIn has a highly-educated, professional user base that's (generally) wealthier than that of most platforms, and thus LinkedIn users are probably willing to spend more. But the big reason, in our mind, is that LinkedIn is by far the best place to advertise *business-to-business*, or *B2B*, products. People browsing their Facebook or Instagram feeds aren't going to enjoy seeing ads for productivity or HR management software, but people on LinkedIn are quite open to that sort of ad. LinkedIn even lets advertisers target ads to specific companies, industries, or job titles — a kind of granularity that's impossible to get anywhere else.[45]

Finally, you might notice that the interest-based social network Reddit and the question-and-answer site Quora have unusually cheap CPMs and CPCs. These platforms are underrated, in our mind. Finding the right subreddits to run an ad on and creating Quora "answers" to promote[46] takes work, but if you're tight on cash, you can get a lot of bang for your buck.[47] (Remember: when you run an ad, you aren't usually dropping a random image on users' screens — you're promoting a post you already created. So your advertising will only be effective if you know how to create an effective post, which is hard for more niche or specialized platforms.)

Retargeting and remarketing

Thinking back to the purchase funnel, most ads seek to push viewers in the funnel a bit further down. Brand ads aim to make people aware of the product, then direct-response ads seek to make them consider and ultimately buy the product (or do whatever other valuable action you have in mind). But there's another way to advertise: picking up people who have leaked out of the funnel. This is the essence of the sister strategies of *retargeting* and *remarketing*.[48][a]

Retargeting seeks to bring back people who viewed your site but never converted. You do this by putting a small snippet of code called a *pixel* on your website. The pixel places a *cookie* of information on a visitor's browser once they visit your site.[49] When the visitor goes elsewhere on the web, the retargeting service (such as Google Ads[50] or Facebook[51]) notices that the visitor has your cookie and shows them an ad for your site.[52] This way, people who visit but don't convert get constantly reminded about your product. Since users who make it to your landing page but don't convert are already familiar with your product, they're already pretty far down the funnel — so getting them to convert isn't that hard.[53]

[a]Speaking precisely, retargeting and remarketing are special cases of direct response advertising, since you're looking to get people to take action immediately.

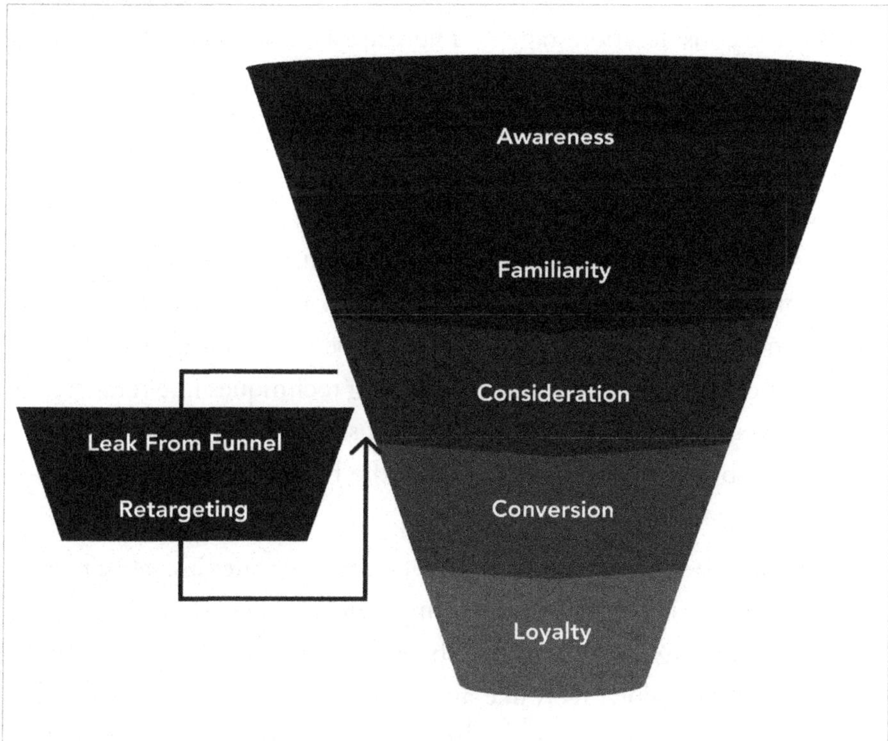

Some users will inevitably leak out of your funnel. Retargeting and remarketing help get them back.

Remarketing is very similar, but it doesn't use pixels or cookies. Instead, it relies on simply sending emails to people who might have signed up for your mailing list but never converted.[54] For instance, if an interior design firm offers people a free ebook when they sign up for the mailing list, the firm can send periodic remarketing emails to everyone who signed up, reminding them of the firm's services.

Retargeting and remarketing are underrated strategies because the purchase funnel is far leakier than any diagram makes it look. Over 95% of the people who visit the average ecommerce site will leave without buying anything — in other words, 95% of the people leak out of the funnel at the consideration stage.[55] There are a lot of potential customers in this 95%, and without retargeting and remarketing it's hard to catch them.

What's more, it's estimated that, for every $92 that businesses spend acquiring customers, they only spend $1 to convert them.[56] In other words, most businesses spend gobs of money stuffing more people into the top of the funnel without considering how to make them stop leaving. Chances are that you'll have plenty of people coming into the top of the funnel — your time is best spent using techniques like retargeting and remarketing to keep them around. To use an analogy, pouring more water into a bucket with a giant hole in the bottom isn't the answer — the answer is to patch up the hole.

That's not to say that you should overuse these strategies. Most people are used to remarketing, but retargeting still seems creepy. The idea of companies planting trackers on your browser, following you around, and never leaving you alone feels like an invasion of privacy to many. This is why there are so many popular browser extensions that get rid of the tracking cookies used in retargeting,[57] and browsers like Mozilla Firefox even block these "third-party" cookies by default.[58] Retargeting is powerful if you can pull it off, but it's become harder than ever.[59] (A possible side effect is that advertisers stop advertising on the web and move to "walled garden" apps like Facebook and Twitter, where it's much harder for users to block ads and tracking.)

Case study: Target's Facebook ads

While conventional retargeting has been somewhat neutered, the concept is still valuable. Nowadays, you can have Facebook "retarget" your ads at people who have previously watched one of your ads but didn't convert yet. These people are so-called *warm leads*; they've been warmed up to your product and can be slowly nudged toward it with a few more ads.[60]

Consider Target, which launched a retargeting-based Facebook ad campaign in 2015. First, they published a video ad for their free app Treatster, which let parents find the best trick-or-treating spots in town.[61] Target then knew that anyone who watched the ad likely had kids who were interested in Halloween. Then Target could advertise a kids-focused Halloween event called the "Sunday Spooktacular," where kids in costume would get "spooky treats and deals," to just those users.[62]

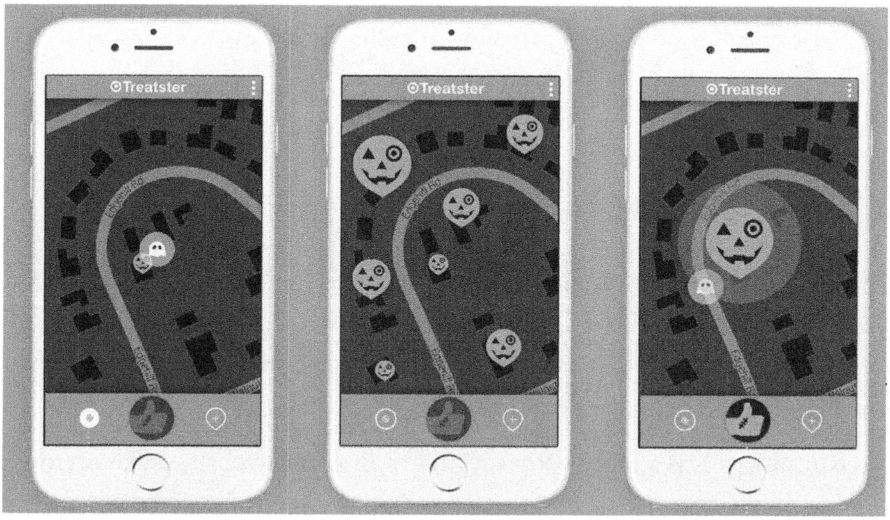

Target's Treatster app let users see and vote on neighborhood houses during Halloween. Users would upvote the houses that gave the best candy; these houses would get bigger Jack-o'-lantern bubbles in the app. Source: Megan Skelly[63]

Because Target had gathered data from the earlier Treatster ad, it could ensure that its Spooktacular ad was only shown to its target audience.[64] Generally speaking, the more precisely you target your ads, the better "bang" you get for your "buck." Think about it this way: your ad is only going to appeal to a narrow slice of the population, so anytime you show an ad to someone who's *not* part of that slice, you're wasting money. Because Target only showed this Spooktacular ad to people in the narrow demographic of "parents of young kids who like Halloween," it could minimize the number of "wasted" ad impressions and thus save money.

Thus, it's helpful to think of ads as a multi-stage campaign instead of one-off blasts. Skillful online advertisers can strategically string together ads to ensure that the last one lands a hefty punch.[65] Target's Treatster ad might have been a money-loser on its own, but it perfectly set up the Spooktacular ad to draw in a lot of valuable paying customers while wasting minimal ad dollars.

The importance of entertaining ads

We've talked about several ways to save money on advertising: choosing platforms with low CPCs and CPMs, precise user targeting, and retargeting. But one critical factor that many people overlook is simply making your ads more entertaining.

Running ads is a risky proposition for apps and websites. Ads are disruptive enough as is — and if users see an especially boring or annoying ad, it's quite likely that they'll leave the app and open up a competing app. Thus, ad platforms like Facebook will charge you a lot more to run ads that people don't engage with much[66] — you have to pay them to counteract the risk they run by putting up your ad in the first place.

In other words, the more entertaining and engaging your ad, the lower your CPCs and CPMs will be, and thus the more money you'll save.

Case study: Dollar Shave Club

A great example of an entertaining ad is the 2012 debut ad by Dollar Shave Club, a startup that sold men's grooming products through a subscription model.[67] Razors are just $1 a month, plus shipping and handling.[68]

In this ad, called "Our Blades are F***ing Great,"[69] the founder, Mike, swaggers his way around a crazily-decorated warehouse. He swings tennis rackets and machetes, cracks deadpan jokes about polio, and rides in a kid's wagon while making a "choo-choo" sound. This manic ad is over a minute and a half long, but most people who watch it — including us, the authors — are transfixed through the whole thing. You can bet that people loved this ad when it first launched, thus netting Dollar Shave Club low CPMs and CPCs.

At the end of the Dollar Shave Club ad, the founder dances with an American flag, costumed bear, warehouse worker, and leaf blower amidst flashing disco lights and flying dollar bills. Source: YouTube[70]

▸ Watch this

Watch the Dollar Shave Club's viral ad.

youtube.com/watch?v=ZUG9qYTJMsI

Entertaining ads don't just play well with ad-pricing algorithms — they can also go viral in their own right. Dollar Shave Club's ad garnered tens of millions of views on YouTube[71] — watch numbers that are more typical of indie band singles than ads for cheap razors. Making your ad go viral is the ultimate bang-for-your-buck, since people will share the ad for you for free. In Dollar Shave Club's case, it worked wonders: Dollar Shave Club got 12,000 signups in just 48 hours after launch.[72]

And finally, there's the notorious fact that the average human has an attention span of just eight seconds, shorter than a goldfish's.[73] If your ad doesn't catch people's attention right off the bat, it's not going to get conversions (for direct-response ads) or strengthen your brand image (for brand ads).

Chapter 34

Growth Hacking

A NEW FORM OF MARKETING was born accidentally in 1996, when the founders of the free email service Hotmail were kicking around ideas to grow their product.[1] They suggested billboards and radio ads,[2] but their investor, the famous venture capitalist Tim Draper,[3] dismissed the ideas. That was an awful lot of money to pay to advertise a free product.

Instead, Draper advised the Hotmail founders to try a simple "hack" to get Hotmail users to advertise the product for free. His hack was to put a small note at the bottom of each email sent from Hotmail, saying, "PS: I love you. Get your free e-mail at Hotmail."[4]

The founders were skeptical, but they gave the idea a try. Within six months of adding the *growth hack*, Hotmail had doubled its user base from 500,000 to one million. A year later, Hotmail had grown to 12 million users[5] — that doesn't sound like much today, but, back in 1998, it was one-sixth the population of the internet.[6] Microsoft bought Hotmail for an estimated $400 million that year,[7] a stunningly successful exit made possible, in large part, by that short note.

A looping funnel

The Hotmail story has become lore around Silicon Valley because it shows the fundamental insight behind this new field of *growth hacking*: that the user funnel isn't one-way.

Marketers used to think that, once customers got to the last stage of the funnel (loyalty), you'd be done with them and would need to move on to finding new users to push through the funnel. Instead, growth hackers realized that there's an additional step after loyalty — *advocacy* — and that, once a user becomes an advocate, they can feed more people into the top of the funnel for you.[8]

Hotmail's genius was finding a way to turn loyal users into advocates automatically, thus building an engine to push new users into the funnel for free. This is the classic definition of growth hacking: building viral features into your product so it can market itself.[9]

The other famous example of classic, viral growth hacking comes from PayPal. Elon Musk explained that PayPal started off by giving people $20 when they opened an account. This was effective, but PayPal's growth really kicked off when they started offering users $20 each time they referred someone else. By doing this, PayPal — like Hotmail — turned loyal users into advocacy machines, driving PayPal's growth to 7-10% per day. You read that right: *per day*. It meant that PayPal doubled its user base about every week.[10] The program wasn't cheap — PayPal shelled out over $60 million — but it sure was effective.[11]

Another benefit of this referral program was that it could be constantly tested, measured, and tweaked. Musk and company got reams of data on how the referral program was working, and when they found the growth rate got too high, they dialed down the incentives to $10 and eventually $5 per referred user.[12] Growth hacking is one of the few forms of marketing that lets you scientifically tweak it after launch — another reason for the huge appeal of this subfield of marketing.

Hacking conversion

The scope of "growth hacking" has grown since Hotmail and PayPal's days. Nowadays, you can growth hack by optimizing the transition between any two stages of the new six-step funnel we laid out. PayPal and Hotmail optimized the flow from loyalty to advocacy, but you can optimize any of the other transitions as well. Any way you patch up holes in your funnel is a form of growth hacking.

One of the more popular applications of growth hacking nowadays is in optimizing the conversion flow: making it as easy as possible for people to take the core actions of your product, from making social media posts to buying products on ecommerce sites.

Case study: Amazon's one-click purchases

In 1999, Amazon invented (and patented) a method of optimizing the transition from consideration to conversion: one-click buying.[13]

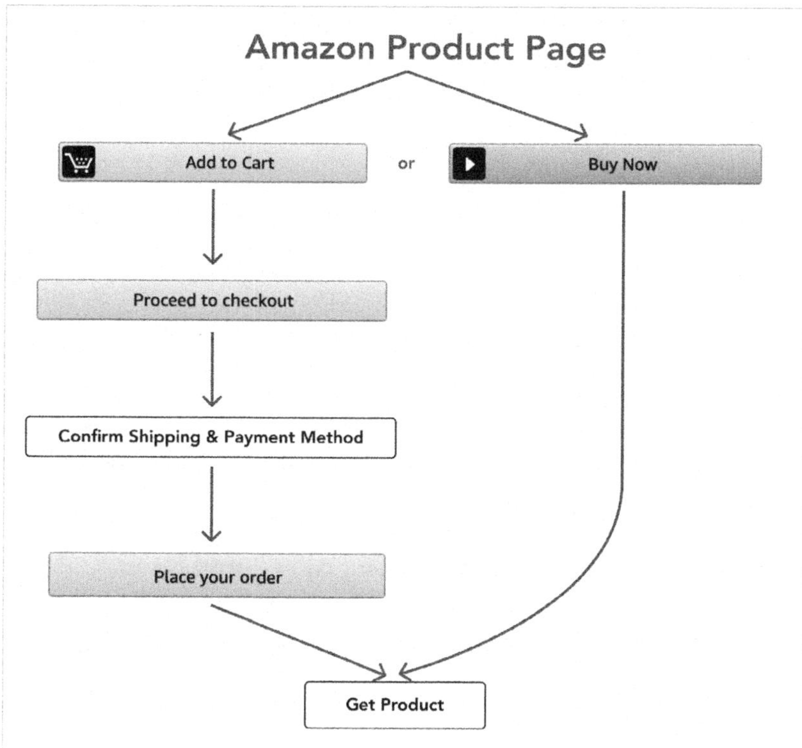

Amazon's one-click buying flow cuts out three steps from the purchasing process.

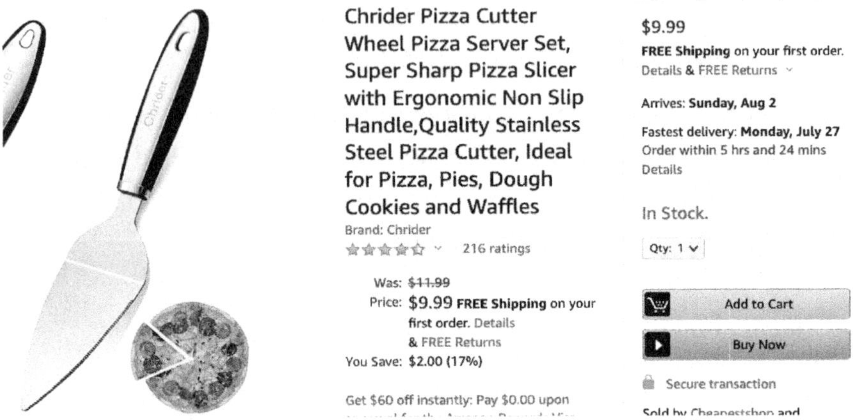

The "Buy Now" button lets you buy an Amazon product with one click — bypassing the cart and payment detail screens entirely. Source: Amazon[14]

Normally, buying a product on Amazon takes at least three clicks: "Add to Cart," "Proceed to Checkout," and "Place Order." Each stage adds a little bit of friction and gives buyers another chance to hesitate and drop out of the buying flow. But one-click buying — where the product is instantly added to your cart, bought with your saved payment method, and shipped to your default address[15] — cuts out most of the friction, making it easier than ever for customers considering a product to pull the trigger and buy it.

It's a simple insight: reducing friction makes things easier, and people will do things more when they're easier. But Amazon found a highly-effective way to apply it. (By the way, other ecommerce websites can use the one-click buying tactic freely: Amazon's patent expired in 2017.[16])

Case study: Music in Instagram and Facebook stories

In 2018, Facebook[17] and Instagram[18] rolled out music for stories. Once you snap a picture or video, you can apply a music "sticker," which lets you embed a clip from a song of your choice in your story.[19]

Instagram lets you add music "stickers" to your stories. Source: Instagram

Parth was the product manager on this feature and noticed that there were large dropoffs in the middle of the funnel. Specifically, people had trouble finding songs, choosing songs, and choosing the right part of each song to include in their stories. This added friction and difficulty meant that a lot of people gave up halfway through the flow.

To streamline the process, Parth's team observed the parts of songs that people picked the most often and built a machine learning model to predict the catchiest parts of new songs (usually the start of the chorus). The music-picking user interface surfaces these suggested clips, thus making it easier for users to get through this stage of the funnel. Streamlining this difficult part of the funnel doubled the completion rate and thus the number of music-enabled stories shared on Instagram.

The shaded box at the bottom of the screen shows the section of the song that will be added to your story. Parth's feature helped users automatically find the best sections, shown as the dots on the line. Source: Instagram

Going back to our looping funnel, the Facebook team was optimizing the "consideration" to "conversion" step: they made it easier for people who were considering making a music-enabled story to actually do it. In this way, it has strong parallels to Amazon's one-click purchasing.

Hacking advocacy

Another key step in the funnel to optimize is the advocacy-to-awareness step. Your users might love your product and want to tell their friends about it, but if they have to text or call all their friends individually, they might have trouble spreading the word. Growth hacks in this area seek to automate or otherwise streamline this word-of-mouth sharing process so you can get more users into the top of your funnel.

Case study: YouTube embeds

YouTube has long offered a great example of optimizing advocacy. YouTube videos have always had short, simple URLs, and anyone can watch a video, whether they're logged in or not. This makes it extremely easy to send video links to friends, thus helping videos go viral and drawing new users into the site.

YouTube's real genius, though, comes from embedding. YouTube offers a short snippet of embedding code on every video; anyone can copy-and-paste this code onto their website to embed the YouTube video. You don't have to get an API key or even log in.

Most people know about YouTube nowadays, but in YouTube's infancy, this embedding strategy helped YouTube spread like wildfire. Whenever the owner of a popular blog or website embedded a YouTube video, all their viewers got exposed to YouTube. And since the embedded YouTube player suggested new videos after the user finished the embedded one, the player quickly drew viewers onto the main YouTube website.[20]

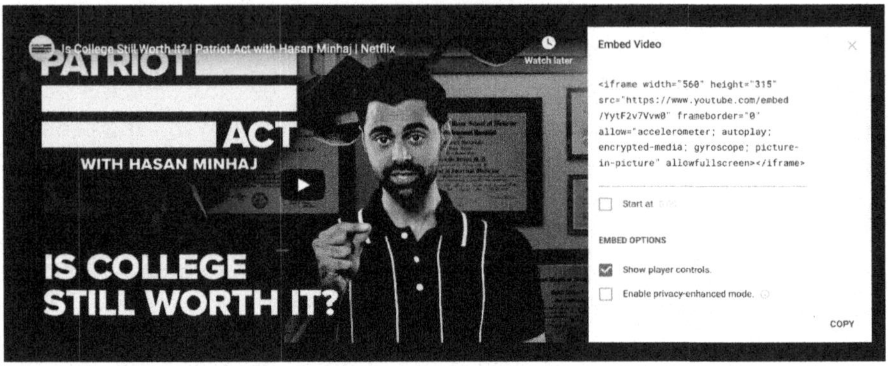

YouTube lets anyone copy and paste a snippet of code to embed any video on their website. This helps expose users on millions of other websites to YouTube. Source: YouTube[21]

YouTube's easy "linkability" and embedding makes it really easy to share YouTube by word-of-mouth. You don't have to text each friend individually; you can just post the link or embed the video on social media or blogs, and then everyone who follows you will see it. Generally, growth hackers want to enable "one-to-many" advocacy, which is more efficient than requiring "one-to-one" advocacy.

Case study: LinkedIn's address book importing

Apps like Snapchat[22] and Houseparty[23] make advocacy easy by letting you invite anyone in your phone's address book with a tap. Like with YouTube, it's far more efficient than making you type out a text to each friend and trying to think of a personalized pitch for the product.

LinkedIn did something similar in the 2000s and early 2010s, when they let users connect their email accounts and send mass invitation emails to all their contacts who weren't already on LinkedIn.[24] This was the epitome of "one-to-many" advocacy: you could let LinkedIn do the work of bringing in your professional connections rather than having to write an individualized email to every single contact. And, because it made advocacy so easy, the feature helped LinkedIn massively expand its user base.[25]

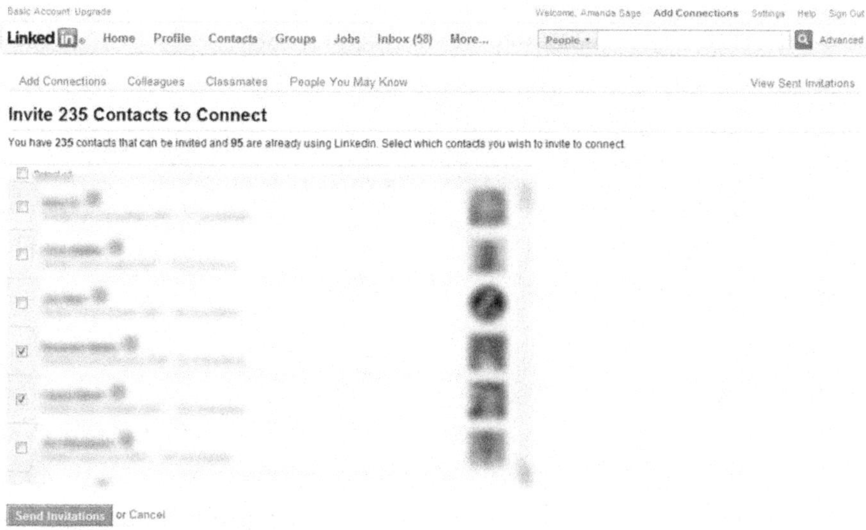

LinkedIn's feature to automatically invite people in your address book. This helped LinkedIn's growth skyrocket. Source: YouTube[26]

LinkedIn's story shows that you shouldn't go overboard with this strategy, though. Once users chose contacts to invite, LinkedIn sent all those contacts an invitation email. But LinkedIn didn't stop there — it started sending second and third follow-up emails to these contacts without the original user's consent.[27] These spammy emails led to a 2015 class action lawsuit against LinkedIn, which LinkedIn had to settle for $13 million.[28] (Chances are good that LinkedIn still came out ahead: $13 million is probably a bargain price for the millions of users that LinkedIn must have gotten from this now-shuttered feature.)

In other words, mass-import tactics are a great way to optimize advocacy, but you have to be careful that you don't veer into spamming territory.

Network effects

Another way to think about growth hacking is as the study of *network effects*, which describes how products, platforms, and other systems become exponentially more valuable as more people use them. Ecommerce websites, *two-sided markets* like Airbnb and Uber, social networks, app ecosystems like Android's, communication systems like email, and many more types of systems have network effects.[29] Think about a new social network: it's entirely useless if you're the only one there, it's barely more useful when a handful of people have joined, and it's extremely useful once it has millions of users.

These positive feedback loops are great for growing companies, but the flipside is that systems with network effects suffer badly from the *chicken-and-egg problem*. Buyers won't join an ecommerce platform if there are no sellers, but sellers won't join unless there are buyers. Developers won't build apps for your operating system unless the OS has users, but users won't use the OS unless developers have built apps yet. And nobody will join a social network unless *others* are on there, but those others won't join unless there are already people on there. Absent a shove, these systems will have trouble getting off the ground.[30]

Case study: Tinder's college recruitment

Growth hackers love finding clever ways to give new platforms that "shove" they need to kick off the virtuous cycle of network effects. A great example of hacking network effects comes from Tinder, which was having trouble attracting its first crop of users when it launched in 2012. Attractive people wouldn't join Tinder unless they already saw *other* attractive people on the app already.

To give Tinder a shove, the company sent an employee to visit college sorority houses, give a presentation on Tinder, and sign up the women in the houses. The employee then went to the "brother" fraternity that was paired with the sorority and showed Tinder to the men there — the men saw their sorority sisters there and eagerly signed up. Soon, the entire campus was downloading Tinder to have a shot at the attractive people on the app. Tinder's strategy worked: after this campaign, Tinder's user base swelled from 5,000 to 15,000.[31]

Convincing a few people to download an app certainly helps you start to get over the chicken-and-egg problem, but the real genius of this strategy was knowing to conquer a small market first before expanding to a larger market. Network effects are only useful if the people in the network are closely-connected: having 100 Tinder users on a single campus is much more useful than having two Tinder users in each of the 50 states (or even ten users in each of 100 countries). So when you're trying to kickstart a platform that could benefit from network effects, you should start by owning a very small, tightly-connected market and expand from there.

In other words, running a Super Bowl ad wouldn't have helped Tinder much: it would have attracted a smattering of users across the US, but a Tinder user in Chicago doesn't care how many Tinder users there are in New Hampshire. Instead, winning the Greek market at a particular campus — where everyone knows (and wants to date) each other — is far easier, cheaper, and more effective. After winning Greek life at the campus, Tinder expanded to the rest of the campus. And you can imagine that Tinder moved next to neighboring colleges, then nearby major cities, and so on.

If this strategy sounds familiar, it's exactly what Facebook did when it was starting in 2004. Mark Zuckerberg knew that people would only use Facebook if people they already knew were on it, so it paid to start with a small, tightly-connected market. So he started by signing up people in Kirkland House, his undergrad dormitory.[32] Then Facebook expanded to the rest of Harvard, then the Ivy League, then colleges nationwide, then high schoolers, then college students worldwide, then everyone on Earth.[33]

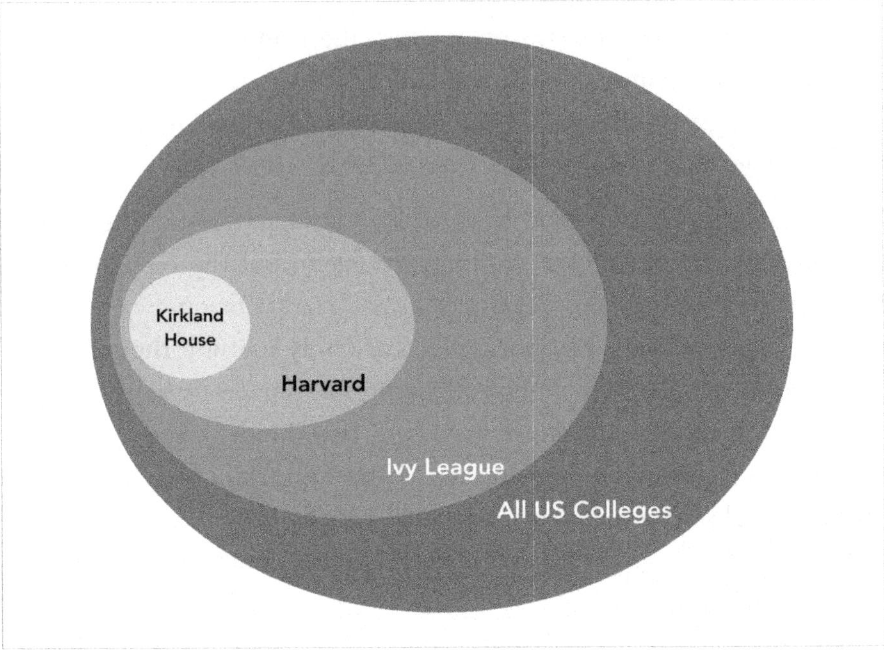

Facebook grew its user base by expanding into progressively large markets. Each market was a foothold into taking over the next one.

Like Tinder, Facebook grew outward in concentric circles. Each time Facebook expanded, it knew that its current user base gave it a toehold in the larger market, which kicked off network effects in the larger market. Most people at Harvard knew someone in Kirkland House, so they'd find value in the social network immediately. Most people in Ivy League schools knew someone at Harvard, and so on.

Colleges aren't the only way to create these "concentric circles" of markets. You can use simple geography for that too: Uber started out in San Francisco, then grew to other coastal American cities like Seattle, Boston, and Washington DC, then expanded to more major American cities, and so on.[34] At each stage, Uber knew that riders from its existing cities would also visit the new cities, thus giving people a reason to start driving for Uber in those new cities.[a]

However you do it, these "shoves" are essential to getting products that require network effects off the ground. Once you get a powerful flywheel going, you'll (hopefully) see lusty growth — and the growth hacker's toolkit can help you get that flywheel spinning.

🎁 Bonus video

Airbnb's founders were some of the most innovative growth hackers in tech history. Watch this video to learn some of the notorious stunts that helped Airbnb become the multi-billion-dollar travel empire[35] it is today.

productalliance.com/videos/airbnb

[a]Techies, Uber's initial target users, seem unable to stop flying in a nonstop loop between San Francisco, Seattle, and New York.

Chapter 35

Persuasion

WHETHER YOU'RE RUNNING ADS, sending out sales teams, or launching growth hacking campaigns, you need to persuade people to download your app, join your mailing list, build for your platform, or otherwise do what you want. Fortunately, there's a common playbook for winning people over: Robert Cialdini's *six principles of influence.*[1]

Cialdini argues that you can persuade people by pulling six key levers: *reciprocity*, *consistency* (also known as *commitment*), *social proof*, *authority*, *liking*, and *scarcity*.[2] If you look carefully, you'll notice that all kinds of tech products use these levers — and yours can too.

Reciprocity

The first lever we'll discuss is *reciprocity*: we'll do things for people who have helped us before, probably because we humans hate being indebted to others.[3] This means that you can persuade potential customers to act by doing something nice for them before asking for anything. For instance, Costco found that adding free samples for products in its stores boosted sales up to 600% because people felt compelled to reciprocate the sample-giver's generosity.[4]

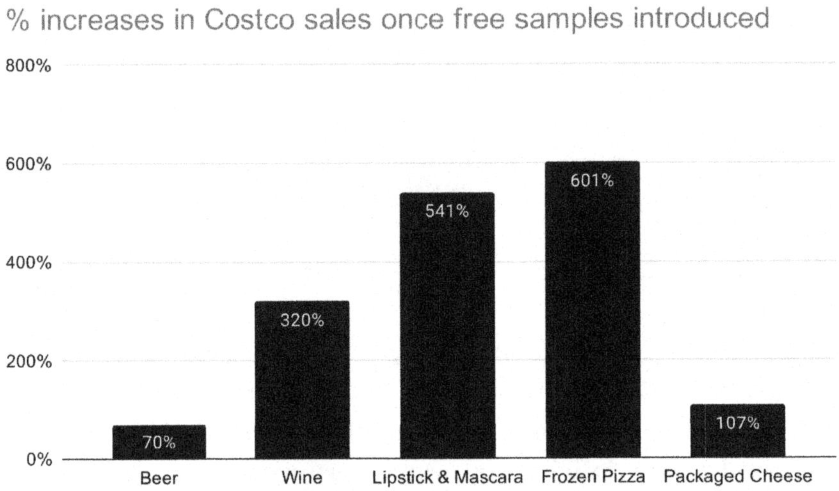

Costco saw huge improvements in the sales of some products once they started offering free samples. Source: The Atlantic[5]

Tech products can't give out free samples that easily, but you can easily give prospective customers free trials, free advice, and free newsletters before you ask them for money. A good example is Microsoft, which gives free Office subscriptions to college students.[6] This not only builds goodwill toward the company, thus making students want to buy Office once they start working jobs, but also helps students build skills in these products, thus making them feel more comfortable using them in place of Google Docs et al. in the future.

This strategy blends with classic public relations work, too. Moves intended to drive good PR, like Uber's giving out 10 million free rides to people affected with COVID-19 in 2020,[7] will make prospective customers think more positively about the brand and thus buy more in the future.

Consistency

The second lever is consistency: once people have made a decision or taken a stand for a particular cause, they'll strongly prefer to behave consistently in the future.[8] Nobody likes the *cognitive dissonance* that comes from acting inconsistently with their past beliefs. Leaving something you signed up for is tantamount to admitting that you made a mistake or misjudged the thing earlier.[9]

This means that, once people sign up for your product or otherwise start a relationship with you, they'll be hesitant to leave. So if you can get someone to do something small for you — like signing up for a free trial — you stand a good chance at keeping them on board for a while. This is one big reason why products like Amazon Web Services,[10] Netflix,[11] and the like offer free trials.

No-obligation offers

You can be more creative than just giving a free month or two of access to the software, though. The eyeglass brand Warby Parker will mail you five free pairs of glasses for five days — no payment or commitment needed.[12] Once you've tried on their glasses, chances are that you'll start thinking up reasons to buy them. Not buying anything would be an admission that you chose a bad vendor — and nobody likes that feeling.

Warby Parker's deal to let anyone try five pairs of glasses — completely free. Source: Scott Sigler[13]

This is closely related to the *foot-in-the-door* strategy, where sellers slowly win over potential customers by getting customers to slowly agree to larger and larger things.[14] First, you can convince people to download a whitepaper from your site. Then you can convince them to sign up for your mailing list, then start a free trial. And finally, you can convince them to start paying for your software. As the requests grow larger, the cumulative amount that the customer has done for you increases, making them likely to keep agreeing at each stage.

Social proof

Third is social proof, which comes from the knowledge that people are inherently herd animals.

In one famous experiment, participants were put in a room with a team of people who were — unbeknownst to the participants — working for the experimenters. The experimenters showed participants a line segment and asked them to choose a match from a group of three line segments of varying lengths. When everyone had to write down their answer, 99% of participants put the right answer.

But when everyone had to speak their answer, the experimenter's allies purposely said the wrong answer. When the participants had to answer, 75% of them gave the wrong answer just to go along with the group.[15] In other words, peer pressure got to them!

This principle works for businesses, of course. Showing the logos of prominent customers, the number of active users, case studies, testimonials, media mentions, awards, and other data showing that you're popular can go a long way toward winning over hesitant customers.[16] There's a reason that almost every enterprise startup has a tidy row of customer logos on their website.[17]

The team collaboration software startup Asana has a classic example of social proof: highlighting its famous customers. Source: Asana[18]

Praise from strangers isn't the only way to get social proof. If you get influencers to talk about your product, people who trust the influencers will feel compelled to check it out.[19]

But the most powerful form of social proof comes from friends and family; if someone you know personally recommends a product, you're very likely to check it out. Social sharing features are very useful for this reason. You can amp up the effectiveness of these strategies by reminding people how closely connected they are to the person sending the recommendation.

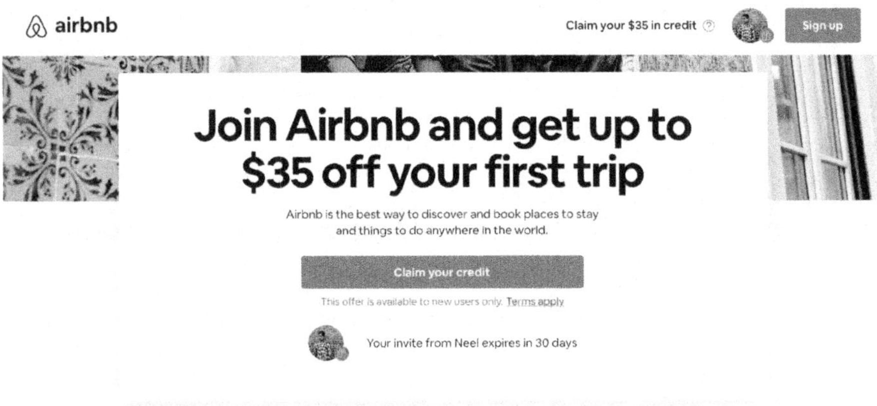

Airbnb's referral pages show the referrer's profile picture to make it feel more personal and amplify the social proof. Source: Airbnb[20]

For instance, Airbnb has long let people refer their friends to the platform, but they decided to revamp it in 2014.[21] As part of the revamp, they started showing new users the profile pictures of the people who referred them, not just their names. This small change boosted the social proof power of the referral and was a big reason why this revamp increased bookings 300% over the original system.[22]

Steering toward tiers

Finally, you can use social proof to get more revenue from your existing users. A common tactic is to label your most profitable pricing tier with "most popular" or "recommended," which steers customers toward buying it.[23]

The enterprise file storage company Box uses social proof to steer customers toward what you can assume is its most profitable tier — Business Plus. Source: Box[24]

Authority

The fourth lever is a twist on social proof: people inherently trust authority figures like doctors, lawyers, professors, and tycoons.[25] It's why frequent flyers love the Briggs and Riley luggage that airline pilots often cart around[26a] and why people listen to those "four out of five dentists approve of this gum" ads.[27] It's also why one Alabama man was able to steal 25 cases of beer from a grocery store in broad daylight — he dressed up as a delivery truck driver and carted the beer out the front door.[28]

For tech products, testimonials from these authority figures carry a lot of weight.[29] Startups can draw plenty of funding and attract top tal-

[a] The lifetime warranties on Briggs and Riley bags are pretty sweet, we must say.

ent just by bragging that a prominent venture capitalist backs them, for instance.[30] (Note that the authority figures that matter to your customer differ based on context. Approval from Al Gore means a lot for a green energy startup but little for a financial technology startup; the reverse is true for a testimonial from the CEO of Goldman Sachs.)

Authority can come from institutions, too; saying your company was founded by Harvard PhDs[31] or ex-Google employees[32] gives it an instant air of legitimacy.

Theranos and the pitfalls of authority

These methods of gaining authority, in fact, are so powerful that they can prop up a company even when its product doesn't work. We're talking, of course, about the infamous blood-testing startup Theranos. Founded by a Stanford dropout,[33] the company partnered with Walgreens[34] and Safeway[35] and even had the former CDC director on its board.[36] Even though its blood-testing machine was an utter failure, it still managed to hoodwink investors on its way to a $9 billion valuation before its inevitable collapse.[37]

Liking

The fifth lever, liking, is a lot more straightforward: we tend to listen to people who we like. Many things go into liking someone, but generally, we like people who are similar to us, people who compliment us, and people we cooperate with to achieve shared goals.[38]

Discord wins over gamers by showing that the creators are also gamers — thus using the principle of liking. Source: Discord[39]

Showing potential customers you're on their side is a great way to win them over. Consider Discord, the popular chat app for gamers. The Discord website proudly advertises that the creators are "a small group of passionate gamers"[40] — a surefire way to make fellow gamers like the app and thus consider using it. Even the humble "About Us" page can be powerful when used this way.[41]

Airbnb does a great job with liking as well. The company highlights the host on its bookings page, going out of its way to tell you about the host's interests, family, and life story. These details don't have that much effect on the quality of the lodgings, but they sure make potential guests like the host — thus making them much more likely to book that Airbnb than a faceless hotel.

Scarcity

Finally, people are drawn to scarcity. We hate the idea of missing out (FOMO is real![42]), and we'll rush to make a decision if we feel like the window of opportunity is closing. In fact, we irrationally overvalue things that we think are scarce: in one famous example, people preferred cookies in a near-empty jar over cookies in a full jar, even though both sets of cookies were the exact same.[43]

An Amazon's daily deal, complete with live countdown clocks marking when it expires. Source: Amazon[44]

You can use this in your products by creating limited-time or limited-quantity offerings. Amazon has different "lightning deals" or "goldboxes" every day, where they offer special discounts on a limited set of products.[45] To drive the scarcity home, Amazon even has a live countdown ticker below each item. You can literally see your time slipping away, second by second. This is one of the only instances of animation on Amazon's website — but it's extremely effective.

To be sure, scarcity is *always* present — most physical goods have a finite quantity, and all deals have some expiration date. But many merchants fail to remind people of that. You can harness this power through liberal use of tags like "while supplies last"[46] or "offer expires in X minutes."[47] Amazon famously writes "only Y left in stock" right next to the "add to cart" button on the pages of hot products to nudge users into buying.[48]

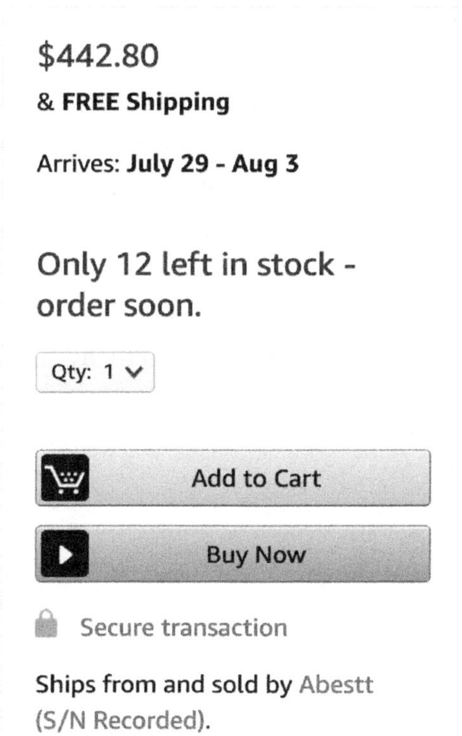

Amazon famously reminds you when there are only a few of an item left in stock. Source: Amazon[49]

By invite only

Scarcity doesn't just help sell things, though. Making new products invitation-only is a remarkably successful way to get a lot of buzz and users when you launch them. The free stock-trading app Robinhood, for instance, didn't open its doors to everyone when it launched. Instead, it made the beta available by invitation only. That simple hack suddenly made access to Robinhood scarce — it was like being part of an exclusive club — and people stampeded to get invites and spots on the waitlist. This tactic helped Robinhood get over one million users signed up before launch.[50]

Similarly, the Android phone maker OnePlus didn't sell its debut phone, the OnePlus One, in stores when it launched in 2014. The only way to buy a OnePlus One was to get an invitation from someone who was already part of the program. People were eager to get invitations — it would signal to the world that they were cool, connected, and "in the know" — and people with invitations were equally eager to share, since it'd make them look generous and powerful. This move was incredibly successful: OnePlus's website got over 25 million views in a month and sold over 1.5 million phones within a year.[51] In other words, *purposely* limiting the distribution of a product can actually make people want it more!

Conclusion

In 2018, Burger King announced a devious new promotion: if you checked into the Burger King app while within 600 feet of a McDonald's, you'd get a Whopper at your nearest Burger King for one cent.[1] The app even opens your mapping app and starts navigating you to Burger King.[2]

It was an act of trolling for the ages, but it was also a highly effective growth hack, literally stealing customers from under McDonald's nose. And it also reinforced Burger King's brand as a playful, edgy, and irreverent company. This is the same company, after all, that posted billboards with moldy Whoppers to show Burger King's commitment to removing artificial preservatives[3] and ran an ad that said, "OK Google, what's the Whopper burger?" to trigger viewers' Google Homes.[4] One Burger King restaurant even "asked" a neighboring Wendy's to prom.[5]

Burger King mocked AI-powered ads by creating this ad, which featured a stilted quote that sounds like a bad AI generated it. Source: Cfx[6]

Burger King is also proud of being the "anti-McDonald's": their press releases brag, tongue-in-cheek, about being "the second largest fast food hamburger chain in the world."[7] This campaign played on, and played up, that rivalry to great effect.

Burger King's method of "hackvertising" is impressive,[8] but we're not trying to show you how to sell fast food. Rather, Burger King's saga shows that some of the best marketing campaigns don't come from conventional social media posts, billboards, and TV ads. People with creativity and a flair for boldness can dream up some of these uniquely brilliant marketing strategies — and as a product manager, that's exactly what you can (and should) be doing. ❦

品 All QR codes from Part VII

In case you skipped over any QR codes from the last few chapters, here's a roundup. Scan them with your phone to watch bonus videos and try interactive demos.

An Old Spice body wash ad that targets women, even though men will be the ones using the product:

youtube.com/watch?v=owGykVbfgUE

The Dollar Shave Club's viral ad, featuring disco lights and a costumed bear:

youtube.com/watch?v=ZUG9qYTJMsI

How Airbnb growth-hacked its way to billions of dollars of revenue:

productalliance.com/videos/airbnb

Conclusion to the Sacred Seven

THAT'S A WRAP for the *Sacred Seven*. Congratulations: you've accumulated the knowledge that will help you design, build, launch, and sell great products while building successful businesses along the way. We hope that what you've learned will help you land your dream job, emerge as a product leader, or lead your company to success (or all of the above!) All that's left is for you to put this into practice. We can't wait to see what you'll achieve!

Before you go, we have a few free online resources to share.

Get the Product Alliance's interview strategy ebook for free

If you're looking for more interview-prep tools to help you stand apart from the competition, we've got you covered. We're excited to offer a free copy of the Product Alliance's 66-page interview strategy ebook, which includes over 70 sample questions written by PMs at top tech companies. **This ebook usually sells for $79**, but we're offering it for free to *Sacred Seven* readers.

Inside, you'll find exclusive strategies to help you crack 17 types of common PM interview questions, including metrics optimization, product growth and pricing, competitive analysis, and algorithm design.

Each section includes sample questions, a custom-designed tool or mental model to break the question apart, and rubrics to grade your responses.

Forget those stale, decade-old frameworks that everyone and their dog uses at PM interviews: this ebook will teach you custom-designed tools like profit trees, portfolio maps, the four-step postmortem process, assumption reversal tables, scenario matrices, and more.

If you share your thoughts on *Product Management's Sacred Seven* in an Amazon review, we'll send you a free copy of this normally-$79 interview strategy ebook. Just email a screenshot of your "verified purchase" **review** to **team@pmsacredseven.com** and we'll send you the ebook.

Get our "Hacking the PM Interview" mini-course for free

We included a handful of mock interview videos throughout this book, but if you're looking to ace your product management interviews, you'll probably want to watch even more. You'll probably also want to get strategic insights from senior PMs at the companies you're interviewing with and guides to crack the most common types of PM interview questions.

The good news is that we've got you covered. We partnered with the Product Alliance to create a PM interview mini-course that contains videos on all those topics and more. You'll get strategy insights, product roadmap teardowns, tricks to impress your interviewer, inside scoops from the top companies, and more. For a limited time, **we're making the mini-course free to all *Sacred Seven* readers!**

Just scan the QR code below or punch in the URL to enroll for free! (Note that enrollment will only be open for a limited time.)

productalliance.com/freecourse

Learn product strategy with *Swipe to Unlock*

If you enjoyed *Product Management's Sacred Seven* and haven't read our earlier books, you might like our first book, *Swipe to Unlock*. The #1 Amazon bestseller covers some of the biggest product management topics we didn't cover in this book: the fundamentals of technology and business strategy.

If you'd like to strengthen your knowledge of essential tech concepts, from cloud computing to collaborative filtering to self-driving cars, and read more case studies exploring product strategy and industry trends, we think you'll love *Swipe to Unlock*. Check it out on Amazon or at **swipetounlock.com.**

Stay in touch!

The three of us share predictions about the future of the tech industry, tips for breaking into tech, and career resources on LinkedIn. Feel free to contact us at:

- Neel: **linkedin.com/in/neel-a-mehta**
- Parth: **linkedin.com/in/parthdetroja**
- Adi: **linkedin.com/in/adityaagashe**

If you write a post about what you liked about *Product Management's Sacred Seven* and tag us, we'll all connect with you and like, comment on, or share your post to help you get more views and followers.

Finally, if you enjoyed this book and would like us to speak at your company or university, email **speaking@pmsacredseven.com** with details about your event and approximate dates. We love meeting our readers and engaging with PMs across the globe, and we look forward to hearing from you!

Whether you've been reading since the days of *Swipe to Unlock* or are just picking up our books now, we appreciate all your support. Thank you again for reading, and until next time, all the best!

— Neel, Parth, and Adi

Acknowledgments

As we like to say, writing a book takes a village. We could not have come anywhere close to completing the *Sacred Seven* without the help, support, guidance, and love of so many of our collaborators, friends, family, and mentors.

Neel

I'm so thankful to have such incredible mentor figures in my life. Your inspiration, guidance, and encouragement have helped me overcome my doubts, find a purpose, and summon the willpower to come as far as I have. I cannot thank you enough: Alex Komoroske, Maciej Michalski, Ritesh Lal, Dacheng Zhao, Tim Feeley, Jeff Meisel, and Nick Sinai.

To Mom, Dad, and Tara: thank you for putting up with me as I set about to write my third book in four years. Your love and support has made all the difference. And to Maitreyee: you help me become a better man every day, and that's more valuable than any writing advice on earth.

And to Adi and Parth: what a partnership it's been. Here's to many more years.

Parth

One day, when I asked my manager during a one-on-one if there was anything on his plate I could help him tackle, he suggested I instead focus on my own personal wellness and practice more self care. He said to do whatever drives you, perhaps write your next book.

I didn't take the suggestion very seriously at first, but it was ultimately the tipping point for me to actually work on researching, refining, and articulating my learnings from helping shape products at Facebook, Microsoft, and Amazon.

Thank you Josh Twist for being an incredible manager and giving me the push I needed to embark on this project. And a special thank you to Henry Soong, Emeka Okafor, Bryan Saftler, Dan Fletcher, Fred Betielle, George Zeng, Will Crew, Volodymyr Krestiannykov, and Davide Di Cillo for your support in my product journey!

A huge thank you to my friends and family for their constant support and encouragement in this endeavor. I'd like to especially thank Krishna Detroja, Nimish Kumar, Hilawi Belachew, Christina Gee, Adam Harrison and Nik Patel for providing their thoughts and feedback to improve this book. A huge shout out to Li Chai, Jennifer Lin, Stephanie Zhu, Peter Luba, Jenny Lee, Winny Sun, Nethra Jayaprakash, and Istvan Kovach for helping us get this book to where it is today.

And finally, thank you to Neel and Adi for being the best co-authors anyone could ever ask for.

Adi

A warm thank you to everyone who has patiently helped us along the way — we wouldn't have been able to do it without your support.

First, a thank you to our *Swipe to Unlock* and *Bubble or Revolution* fans — we are so grateful for and inspired by your enthusiasm and genuine interest in our content. Thanks for sharing your stories - hearing how we've played a small part in helping you out has been one of the most rewarding things I have experienced. We certainly wouldn't keep writing if it weren't for you.

A huge thank you is in order for all the friends and family who helped us get this book to where it is today. I'd like to especially thank Sai Naidu, Sandeep Gupta, Unnati Shukla, Arun Job, Juhee Lee, Aditi Jain, Young Chen, Katie Han, Bowen Zhang, Jimmy Xia, Ji Hun Kim, Holly Deng, Jeanne Lee, Andrej Safundzic, Serguei Balanovich. These kind people provided their valuable time, skills, opinions, and insights on everything from content to design to marketing.

And to Mom, Dad, and Athu — thanks for your continual encouragement and love throughout this journey. I am incredibly grateful for having the support of such amazing family and friends.

And to my fantastic co-authors Parth and Neel, who have been some of the best friends and colleagues. Can't wait to see what's next!

All of us

A huge thank you to the 67 product leaders from around the world who helped us craft the vision for this book. Several of the companies represented in our research have strict policies around describing what they look for in talent, so we've promised all our interviewees anonymity so they could freely speak their minds. While we can't thank them all individually, know that this book would have not existed without these brilliant people generously donating their time to speak with us.

We'd also like to thank everyone who gave us strategic advice; sourced case studies; identified people to interview; gathered feedback on our designs; and helped edit chapters. It has been such a pleasure working with you, and you made this book happen. Thank you Li Chai, Jennifer Lin, Unnati Shukla, Stephanie Zhu, Peter Luba, Jenny Lee, Winny Sun, Nethra Jayaprakash, and Istvan Kovach for helping us get this book to where it is today.

And finally, we'd like to thank you, the reader! We hope you enjoyed reading *Sacred Seven* as much as we enjoyed writing it. ❦

Citations

WE COULD HAVE WRITTEN entire books about each chapter in *Product Management's Sacred Seven.* There's so much to explore about each topic we wrote about, and we only just scratched the surface.

So we're providing links to every single source we used during our research for this book. Printing the citations here would add a hundred pages or more to this book, so we've put them online. Just scan the QR code below or punch in the URL. If a particular fact or opinion piques your interest, we encourage you to read the source and dive deeper into the material!

pmsacredseven.com/notes/1.4.0

Made in the USA
Coppell, TX
24 August 2022

81993184R00402